Foreword

This masterful work has already gained stature as the definitive accounting of the creation and establishment of the United States Air Force. As such, it is fitting that it is now released in a new and expanded edition, in honor of the fiftieth anniversary of the creation of the USAF as a separate military service.

As author Herman Wolk demonstrates, the creation of the USAF was hardly the product of casual intent. The creation represented the fulfillment of both a desire and a need dating back to the experiences of the Army Air Service in the First World War, the doctrinal controversies of the interwar years, and the crucible of global combat in the Second World War. It was this legacy of struggle and effort that shaped the service and its leadership. If for no other reason than this, the creation of the United States Air Force can thus be seen as far more than merely the result of the emergence of atomic weaponry and a bipolar post–Second World War global environment, or that of enthusiastic impulse borne of America's wartime air power experience.

But if the Air Force necessarily represented the product of a long tradition of air power thought and activity, it had nevertheless purchased its birthright with the blood and sacrifice of innumerable air and ground crews in combat around the world. In 1943, General George C. Marshall, the Chief of Staff of the U.S. Army, had seen fit to issue the then-Army Air Forces with its Declaration of Independence: FM 100–20, which recognized the co-equality of air and land power. Two years later, his successor, General of the Army Dwight D. Eisenhower, was one of the strongest proponents of Air Force independence. He was in a position to know: in June 1944, after D–Day, he had remarked to his son John (a newly minted Army second lieutenant visiting his father in Normandy), "Without air supremacy, I wouldn't be here." It was the Army Air Forces that had secured that air supremacy. Given the significance of air power in the modern world, he well recognized that the best means of projecting that air power and meeting the increasing global requirements thrust upon the United States was via a strong, well-led, well-equipped, and well-trained independent Air Force.

Today the United States Air Force reaches globally to project power and presence, and Air Force-launched and managed space-based systems provide global air force, and it is America's "911" for responding to crises and contingencies anytime, anywhere. That it is so is a tribute to those who labored long and hard to create it. Their story is admirably told in this remarkable book.

Richard P. Hallion
Air Force Historian
June 26, 1996

THE STRUGGLE
FOR AIR FORCE
INDEPENDENCE
1943–1947

Herman S. Wolk

Air Force History and Museums Program
Washington, D.C., 1997

Library of Congress Cataloging in Publication Data

Wolk, Herman S., 1931–
    The Struggle for Air Force Independence, 1943–47.

    Bibliography
    Includes index.
    1. United States. Air Force—Organization.
    2. United States. Army Air Forces—History.
    I. United States. Air Force. Air Force History and Museums Program.
II. Title
    UG773.W64 1982 358.4'13'0973 82–22398

Revised edition of *Planning and Organizing the Postwar Air Force, 1943–1947*, published in 1984 by the Office of Air Force History.

The Cover: Photo montage includes (clockwise from upper left) Dwight D. Eisenhower, Carl A. Spaatz, James V. Forrestal, Stuart Symington, Henry H. (Hap) Arnold, Lauris Norstad, Hoyt Vandenberg, and Ira C. Eaker.

For sale by the U.S. Government Printing Office
Superintendent of Documents, Mail Stop: SSOP, Washington, DC 20402-9328
ISBN 0-16-049066-9

Preface

World War II marked a culminating point in the long struggle of the Army airmen to establish an independent Air Force. The impressive contribution to allied victory made by the United States Army Air Forces (AAF) provided a decisive impetus to the drive to create a United States Air Force. Despite the retrospective judgement that the formation of a separate Air Force after World War II was all but a foregone conclusion, the fact remained that a great deal of difficult work needed to be accomplished in 1945–1947 in order to make this a reality.

World War II had uncovered shortcomings in the organization of military forces which fortunately were overcome by the genius of American productivity, the outright skill of military leadership, and the tenacity and courage of the American fighting man. The postwar period was unprecedented in American military history, a time when the administration and the nation decided to build a permanent peacetime military establishment based upon the concept of deterring war.

General Henry H. (Hap) Arnold, Commanding General, AAF, with prescience, laid the conceptual framework for the postwar Air Force. Early in the war, he recognized the critical need to plan an organizational structure that would be appropriate for the postwar Army Air Forces. Moreover, in the compact pre-war Army Air Corps, Arnold from his long experience made it a top priority to identify those who would be well-suited to key command and planning positions. He accelerated this planning after the war in Europe erupted and President Franklin D. Roosevelt ordered a military buildup.

In the spring and summer of 1943, General Arnold directed the formation of formal planning groups in the Headquarters Army Air Forces. These were the post War Division and the Special Projects Office. Arnold also had created an Advisory Council in 1942 which, among other issues, considered the subject of postwar planning.

Although in 1943–45 General Arnold was under great pressure in Washington to produce results in the theaters of war commensurate with the substantial resources being devoted to the AAF, he nonetheless placed considerable emphasis upon this planning for the postwar Air Force. Arnold, his successor, Gen. Carl A. (Tooey) Spaatz, and Lt. Gen. Ira C. Eaker, Deputy Commander, AAF, were among those who had fought the bureaucratic battles for more autonomy from the War Department during the interwar years. Once the war was over in 1945 the AAF leaders were determined to succeed with the establishment of an independent Air Force. The passage of appropriate unification legislation was only one of the many crucial concerns facing the Army Air Forces after the war. Setting reorganization and planning force structure were extremely vital parts of the AAF drive for autonomy, as was the question of roles and missions. This story focuses on these concerns and seeks to show the connections between them.

When the Army Air Forces reorganized in March 1946, it did so in such a way that when the AAF became an independent service, it did not have immediately to revamp its major commands once again. This major reorganization of 1946, creating the basic combat commands of the Air Force, grew out of discussions and eventual agreement between Spaatz and Gen. Dwight D. Eisenhower, Army Chief of Staff. The key issue to be settled between them was how to organize the AAF's tactical air elements. Similarly, Spaatz and Eisenhower had discussed the idea of forming an Air Board to advise the Commanding General, AAF, on air policy. Spaatz ordered the establishment of the Air Board—marking the beginning of the modern postwar Air Board system—in February 1946. These events illuminated a salient feature of this period of Air Force history: namely, that frequently relatively few men were involved in the process by which crucial decisions were made.

Planning for the 400,000-personnel, 70-group program had in the final analysis been ordered by the War Department and had been progressively scaled down from much higher figures. The airmen viewed the 70 groups as the minimum structure for the standing postwar Air Force. As the reader will understand, it was specifically this view which put the AAF leaders in conflict with the War Department hierarchy over the universal military training (UMT) program.

This concerted postwar planning—for unification and a separate Air Force, roles and missions, force structure, and reorganization—took place amid the confusion of massive immediate postwar demobilization. It is no exaggeration to say that the air planners sought to build and tear down their forces at the same time. Their tasks were tremendously complex. Plans had to be drawn rapidly and yet without concrete guidance as to the shape of future domestic and foreign policies. "Almost every endeavor was interrelated to every other action," noted General Jacob E. Smart, who after the war was Secretary to the Air Staff. "Plans and programs were in a state of flux and frustration was the normal condition."

Perhaps the only recognizable certainty was that austerity would mark the postwar milieu. Yet, even here the AAF and War Department officials differed in their estimates and definitions of postwar austerity. The War Department reflected the view of Gen. George C. Marshall, Army Chief of Staff, that the American public would not sustain a large standing army. Moreover, he did not believe it could be recruited by the military in the first place.

This detailed narrative of the resolution of the 70-group program, the postwar reorganization of 1946, and the Headquarters reorganization of October 1947 are stories that have not previously been related, stressing the interrelationship between them. As will be seen, this interplay was often the result of unusually close relationships between the top wartime commanders. For example, Arnold, enjoyed a long-lasting friendship with Marshall going back before World War I. They understood each other and worked well together. Even so, this did not stop Arnold from opposing Marshall on UMT, arguing that in the future a substantial standing Air Force should not be sacrificed to the UMT program. Similarly, General Eisenhower thought highly of General Spaatz and indeed considered him as his own airman. These particular relationships were crucial to the postwar creation of the United States Air Force (USAF).

General Eisenhower was in a very real sense a founder of the Air Force. Returning to the War Department in Washington after leading the "Great Crusade" in Europe, he emphasized to the Congress that in his view "no sane person" could any longer reject the idea of an independent United States Air Force. Based on the experience of World War II, the Army air arm deserved coequality with the land and naval forces. Eisenhower's advocacy was also based upon his conviction that unity of command had become absolutely essential and that a unified defense establishment would foster economy. In peacetime, the nation could no longer afford the brutal competition for resources.

Also of great importance to the autonomy drive were the history of the Air Corps between the wars and the airmen's ideas about air power and air organization as formed over the decades since World War I. These had great influence after World War II on the collective frame of mind of the airmen and their approach to the question of air independence.

However, it was the cataclysmic events of the second World War that propelled the AAF into what the air leaders deemed a pre-eminent position. With the war over, the air leaders felt that the AAF had replaced the Navy as "the first line of defense." The war had given them the chance to demonstrate the effectiveness of air power. They thought their war record entitled them to a position coequal with the Army and Navy. Their resolution of the questions of force structure, internal reorganization, and roles and missions, first took into consideration the belief that the Army air arm had become the premier component of the defense phalanx. The organizational and force planning accomplished by the airmen in 1943–47 were enormously complicated. It was not only the substance of the issues themselves which was so difficult; the air planners also had to coordinate and gain approval for force deployment plans through the War Department. Subsequently, of course, final approval would have to be won through the Joint Chiefs of Staff. Along with planning internal reorganization, the end result of this lengthy process was the air leaders had the Air Force relatively in place when the United States Air Force was formed in September 1947.

Generals Henry H. Arnold and Carl A. Spaatz, successive commanders of the AAF, gave heavy responsibilities to Maj. Gen. Lauris Norstad. Having planned air campaigns in North Africa and Italy during the war, and then serving as Chief of Staff of the Twentieth Air Force, that conducted the B–29 campaign against Japan, Norstad brought experience and an appropriate temperament to these postwar tasks. During 1945–47, Norstad played a key role in planning and organizing the postwar Air Force and in negotiating with naval leaders the unification legislation that led to the National Security Act of 1947.

Not surprisingly however, troubles failed to disappear with the creation of the USAF. To the contrary, the roles and missions controversy with the Navy grew more bitter and intense; difficult aircraft production decisions lay ahead; and the Air Force faced a period of two years during which critical support functions would have to be transferred from the War Department. Nevertheless, Stuart Symington, the first Secretary of the Air Force, and General Spaatz, the first Air Force Chief of Staff, enthusiastically assembled their staffs and began to organize and operate the Department of the Air Force and Headquarters USAF.

The author has not tried to describe the many organizational changes within AAF Headquarters or in the commands. The approach has been primarily to center on the crucial roles played by Air Force leaders and officials in the overall organizational planning of the postwar Air Force. A new epilogue describes important national security legislation and Air Force organizational changes in the half-century since the establishment of the Air Force. New material has also been interspersed in the various chapters throughout this book. The appendices include major sequential documents that were important to the establishment of the conceptual framework and organizational structure of the USAF.

Acknowledgments

Dr. Richard P. Hallion, the Air Force Historian, reviewed and commented on this manuscript. Mrs. Anne Johnson Sachs edited and formatted the manuscript. Cynthia Wyche Umstead scanned the original edition and cleaned the files. Lori Crane designed the book cover and Protean Gibril created the electronic photo montage.

The following colleagues commented on the manuscript: Thomas A. Sturm, John Greenwood, Jack Neufeld, Charles Hildreth, Richard Kohn, Maj. Gen. John Huston, Marcelle Knaack, H. O. Malone, Stanley L. Falk, Lt. Col. Drue DeBerry, Col. John Schlight, Warren Trest, and Prof. Edward Homze.

The following reviewed parts of the manuscript and provided important insights: Secretary of the Air Force W. Stuart Symington, Gen. Ira C. Eaker, Gen. Curtis E. LeMay, Maj. Gen. Haywood Hansell, Jr., John F. Loosbrock, Robert Childress, Robert M. Kipp, Gerald Cantwell, Gerald Hasselwander.

Eugene Sagstetter edited the original edition.

The Author

Herman S. Wolk is the Senior Historian at the Air Force History Support Office in Washington, D.C. Before joining the Headquarters Air Force history program, he was an historian at the Strategic Air Command Headquarters (1959–1966). He holds BA and MA degrees from the American International College, Springfield, Massachusetts, and studied at the Far Eastern and Russian Institute, University of Washington, under a Ford Foundation Grant. In 1974–1975 he served as a member of the Office of the Secretary of Defense Special Project on the History of the Strategic Arms Competition. He is a Fellow of the Inter-University Seminar on Armed Forces and Society. Among his many publications are *Strategic Bombing: The American Experience* (1981), *Evolution of the American Military Establishment Since World War II* (co-author, 1978), and several essays on the career and contributions of General George C. Kenney. He is also the author of "General Arnold, the Atomic Bomb, and the Surrender of Japan," to be published by the Louisiana State University Press, in *The Pacific War Revisited* (1997).

Contents

Illustrations

Charts

THE STRUGGLE
FOR AIR FORCE
INDEPENDENCE
1943–1947

**Generals Carl A. (Tooey) Spaatz and Henry H. (Hap) Arnold,
architects of the postwar Air Force.**

1

Roots of AAF Organization

I don't believe any balanced plan to provide the nation with an adequate, effective Air Force. . .can be obtained, within the limitations of the War Department budget, and without providing an organization, individual to the needs of such an Air Force. Legislation to establish such an organization. . .will continue to appear until this turbulent and vital problem is satisfactorily solved.

Maj. Gen. Frank M. Andrews
Commanding General
General Headquarters (GHQ) Air Force
April 1937.

The roots of Army Air Forces' (AAF) planning for post-World War II organization, the 70-group force, and independence lay mainly in the AAF's experience in World War II and in the history of the Air Corps between the two world wars. To the air leaders, World War II and its alleged lessons determined the character of formative postwar planning in 1943–45. The work of AAF planners over these years formed the foundation for later decisions leading to the postwar reorganization in March 1946 and to the establishment and organization in September 1947 of the Department of the Air Force and Headquarters United States Air Force (USAF).*

---

*As it appears in the title of this chapter, the word "organization" is defined in a broad sense. During 1943–47, the term "organization" became inseparable from the subjects of force levels and the struggle for autonomy.

THE STRUGGLE FOR AIR FORCE INDEPENDENCE

Wartime planning also afforded the basis for actions in 1945–46 which fixed force levels. Although the AAF's 70-group goal evolved at the direction of the War Department in August 1945, force planning had begun in the summer of 1943. Similarly, while the major peacetime reorganization of March 1946 set the combat commands as the Strategic Air Command (SAC), Tactical Air Command (TAC), and Air Defense Command (ADC), definitive planning for the command structure had begun in 1944. Moreover, planning for legislation leading to a National Military Establishment including a separate Air Force began to take shape during 1943–45. The impetus came from studies by the military services and the pressure of Congressional hearings.

Despite the importance of the war experience to the drawing of postwar plans, no discussion of the ideas and concepts behind postwar organization would be complete without an understanding of the history of the Army air arm between the two world wars.* This history played a crucial part in the gestation of the air leaders' ideas about a separate air organization and the role of air power. Between the wars the air leaders refined air doctrine, tested new aircraft and equipment, and became convinced of the need for a separate air force. The movement for air autonomy was well under way long before the start of World War II. Among the major issues confronted by the Air Corps before the war were the same two questions to be dealt with by the Army Air Forces during and after World War II: To the airmen, the seeming validity of the independent mission;

---

*Among the works of Air Force history that consider the interwar period are these: Maurer Maurer, *Aviation in the U.S. Army, 1919–1939* (Washington, D.C., 1987); Martha Byrd, *Chennault: Giving Wings to the Tiger* (Tuscaloosa and London, 1987); R. Earl McClendon, *Autonomy of the Air Arm* (Maxwell AFB Ala., 1954) [new edition by the Air Force History and Museums Program, 1996]; DeWitt S. Copp, *A Few Great Captains*, (Garden City, N.Y., 1980); John F. Shiner, *Foulois and the U.S. Army Air Corps, 1931–1935* (Washington, D.C., 1982); Alfred Goldberg, ed., *A History of the United States Air Force, 1907–1957* (New York, 1957); Robert F. Futrell, *Ideas, Concepts, Doctrine: A History of Basic Thinking in the United States Air Force, 1907–1964* (Maxwell AFB, Ala., 1971); Thomas H. Greer, *The Development of Air Doctrine in the Army Air Arm, 1917–1941* (USAF Hist Study 89, Maxwell AFB, Ala., 1953); Henry H. Arnold, *Global Mission* (New York, 1949); Claire L. Chennault, *Way of a Fighter: The Memoirs of Claire Lee Chennault* (New York, 1949); Benjamin D. Foulois and Carroll V. Glines, *From the Wright Brothers to the Astronauts: The Memoirs of Major General Benjamin D. Foulois* (New York, 1968). The most comprehensve work on the AAF in World War II is Wesley F. Craven and James L. Cate, eds., *The Army Air Forces in World War II*, 7 vols (Chicago, 1948–1958, reprinted Washington, 1984). A more broad, popular approach, quite useful and readable, is Geoffrey Perret, *Winged Victory: The Army Air Forces in World War II* (New York, 1993).

and the shape of potential legislation to make the air arm independent. And a striking continuity is also apparent in the air leaders themselves. The men who led and organized the Army Air Forces in the drive for independence after World War II had fought the bureaucratic, political, organizational, and technological battles of the 1920s and 1930s. General Henry H. Arnold, who headed the Army Air Forces in the second World War, gained his early flying experience from the Wright School in Dayton, Ohio, and was himself an air pioneer. He held key command and staff positions between the wars and in 1938 became Chief of the Air Corps after Maj. Gen. Oscar Westover died in an air crash.

General Carl A. Spaatz, who in World War II commanded the United States Strategic Air Forces in Europe and briefly the United States Strategic Air Forces in the Pacific, had distinguished himself in command and combat during World War I. Likewise an air pioneer, he performed important command and staff duties in the Air Corps through the 1920s and 1930s. With Arnold's retirement in early 1946, General Spaatz became Commanding General, AAF; spearheaded the postwar drive for an independent Air Force and for internal air organization; and eventually was named the first Chief of Staff, United States Air Force.

Lt. Gen. Ira C. Eaker, AAF Deputy Commander in 1945–47, flew with the Air Corps in the 1920s and 1930s and occupied significant staff positions over these years. During the war, he successively commanded the VIII Bomber Command, Eighth Air Force, and the Mediterranean Allied Air Forces. Returning to AAF headquarters in the spring of 1945, Eaker was in the forefront in developing force structure, redeployment plans, and organizational plans for the postwar Air Force. Arnold, Spaatz, and Eaker were the top men in command in 1945–47, when the AAF fought the successful battle for a separate Air Force. Among many other prominent airmen and air advocates who made vital contributions to AAF organizational planning in 1944–47 were: Stuart Symington, Assistant Secretary of War for Air, 1946–47, and the first Secretary of the Air Force in September 1947; Robert A. Lovett, Assistant Secretary of War for Air, 1941–45; Lt. Gen. Hoyt S. Vandenberg, Assistant Chief of Air Staff, Operations, Commitments and Requirements, and successor to Spaatz in 1948 as Air Force Chief of Staff; Maj. Gen. Lauris Norstad, Assistant Chief of Air Staff, Plans, in 1945, who later helped draft a unified command plan and unification legislation; and Maj. Gen. Laurence S. Kuter, Assistant Chief of Air Staff, Plans, 1943–45.

Early Air Organization

The United States Army air arm antedated the first World War, having been created in 1907 as the Aeronautical Division, Office of the Chief Signal Officer, "to take charge of all matters pertaining to military ballooning, air machines and all kindred subjects." As originally formed, the Aeronautical Division consisted

General Henry H. (Hap) Arnold

An aviation pioneer, General Arnold began his flying career when aircraft were in their infancy. He is shown in a Wright "B" airplane at the Army's first flying field, College Park, Maryland, in 1911 *(adjacent page, top)*. At San Diego Air Depot, he examines the first Liberty engine, built by the Ford Company in World War I *(adjacent page, bottom)*. Maj. Thomas DeW. Milling, another military aviation pioneer, appears with Arnold *(below)* to celebrate a reunion by flying together in an army observation plane in 1930.

of one officer and two enlisted men. In 1913, the first bill to recommend a change in the status of military aviation was introduced into the House of Representatives. It proposed to remove aviation from the Signal Corps and establish an Aviation Corps under the Army Chief of Staff. One officer and former pilot, Lt. Paul W. Beck, supported this legislation, observing that aviation did not belong in the Signal Corps.* Lt. Benjamin D. Foulois, to become Chief of Air Corps, 1931–35, opposed this bill, noting that military aviation had not yet sufficiently advanced to be organized into an Aviation Corps. The War Department opposed this legislation. In July 1914 the Aviation Section of the Signal Corps was established by Congress with authorized strength of 60 officers and 260 enlisted men. Due chiefly to the potential shown by the airplane in World War I, the Air Service was formed in May 1918.

Although air power's wartime contribution had been minor, some airmen considered the airplane an ultimately decisive instrument to wage war. Aircraft had been used in World War I primarily for observation and support of ground units. Potentially however, aircraft could strike the enemy's war-sustaining resources (transportation, communications, industry and population) and break his will to resist. This became known as the independent or strategic mission, as opposed to the tactical mission of attacking the enemy's ground or naval forces.[†] In future conflicts the trench slaughter of World War I could be avoided. As bombers of much better performance were developed, air leaders even more intensively advocated the independent mission, connecting it directly to their advocacy of autonomy.

Also, airmen knew that Britain's Royal Air Force (RAF) had been created during World War I. While in 1916 Winston Churchill had declared in the House of Commons that "ultimately, and the sooner the better, the Air Service should be one unified, permanent branch," it had taken the German air attacks on England of 1917 to impel the drive for separation. Following these raids, a commit-

---

*Beck, one the earliest flyers, who also appreciated the potential military application of aviation, was removed from flying status in 1932 becuase of the so-called "Manchu Law." This act of Congress required that officers alternate between line and staff positions for specified periods. Beck served with the Infantry in World War I, returning to aviation after the war. Lt. Col. Beck was commanding Post Field at Ft. Sill, Okla., in April 1922, when he was shot and killed by a friend during an altercation generated by Beck's relationship with his friend's wife.

[†]Maj. Gen. Hugh M. Trenchard, commander of Britain's Royal Flying Corps, in 1918 had established an Independent Air Force. This force was not under the command of division, corps, or army commanders, but could conduct operations against industry, transportation, communications, and supply centers.

tee headed by Lt. Gen. Jan C. Smuts recommended to the British cabinet that an Air Ministry be formed. Further, since independent air operations gave promise of becoming a major means of conducting warfare, a separate air service should be set up.

The Smuts report afforded Prime Minister Lloyd George needed support to silence conservative military opposition. On January 1, 1918, the Air Ministry was organized and on April 1, 1918, the Royal Air Force came into being, combining the Army's Royal Flying Corps and the Royal Naval Air Service. After the war, the British army and navy attempted to regain their air arms, but failed.* In retrospect, the RAF's Air Marshal Sir John C. Slessor described this battle to maintain the RAF as fought "tooth and nail against the most powerful, the most determined and sometimes the most intemperate obstruction by the forces of military conservatism." Arnold, Spaatz and Eaker remembered this British military history. It tremendously influenced their thinking about autonomy.[1] They kept in touch with their RAF counterparts, especially after World War II. Nonetheless, in the United States the prevailing opinion was that air forces should be trained and maintained to support field armies. The postwar Dickman Board, appointed by Gen. John J. Pershing, came to such a conclusion as did Secretary of War Newton D. Baker, Assistant Secretary of War Benedict Crowell, and Army Chief of Staff Gen. Peyton C. March.

As U.S. Army commanders understood, the support of the ground troops was a useful role for the Air Service. When airmen argued that sustained bombardment of the enemy's war-making industry had not really been tried and that trench warfare was self-defeating they were deemed visionaries. As General Eaker recalled: "We were just sort of voices in the wilderness. A great many military people considered us crackpots."[2] The wartime Chief of Staff, General Peyton March, concluded: "The war had taught many lessons; the principles of warfare, however, remained unchanged. It was not won, as some had predicted it would be, by some new and terrible development of modern science; it was won, as had every other war in history, by men, munitions and morale."[3]

Army Command and General Staff School textbooks described the airplane's role as being observation. Although eight bills to establish a Department of Aeronautics had been introduced in Congress during 1916–20, the Reorganization Act of 1920 recognized the Air Service only as a combatant branch of the U.S. Army. The Navy, with its battleships, remained the first line of defense. However, men like Brig. Gen. William (Billy) Mitchell, the Army's flamboyant airman of

---

*That both the Army and Navy air arms were integrated into the RAF would not be lost upon the postwar leaders of the U.S. Navy. The Royal Navy regained its air arm prior to World War II.

World War I, argued that the airplane was more economical and militarily effective than the battleship and that an independent air service was the best way to exploit aircraft.* In June-July 1921, Mitchell seemed to prove his point. Bomber planes under his command destroyed some obsolete warships off the Virginia capes, including the allegedly unsinkable battleship *Ostfriesland* with its four layers of steel and watertight bulkheads.

After the war the Army's airmen refined their doctrine, based on what they considered to be the war's lessons. Major Carl Spaatz,[†] Commanding Officer, 1st Pursuit Group (Selfridge Field, Mich.), in 1923 stressed in an unpublished study the part of military aviation known as "Air Force." Whereas aviation observation forces worked with the ground armies, Air Force comprised pursuit, bombardment, and attack aviation. Spaatz defined pursuit aviation as the branch that sought to destroy the enemy's air force. Its mission was to gain air supremacy. The branch called attack aviation attempted to strike enemy forces and military objectives on the ground or water with machine gun fire. Bombardment forces tried to destroy military objectives by bombing targets on the ground and on water.[4]

Spaatz observed that since the war the concept of Air Force continued to develop. He pointed to advances in the design of aircraft, bombs, and machine guns. As far as using bombing as a means to defeat the enemy, Spaatz noted that this was undertaken only late in the war. However, in his opinion the results were so successful that they demanded an air force role apart from support of the armies on the ground.

Instructors at the Air Service Field Officers School (established at Langley Field, Va., in October 1920) also promulgated air doctrine based principally upon the idea of independent air operations.[**] In 1926 the tactical school published *Employment of Combined Air Force* (subsequently revised under the title *Air Force*), which for the first time formally articulated the idea that the basic air objectives were the enemy's "vital centers" and his air force. Contemporary scholarship suggests General Giulio Douhet's influence, an English translation of his *Command of the Air* (1921 edition) being available at the school as early as 1923. *Employment of Combined Air Force* borrowed heavily from Douhet, stressing

---

*During the war, Mitchell was successively chief of air service for several units of the American Expeditionary Force. He was promoted to brigadier general in October 1918 and made Chief of Air Service for First Army Group.

[†]At this time Spaatz actually spelled his name "Spatz." He changed it to Spaatz in 1938 because people frequently pronounced it "spats" rather than "spots."

**In November 1922, the school's name was changed to the Air Service Tactical School, and in 1926, when the Air Service became the Air Corps, to the Air Corps Tactical School (ACTS). In July 1931, it moved from Langley to Maxwell Field, Ala.

that attacks on "morale" (population) should be made at the outset of war. Also like the Italian theorist, it underscored the importance of neutralizing the enemy's air force.[5]

Meanwhile, in the 1920s several boards studied the organization of military aviation. Maj. Gen. Mason M. Patrick, Chief of the Air Service, favored air autonomy within the War Department structure. He opposed permanent assignment of air units to the ground forces. The Lassiter Board report of 1923, which approved the idea of a General Headquarters Air Force, marked the Army's first acknowledgment that the independent air mission might serve a useful role. Nevertheless, the Morrow Board report of November 1925 opposed establishment of a Department of Aeronautics. This board—convened in the wake of Mitchell's protestations that the air arm was unprepared for war—remarked that air power had yet to prove the value of independent operations. Such missions could better be done under the command of Army or Navy officers. Moreover, as to air defense, the United States had no reason to fear an enemy attack:

> No airplane capable of making a transoceanic flight to our country with a useful military load and of returning to safety is now in existence. . . .with the advance in the art. . . it does not appear that there is any ground for anticipation of such development to a point which would constitute a direct menace to the United States in any future which scientific thought can now foresee. . . .The fear of such an attack is without reason.[6]

In December 1925 the Lampert Committee recommended that a Department of National Defense be created under a civilian secretary. Implied was the idea of three coequal services. Neither the War Department nor Congress acted. The Air Corps Act of 1926 created the Army Air Corps from the Army Air Service. The act also sanctioned Air Corps representation on the War Department General Staff (WDGS). In addition, the Office of Assistant Secretary of War for Air was created (first held by F. Trubee Davison), only to be abolished in 1933 by President Franklin D. Roosevelt.* These were years of the depression, military budgets were held to a minimum by Congress, and international commissions were convened to pass resolutions restricting planes in wartime to attacking only military targets. Besides, protected by oceans, American citizens saw little need for increased military strength. The Navy remained the first line of defense.

---

*Just prior to graduation from Yale in 1918, Davison, whose father was a partner of J. P. Morgan and Company, had suffered permanent damage to his lower legs in a plane crash. He received a law degree from Columbia University and in 1922 was elected to the New York State Assembly. He had resigned in the fall of 1932 to run for Lieutenant Governor of New York. In June 1933 the Roosevelt administration announced that the position of Assistant Secretary of War for Air would not be filled. This news did not displease the War Department General Staff.

Military aviation advocates during the interwar years: Brig. Gen. H. H. (Hap) Arnold *(above, left)*; **Maj. Carl A. Spaatz** *(above, right)*; **and Capt. Ira C. Eaker** *(below)*.

Wreck of the dirigible *Shenandoah* in September 1925.

Brig. Gen. William (Billy) Mitchell, a strident supporter of air power, with Maj. Gen. Mason M. Patrick, Chief of the Air Service, 1922.

Meanwhile, Billy Mitchell's attacks grew more intense. After naval aviation disasters involving disappearance of an aircraft in the Pacific and the crash of the dirigible *Shenandoah*, he charged that the War and Navy Departments were guilty of "incompetency, criminal negligence and almost treasonable administration of the National Defense."[7] As a result, President Calvin Coolidge himself preferred charges and the War Department announced that Mitchell would be court-martialed. The trial began in October 1925 and the guilty verdict with sentence of five years suspension without pay was delivered in December, two weeks after the Morrow Board report appeared. Afterwards, Coolidge lessened the verdict to five years at half pay. On February 1, 1926, Mitchell resigned. Ahead of his time, Billy Mitchell was a brilliant technologist, impatient because others would not share his confidence in machines that had yet to demonstrate their decisiveness in war. After Franklin D. Roosevelt became President, Mitchell tried to influence a change in air policy—more money and resources should be devoted to the air arm—but failed. Roosevelt in fact had opposed a separate air arm ever since 1919, when he served as Assistant Secretary of the Navy. Mitchell died in February 1936, convinced to the end that in any future war air forces would ultimately prove decisive.

General Headquarters Air Force

In October 1933 the Drum Board,* among other things, determined the Army's responsibility for the coastal air defense mission and recommended formation of a General Headquarters Air Force. The basic idea was to have a unified air strike force directly under a General Headquarters. This strike force could either be used for independent strategic operations or in support of ground troops.[†] However, the Drum Board report emphasized that the Air Corps should stay under Army control. Following a series of air crashes after the Air Corps was suddenly ordered to take over mail routes,** a board was created under for-

---

*Maj. Gen. Benjamin D. Foulois, Chief of the Air Corps, was the sole airman on the board. Other members were Maj. Gen. Hugh Drum, War Department Deputy Chief of Staff; Maj. Gen. George S. Simonds, Commandant of the Army War College; Brig. Gen. Charles E. Kilbourne, Assistant Chief of the War Plans Division, and Maj. Gen. John W. Gulick, Chief of the Coast Artillery.

†The Air Corps had advocated the mission of strategic bombardment and the destruction of the enemy's fleet. Advocacy of the coastal air defense mission was less controversial. Army aviators considered the coastal defense mission as important and legitimate. The bomber could strike aircraft carriers as well as the the enemy's airfields and industry.

**For an excellent discussion of the Air Corps' tribulations in flying the mail, see John

Courtesy National Archives

President Franklin D. Roosevelt, long-time opponent of a separate air arm.

mer Secretary of War Baker to investigate the organization of military aviation. This board was against an independent air mission and separate air arm, accenting that independent operations could not decide wars. It opposed creation of a Department of Aviation or a Department of National Defense, but did recommend setting up a GHQ Air Force. James H. Doolittle[*] filed a dissent to the majority report:

F. Shiner, *Foulois and the Army Air Corps, 1931–1935* (Washington, D.C.: Office of Air Force History, 1982), Chapter V.

    *When the Baker Board report was published, Doolittle was a major in the Air Corps Reserve. Commissioned a second lieutenant in the Aviation Section of the Signal Corps in March 1918, he resigned from the Air Corps in December 1930 to become manager of the Aviation Department of the Shell Petroleum Corporation. An aeronautical engineer and a crack racing pilot, Doolittle set a number of important aviation records in the 1920s and early 1930s. During World War II, he achieved fame as the leader of the Tokyo raid of April 1942. He went on to command the Twelfth Air Force, North African Strategic Air Forces, Fifteenth Air Force, and the Eighth Air Force.

> I believe that the future security of our nation is dependent upon an adequate air force. This is true at the present time and will become increasingly important as the science of aviation advances. I am convinced that the required air force can be rapidly organized, equipped and trained if it is completely separated from the Army and developed as an entirely separate arm.[8]

Doolittle and the Air Corps leaders were well aware that Air Corps strength had lagged behind the objectives of the 1926 Air Corps Act. Mid-1932 should have marked the end of the Air Corps' five-year expansion program. By that time the Air Corps had about 1,300 officers, 13,400 enlisted men, and 1,646 aircraft rather than the 1,650 officers, 15,000 enlisted men and 1,800 serviceable planes called for in the Air Corps Act. But, noted Doolittle, should the Air Corps remain part of the Army, it ought to have its own budget and promotion list and be removed from General Staff control. The desire for a separate budget and promotion list subsequently became a sustained theme of the air leaders.

The Drum and Baker Board reports supplied the crucial impetus to the drive for a GHQ Air Force. Another vital force was Maj. Gen. Benjamin D. Foulois, Chief of the Air Corps, who had long fought for a separate Department of Aeronautics.* After repeated attempts, he had finally convinced the War Department by 1933 of the need to assign the aerial coast defense mission to the Air Corps. Foulois' recommendation was approved in January 1933 by Army Chief of Staff Gen. Douglas MacArthur.[9]

Based on the Baker Board Report, the GHQ Air Force was created on March 1, 1935, with Brig. Gen. Frank M. Andrews named commanding general.† Andrews was a former commandant of the Advanced Flying School and had been chief of the Training and Operations Division in the Office of the Chief of the Air Corps (OCAC). He had served with the War Department General Staff before becoming General Headquarters Air Force commander. Formation of a GHQ Air Force in peacetime was unprecedented. During World War I the Air Service's offensive aircraft were organized under a single officer, responsible to the commander of Army Field Forces. As mentioned, in 1923 the Lassiter Board recommended organization of bomber and pursuit planes directly under General Headquarters. Also, Army Regulations 95–10 (March 1928) described bomber and pursuit aircraft organized into "GHQ aviation" under command of an air officer reporting to the commander of Army Field Forces. Notwithstanding, the Army had not shaped its air element this way.[10]

---

*Foulois in 1913 had opposed a separate department.

†The post of Commanding General, GHQ Air Force, was made a major general's slot. Andrews became commander as a brigadier general because the 1926 Air Corps Act restricted temporary promotion to two grades above an individual's permanent rank.

Air Corps units in the United States had been under operational control of Army corps area commanders in whose territory they were stationed. There were nine such corps areas, each commanded by a ground officer. In similar fashion to the Chief of Infantry and other Chiefs of Arms or Services, the Chief of the Air Corps had been responsible for support of his units—the design and procurement of aircraft, personnel, training, and doctrine. The Chief of the Air Corps was therefore not really an operational commander. With establishment of GHQ, General Andrews gained operational control of tactical units, which were formed into three wings.* Brig. Gen. Henry H. Arnold commanded the 1st Wing at March Field, Calif.; Col. Henry Conger Pratt headed the 2d Wing at Langley Field, Va.; and Lt. Col. Gerald C. Brant commanded the 3d Wing at Barksdale Field, La. The Chief of the Air Corps and the GHQ commander were on the same echelon of command, and each reported separately to the War Department. Here was a situation in which the Office of the Chief of the Air Corps controlled funds, personnel, and procurement of equipment. GHQ Air Force was responsible for combat efficiency and results, but did not have the controlling voice to gain the means to accomplish this end. Administratively, tactical bases were under the Army corps area commanders. Thus, when handling air matters, the Army Chief of Staff and the War Department General Staff dealt with the commander of GHQ Air Force, the Chief of the Air Corps, and the corps area commanders.

Obviously, this type of organization severely divided authority between the Office of the Chief of the Air Corps and the GHQ Air Force. Consequently, the air arm found it difficult to establish a single position when dealing with the War Department. In January 1936 the Air Corps' Browning Board[†] report noted:

> This organization has damaged Air Corps morale and has split the Air Corps into two factors (OCAC and GHQ Air Force). . . .the board believes that the present organization is unsound. . . .a consolidation of the Air Corps under one head will permit the Commanding General, GHQ Air Force to devote his maximum effort to training and a minimum to administration.[11]

The Browning Board proposed that the GHQ Air Force be consolidated under the Office of the Chief of the Air Corps. The board's report also recommended placing "all AAF stations and all personnel and units solely under the Air Force chain of command."[12] General Andrews of course firmly supported this last proposal. The War Department approved it in May 1936, thereby exempting Air

---

*The three wings together consisted of nine groups of thirty tactical squadrons— twelve bombardment, six attack, ten pursuit, and two reconnaissance.

[†]After Col. Williams S. Browning of the Air Corps Inspector General's Office who headed the study.

Corps stations from corps area control.[13] However, no immediate action was taken on the recommendation to place GHQ Air Force under the Chief of the Air Corps.

Determined to make GHQ a combat-ready striking force, General Andrews increased the flying time of GHQ pilots. A fine flyer himself (Eaker called him perhaps the best blind-flying pilot in the Air Corps) and convinced of the importance of an all-weather force, he insisted that pilots be qualified to fly by instruments. He inherited a force in which few pilots could do so, but after a year of GHQ almost all flyers were instrument qualified. Aerial navigation without use of known reference points and night flying were also emphasized. "The Air Force," General Andrews observed, "cannot be improvised after war is imminent. It takes years to build bases and airplanes and to train personnel."[14] Thus GHQ stressed combat readiness. The keys were mobility and effectiveness. A unit should be able to take off from its home station with all planes within forty-eight hours, fly to a specified area with minimum stops for fuel and oil, and then take off on a combat mission within twenty-four hours.[15]

Mobility of this "striking force of the air" called for rapid concentration of force in the Army's major corps areas. Strenuous training was designed to prepare forces to repel an enemy approaching U.S. coasts if the Navy could not cope with the situation (the Army and Navy had fought a constant battle over the coastal air defense mission). Also, GHQ would be set to strike enemy ground forces should they approach U.S. borders. Formation of GHQ was significant because it gave airmen the chance to coordinate air operations with ground forces. This was a step towards unified direction. Thus, the objectives, organization, and training of the General Headquarters Air Force were in a way harbingers of the development of air power and air organization during World War II. Of more immediate importance, creation of GHQ Air Force marked a workable compromise between those airmen who advocated an independent air arm and those on the War Department staff who continued to argue that the function of Air Forces was to support the ground element. Some Army officers thought forming GHQ Air Force would deflate the airmen's advocacy of a separate Air Force. After Andrews was reassigned in February 1939, GHQ was finally placed under the Office of the Chief of the Air Corps. This was a major move that seemed to solve a problem that had afflicted Army air organization since formation of the GHQ Air Force. Functions of the GHQ Air Force commander were unaffected, but his immediate responsibility was to the Chief of the Air Corps and not to the War Department Chief of Staff.

During his command of GHQ, Andrews made clear his conviction that air power should be separately organized and that bombardment aviation should be the basic element of the air forces as the infantry and battleship were the primary divisions of the ground and sea forces. Among other things, the development of the B–17 long-range bomber in the 1930s persuaded him that bomber forces

(Above) Commander of GHQ Air Force, Maj. Gen. Frank M. Andrews.
(Below) Maj. Gen. Benjamin D. Foulois, Chief of the Air Corps, with Brig.
Gen. Henry C. Pratt, during the Ft. Knox, Kentucky, exercises.

would play an important role in wars of the future. "Though both the Army and Navy have a requirement for auxiliary aviation to complete their combat teams," Andrews stressed,

> it must be remembered that the airplane is not just another supporting weapon. . . .It is the only weapon that can engage with equal facility land, sea, and other air forces. It is another means, operating in another element, for the same basic purpose as ground and sea power—destruction of the enemy's will to fight.[16]

He further argued that an adequate air defense could not be built under the existing organization. The United States was a secondary air power, this being true of any Air Corps that was an integral part of an Army or Navy.[17] The Air Corps, with its own budget, should be organized under the Secretary of War on a basis coequal in authority with the Army.*

General Andrews' views had brought him into conflict with the Chief of the Air Corps, General Westover, who opposed separation from the Army.[†] Westover thought that in the years after World War I, when the budget was slashed, all branches had suffered, not primarily the Air Corps. He considered much of the criticism of the War Department by his airmen unjust. These years were difficult, he insisted, and would have been so even if a separate agency had control of Army aviation. Westover remarked that the Army had made a good record in support of aviation. He charged that critics both within the military and without, who vigorously criticized the War Department, were in fact professional agitators. Additional criticism came from those who were ignorant of the issues or misunderstood the facts. To Westover, the War Department "need not feel ashamed of the showing it made in the air."[18]

Meantime, while the battle raged in the 1930s over organizing the Army's air arm, the Air Corps itself did not neglect doctrine. In the Air Corps Tactical School and elsewhere. the precision daylight bombing doctrine gained ascendancy and air theorists debated whether or not escort fighters were necessary. By 1935 bombardment officers accented speed, range, and altitude, and believed that fighter escorts would not be required. With an austere budget and better bomber

---

*After his tour as Commanding General, GHQ Air Force, Andrews reverted to his permanent rank of colonel. General Marshall then brought Andrews to the War Department General Staff as Assistant Chief of Staff for Operations and Training, promoting him to brigadier general. Andrews was the first Air Corps officer ever to hold this position. Later on, Andrews became CG, Panama Canal Air Force; CG, Caribbean Defense Command; CG, U.S. Forces in Middle East; and in February 1943 CG, U.S. Forces in European Theater. In May 1943, Lt. Gen. Andrews was killed in air crash in Iceland.

†Westover was killed in an air crash in 1938 and was succeeded by Arnold.

performance, pursuit aviation lost ground. By 1932 the Air Corps had started to test the Boeing B–9 and Martin B–10 bombers. The B–10 was an all-metal monoplane with a speed over 200 miles-per-hour, a ceiling of 21,000 feet, and a 900-mile range. This craft would open the way for development of larger and faster bombers.*

By 1934 the Air Corps had started engineering studies and announced design competition to build a long-range, multi-engine bomber capable of carrying a 2,000-pound bombload. Only the Boeing Airplane Company submitted a design for a four-engine aircraft. Its Model 299, featuring great range, substantial carrying capacity, and high speed, became the prototype of the B–17 Flying Fortress. The XB–17 went through flight testing in 1935, and on August 20, 1935, it flew from Seattle to Dayton at an average speed of 252 miles-per-hour, setting a nonstop record for the 2,100 miles. By August 1937, thirteen YB–17s had been delivered to the Air Corps.

As mentioned, air leaders were of course aware of the gap separating doctrine from available weapons. Geography and technology continued to be constricting factors. An enemy attack on the United States would have to be made by an expeditionary army supported by naval units or by aircraft launched from bases in the Western Hemisphere. As noted, the defensive mission of the bomber had drawn Army aviation into conflict with the Navy over the responsibility for aerial coastal defense.

This interservice dispute erupted after the war and lasted through the 1920s and 1930s. In January 1931 a meeting between Army Chief of Staff Gen. Douglas MacArthur and Chief of Naval Operations Adm. William V. Pratt led to an informal agreement spelling out the services' responsibilities. Naval air was to conduct missions directly connected with fleet movements; land-based Army air would defend the home coasts (and overseas possessions) and conduct reconnaissance and offensive operations beyond the lines of ground forces.

However, the MacArthur-Pratt understanding did not endure because Pratt's successor, Adm. William H. Standley, repudiated the agreement. And in 1934 the Joint Board, in "Doctrines for the Employment of the GHQ Air Force," stated that the fleet maintained primary responsibility for coastal defense and implied that the Army air arm would be used solely in cases of insufficient naval power to deal with a situation at sea.

In May 1938 this dispute broke dramatically when, during joint maneuvers, three B–17s flew six hundred miles into the North Atlantic to intercept the Italian liner *Rex*, bound toward New York. It was located and the Air Corps made cer-

---

*Also, development of the Norden (1931) and Sperry (1933) bombsights gave bomber advocates what they needed for precision bombing.

Gen. Douglas MacArthur, Army Chief of Staff.

tain that details of this operation found their way to the press.* The fury of naval authorities prompted the War Department to issue a verbal directive prohibiting Army air operations more than one hundred miles from the coast. Gen. Malin Craig, who replaced MacArthur in October 1935, sought to limit the Air Corps' coast defense activities. He wanted the Air Corps to concentrate on the support of Army field forces. Craig made a personal agreement with the Chief of Naval Operations in 1938 limiting the Air Corps to operational flights of no more than one hundred miles from shore.

Meanwhile, as noted, bombardment theorists at the Air Corps Tactical School—confident that long-range bombers carrying heavy bomb loads would be produced—had formulated the high-altitude daylight precision concept. The idea was to attack the enemy's economic structure and ultimately, if necessary, mo-

---

*A similar escapade had occurred in August 1937 when the War Department and Navy agreed to a secret exercise to determine if Air Corps bombers could locate and bomb Navy ships. In a test, Gen. Andrews' bombers spotted the U.S. Navy's battleship *Utah* and successfully "bombed" it. Subsequently, the secrecy of the contest was violated when a newscaster announced the verdict. Navy officers were outraged.

Chief of the Air Corps, Maj. Gen. Oscar Westover, opposed separating the Air Corps from the Army.

rale. Instructors at the school stressed that "no barrier can be interposed to shield the civil populace against the airplane." The objective was "to force an unwilling enemy government to accept peace on terms which favor our policies. Since the actions of that hostile government are based on the will of the people, no victory can be complete until that will can be molded to our purpose."[19] This meant using air power strategically. American airmen had been trained to sink ships, and Mitchell's demonstration against obsolete warships seemed to prove that precision bombing would work. Even so, aircraft were not yet able to bomb effectively at night, and illuminated bombsights would not be developed until World War II. Despite these drawbacks, precision bombing was also stressed because of the public's aversion to population bombing.*

In the 1930s then, with better performing bomber and pursuit planes being developed and produced, and with doctrine being refined, the debate over how to

---

*Air historians have often observed that the precision concept owed much to the American tradition of marksmanship. This may have been a factor, but a more persuasive case needs to be made for the climate of opinion in the 1920s and 1930s which was strongly opposed to bombing cities. General Arnold, a perceptive judge of opinion, was impressed with this public feeling.

organize air forces intensified. Traditionalists in the War Department still refused to accept strategic bombing as a way to avoid the carnage of the battlefield. The War Department General Staff believed that air autonomy would result in decreased funds for the rest of the Army's components. The leadership of the War Department held that independence for the air element would mean less than adequate air support for the ground Army. On the other hand, the aviators felt that only when they administered and controlled their own forces could aviation experience the requisite growth. In retrospect, Brig. Gen. Haywood S. Hansell, Jr., instructor at the Air Corps Tactical School, AAF war planner, and World War II commander, noted that "proponents of the two ideas soon lost all sense of proportion in the very intensity of their zeal. There was a tendency of the airmen to advocate strategic bombing to the exclusion of all else; and of the ground soldiers to view bombardment simply as more artillery." Hansell added that if the General Staff belittled the airmen's claims, "it must also be admitted that at least in some very small measure we may possibly have overstated our powers and understated our limitations."[20]

Air Organization in World War II

However, these arguments were giving way to the pressure of events. With Britain in a desperate struggle against Nazi Germany, air operations were already becoming important to U.S. war planning. President Roosevelt had ordered a huge expansion of aircraft production. "Military aviation," he said, "is increasing at an unprecedented and alarming rate." Nonetheless, the airmen received a setback in November 1940, when the GHQ Air Force was removed from the jurisdiction of the Office of the Chief of the Air Corps. In July 1940, Gen. George C. Marshall had activated a General Headquarters under the command of Maj. Gen. Lesley J. McNair, to train tactical units through the four field armies. The Army Chief of Staff then asked General Arnold to submit his ideas on organization. Arnold recommended three Deputy Chiefs of Staff for the Army—ground, air, and service forces. The Deputy Chief for Air would command all OCAC and GHQ air forces except those in the war theaters. Arnold's proposal was opposed by the War Department General Staff. In October 1940, Marshall decided to appoint Arnold as Acting Deputy Chief of Staff for Air, a position from which he could mediate between OCAC and GHQ Air Force. However, GHQ Air Force was assigned to the ground-controlled General Headquarters and placed under the direct control of the Commander of Army Field Forces. Also, air station complements again came under the control of corps area commanders. With Arnold as Deputy

Chief of Staff for Air, Maj. Gen. George H. Brett became Acting Chief of the Air Corps.*

Thus the drive for air independence suffered a blow. This reversion to split command would exist until June 1941, when the Army Air Forces would be established, with Arnold as Chief. Still, the impact of this setback of November 1940 was somewhat softened by Arnold's close relationship to General Marshall, Army Chief of Staff, and by the appointment in December 1940 of Robert A. Lovett as Special Assistant to the Secretary of War (to be redesignated as Assistant Secretary of War for Air in April 1941). Meanwhile, the difficulty of getting prompt action on air matters from the War Department General Staff induced General Marshall and Secretary of War Henry L. Stimson to consider reform of air administration. Arnold had already informed Marshall of the need for decisions to accelerate the arduous task of rapidly building up the air arm. Action must be taken, Stimson directed,

> to place our air arm under one responsible head and. . .plans should be worked out to develop an organization staffed and equipped to provide the ground forces with essential aircraft units for joint operations while at the same time expanding and decentralizing our staff work to permit Air Force autonomy in the degree needed.[21]

Accordingly, in late March 1941, Marshall ordered General Arnold, Deputy Chief of Staff for Air, to coordinate all air matters. Marshall wanted a simpler system with direct lines of authority. In April, Marshall, Arnold, and Lovett, now Assistant Secretary of War for Air, agreed that for the time being, quasi-autonomy for the air arm was preferable to separation from the Army. They did not want to generate a harsh debate when the Air Corps faced the formidable task of expanding its forces. Hence, a compromise was reached through a revision of Army Regulations (AR) 95–5. On June 20, 1941, the Army Air Forces was established, the first major organizational step toward autonomy since formation of the GHQ Air Force in 1935.

Army Regulations 95–5 stipulated that the AAF "shall consist of the Headquarters Army Air Forces, the Air Force Combat Command, the Air Corps, and all other air units."[22] The Chief of Army Air Forces—also to be Deputy Chief of Staff for Air—would be directly responsible to the Secretary of War and the

---

*Brett graduated from the Virginia Military Instutute in 1909, joined the Cavalry in 1911, and turned to aviation in 1915. He commanded airfields after World War I, built a reputation in the materiel field between the wars, and was appointed commanding officer of the 19th Composite Wing in mid-1936. Prior to becoming Acting Chief of the Air Corps, he had been Chief of the Materiel Division at Wright Field and then also held the top materiel position in the Office of the Chief of the Air Corps.

Army Chief of Staff for making aviation policies and plans. He would also coordinate the Office of the Chief of the Air Corps agencies and an Air Force Combat Command (AFCC), a redesignated GHQ Air Force. According to AR 95–5, the Commanding General, Air Force Combat Command, when directed by the Chief of the Army Air Forces, was to prepare plans for defense against air attack on the continental United States. The AFCC was further responsible for operational training and development of air doctrine.[23] The Chief of the Air Corps would supervise research and development, procurement, supply and maintenance. He would in addition supply the War Department with the "basis for requirements of personnel, equipment and stores to be furnished by arms and services to the Army Air Forces."[24]

Also, the Air Council was created to review periodically all Army aviation projects and matters of aviation policy. The council comprised the Assistant Secretary of War for Air; the AAF Chief (President); Chief, War Plans Division (War Department General Staff); Commanding General, Air Force Combat Command; and the Chief of the Air Corps. From the AAF's view, AR 95–5 was

Maj. Gen. H. H. Arnold and Gen. George C. Marshall at Randolph Field, Texas, 1941. The close relationship between the two advanced the cause of strengthening the air arm.

Courtesy National Archives

Henry L. Stimson, Secretary of War, advocated limited autonomy for the Air Corps.

just an interim solution to the problem of gaining even more autonomy, although this directive gave the new AAF chief an Air Staff. The utility of the Air Staff lay in its assisting the Chief of the Army Air Forces to deal with aviation matters and to form air policy. Creation of the Air Staff could be seen to stem from Stimson's desire to afford the Air Forces more autonomy.

The Army Air Forces also enhanced its authority on July 10, 1941, when the Joint Army–Navy Board added to its members the Deputy Chief of Staff for Air as well as the Navy's Chief of the Bureau of Aeronautics. Perhaps the most meaningful gain occurred in August 1941 when General Arnold accompanied President Franklin D. Roosevelt to the Atlantic Conference meeting with British Prime Minister Winston Churchill. Arnold was present because the British were represented by their air, ground, and naval chiefs (the Royal Air Force was an independent service), and it was therefore necessary for Roosevelt to have his chief airman there. But it was equally true that the President had ordered a substantial expansion of aircraft production and that American airmen were drafting major offensive air plans. Thus, when the war began, Arnold took his place as a member of the U.S. Joint Chiefs of Staff (JCS) and the Anglo-American Combined

Chiefs of Staff (CCS). * This implied recognition that the Air Forces had become the equal of land and sea forces.

While this air buildup was proceeding, the Air Corps had taken a number of actions designed to strengthen its forces. The War Department had formed an Air Defense Command in early 1940 under Brig. Gen. James E. Chaney. This command was a planning agency; responsibility for continental air defense remained with the GHQ Air Force. In the spring of 1941, the War Department established the Northeastern, Central, Southern, and Western Defense Commands to plan for the complete defense of these areas. At the same time, air districts were redesignated the First, Second, Third, and Fourth Air Forces. They were given the responsibility for air defense planning and organization along the east coast; in the northwest and the mountain areas; in the southeastern region; and along the west coast and in the southwest. In late 1940 and early 1941, moves were also taken to strengthen the air forces in such places, among others, as the Caribbean and Hawaii. A Caribbean Defense Command was created and in Hawaii the Hawaiian Air Force was activated.

Of enduring importance to the AAF's rising influence in high councils was the personal relationship of Arnold to Marshall, resting on mutual respect and confidence. They had come to know each other in 1914 during their Army service in the Philippines. Marshall trusted Arnold's judgment in air matters and what General Arnold proposed, Marshall, if possible, usually accepted. As Marshall noted, during the war he had tried to make Arnold "as nearly as I could Chief of Staff of the Air without any restraint although he was very subordinate. And he was very appreciative of this."[25] Marshall remarked that one of his problems early in the war was the immaturity of Arnold's staff. He referred not necessarily to age, but to lack of experience in staff work. Additionally, Marshall took exception to the airmen's agitating over promotions (they were not coming rapidly enough) and the need for a separate air force. Separation, asserted Marshall, "was out of the question at that time. They didn't have the trained people for it at all. . . .When they came back after the war, the Air Corps had the nucleus of very able staff officers but that wasn't true at all at the start."[26]

General Marshall linked the air leaders' desire for more freedom with his own conviction that it was time to decentralize the General Staff's operating responsibilities. The staff, he noted, had "lost track of the purpose of its existence. It had become a huge, bureaucratic, red tape-ridden, operating agency. It slowed down

---

*The Joint Chiefs of Staff commenced formal meetings in February 1942. During the war, an official charter establishing the U. S. Joint Chiefs was never promulgated. For a succinct consideration of the development of the Joint Chiefs and the Combined Chiefs of Staff, see Ray S. Cline, *The War Department, Washington Command Post: The Operations Division* (Washington, 1951), pp 98–106.

ARMY AIR FORCES ORGANIZATION
24 DECEMBER 1941

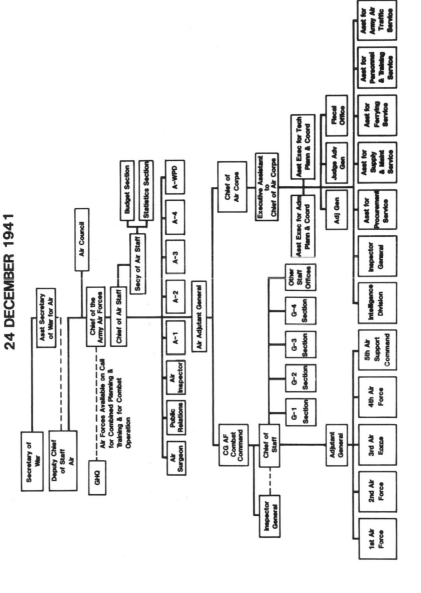

everything."[27] Many staff officers had to coordinate on papers winding their way through the echelons of the War Department. The chief and his three deputies had become mired in detail and paperwork. Marshall was determined to replace the horizontal bureaucratic structure with a vertical one. He could then devote his time to planning strategy and directing the war. And Arnold, of course, looked upon AR 95–5 as just another step in the direction of autonomy. The Air Staff still had to answer to the War Department General Staff. The AAF did not control its own budget and promotion system, a constant frustration to the airmen.* Relations between the Air Force Combat Command and AAF continued to be unsatisfactory just as those between the Chief of the Air Corps and GHQ Air Force had been divisive.

Arnold wanted to reorganize to eliminate these troubles and guarantee the proper exploitation of air power by air officers. In October 1941, with Arnold's approval, Brig. Gen. Carl A. Spaatz, Chief of the Air Staff, recommended that the War Department create three autonomous commands—air forces, ground forces, and service forces. Although the War Department rejected this proposal. Arnold in November suggested a similar reorganization. This plan centered on the complementary relationship of ground and air forces in modern warfare. In an unprecedented passage, stressing the interdependence of the principles of strategy and organization, General Arnold emphasized the unity of command:

> The development of the Air Force as a new and coordinated member of the combat team has introduced new methods of waging war. Although the basic Principles of War remain unchanged, the introduction of these new methods has altered the application of those Principles of War to modern combat. In the past the military commander has been concerned with the employment of a single decisive arm, which was supported by auxiliary arms and services. . . .Today the military commander has two striking arms. These two arms are capable of operating together at a single time and place, on the battlefield. But they are also capable of operating singly at places remote from each other. The great range of the air arm makes it possible to strike far from the battlefield, and attack the sources of enemy military power. The mobility of the air force makes it possible to swing the mass of that striking power from those distant objectives to any selected portion of the battle front in a matter of hours, even though the bases of the air force may be widely separated.[28]

---

*One reason why the Air Corps wanted a separate promotion list was that advancement in the Army depended on length of commissioned service. Most aviators, being relatively young, ranked considerably down the Army's single promotion list. Also, flyers underwent longer training than ground officers prior to commissioning. This meant the airmen as a group fell behind in the promotion cycle.

According to Arnold, unity of command had in effect been achieved within the AAF, but not yet between the ground forces and air forces. A "superior" commander was now required to determine the proper use of forces for maximum results. Also needed was a superior coordinating staff, embracing both air and ground personnel. Arnold further recommended that the air forces and ground forces should have equal access to the common services and supply arms.[29]

The War Plans Division of the War Department General Staff approved Arnold's plan in principle, but before action could be taken the Japanese attacked Pearl Harbor and the United States was at war. However, partly owing to Arnold's proposal, Marshall in January 1942 appointed Maj. Gen. Joseph T. McNarney of the Air Corps to head a War Department Reorganization Committee. Serving under McNarney were Col. William K. Harrison, Jr., and AAF Lt. Col. Laurence S. Kuter.*

Out of this committee's deliberations came War Department Circular 59, *War Department Reorganization*, March 2, 1942, by which the Army Air Forces under Arnold achieved the kind of autonomy that Stimson and Marshall had envisioned. Effective March 9, this reorganization was for the duration of the war plus six months under the First War Powers Act of December 18, 1941. Most important from the AAF view, Circular 59 made the Army Air Forces one of three autonomous Army commands, along with the Army Ground Forces (AGF) and the Services of Supply [subsequently Army Service Forces (ASF)], the structure that had been recommended by Arnold and Spaatz. General Marshall remained as Chief of Staff of the War Department. Below the Chief of Staff were Lt. Gen.

---

*Kuter, a 1927 graduate of the U.S. Military Academy, had taught at the Air Corps Tactical School in the late 1930s and had functioned as a planner with the War Department General Staff from 1939-42. His intellectual capacity was highly regarded by senior officers. Marshall had been impressed by Kuter as a young staff officer. He had asked Arnold why he didn't make Kuter a general. According to Marshall, General Arnold had replied that he could not because he would lose all his staff. They would all quit on him if a man that young was made a general. So, recalled Marshall, "the next list that came in, I just wrote the officer's name on it. Within one month he was a lieutenant colonel. A month after that he had his first star." (Forrest C. Pogue, *George C. Marshall: Ordeal and Hope* (New York, 1966), p 291.) General McNarney was a distinguished officer, a graduate of West Point who had been commissioned a second lieutenant in the infantry in 1915. In World War I, McNarney served with the 1st Aero Squadron. He saw service with the War Department General Staff and in the early 1930s was commandant of the Primary Flying School, March Field, Calif. In 1935 he went to Langley Field, Va., as Assistant Chief of Staff, to help organize the GHQ Air Force. Prior to World War II, he was a member of the War Plans Division, WDGS.

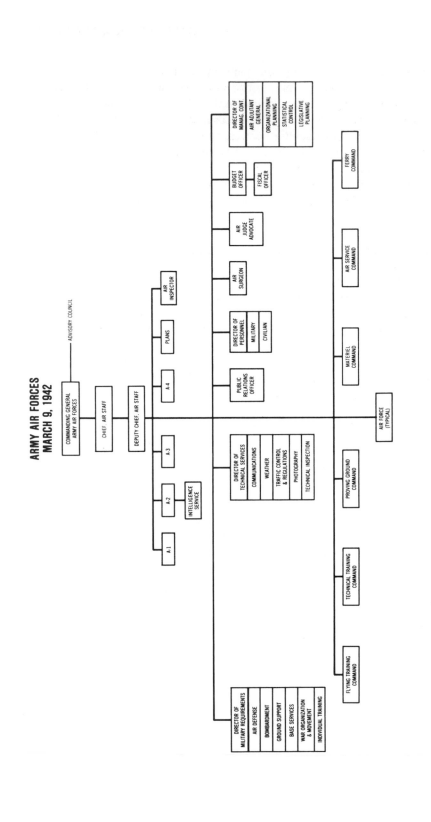

ARMY AIR FORCES
MARCH 9, 1942

Henry H. Arnold, Commanding General, Army Air Forces; Lt. Gen. Lesley J. McNair, Commanding General, Army Ground Forces; and Maj. Gen. Brehon B. Somervell, Commanding General, Services of Supply. The functions of the Commanding General, Air Force Combat Command and the Chief of the Air Corps were transferred to the Commanding General, Army Air Forces.* Circular 59 described the mission of Army Air Forces as "to procure and maintain equipment peculiar to the Army Air Forces, and to provide air force units properly organized, trained and equipped for combat operations. Procurement and related functions will be executed under the direction of the Under Secretary of War."[30]

Among duties assigned to Army Air Forces were the operation of replacement training centers and schools; organization of tactical units as directed by the War Department; development of tactical and training doctrine, tables of organization, military characteristics of aircraft, weapons, and equipment, and operational changes needed in equipment, aircraft, and weapons of the Army Air Forces; and also development (jointly with the Commanding General, Army Ground Forces) of ground-air support, tactical training, and doctrine in conformity with policies prescribed by the War Department Chief of Staff.[31] After March 1942, the Air Corps—which had been established by law—remained the chief component of the AAF, but the OCAC and AFCC were abolished, their functions taken over by AAF Headquarters. Officers continued to be commissioned in the Air Corps. This so-called "Marshall reorganization" enabled the Chief of Staff to plot strategy and direct global forces while the commands controlled administration and executed policy. McNarney observed that decisions would now be based upon a more deliberate consideration of the issues. Thus, the AAF had attained a substantial measure of autonomy within the structure of the War Department, a reorganization that Maj. Gen. Otto L. Nelson, Jr., of the War Department General Staff called "the most drastic and fundamental change which the War Department had experienced since the establishment of the General Staff by Elihu Root in 1903."[32] But this setup would expire six months after the close of the war, in accordance with the First War Powers Act of December 18, 1941.

Despite this restructuring, administrative problems persisted. Coordination within Headquarters AAF at times suffered since it was hard to fix final responsibility for various actions. Complaints from the field continued, the most prevalent being that the headquarters organization was confusing. With the AAF buildup going on, even more decentralization became a major objective. In consequence, after several headquarters studies, and proposals by General Arnold, a major reshuffling ensued. This new organization of March 29, 1943, abolished

---

*After this March 1942 reorganization, General Arnold, Commanding General, AAF, formed an Advisory Council—separate from the Air Staff—to report directly to him. See Chapter 2.

directorates and combined policymaking with control of operations in six recon-figured Assistant Chief of Air Staff (A–staff) offices: Personnel; Intelligence; Training; Materiel, Maintenance, and Distribution; Operations, Commitments and Requirements; and Plans. In addition, there were three deputy chiefs of air staff formed in 1943 and four from 1944 on.[33] The AAF reorganization of March 1943 was the last major wartime headquarters realignment.

As noted, the status of Army Air Forces had been enhanced by Arnold's membership on the Joint Chiefs of Staff and the Combined Chiefs of Staff, where the AAF Commander was privy to—and could attempt to influence—policy and plans.* The AAF's status and prestige received another boost from publication of War Department Field Manual (FM) 100–20, *Command and Employment of Air Power*, July 21, 1943. This manual established the strategic, tactical, and air de-fense roles as the primary functional missions of the air forces. General Kuter played a significant part in drafting this manual, having shown the interdepen-dence of ground and air forces in North African operations and having convinced the War Department of the need to state this in such a publication.[†] "Land power and air power," stated FM 100–20,

> are co-equal and interdependent forces; neither is an auxiliary of the other. . .
> the gaining of air superiority is the first requirement for the success of any
> major land operation. . . .Land forces operating without air superiority must
> take such extensive security measures against hostile air attack that their mo-
> bility and ability to defeat the enemy land forces are greatly reduced.[34]

The key tenet was that air forces should be used primarily against the enemy's air forces until air superiority was gained.

Based on the evolving experience of World War II, especially in the North African theater, this War Department directive defined command of air and ground forces in a theater of operations. Control of air power, it pointed out, must be centralized and command exercised through the air force commander. As for the responsibility of a theater commander:

---

*For an assessment of Arnold's wartime leadership, see Maj. Gen. John W. Huston, "The Wartime Leadership of Hap Arnold," in *Air Power and Warfare*, Proceedings of the 8th Military History Symposium, U.S. Air Force Academy, October 18–20, 1978 (Wash-ington, 1979).

†Brig. Gen. Kuter was named Assistant Chief of Air Staff, Plans, in May 1943. Pre-vious to this assignment, Kuter was Commanding General, Allied Tactical Air Forces and then American Deputy Cmmander under Air Vice Marshal Sir Arthur Coningham, Com-mander in Chief of the North African Tactical Air Forces. They successfully demon-strated the concept of unity of command of all air elements under a single air commander, working closely with the ground forces.

The command of air and ground forces in a theater of operations will be vested in the superior commander charged with the actual conduct of operations in the theater, who will exercise command of forces through the air force commander and command of ground forces through the ground force commander. The superior commander will not attach Army Air Forces to units under his command except when such ground force units are operating independently or are isolated by distance or lack of communication.[35]

Usually there would be one air force—the largest AAF tactical unit—in a theater of operations. Normal composition of an air force, under FM 100–20, included strategic, tactical, air defense, and air service elements. AAF tactical (offensive and defensive) air units were designated flight, squadron, group, wing, division, command, and air force.[*] The major aim of the strategic air force was to defeat the enemy nation. Selection of strategic objectives was done by the theater commander. He would as a rule assign a broad mission to the strategic air force commander and follow with specific directives.

FM 100–20 stipulated five kinds of tactical aviation: bombardment, fighter, reconnaissance, photographic, and troop carrier. Basic tasks of combat operations included: Destroy hostile air forces; destroy existing bases; operate against hostile land and sea forces; wage offensive air warfare against sources of enemy strength, military and economic; and operate as part of task forces in military operations.[36] Until the close of the war, FM 100–20 was the definitive War Department directive on employment of air power in joint operations. Mostly, it defined the tenets of unity of command in theaters of operations. The issue of unity of command in theaters and in the various headquarters in Washington, entwined as it was with roles and missions, would become a key issue during the postwar unification struggle.

---

*The flight, the basic tactical unit, consisted of two or more planes, the squadron comprised three or more flights; the group was composed of three or more squadrons; two or more wings formed an air division; an air command, which was both tactical and administrative, might have divisions, wings, groups, and service and auxiliary units. The group, made up of three or four squadrons and support elements, was the basic AAF combat unit. The group would consist of 35–105 planes and from one thousand to two thousand men. During the war, reflecting the influence of the RAF, the command became the major en- tity for coordination between the air commander and his groups. The wing served chiefly for tactical control.

Anticipating Postwar Reorganization

Thus, although changes in the organization of the War Department and the Army Air Forces had been made; and the importance of unity of command had been recognized and at least in part acted upon; the global scope of this conflict, with its concomitant organizational demands, forced military leaders to anticipate even more sweeping changes once the war ended. General Marshall held strong opinions on the subject of organization.

For the postwar period, he favored a single Department of Defense with co-equal ground, air, and naval elements. In November 1943, Marshall had formally approved the basic idea of a single department and referred it to the Joint Chiefs of Staff. "The lack of real unity of command," his War Department planners said, "has handicapped the successful conduct of this war." Unified command at top echelons had been pursued by means of joint committees to coordinate Army and Navy policies. Given separate military departments, these committees were perhaps the best solution possible during the war. But neither the War Department nor the AAF considered them to be a completely satisfactory answer to a thorny problem.[37] The War Department argued that: "Any system which depends upon committee action for high-level military decisions in time of stress is unsatisfactory, as it lacks the quality of prompt and decisive action that springs only from true unity of command."[38] Both the War Department and the Army Air Forces wanted a single department headed by a strong administrator with substantial powers at his command. Navy Department officials supported improvement of the existing system of coordination within the Joint Chiefs of Staff.*

As mentioned, the War Department General Staff had been impressed by the necessity for combined ground, air, and sea operations whose success depended on unity of command under a single commander. Moreover, as stressed in FM 100–20, effective coordination must not only exist at the highest level, but down through the command chain to task force commanders who directed forces of more than one service. The United States had entered the war unprepared for large-scale combined operations. Since the exigencies of war had forced the services into combined, coordinated operations, the single department conceivably could be the answer in the postwar period.[39]

During the war, General Marshall had frequently said that the postwar environment would be austere. He recalled the chaos created by demobilization after the first World War, and remembered that Congress in 1916 and again in 1920 had rejected the concept of a large standing army. So in November 1941, Marshall had brought Brig. Gen. John McAuley Palmer out of retirement, at the age of 71, to be his personal adviser on organization and to serve as liaison with the

---

*See Chapter 3.

the National Guard.[*] Marshall and Palmer had served together with General Pershing. Marshall knew that Palmer, unlike some Regular Army men, believed that in wartime the Army should be a citizen army, drawn from the reserves. Palmer advocated the citizen army approach and a system of universal military training (UMT). After the Japanese attack on Pearl Harbor, Palmer devoted nearly all of his time to postwar planning.[40] While Marshall, Palmer, and Secretary of War Henry L. Stimson strongly backed UMT, the Army staff opposed reliance on the citizen reserve Army.[†] Yet, as long as Marshall was Chief of Staff, the War Department firmly supported UMT in its official positions and before the Congress. Marshall did not believe that the public would go along with a postwar army larger than 275,000 men. Set on having peacetime plans ready for congressional consideration, Marshall in June 1942 formed a Post-War Planning Board to deal with the question of organization. And in April 1943, Marshall instructed General Somervell to begin a study of demobilization planning. Somervell set up a Project Planning Division in the Office of the Deputy Commanding General for Service Commands to recommend an appropriate organization to supervise demobilization. Then in May the War Department General Staff's Special Planning Division (SPD) was created to review postwar organization.

Too, War Department Circular 347 of August 1944, prepared by Palmer, prescribed that in its postwar plans the War Department would adhere primarily to a "professional peace establishment" of trained militia—the National Guard and Reserve forces.[41] This circular mirrored Marshall's views, describing a temporary standing army in the immediate postwar period. It defined the permanent military establishment as those forces related to a later period "when the future world order can be envisaged."[42] The peace establishment would be based upon a system of universal training. The large standing army organization, such as flourished in Germany and Japan, had no place in the United States. This country, with its democratic heritage, required forces no larger than necessary to meet normal peacetime needs. As viewed by General Marshall, the advantage of the small standing army was that its leadership could be drawn from the whole of society.[43] However, the Army staff generally favored a larger standing army than Marshall thought realistic and it was also known that General Dwight D. Eisen-

---

*For a consideration of John McAuley Palmer, see Irving B. Holley, Jr., *General John M. Palmer, Citizen Soldiers, and the Army of a Democracy* (Westport: Greenwood Press, 1982).

†For a detailed treatment of the the views of Marshall and the Army staff, see James E. Hewes, Jr., *From Root to McNamara: Army Organization and Administration, 1900–1963* (Washington, 1975), pp 136–37.

ARMY AIR FORCES
OCTOBER 1943

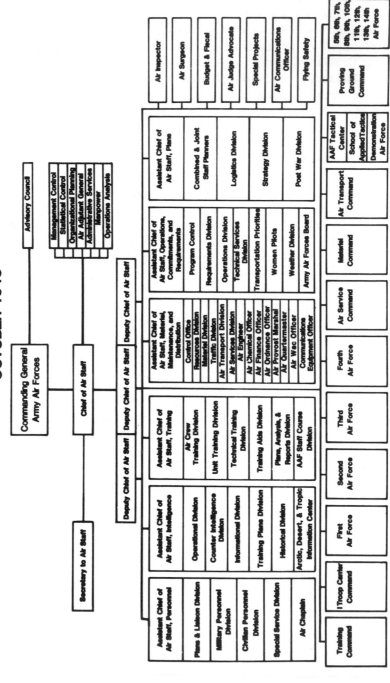

hower, to become Army Chief of Staff in November 1945, regarded Marshall's postwar planning figures as inadequate.[44]

According to War Department planners, austerity would require a determined elimination of overlapping functions. For example, economy would demand centralized control of military supplies in peacetime.[45] In late 1943 the planners recommended that a single Department of War should be headed by a Secretary of War with four Under Secretaries, organized into Ground Forces, Air Forces, and Naval Forces. There would be a common Supply Department. They also suggested a Chief of Staff to the President, a post held during the war by Adm. William D. Leahy. The Chief of Staff would head a General Staff composed of the three services (and the Chief of Supply).[46]

The planners urged the War Department to propose through the Joint Chiefs to the President the appointment of a commission. It would survey in detail the Army and Navy establishments and make recommendations for efficient and economical operation under a single department.[47] This should be done when consideration of such a proposal would not adversely affect the prosecution of the war.* Doing away with duplication and the importance of crusading for economy became recurrent War Department themes. Brig. Gen. William F. Tompkins, Marshall's top postwar planner and Director, Special Planning Division, testified in April 1944 to the House Select Committee on Post-War Military Policy (Woodrum Committee):

> We realize that in the post-war era this Nation will be struggling under the burden of a large public debt and that while the Nation will require adequate national security it will also demand that measures for this security be such as to provide for maximum efficiency and economy in the elimination of overlapping and duplication and competition between agencies.[48]

By 1945, with the war in its final stages, General Marshall (like General Eisenhower) thought that the most meaningful lesson of the war was that unified command had become a necessity. The way to assure unity of command was to create a single Department of National Defense. This view had been espoused by the War Department before the Woodrum Committee. Since then, Marshall had become more certain than ever that the single Department was the best way to achieve unification. Defense problems were not susceptible to solution by independent action of each service. Duplication could be held to a minimum and major economies realized by unification through standardizing policies and procedures in fields such as procurement, supply, and construction.[49] Mainte-

---

*In 1944 the Joint Chiefs formed a JCS Special Committee for Reorganization of National Defense. In its April 1945 report the committee recommended a single Department of Defense with a separate Air Force. See Chapter 3.

nance of a large standing peacetime army would not be possible. The military would rely upon a system of universal military training. The postwar military establishment would comprise the Regular Army, the National Guard, and the Organized Reserve.[50] The UMT system would furnish the trained manpower reserve. Marshall's concept was for Reserve officers to train young men in the UMT program. Thus, a substantial Reserve Officer Training Corps (ROTC) would be needed as well as officer candidate schools.[51]

Both Marshall and Eisenhower supported a separate Air Force.* However, because Eisenhower became Army Chief of Staff in November 1945, he would carry the burden of the Army's postwar leadership in advocating an independent Air Force. General Eisenhower had become convinced that there should be an Air Force coequal to the Army and Navy. He called this the principle of the "three-legged stool," with each leg equally importantøArmy, Navy and Air Force. Eisenhower's opinion was based upon his own experience as Supreme Commander in Europe, where he had witnessed the effectiveness of air forces in both the tactical and strategic roles. He was quick to remind people that the successful invasion of the European continent would have been impossible without air superiority.[52] Also, Eisenhower had enjoyed an especially fine relationship with his top airman, General Spaatz, and the Supreme Commander appreciated the vast capabilities of air power under theater command.

Lt. Gen. Ira C. Eaker, who as AAF Deputy Commander was instrumental in the planning and organizing of the postwar Air Force, observed that the relationship between Eisenhower and Spaatz "undoubtedly was primary" in the support that General Eisenhower gave to the drive for air autonomy.[53] Eisenhower admired Spaatz' quiet competence, dedication to mission, and loyalty. Beyond question, Eisenhower was now an advocate for air power. In addition, he firmly believed that unification was needed to ensure American security and to reduce the duplication so prevalent during the war. Upon returning from Europe, Eisenhower told his staff and commanders that he expected them to support the defense reorganization program, including a separate Air Force.

However, naval leaders thought otherwise. Before the end of the war, the Navy had taken a firm position opposed to unification (a single Department of National Defense) and an independent Air Force. James V. Forrestal, Secretary of the Navy, Adm. Ernest J. King, Chief of Naval Operations, and Adm. William D. Leahy, Chief of Staff to President Roosevelt, argued that sufficient unity of command had been secured during the war. Evolution of the Joint Chiefs of Staff

---

*While during the war Marshall generally submerged this view to the paramount goal of winning the war, there is no doubt that he favored a separate Air Force coequal to the Army and Navy. See Forrest C. Pogue, *George C. Marshall: Organizer of Victory, 1943–1945* (New York, 1973), Chap IV; memo, Eaker to Wolk, Feb 3, 1977.

Naval leaders opposed unification of the armed services and establishment of an independent Air Force. *Above:* Secretary of the Navy James Forrestal *(second from left)* examines photographs of the fourth atomic bomb burst on Bikini Atoll. With the secretary are Col. Paul T. Cullen *(left)* and Commodore Ben H. Hyatt *(right, bending).*

(*Left*) Adm. Ernest J. King, Chief of Naval Operations.

(*Right*) Adm. William D. Leahy, Chief of Staff to the President.

itself and creation of the various JCS committees, which allegedly fostered coordination, rendered undesirable what the Navy termed "revolutionary" reorganization. In the various and increasingly frequent proposals for unification and a separate Air Force, naval leaders detected a distinct threat to the existence of the Fleet Air Arm and the Marine Corps. The Navy likewise feared that eventually decisions on naval weapons and naval affairs would he made by officials without the requisite knowledge, or even worse by people who would not have the Navy's best interests foremost in mind. To men like Forrestal, King, and Leahy, these issues were real and threatening. They were determined generally to preserve the wartime organization.

General Arnold also held firm views on postwar organization. He naturally championed a separate Air Force coequal with the Army and Navy. He agreed with Marshall on the need for a military structure geared to unity of command. Both men wanted to avoid the chaos that accompanied demobilization after World War I. In April 1943, Arnold had set up the Special Projects Office to evolve postwar plans and to coordinate them with the War Department. And in July 1943, he had directed Brig. Gen. Laurence S. Kuter, Assistant Chief of Air Staff, Plans, to form a Post War Division.* Whereas Marshall saw the need for universal military training as opposed to a large standing army, Arnold promoted the idea of a substantial Air Force in being that could swiftly expand.

The question of a large postwar standing arm versus the concept of UMT had not been confronted by the services during the early part of the war. But as the conflict reached the final phase, this matter naturally grew more active and controversial.[†] In the spring of 1945, Arnold tackled this issue head-on. He informed Marshall that UMT should not be substituted for an M–day force, i.e., an adequate standing Air Force. Reserves simply could not match combat units which should be instantly ready for employment. In case of war, rapid expansion of forces should be anticipated and therefore a sizable standing training establishment would be needed.[54] With approval of the 70-group program in August 1945, a reduction from a 105-group plan, the leadership of the Army Air Forces would staunchly oppose the UMT program, ultimately championed by both General Marshall and President Harry S. Truman.

Arnold had other matters on his mind reinforcing his resolve to move ahead with postwar plans and eventually to gain independence for the Army air arm. He and the other AAF leaders were products of what they considered to have been

---

*See Chapter 2.

[†]See Perry McCoy Smith, *The Air Force Plans for Peace, 1943–1945* (Baltimore, 1970). Smith broke new ground with this insightful book, although it should be emphasized that the 400,000-man figure was basically directed by the War Department rather than selected by the Army Air Forces.

the unfulfilled years between the wars. They well remembered the bureaucratic and organizational battles with the War Department and the struggles in the Congress as to how military air power should be organized. World War II gave these airmen the chance to show the potency of air power and to prove their case for autonomy. The air leaders made the most of their opportunity. Air powerøstrategic, tactical and supportøvitally contributed. The road had been hard, and the AAF commanders had found it necessary to change doctrine and strategy when their plans were not working. In March 1945, for example, Maj. Gen. Curtis E. LeMay commanding the XXI Bomber Command, was pressured by Arnold to achieve results. Realizing that high-altitude daylight bombing was not succeeding against Japan, LeMay switched to low-altitude, night incendiary bombing. The results were dramatic.

Illustrative of his abiding faith in conventional bombardment forces, General Arnold in July 1945 at Potsdam, took the view that it was not necessary to drop the atomic bomb to end the war.[55] He thought that Japan would capitulate by October 1945 under the continuing conventional bombing assault which was smashing its war industries and urban areas. For years air leaders had argued that air power could defeat nations. Invasions were not required. The atomic bombs, Arnold wrote, "did not cause the defeat of Japan, however large a part they may have played in assisting the Japanese decision to surrender." Japan fell, in his view, "because of air attacks, both actual and potential, had made possible the destruction of their capability and will for further resistance. . . .Those. . .attacks had as a primary objective the defeat of Japan without invasion."[56]

Airmen were convinced their weapon had proved to be the indispensable instrument of modern warfare. Nonetheless, despite air power's achievements in the European and Pacific theaters, General Arnold remained apprehensive that this impressive record had not been sufficiently recognized. "We were never able," he wrote Spaatz, "to launch the full power of our bombing attack. . . .The power of those attacks would certainly have convinced any doubting Thomases as to the capabilities of a modern Air Force. I am afraid that from now on there will be certain people who will forget the part we have played."[57] Nevertheless, beyond a doubt, the American public and press were in fact impressed by the contributions of the Army Air Forces. *The New York Times* noted that "the place of air power in war now is. . .well recognized." The paper emphasized, "just how great a part" the AAF had taken in victory.

Arnold was also haunted by the fact that the United States had not been prepared for war. Victory had not come easily:

> As a nation we were not prepared for World War II. . . .we won the war, but at a terrific cost in lives, human suffering and materiel, and at times the margin of winning was narrow. History alone can reveal how many turning points there were, how many times we were near losing and how our ene-

Scientific advisor Dr. Theodore von Kármán led the planning of a long-range research and development program for the Army Air Forces.

mies mistakes often pulled us through. In the flush of victory some like to forget these unpalatable truths.[58]

He was determined to do all he could to make certain that the Air Force would not again be caught unprepared. Long before the war ended, Arnold started to plan for the future. He called upon Dr. Theodore von Kármán, the scientist. They had been close friends since the early 1930s when Arnold commanded March Field and von Kármán headed the California Institute of Technology's rocket research project. In 1940, von Kármán was appointed a part-time consultant to Arnold and a special adviser at Wright Field. Whenever Arnold needed help with a difficult scientific problem, he often requested von Kármán's advice.

In November 1944, Arnold asked von Kármán to form a scientific group to chart a long-range research and development program for the Air Force. "I am anxious," Arnold wrote von Kármán,

> that the Air Forces post war and next war research and development programs be placed on a sound and continuing basis. These programs should be well thought out and contain long range thinking. They should guarantee the security of our nation and serve as a guide for the next 10-20 years.[59]

In November, General Arnold formally established the AAF Scientific Advisory Group to create a long-range research and development program. The group's report, *Toward New Horizons* (33 volumes), was given to Arnold on December 15, 1945. Von Kármán's introductory volume attempted to chart the Air Force's future research and development requirements and to make recommendations as to the organization of research and development.[60] The report was distributed to the Air Staff in January 1946, Arnold calling it the first of its kind ever published. So before being succeeded by Spaatz in February 1946, Arnold warned that the Army Air Forces must stress plans for the future. The country needed to rely on technology rather than manpower. "The weapons of today," he admonished, "are the museum pieces of tomorrow."[61]

General Spaatz, who had commanded the Strategic Air Forces, had no doubt about strategic air power's effectiveness and its future role. In this view, he generally had wide support from the public and the press. The New York Times, noting the Army Air Forces' record in the war and the existence of the atomic bomb, observed editorially that "the era of continental bombing is with us."[62] Spaatz thought that the major lesson of the war was that prolonged ground wars of attrition could now be relegated to the past. Other airmen of course shared this view, outstanding among them being Marshal of the Royal Air Force, the Viscount Trenchard, who in World War I had created the Independent Air Force. He pointed up the difference between the two world wars. The First World War featured the stalemate of trench warfare. In Trenchard's thinking, the relatively lower casualties of the western democracies in the Second World War were chiefly due to the impact of air power. What he termed this war of "movement and maneuver" signaled a fundamental change in the nature of warfare."[63]

To Spaatz, strategic air power was the key: "Strategic bombing is thus the first war instrument of history capable of stopping the heart mechanism of a great industrialized enemy. It paralyzes his military power at the core."[64] Spaatz said the concept of strategic warfare was to shorten the conflict by striking directly at the enemy's industrial, economic, and communications organizations.[65] The prototype of a postwar force with such a mission was the Twentieth Air Force, which had pressed the B-29 strategic bombing campaign against Japan.* This force should be closely controlled, under command of the Commanding General, Army Air Forces, and should operate directly under the Joint Chiefs of Staff, as had the Twentieth Air Force.

The United States had come out of the war as the most powerful nation in the world, possessor of the atomic bomb. Even before the atomic bombs were dropped on Japan and the war ended, Army Air Forces leaders adhered to the be-

---

*See Herman S. Wolk, "The B–29, the A–Bomb, and the Japanese Surrender," *Air Force Magazine*, February 1975

(Above) In England during World War II, Lt. Gen. Carl Spaatz (center) confers with other generals of his command. They are (left to right) Maj. Gen. Ralph Royce, Maj. Gen. Hoyt S. Vandenberg, and Maj. Gen. Hugh J. Knerr.

(Left) Air power proponents Lt. Gen. H. H. Arnold and Brig. Gen. James Doolittle, ca 1942.

(Left) As a major general, Laurence S. Kuter proposed that the nation's strategic air forces be placed under the total authority of an independent Air Force.

(Below) Royal Air Force Marshal Viscount Trenchard and Maj. Gen. Ira Eaker in England, 1943. The RAF leader believed that the rise of air power was transforming the very nature of warfare.

lief later voiced publicly by Assistant Secretary of War for Air Stuart Symington: "To ever relegate strategic air again to a secondary position under the Army would be to insure the failure of adequate national defense." This was self-evident, he said, to "anyone who has no axe to grind."[66]

In June 1945, Maj. Gen. Laurence S. Kuter—from his post as Deputy Commanding General of the AAF, Pacific Ocean Areas—wrote Arnold to stress the importance of having the Strategic Air Forces recognized as on the "same level" with the Army and the Navy. In General Kuter's view, the Joint Chiefs of Staff had in fact made a "gesture" towards the AAF by establishing the Twentieth Air Force under the direct control of the Commanding General, Army Air Forces. What was now required, according to Kuter, was complete logistical and administrative authority for the Strategic Air Forces. Administrative control meant the Strategic Air Commander could make his personnel requirements known directly to the War Department. As things now stood, for example, such requirements were screened in the Pacific by General MacArthur. Logistical control was exercised by the JCS and the best that Kuter could hope for here was that the Commanding General, U.S. Army Strategic Air Forces, be given equal representation with the Commander in Chief, Army Forces in the Pacific and the Commander in Chief, Pacific Command (CinCAFPAC and CinCPAC). What Kuter emphasized to Arnold was that the postwar Strategic Air Force should be completely independent of the War Department and the JCS and should be under the total authority of the Commanding General of the Air Force.

The airmen were now agreed that an air power revolution had been consummated. World War II had been the costliest war in men and materiel in the history of the United States. Air leaders avowed that air power had been established as decisive in modern warfare. Scientific reports, such as von Kármán's, forecast an increasingly destructive role for air power in future conflicts. Not only was the atomic bomb a harbinger of potentially an even more destructive war, but scientists alluded to the future development of guided missiles and rockets equipped with atomic warheads. Nonetheless, for the present the long-range bomber remained the most effective carrier of the atomic weapon. Another of the war's lessons stressed by the AAF was that modern wars almost always began with air offensives and counteroffensives. Future conflicts would be decided in the air, not by mass armies on the ground, nor by naval forces on the high seas.

Army Air Forces leaders believed that a future war would start inevitably with an air offensive against the United States, perhaps over the so-called polar frontier. They claimed that the best way to prevent such an attack was to maintain an Air Force in being strong enough to deter the potential enemy from launching one. The Air Force, not the Navy, was the first line of defense. As Lt. Gen. James H. Doolittle stressed to Eaker:

It is obvious the Navy is aware that the capital ship is not the "First Line of Defense" of the future and, in order to maintain its prestige, is determined to retain and augment its air arm and ground component.

It is also apparent that the Navy fears an autonomous Air Force which would absorb the Navy's land-based aviation, and particularly fears a Single Department of National Defense which would apportion the drastically reduced defense appropriations between the services, according to their value and importance to National Security.[67]

The airmen contended that the nation's safety hinged upon having an independent Air Force coequal with the Army and Navy. It was to this task that they dedicated themselves.

2

Planning for 70 Groups

Two years of planning in the Air Staff have resulted in the firm conviction that the 70 Group Air Force (which excluding overhead for training civilian components has been squeezed into a 400,000 tentative Troop Basis) is the bedrock minimum with which the Air Force can accomplish its peacetime mission.

Brig. Gen. Glen C. Jamison
Army Air Forces Member
Special War Department Committee on
Permanent Military Establishment
November 1945

Early Postwar Planning

In 1943, Army Air Forces' Headquarters began concerted postwar planning. Between 1943–46, this activity involved a number of offices and sections and was primarily concerned with three kinds of planning: Force level and deployment planning, eventually culminating in August 1945 with establishment of the 70-group objective; legislative planning for a single department of national defense and an independent Air Force; and planning to organize Air Force Headquarters and the major commands. Postwar planners from several offices worked on these programs concurrently; indeed, the work was interlocking, the force planning, for example, impacting upon plans for a separate Air Force and for organizing the major commands. Especially at the higher echelons, planners worked simultaneously on more than one program. This work was immensely complex, frequently tentative, and influenced by the diverse views of the planners as well as by unforeseen events. The difficulty of this planning was heightened in 1945–46 by the rush of events—the end of the war and the concomitant beginning of the atomic era—and the need for speed in resolving the major planning issues. Although considerable postwar planning had been accomplished in 1943–44, some of it ultimately had to be discarded as unrealistic because of anticipated postwar austerity. Also, after the war, the confluence of massive demobilization and the requirement to plan the AAF's force in consonance with War Department projections made the planners' task even more complicated.

As mentioned, these Army Air Forces plans were subject to War Department scrutiny. Both the AAF and the War Department had their own postwar planning sections. Although ultimately liaison usually existed between these sections, draft plans were sometimes published independently and thus at first there was not always a great deal of compatibility between them. For example, the War Department several times ordered the AAF to scale down its force structure recommendations. Sometimes contradictions could be worked out at higher echelons, and in the most important cases it would be left to Generals Marshall and Arnold to settle the differences.

Thus, the character and substance of postwar planning in the War Department and the Army Air Forces were influenced by varied assumptions and opinions not always in harmony. Ingrained attitudes had been reinforced by experience. Simplistically, these differing attitudes were best exemplified by Marshall and Arnold. Naturally, divergent ideas and conclusions were also apparent between the War Department General Staff and the Air Staff. Finally, the march of events frequently influenced the planners in ways they could not have foreseen.

The Army Air Forces' major goal in the postwar period was to establish an independent Air Force. Other key considerations such as force planning, had to be judged on their relation to the objective of a separate Air Force. Postwar planning of organization and forces was also primarily based upon the lessons of the war as seen by the airmen, and on expected occupation responsibilities. General Arnold was determined that the air arm gain autonomy and he realized the necessity of wartime planning towards this end. Consequently, he gave high priority to detailed plans for organization, force structure, and deployment of the postwar Air Force. Moreover, the intense interest of Congress in postwar military organization (reflected, for example, in the Woodrum Committee hearing of 1944) put additional pressure on the AAF to produce postwar plans. The Army Air Forces required firm positions on postwar organization and structure to present to the War Department and Congress, and to ensure an independent Air Force.

In 1943, Army Chief of Staff General George C. Marshall had directed the War Department to begin detailed, sustained, postwar planning. General Arnold created two offices in the Air Staff to do most of the AAF's postwar planning. He formed the Special Projects Office under Col. F. Trubee Davison in April 1943 to coordinate planning with the War Department. In July 1943, Brig. Gen. Laurence S. Kuter, Assistant Chief of Air Staff, Plans, established a Post War Division under Brig. Gen. Pierpont M. Hamilton.* However, Hamilton headed the Post War Division for only a few months. His successor, Col. Reuben C. Moffat, served in this position throughout the war.[†] Eventually, as the Special Projects Office became increasingly involved with demobilization plans, the Post War Division assumed the bulk of postwar force planning. In addition to the planners working under Davison and Kuter, Arnold's personal staff, called the Advisory Council, actively engaged in postwar planning during 1942–44. Among the members at various times were Cols. Jacob E. Smart, Fred M. Dean, Emmett O'Donnell, Jr., Charles P. Cabell, and Lauris Norstad.

The Advisory Council, formed by Arnold in March 1942, consisted of several carefully chosen officers, reporting directly to the Commanding General, AAF. They were General Arnold's idea men, and as such they had no specified assignments. Arnold, at times uncomfortable with his large Air Staff, felt free to call upon members of the council for ideas and suggestions. Many years later, General Jacob Smart recalled that General Arnold had admonished him to spend absolutely all of his time "thinking." However, after Arnold had upon one specific occasion failed to convince General Marshall of something or other, Arnold emphasized to Smart: "From now on, you spend thirty percent of your time thinking and seventy percent on how to sell an idea."[1]

Actually, as early as April 1943, Brig. Gen. Orvil A. Anderson, Assistant Chief of the Air Staff for Operational Plans,** had afforded perhaps the first detailed view of Air Staff postwar thinking. His work, "A Study to Determine the Minimum Air Power the United States Should Have at the Conclusion of the War in Europe," dated April 1943, concentrated upon a recommendation for the proper AAF structure after Germany's surrender. The study did not try to describe a complete postwar AAF in terms of personnel, planes, and deployment.

"Military forces," wrote General Anderson, "are justified only as a necessary means of implementing national policies for the accomplishment of national objectives." He pictured U.S. postwar objectives as avoidance of chaos in Europe; restoration of sovereign rights and self-government to those forcefully deprived of them; creation of Western Hemisphere solidarity and security under United States' leadership; assurance of permanent world peace and a stabilized world economy through use of an international military force; and an orderly transition from wartime to peacetime of the industrial organization of the United States and

---

*Hamilton had won a Medal of Honor for heroism in action in North Africa in November 1942.

[†]Moffat attended Cornell University for three years during World War I. He then enlisted in the Army and became a flyer. A graduate of the Air Corps Tactical School and the Command and General Staff School at Fort Leavenworth, Moffat was seriously hurt in an aircraft accident early in the war and never returned to flying status.

**In June 1943, this office became known as the Assistant Chief of Air Staff, Plans.

the world.[2] According to Anderson, American influence would depend upon military strength, the extent to which the U.S. shared in the control of formerly Axis areas, and the contribution the United States could make to the war-torn countries of Europe.

Upon Germany's surrender, the United States should be prepared to contribute the principal portion of the air component (chiefly bombers) of the United Nations' force. His idea was to offset Soviet ground forces by what he termed preponderant air strength.[3] The Soviets' postwar objectives, he emphasized, were as yet unknown.

After the war in Europe, General Anderson proposed there should be an AAF air strength of 6,000 heavy bombers, 4,000 medium and light bombers, 7,000 fighters, and 7,500 cargo craft. He noted that a powerful air offensive was the most practicable means to win the war in Europe and the Pacific, with a minimum loss of life.[4]

Within the War Department, the Operations Division and the Special Planning Division took over demobilization and postwar organizational planning. At Marshall's direction, the War Department's Special Planning Division in the summer of 1943 developed a tentative outline of a permanent military establishment.* This outline was sent to General Marshall in October 1943. Maj. Gen. Thomas T. Handy, Chief of the War Department's Operations Division, had remarked that this plan would not

> provide expeditionary or task forces. . . for prompt attack in any part of the world in order to crush the very beginnings of lawless aggression, in cooperation with other peace-loving nations. . . .To crush the very beginnings of . . . aggression requires a force in being, not a potential one.[5]

Marshall's written reply to this was that formation of a substantial ground expeditionary force would be impractical. "Having air power," he observed, "will be the quickest remedy."[6] Handy noted that the tentative outline seemed to have taken the view of the Ground Forces:

> Although it may be considered that the outline covers Air Forces as well as Ground Forces, I believe the Army should be divided into these two categories and covered separately, since their problems particularly as to reserves, training and equipment are not identical.[7]

Marshall agreed with Handy's comment.

Based on the Special Planning Division's outline (and Marshall's reaction to it), General Arnold, on November 8, 1943, requested Kuter to prepare a study on

---

*General Arnold appointed Col. F. Trubee Davison as air advisor to the Director, Special Planning Division.

(Above) Brig. Gen. Orvil A. Anderson prepared a detailed study on the degree of air strength needed to ensure peace in the postwar period.

(Left) Army Chief of Staff Marshall — the impetus for post-war planning in the AAF.

the organization and composition of the postwar air force. This preliminary study, submitted to the Chief of Air Staff on November 13, proposed an M–day (first day of mobilization) force of 105 groups, deployed in five Air Forces (changed to six in December). It assumed that fifty percent of the active duty M–day force should consist of professional soldiers and career officers and fifty percent universal service enlisted personnel and short-term officers.[8] A December 1943 revision of the preliminary study delineated troop requirements of 530,000 officers and enlisted men for a force of 105 combat groups:[9]

	Atlantic-Pacific	Pacific Far East	U.S.-Alaska-Caribbean	Total
Bomb, Very Heavy	10	25	5	40
Bomb, Heavy	0	1	1	2
Bomb, Light	0	0	4	4
Fighter	10	25	10	45
Reconnaissance	0	1	2	3
Troop Carrier	1	6	4	11
	21	58	26	105

Drawing on Kuter's study, the Army Air Forces forwarded to the War Department in February 1944 the first tentative plan for a postwar Air Force. Known as Initial Postwar Air Force–1 (IPWAF–1), this plan was influenced by Handy's guidance that an estimate of the interim forces (Army) six months after Japan's defeat and eighteen months after Germany's defeat would be about 1,571,000 with 105 air groups. The Army Air Forces IPWAF–1 comprised one million men (with an additional million in an Organized Air Reserve) in 105 air groups, distributed the same as above, according to aircraft type.

Approved by Arnold on February 5, 1944, IPWAF–1 was portrayed by Kuter as recommending a large force "according to former peacetime standards, and large in proportion to the conventional concepts of ground forces and naval establishments, but it is what we foresee will be needed to keep us out of a new war during the initial period of peace."[10] As Kuter admitted, AAF planners paid no attention to cost because in their view the alternative eventually might well be another war.[11] In other words, the planners proceeded on the assumption of proposing whatever they thought necessary to avoid future hostilities.

However, the War Department requested a more modest and less expensive plan based on a new outline for a permanent military establishment with a peacetime Air Force ceiling of 700,000 men and a 900,000-man Air Reserve. This second AAF plan, PWAF–2, envisioned a postwar Air Force of 635,000 (75 groups), contingent upon the existence of an international security organization to regulate world armaments. According to Kuter, it was presumed that such a world organization would be functioning at some unspecified future date. Only at that time could the final step be taken in progressive demobilization from war strength to complete peacetime status. Thus, in this early plan the Army Air Forces relied heavily upon the assumed policing powers of a world security organization. The Special Planning Division accepted this condition as a planning premise and the 75-group plan was incorporated into the War Department's postwar troop basis—1.7 million men—of August 11, 1944.[12] Kuter commented that both these plans were predicated upon "continued standards of quality, Air Force autonomy within a single Department of National Defense, universal military training and integration into the Air Force of the ASWAAFs (Arms and Services with Army Air Forces) and anti-aircraft artillery."[13]

Meanwhile, even though postwar planning (including demobilization and redeployment plans) remained a major function of both the Special Projects Office and the Post War Division, the Air Staff recognized the duplication and jurisdictional problems latent in this split responsibility. The Assistant Chief of Air Staff, Operations, Commitments, and Requirements also frequently contributed to postwar planning. And, as noted, General Arnold's Advisory Council likewise took part. Further, duplication abounded between the several offices in the Air Staff involved in the AAF's operational planning.

In September 1944, Brig. Gen. Byron E. Gates. the AAF's Chief of Management Control, proposed to Lt. Gen. Barney M. Giles, Deputy Commander, AAF, and Chief of Air Staff, that these defects be corrected by creating what Gates termed an "AAF OPD." Gates' idea was to form a single AAF agency above the level of the Assistant Chiefs of Air Staff to correspond to the War Department General Staff's Operations Division. Gates stressed that this would correct, among other things, the overlap in logistical and personnel planning. Logistical planning and the determination of total personnel requirements should be transferred to the office charged with operational planning. Gates suggested naming this new activity the Operational Plans Office. It would be directly under a Deputy Chief of Air Staff.[14]

At the same time, Gates suggested formation of a Special Plans Office to handle postwar civil aviation and demobilization planning. This office would parallel the War Department's Special Planning Division and would take over the duties performed by the AAF's Special Projects Office under Davison. Gates said this entire concept assumed that the Air Staff office responsible for fighting the war need not and should not be responsible for developing postwar plans, and that normal staff coordination would link the two functions. When the hostilities were over, the two functions would join in an office similar to the War Plans Division.[15] Giles and Arnold did not approve Gates' plan, preferring the present organization. They thought that the basic functional division, despite duplication, still served the AAF's major purposes as well as any other recommended organization. Arnold had previously made clear that he considered the Office of the Assistant Chief of Air Staff, Plans, as the primary planning agency in the Air Staff.

Thomas T. Handy, one of General Marshall's chief post-war planners, as a lieutenant general.

The Special Projects Office would continue to be the point of contact with the War Department's Special Planning Division.

Marshall Orders a Resurvey

In December 1944, General Marshall decided that the cost of this Army (a total of 4.5 million troops with reserves) was prohibitive, and a force of this size would be impossible to attain by voluntary enlistments in peacetime. He directed creation of a committee to "resurvey" postwar planning and to come up with a new troop basis, contingent in his view on a more realistic opinion of what Congress and the citizenry would support. The Army Chief of Staff ordered that this resurvey be based upon a Universal Military Training program, which he deemed absolutely vital to the success of any postwar military program. General Handy, acting on Marshall's guidance, had the Special Planning Division make UMT a basic assumption. No mention was made of an international security organization.[16]

The resurvey committee adopted these ideas in the "War Department Basic Plan for the Post-War Military Establishment," approved by General Marshall on March 13, 1945. This plan defined the postwar establishment as that organization to be in existence with the return to peacetime. The document was not meant to describe the requirements of the period of transition from war to peace. While agreeing that the United States needed adequate military forces, the War Department planners insisted that such adequacy would hinge upon the character of the postwar world. They could not foresee what postwar international obligations the United States would have to meet. This plan stated that the postwar military establishment would maintain the security of the continental United States during the initial phases of mobilization, support international obligations, defend strategic bases, and, when required, expand rapidly to full mobilization.[17]

Central to the War Department's plan for a postwar establishment was Marshall's familiar and oft-repeated concept of a "professional peace establishment." This meant a military structure no larger than necessary to meet normal peacetime requirements, to be reinforced promptly during an emergency by units from a citizen Army Reserve. The plan emphasized that the War Department would support a Universal Military Training Act to institute the principle that every "able-bodied American is subject to military training, and to furnish a reservoir of trained Reserves."[18] The War Department included a section, "Post-War Relationship Among the Principal Nations." Its major assumptions embraced the creation of an international organization, controlled by the major powers, to keep the peace and to control armaments. There were to be major power spheres of influence, each power to control its own strategic area.[19] The character of future conflict was described in these terms:

> the actual attack will be launched upon the United States without any declaration of war; that the attack will represent an all out effort on the part of the enemy; that the war will develop into a total war; that the United States will be the initial objective of aggressors in such a war and will have no major allies for at least 18 months. However, it will be further assumed that the United States will have cognizance of the possibility of war for at least one year, and during this year preparatory measures will be inaugurated.[20]

The War Department's basic plan presumed that Congress would enact a UMT program whereby young men would serve in the Reserves for a reasonable time after being trained. The plan also supposed that after M–day the military establishment could quickly expand to 4,500,000 troops.[21] General Marshall's advocacy of universal training was rooted in his philosophy and experience. The practice and tradition of democracy signified that the people of the United States would not support a large standing peacetime army. Nations like Germany and Japan maintained huge peacetime forces. Such a practice produced formidable military strength, but the Army Chief believed it would not be tolerated by members of a democratic state. Here at home a large peacetime force would be looked upon as a threat to our democratic foundations. Marshall further argued that the inevitable postwar slashing of the budget by the Congress, under pressure from the public, would thrust economy on the military services. Military forces would be reduced. Austerity would be imposed.[22] This happened after World War I and Marshall was absolutely certain that this cycle would be repeated.

Hence a system of Universal Military Training would be required:

> As all our great wars have been fought in the main by citizen armies, the proposal for an organized citizen Army reserve in time of peace is merely a proposal for perfecting a transitional national institution to meet modern requirements which no longer permit extemporization after the outbreak of war.[23]

According to this view, in a crisis the citizen Reserve could be swiftly mobilized. Thus, one advantage of UMT would be an Army not composed exclusively of the professional military class. The War Department expected the Congress to be receptive to this point.

Marshall and Maj. Gen. William F. Tompkins,* Director of the War Department's Special Planning Division, envisioned that sometime between the ages of seventeen and twenty, youths would enter the UMT program. During this training, they would not be part of the armed forces. Afterwards, they could only be called up for service during a national emergency declared by Congress. Registration, examination, and selection of trainees would be administered by civilian agencies. The training itself, given by the military services, would last one year. After completion, trainees would become members of the Reserves for five years or could enlist in one of the Regular military services, the National Guard or the Organized Reserve.[24] The Army Chief and some of his WDGS planners had little doubt that UMT would prove popular with Congress as an alternative to large standing forces. They fully counted on a UMT program being enacted. As a result, the War Department did not immediately draw definitive, detailed plans based upon UMT's possible failure.

In early 1945 the preliminary report of the War Department resurvey committee recommended a postwar troop basis containing a small, token Air Force—only 16 groups. Handy approved the report as a basis for additional planning; General Marshall noted this without formally approving the report himself. As a planning factor, the committee used an estimate from various economists that just $2 billion would be available annually for defense. While the committee later used a $5 billion figure as the maximum available (also for funding UMT), it funded merely $1.1 billion for the Regular Army of 155,000 and an Air Force of 120,000 men, enough for only 16 air groups.[25]

---

*Tompkins was Arnold's classmate in 1929 at the Command and General Staff School, Fort Leavenworth, Kans.

AAF Protests Resurvey

As would be expected, Headquarters Army Air Forces strongly disapproved of the resurvey committee's report. The AAF charged that the report's authors had failed to weigh the task to be performed; had not considered phased reduction in the size of the postwar Army in line with probable world developments and the domestic situation; and in addition had not provided for alternate plans to meet various possible major contingencies. Kuter suggested to Arnold that UMT might weaken the Regular, standing forces:

> Assuming a limited peacetime appropriation for aviation, if too great a proportion of the total effort is devoted to building up. . .a reserve of trained personnel. . .then it may be that the resulting regular establishment will be found in a sudden emergency to be too small to prevent a serious set-back. . . therefore the reserve components can be successfully mobilized and brought into action.[26]

In January 1945, General Giles, AAF Deputy Commander, and Chief of Air Staff, had reacted to the survey, based on a draft paper written by Colonel Moffat, head of the Post War Division. Giles informed General Tompkins, Director, Special Planning Division, that the postwar Army's size should not be grounded in an estimate of the peacetime national budget (assuming UMT and a balanced budget). Rather, the military should first set forth their minimum needs and then Congress should arrive at the budget. The AAF could not agree, Giles asserted, that planning predicated on limited men and funds was realistic if such plans failed to recognize the requirements of national defense.[27] Moffat had noted in his draft that there were known national commitments for defense, both of the Western Hemisphere and American interests in the Pacific. These dictated the minimum requirements for the peacetime Regular military establishment, when approached with an appreciation of possible developments in the world's military and political situation.[28]

An Air Force of 16 groups, Giles averred, would be incompatible with the War Department's UMT program to train 200,000 enlisted Reserves annually in the Army Air Forces. It would take additional groups to train the Reserve force. Eighteen months was needed to train a pilot for an operational squadron. And more training would be required for a Reserve officer pilot, for assignment in an emergency without further training. Moreover, Giles contended that an Air Force of 16 groups could not carry out its mission. He was likewise disturbed by the assumption that in the future the Navy would need a larger share of military funds than the Army. The size of the Air Force should not be tied to a split, "however generous, of the Army's traditional short end of the peacetime defense appropriations."[29]

General Giles recommended that before plans were drawn for the peacetime military establishment a political and military estimate should be prepared, so that the War Department could ascertain its minimum peacetime requirements and then draw up an appropriate plan. Such a plan should include forces ample for an Air Force to maintain peace by being prepared for action against a first strike by a potential enemy, and to repel attacks over a longer period while forces were mobilized and deployed.[30]

The 16-group proposal also aroused General Arnold's ire. The AAF Commander thought that the time had arrived to take his case directly and forcefully to General Marshall. As he saw it, UMT was becoming a threat to the necessity of maintaining an Air Force sufficient in numbers and overall strength to perform its mission. "There exists," Arnold said,

> a clear and inescapable requirement that a realistic basis for planning the postwar Air Force be found and agreed upon....At this moment we can do no more than set up a schedule of progressive demobilization based on definite phases which can be foreseen. But we should not do less.[31]

He told Marshall that the peacetime Air Forces should be able to support a quality M–day task force—mobile, effective, and capable of rapid expansion. Sixteen groups would not be nearly enough, seeing that the President had approved a Joint Chiefs' proposal to build a network of bases for hemispheric defense, now being negotiated by the State Department. It was contradictory to plan such a system of bases without an adequate force to protect them. To Arnold, national defense and hemispheric defense were synonymous. This 16-group proposal, Arnold charged, "would amount to virtual disarmament in air strength." An Air Force so small would be merely a token force, acceptable under world conditions which seemed highly improbable.[32]

The AAF Commander next turned to a point that had greatly troubled him and General Giles—the potential substitution of UMT for the M–day force. Arnold avowed that Reserve elements could not be equated with Regular combat units ready for M–day employment. Training was the critical factor. In the event of war, the need for a quick expansion of forces would demand a substantial training establishment to ready aircrews and operational units. UMT should not be regarded as the major ingredient in the military structure:

> If an aggressor is allowed to mount and launch a surprise attack, it is unlikely that there will be opportunity for our gradual mobilization....Our elaborate mobilization plan could be buried. . . .UMT. . .is a good thing, but only insofar as it supplements other military measures in proper proportion. If it can only be maintained at the expense of so great a portion of the peacetime regular establishment that the available M–day force will he unable to prevent our quick overthrow before the nation can be mobilized, then universal military training will defeat its purpose.[33]

(Above) Gen. H. H. Arnold and Gen. George C. Marshall, Cairo, 1943. (Below) Chief of Air Staff, Lt. Gen. Barney M. Giles (left) and Brig. Gen. Russell H. Randall seated in a liaison plane, July 1944.

If war came the United States could well be the target of a surprise attack. Consequently, there might be too little time to mobilize. Trained Reserves might never have a chance to enter the battle. The way to prevent such a failure, Arnold stressed, was to counteract it at once with superior air power.[34] An Air Force of 16 groups would be insufficient to train the 200,000 airmen each year, desired by the War Department under the UMT program. Aircrew training was geared to the number of units in the standing Air Force.

The Air Force had to be fully trained, ready to react in an emergency. Regarding the danger of a large peacetime force to the nation's economy and democratic tradition, it was judged secondary to a grave external threat to the country. Arnold, like Giles, noted that it took eighteen months to train individuals plus another year's experience in a tactical squadron; thus these men could not be expected to be effective upon mobilization. Reserve units could not be deemed equivalent to an M–day force. The AAF in no way accepted UMT as an alternative to a solid group program. There was no choice in the AAF's view between a large Regular force, ready to act instantly, and a much smaller force buttressed by UMT.[35] General Arnold's opposition to universal training, stated directly to Marshall, marked a significant departure. This was the first time that Arnold had presented his detailed case against reliance on UMT in writing to the Army Chief of Staff. This reluctance had obviously been due to General Marshall's strong, long-time support for AAF autonomy. Also, of great importance in March 1945, operations in both the European and Pacific theaters were entering critical phases that lent emphasis to postwar planning in Washington. Arnold, acutely sensitive to the connection between operations—especially the impact of major air campaigns—and postwar plans, felt this was the time to raise the crucial UMT issue with Marshall. Put simply, the AAF perceived UMT as endangering its plans for a large standing Air Force.*

At War Department direction the AAF would go on planning for UMT (in addition to 70 groups) over the next several years. But in 1945 it was already becoming clear in the Congress that, given the proven wartime potency of air forces, the AAF's opposition was going to make passage of a UMT program much more difficult than Marshall and the War Department planners had foreseen.

Arnold argued that should UMT be the only plan presented to Congress by the War Department, then "people may well look to the Navy to provide total secu-

---

*In September 1944, Arnold had told the American Legion convention in Chicago that the military required trained men prior to the outbreak of war. The way to accomplish this, he said, was to accept "the policy of universal training. . . .We may not always have time to prepare." (excerpt from address by Arnold to American Legion National Convention, Chicago, Sep 18, 1944, in Gen. H. H. Arnold Collection, Box 45, Post War Planning Folder, LC.)

rity in the air, as already advocated by many Navy enthusiasts." He could not imagine that the War Department would propose or condone a policy which might lead to the Navy's providing the M–day air force. Arnold suggested that the Army ascertain the composition being planned for naval aviation and what assumptions should be jointly agreed upon for naval aviation's peacetime mission. Arnold recommended an outline plan to serve as a model for demobilization of the armed forces. It specified three phases of air strength. In the first phase, before the defeat of Japan, the Army Air Forces would need 215 air groups with 14,092 tactical aircraft. The second phase (Initial Postwar Air Force), after the defeat of Japan but prior to creating an effective World Security Organization, would demand no fewer than 105 groups and 7,296 aircraft. Phase III, distinguished by an effective world organization, would require 75 groups with 4,233 aircraft. Arnold concluded that the War Department should accept his demobilization plan in successive phases as a model and should evolve a program around his premises.[36]

The War Department and UMT

In May 1945, Army Deputy Chief of Staff Handy responded to General Arnold. The reply—based upon opinions from Tompkins' Special Planning Division—as well as the Operations Division—was for the most part a restatement mirroring Marshall's view of what the public would likely support in the postwar milieu. Handy agreed with Arnold that planning should embody a progressive demobilization with reduction only as justified by world events. Once this initial postwar period had ended, Handy echoed Marshall's long-held view that the military would then face a situation similar to post–World War I. This meant austerity, paying off the public debt. Handy warned:

> Military appropriations will be greatly reduced. The burden of our national debt, the pressure to greatly reduce taxes and the necessity for the use of available funds for nonmilitary purposes will quite likely force the Congress into this position (austerity) even though Congress itself may desire something better in the way of national security.[37]

So postwar planning realistically should shape a military establishment to conform with such an environment. The Army Deputy Chief of Staff saw only a slight chance of having a standing Army in peacetime that could furnish the kind of national defense that the country deserved.[38] Thus, the War Department (with what it thought would be support from Congress) looked to UMT for the requisite military strength. This view, of course, clashed with General Arnold's conviction that the military should make clear what it needed, even in the face of possible austerity. The key to the AAF's view was provision for an M–day striking force which could fulfill international commitments.

General Handy contested Arnold's opinion that Reserves could not be considered equal to a ready M–day force. The War Department, Handy reasoned, would lack the funds to keep a Regular Army big enough to field a strong M–day force. Clearly the critical question was how well could the Reserve units be expected to perform. The War Department's position pivoted upon the potential existence of a successful UMT program with Reserve components trained and equipped to become part of the available M–day force. If this should prove to be the case, Handy said, then the Army would have a larger and less expensive M–day force than without UMT, depending entirely on what size Regular Army the Congress would approve.[39]

Arnold insisted that national security called for a statement of minimum military requirements (Congress and the public had a right to know), no matter what funds might be obtainable. Handy countered that it was impossible to predict future needs. It was the War Department's stand that after the war there should be a gradual demobilization with the Army being reduced only as justified by world events. Handy thought this would elicit congressional support for perhaps several years after the war so long as occupation forces stayed overseas and the world situation was fluid. Later on, however, the Army would find itself in the same position as after World War I—a sharp cutback in standing forces. To Handy and Marshall, the crucial element was still funds. Based on past experience, they were absolutely certain money for the military would be in very short supply.

Tompkins had pointed out that an Army Air Forces of 16–20 groups appeared to be as much as the peacetime national budget would allow. It also approached the ceiling which could be supported by recruiting. The cost of the postwar establishment—330,000-man Army, UMT, and support for the Reserves—was estimated by Tompkins at about $2.8 billion. This amount, he observed, "together with cost allocable to the Navy, represent a charge against the national budget which it is expected will be exceedingly difficult for the Congress to support with appropriations."[40] Nonetheless, the War Department was going to prepare a tentative alternate troop basis (composition) for the Permanent Postwar Army, resting on the premise that UMT would fail to become a reality.[41] As to the AAF's fear that after the war there would continue to be an even split in funds between the War Department and the Navy, Handy agreed that planning assumptions should be worked out with the Navy. And General Tompkins cautioned that the War Department should not permit itself to be placed in an inferior position relative to the Navy. Thus, the details of the permanent postwar Army troop basis should not now be disclosed. At this time, Tompkins emphasized, the War Department should not commit itself publicly on the composition of the postwar Army.[42]

General Tompkins claimed that the root problem of the postwar military organization was how to speed sufficient reinforcements to a small peacetime Army.[43] In May 1945, Tompkins outlined the foundations of the War Department's postwar program: An in-being postwar military establishment comprising the Regular Army, National Guard, and the Organized Reserve, to form the nucleus for initial mobilization if Congress declared a national emergency; Universal Military Training to mobilize a reserve of trained manpower during a national emergency; an adequate military intelligence network; an efficient industrial mobilization plan; and a satisfactory research and development program.[44]

The War Department's stance, as reiterated by Tompkins, was that American military tradition did not countenance a large standing peacetime Army, nor had the Congress over many years backed one.[45] On the other hand, the War Department did not want to see anything like pre–World War II Army strength: "In 1935, for example, we could have placed all the Regular Army in the continental United States, including the non-combat elements, in the Yankee Stadium and still have had empty seats. We will need a real force."[46] However, in May 1945

Maj. Gen. William F. Tompkins *(second from left)* **meets with** *(left to right)* **Brig. Gen. Kendall J. Fielder, Maj. Gen. Russell L. Maxwell, and Brig. Gen. M. W. Watson, Hickam Field, February 1945. General Tompkins was then director of the War Department's Special Planning Division.**

with the war still going on, the War Department planners admitted that too many unknown factors persisted to settle on the precise size of the postwar Army.

Although the War Department could not calculate the postwar Army's size, it harbored no doubt about the need for UMT. Without Universal Military Training, the standing Regular Army would have to be expanded. This larger force would be costly, voluntary enlistments could not sustain it, and it would not be in harmony with American ideals and tradition. Only by peacetime conscription or by financial inducements to encourage voluntary enlistments could such a large force be maintained. General Marshall, of course, did not consider either of these methods feasible. Tompkins accordingly turned to a system of UMT as the logical answer to the problem:

> In the event of a national emergency, we must place our principal reliance, as in the past, on our citizen soldiers. However, it is essential that these citizen soldiers be ready and effective if and when the necessity for mobilization arrives, and our plans for the size and composition of the post-war army must be based on these fundamental principles.[47]

As part of its postwar planning, the War Department highlighted the National Guard. Tompkins said the National Guard should be capable of immediate expansion to wartime strength, able to furnish units trained and equipped for service anywhere in the world. Eventually, the Guard should be able if necessary to help the Regular Army defend the United States.[48] Again, the key was UMT, which could place the National Guard in a position to recruit volunteers who had completed their year's training under the UMT program. In addition, the War Department was planning an Active as well as Inactive Reserve. In case of emergency, the Active Reserve would contribute units for rapid mobilization and deployment. The Inactive Reserve would supply manpower for assignment as needed. Reserve officers would aid in training young men in the UMT program.[49]

Even so, the Army Air Forces held to its previously stated view that the potential Universal Military Training program depended upon available aircrews and aircraft. Ground crews and technicians were but part of a balanced Air Force. Therefore, in planning for expansion and the most efficient use of UMT trainees, a proper ratio of aircrews must be trained.[50]

The Air Force portion of the 4,500,000-man Army to be mobilized within twelve months after M–day was 1,500,000. This would require the Air Force to train 200,000 men a year, absorbing nearly the whole Army of 330,000 proposed by General Tompkins' Special Planning Division. The AAF argued that the projected Army of 330,000 would not yield the M–day force essential for meeting possible international commitments.[51]

Establishing the 70–Group Goal

Meanwhile, with the war in Europe over, the War Department General Staff in the spring of 1945 started planning for an interim force to undertake occupation duties in Europe and subsequently in the Far East, after Japan's anticipated capitulation. For his part, General Arnold, determined to assign the appropriate officers to key postwar planning positions, reassigned Maj. Gen. Laurence S. Kuter from his planning post in Washington to become Deputy Commander of the AAF, Pacific Ocean Area. Maj. Gen. Lauris Norstad replaced Kuter as Assistant Chief of Air Staff, Plans. In 1942, as a colonel, Norstad had served on General Arnold's Advisory Council. Next, he was a planner for the Twelfth Air Force and the Northwest African Air Forces. From January to June 1944, he was Director of Operations for the Mediterranean Allied Air Forces. In 1945, based in Washington as Chief of Staff of the Twentieth Air Force, he worked directly under Arnold in planning the strategic bombing campaign against Japan. Norstad, in fact, was a protege of Arnold's. When Arnold summoned him from the Mediterranean to become Chief of Staff of the Twentieth in Washington, Norstad proclaimed his reluctance, not wanting to leave the Mediterranean Allied Air Forces just when the end of the war was in sight. General Arnold made clear to Norstad that as Assistant Chief of Air Staff, Plans, he should take the lead in planning the postwar organization and make certain that it would be compatible with an independent Air Force.

Also, Arnold transferred Lt. Gen. Ira C. Eaker from his Mediterranean command to Washington, as Deputy Commanding General, AAF, and Chief of Air Staff. In his new post, Eaker would control planning for the AAF's interim and permanent force structures. He would likewise have a dominant role in establishing the AAF's position on unification legislation. On May 31, 1945, Eaker approved and sent to the Special Planning Division an Interim Air Force plan consisting of 78 groups and 32 separate squadrons, totaling 638,286 military personnel. This plan was designed for the period from the end of demobilization to V–J Day plus three years. Still another plan, called the "V–J Plan," was created by Brig. Gen. Davison's Special Projects Office in mid-July. This demobilization plan, to be activated upon the defeat of Japan (which was assumed to be August 31, 1945), set the 78-group figure as the point at which demobilization would end. It called for 78 groups, 32 separate squadrons, and a total of 654,000 enlisted and officer personnel.[52] In completing these plans, Eaker was complying with War Department guidelines, stipulating that the Air Force would receive one year's notice of impending war. The important thing was for the Air Force to retain enough men to build an effective in-being force.

Meantime, in the summer of 1945, Navy Secretary James V. Forrestal proposed legislation to increase the permanent postwar strength of the Navy and Marine Corps. Forrestal's move disturbed both Marshall and President Truman.

It followed by a short time the publication of a report by the JCS Special Committee on Reorganization (Richardson Committee), scoring the absence of interservice coordination as one of the major deficiencies in wartime.* Marshall observed that Forrestal's attempt to enlarge naval strength by statute was a prime example of a military service going its own way and a demonstration of the need for unification once the war ended. Truman reacted by directing his personal military adviser, Adm. William D. Leahy, to order all the military services to rethink their requirements. "This review," the President said, "should consider our international commitments for the postwar world, the development of new weapons, and the relative position of the services in connection with these factors."[53]

As a result of Truman's request, the services quickly defined and formulated their postwar requirements. General Arnold instructed Spaatz, Vandenberg, Norstad, and Eaker to set the AAF's permanent peacetime force objective. On August 28, 1945, General Eaker approved the goal of a 70-group Air Force (550,000 men), a reduction from 78 groups. This landmark decision was not solely arrived at by deliberations of the AAF leaders. It reflected the War Department's decision of August 27 that the AAF would have to settle for a 70-group program within a 574,000-man figure. The 70-group, 574,000-man figures were broken down by the War Department as follows:[54]

Area	Total AAF Military Personnel	Number of AAF Groups
Pacific	174,000	29
Alaska	14,000	3
China-Burma-India	12,000	0
Africa/Middle East	1,000	0
Europe	97,000	20
North Atlantic	4,000	0
South Atlantic	18,000	5
Continental U.S.	194,000	3
Strategic Reserve	60,000	10
	574,000	70

The Army Air Forces disagreed with the location of specific AAF groups; for example, it was reconfiguring the number of groups to be stationed in Europe.[55]

This War Department personnel ceiling of 574,000 was specified for the Interim Air Force as of July 1, 1946, exclusive of students and replacements. The AAF was enjoined to reduce this number to 550,000 including students and replacements, as soon as possible thereafter.[56] At the same time, Eaker directed that the AAF would accept about 100 B–29s which were virtually completed.

---

*See Chapter 3.

Production of all other B–29, P–47, and P–51 aircraft not needed to meet the 70-group program would be canceled. General Eaker decided on 25 very heavy bomb groups of B–29s in lieu of the previously planned 40 groups. Of the already scheduled 40 very heavy bomber (VHB) groups, 28 were to be deployed to Asia (including the western Pacific), 4 to Hawaii, 1 to Alaska, 2 to the Caribbean, and 5 in the United States.[57] This deployment change by Eaker in late August meant that 12 very heavy bomb groups would be kept in the Pacific (25 VHB groups were there at the end of August); 1 VHB would be stationed in Alaska, 2 in the Caribbean, 5 in the United States, and 5 sent to Europe.[58] Very heavy bomb groups picked for Europe were the 44th, 93d, 448th, 467th, and 485th. Departure of these five units, scheduled for October 1945, was postponed to December and then to summer 1946. The delay was due to the need to replace many personnel of these groups lost through demobilization.[59] The War Department approved Eaker's very heavy bombardment deployment plan on September 1, 1945.[60]

The rest of the very heavy bombers would be used in the training program or kept in depots as a reserve. Long-range reconnaissance needs were to be met by rotating one squadron of each VHB group. Subject to reductions that might be necessary to meet the 70 groups, there would be 25 fighter groups, 5 of them flying P–80s.[61] In September the Joint Chiefs of Staff endorsed the 70-group figure, to be reached by July 1, 1946.

Also in September, Norstad explained the rationale that would be used to justify the 70-group Air Force. Two considerations were paramount. First, a substantial standing Air Force would have to be maintained because of the increasing American interest in international economics and politics. Norstad called this the "broadening" of the U.S. sphere of influence. Second, the time when an Air Force or an Army could be equipped and trained almost overnight was gone. "In the next war," General Norstad emphasized, "we will be in the midst of an all-out war from the start." Norstad specified the AAF's requirements as long-range reconnaissance, strategic bombing, air defense, support of ground forces, and the contribution of air forces to a United Nations organization. Perhaps the major consideration, he noted, would be the state of the postwar economy. To support a postwar Air Force of 550,000 would be inexpensive compared to the cost of conducting a future war.

In November, General Vandenberg, Assistant Chief of Staff for Operations and Training, apprised Eaker that the War Department General Staff had designated only 400,000 troops for the AAF. If accepted by the AAF, Vandenberg said, the War Department would freeze this figure until February 1947, when reductions might occur if Congress cut the Army's overall one million-man ceiling. Vandenberg approved of the 400,000 level, asserting that the War Department would permit 70 groups if strict economy ruled in the use of personnel.[62]

While these important decisions were being made, General Davison's Special Projects Office phased out in September 1945. Norstad, Assistant Chief of Air Staff, Plans, had assumed a far larger role in the planning process and would now monitor changes in the size and composition of the postwar Air Force. Davison's Special Projects became the Special Planning Division (under Col. Reuben C. Moffat) of the Assistant Chief of Air Staff, Plans.[63]

With the war ended and Eaker having formally established the AAF goal of 400,000 men as directed by the War Department, Headquarters AAF revised its V–J Plan on September 19, 1945. This revision of "Assumptions and Ground Rules" specified three periods: I, July 1945 to September 2, 1945 (V–J Day which had already passed); II, from September 2, 1945 to July 1, 1946; and III, from July 1946 to July 1948. The revision delineated an Interim Air Force during Periods I and II of a size and composition necessary to furnish occupational forces in Asia and Europe; provide a firstline defensive striking force and a strategic reserve; supply a military air transport service, operated by the Air Force for all the services; and maintain training and research facilities.[64] The strategic reserve was defined as that part of the Interim Air Force to be available immediately to reinforce units anywhere in the world.[65] The Mobilized Air Force referred to the 1,500,000 personnel for forming 131 groups that could be mobilized within twelve months during an emergency.

Thus, the Interim Air Force would exist until July 1, 1948, composed of 574,000 personnel exclusive of students and replacements. It would stabilize as

As Deputy Commander and Chief of Air Staff, Lt. Gen. Ira Eaker played a key role in planning the structure of the postwar Air Force.

Maj. Gen. Lauris Norstad. A member of the AAF's peace-time planning team, he foresaw the need for a large standing Air Force.

soon as possible thereafter at a period III strength of 550,000 including students and replacements. The September 19, 1945 plan also stated that the Interim Air Force would be organized so as to "facilitate early implementation of the basic recommendations of the Richardson Committee with respect to the establishment of a single Department of National Defense."*[66] This September 1945 plan in large measure bore the stamp of General Norstad, Assistant Chief of Air Staff, Plans. He suggested that the AAF take the lead in proposing a military air transport service, and encouraged Eaker to plan for the eventual integration of ASWAAF personnel into the Air Force. These recommendations fit into Norstad's larger framework calling for greater attention to planning for the transition to the peacetime Air Force.[67] Moreover, Norstad emphasized that the thrust of all postwar planning would be to foster the early implementation of the recommendations of the Richardson committee to create a single Department of National Defense and a separate Air Force coequal with the Army and Navy.

After President Truman had asked for the services' requirements, the War Department in August had created the Special War Department Committee on the Permanent Military Establishment, headed by Brig. Gen. William W. Bessell,

---

*See Chapter 3 for a discussion of the recommendations of the Richardson Committee.

Jr.* The Bessell Committee's report (revised many times in September and October) underscored that its recommendations should in no way compromise the goal of a single Department of the Armed Forces, if that is what should be decided upon. This committee also stated that the United States would undoubtedly keep a peacetime force and, in the event of an emergency, mobilize industry and the citizen army. The Regular establishment would be supported by the National Guard and the Organized Reserve. Adequate manning and training of these Reserve components could only be done by a system of Universal Military Training.[68]

The committee acknowledged the difficulty of planning the future organization of the military establishment as well as defining roles and missions:

> It is impossible at this time to envisage precisely the nature of the military establishment with which we will enter the next war. In the first place the decision as to whether or not there will be a single Department of Armed Forces will have a profound effect. In the second place the rapid strides which are currently being made. . .in the research and development of new weapons are such that our present concept of military organization, tactics and strategy may have to be materially altered. In the third place National Policy, on which military policy is based, is itself fluid.[69]

The committee's report thought it unlikely that the atomic bomb would be employed except in a conflict with a major power. For other wars, forces would be organized to use conventional weapons.[70] So, a series of arbitrary assumptions were made as to what the Army must deliver: minimum forces to protect strategically located bases in outlying areas of responsibility; sufficient air and ground striking forces in the United States, able to move rapidly to any area; and a nucleus of trained officers and men held in reserve in the United States.[71] General Marshall, however, found the committee's interim report unrealistic in that he was convinced that the cost to support such a permanent military establishment would not he voted by a peacetime Congress. Furthermore, personnel to support such a program could not be obtained by a voluntary enlistment program. Brig. Gen. Henry I. Hodes, War Department Assistant Deputy Chief of Staff, told the Bessell Committee in October that its suggested figures were unnecessarily large since the committee had yet to weigh the thrust of UMT. Hodes said that once a UMT program had been established, National Guard units could be ready on or shortly after M–day. Organized Reserve units could be made combat ready more

---

*Besides Chairman Bessell from the Operational Plans Division, the committee included Brig. Gen. Edwin W. Chamberlain, G–3; Brig. Gen. Reuben E. Jenkins, Army Ground Forces; Brig. Gen. Glen C. Jamison, AAF; and Brig. Gen. Henry C. Wolfe, Army Service Forces.

quickly than before, and the strength of a "skeletonized" Regular Army could be expanded as need be. He asserted that

> the requirement for an air force in being and strategically deployed, as well as for a high percentage of technical and specialized training, will require a corresponding increase in strength. Those units serving overseas may have to be manned at greater strength than those stationed within the continental limits of the U.S.[72]

Hodes directed that the special committee should emphasize: the effect of the atomic bomb and new weapons on warfare and the resultant changes in unit needs; an analysis of how many personnel might be procured by voluntary enlistment; the demand for stringent economy; the impact of Universal Military Training; maximum "skeletonization" of units in the permanent establishment; and maximum use of civilians. Hodes also wanted the special committee to keep in touch with the Patch Board, which was conducting hearings to recommend a reorganization of the War Department.[73]

In line with Hodes' directive, General Bessell advised the committee that AAF planning should be guided by the policy that air units in the continental United States would either be kept at 50 percent strength or the number of groups would be reduced. Overseas air units would be held at 80 percent or less or similarly the number of units would be pared. Bessell next presented figures totaling 435,000 men: Army Air Forces, 150,000; Army Ground Forces, 100,000; Army Service Forces, 60,000; overhead, 15,000; training, National Guard, Organized Reserve, and UMT, 110,000.[74] Bessell's guidance of course conflicted with the AAF's objective of a 70-group, 400,000-man Air Force.

In early November 1945, General Bessell pressed for a Regular Army ceiling of 500,000 with 200,000 of this figure allocated to UMT, National Guard, and the Organized Reserve. The remaining 300,000 would be divided as follows: AAF, 165,000; AGF, 100,000; and ASF, 35,000.[75] At this juncture, Brig. Gen. Glen C. Jamison, the AAF committee member, apprised General Norstad of Bessell's guidance which fell far short of what the AAF believed it needed. Norstad (now the primary focus for Air Staff planning since General Davison's departure from the Special Projects) Office) ordered Jamison to draw up a formal reply to Bessell's request. This meant assisting the committee with such information as needed. Nevertheless, Norstad instructed Jamison that under no circumstances would the AAF accept less than 70 groups and 400,000 personnel. The ceiling of 165,000 would in no way be a recommendation of the Army Air Forces nor would the AAF accept such a figure.[76] General Jamison followed Norstad's direction and on November 17 sent the committee information supporting a plan for an Air Force of 22 groups and 34 separate squadrons. Simultaneously, Jamison stressed the AAF's adherence to the 400,000-man, 70-group program.[77]

Jamison's Dissent to Bessell Committee

On November 29, 1945, having revised its figures once again. the Bessell Committee proposed to General Marshall a War Department troop basis of 562,700 including 203,600 AAF personnel, organized into 25 1/2 groups in the United States and 8 1/2 groups overseas. General Jamison filed a minority report suggesting acceptance of the 400,000 AAF troop basis.[78] Jamison noted that so far attempts by the AAF to receive approval for its force structure of 400,000 had failed. Typically, the War Department continued to recommend a ceiling considerably below what the Army Air Forces considered to be the minimum. Jamison pointed out that "after the second major war in this century and the costliest ever suffered by this nation, it is desperately necessary that we lay well-conceived plans for a military security force that will effectively guarantee the peace and safety of the U.S."[79] Like General Arnold, Jamison argued that the AAF would fail to fulfill its obligations if it did not make plans, aside from arbitrary budget estimates. The Army Air Forces owed the nation a realistic assessment of air requirements. Two considerations were paramount. The first was national security and the second was the economy. Air Staff plans since 1943, Jamison asserted, "have resulted in the firm conviction that the 70-Group Air Force (which. . . .has been squeezed into a 400,000 tentative Troop Basis) is the bedrock minimum with which the Air Force can accomplish its peacetime mission."[80] Reduction of Air Force strength from 400,000 to 203,600 meant a considerable diminution of the striking force. It was simply not acceptable to the Army Air Forces.

Jamison depicted the peacetime mission as building a ready striking force that could operate instantly on a global scale and at the same time protect mobilization at home. Overseas bases (with intermediate fields) would likewise be needed. It was contradictory to plan a network of overseas bases, as the administration was doing, and yet simultaneously slash the AAF below 70 groups, thus neglecting to allocate the requisite units to maintain such bases. Moreover, "stripping the Air Force of the units needed for its mission will be an admission that this country must rely for security in the air on the Naval Air Forces, which is a more expensive and less effective way of attacking the problem of air security."[81] The proposed Regular Air Force would be too small to meet its major responsibility—replying to a surprise, all-out attack. And again bearing down on one of the AAF's chief arguments, a point which General Arnold refused to compromise: a thoroughly trained combat force was required. The number of pilots having experience in combat units before entering the Reserves must be balanced with the output from UMT.[82]

Meanwhile, the long-time proponents of UMT, of whom General Marshall had been the most important and conspicuous, received a tremendous boost from the President.* Mr. Truman, who profoundly respected Marshall, was known to favor universal training. At a press conference in June 1945, he had pointedly mentioned that he held strong views on this subject, which he said he would subsequently make known. On October 23 the Commander in Chief delivered a formal address on UMT to a joint session of Congress. He said that the war just ended had made one point clear: If attacked in the future, the United States would not have time to adequately arm itself. Consequently, Truman said that the nation could either maintain a large standing Army or rely on a small Army supported by trained citizens, able to be speedily mobilized. To President Truman, the proper course was clear. The country should depend on

> a comparatively small professional armed force, reinforced by a well-trained and effectively organized citizen reserve. The backbone of our military force should be the trained citizen who is first and foremost a civilian, and who becomes a soldier or a sailor only in time of danger—and only when Congress considers it necessary. This plan is obviously more practical and economical. It conforms more closely to long-standing American tradition. The citizen reserve must be a trained reserve. We can meet the need for a trained reserve in only one way—by universal training.[83]

Truman recommended that the postwar military organization consist of comparatively small Regular forces, a strengthened National Guard and Organized Reserve, and a General Reserve composed of all male citizens who had received Universal Military Training. The General Reserve, as proposed by Truman, could be quickly mobilized, but would not be obliged to serve unless called up by an Act of Congress. To man the General Reserve, he proposed adoption of UMT, under which citizens would be trained for one year. Young men would enter training upon graduation from high school or at the age of eighteen, whichever was later. The President argued that this system would give the nation "a democratic and efficient military force." The atomic bomb, he stressed, was of little value without a strong Army, Navy, and Air Force. Truman urged Congress to pass UMT legislation promptly.[84]

---

*Secretary of War Robert P. Patterson was also an advocate of UMT. He generally supported Marshall's views and also emphasized the way UMT would stimulate a sense of responsibility and of duty on the part of the nation's youth. Patterson believed that "service in the ranks should be obligatory before young men could qualify for officers' commission." (Ltr, Patterson to Herbert Pell, Nov 29, 1945, in Patterson Papers, MD, LC, Box 21.)

Arnold Urges 70 Groups

Arnold, however, was not deflected from promoting the 70-group program. To the contrary, he renewed the AAF's attack on UMT and the Bessell Committee report. In December 1945, he underscored to Army Chief of Staff General Eisenhower that Headquarters AAF concurred with Jamison's minority report. A 203,600-man Air Force would yield a force in being that could neither sustain national security nor properly support ground and naval operations. Until the reorganization or unification of the armed forces, the minimum strength of the AAF to discharge its postwar mission was 70 groups with at least 400,000 men.[85]

Besides, Arnold strenuously objected to the way in which postwar requirements were being drafted by the services. President Truman had requested in August 1945 that the Joint Chiefs of Staff review the Navy's demands relative to the peacetime needs of all the services. Truman wanted nothing less than a comprehensive plan, but the question was how to develop it. Arnold opposed devising this plan by having each of the services independently arrive at their wants and afterwards forcing them to make minor revisions. The AAF Commander reiterated that the President wanted the Joint Chiefs first to consider the postwar mili-

Bessell Committee member, Brig. Gen. Glen C. Jamison, AAF, attacked the committee's recommendations and supported the 70-group, 400,000 military personnel program.

Courtesy National Archieves

President Truman and Gen. Dwight D. Eisenhower. The president favored maintaining a small standing Army, supported by trained citizen reserves.

tary organization the country needed, and then to figure out the forces required for such an establishment. Having the services work out their needs on their own, Arnold argued, was bound to spawn duplication and excessive requirements. It was simply not an efficient way to do business. As an example, Arnold pointed to the existence of two air transport services, the Navy's and the AAF's.* Such duplication was costly and Arnold suggested that the money would better be spent on research and development.[86] Over and above all other considerations, he thought the AAF might not receive the forces it required if the services continued independently to assess their needs. He wanted air requirements to be generally recognized as preeminent.

General Arnold repeated his preference for a single Department of National Defense as recommended by the April 1945 report of the JCS special committee. He said that this committee, whose sole purpose was to suggest a postwar organization for the nation's defense, consisted of members from all the services. He also emphasized that forces being proposed by the War Department for the post-

---

*They would be combined in June 1948, with creation of the Military Air Transport Service, under General Kuter. See Chapter 7.

ESTIMATED AIRCRAFT REQUIREMENTS
FOR 70-GROUP PEACETIME AIR FORCE

Regular Air Force Unit Equipment		Air National Guard, Air Reserve, Air ROTC Unit Equipment	
Combat	4925	Combat	2657
Transport	496		
Training	2040	Training	3000
Utility	697	Utility	500
Total	8158	Total	6157

Aircraft Reserve		*Aircraft Reserve*	
Combat	2634	Combat	266
Transport	50		
Training	204	Training	300
Utility	70	Utility	50
Total	2958	Total	616

Total All Components	
Combat	10,482
Transport	546
Training	5,544
Utility	1,317
Total	17,889

Estimated New Aircraft per Year	
Combat	2,600
Other Types	1,100
Total	3,700

war Air Force were wholly inadequate. Due to War Department restrictions—witness the Bessell Committee deliberations—the AAF lacked the latitude to draw up its own requirements, thus giving the Navy an unfair advantage in stating its aviation needs. In addition, the AAF had to have ample forces to support the planned international Air Force under the United Nations.[87]

The positions put forth by General Arnold and other AAF leaders were persuasive. They were highlighted in November 1945 when AAF and War Department planners discussed the overall War Department troop basis and the Army Air Forces' contribution to it. General Staff members, no doubt swayed by the new Army Chief of Staff Eisenhower's view on the significance of air warfare, became persuaded that the AAF must have sufficient forces to accomplish its postwar tasks. They agreed to the 400,000-man ceiling, to encompass students, "pipeline population," and other personnel in support of the 70-group program.[88] The 400,000 would be frozen from June 30, 1946, until February 1, 1947, when a reduction might be dictated should Congress then decrease the Army below one million personnel. Army Air Forces planners assented to this approach with the understanding that 400,000 would remain constant unless selective service or enlistments failed to meet the overall troop program.

However, UMT persisted as a major concern. The Army Air Forces wanted to be sure it would not have to support UMT out of the 70-group program. The AAF estimated a need for 70,000 additional men to support UMT, National Guard, and the Reserve. General Arnold regarded 400,000 as the minimum for 70 groups. The extra 70,000 would therefore have to be met from other sources.[89] Arnold next met with Eisenhower, who approved the AAF's position that 400,000 would not embrace UMT or other civilian components.[90] This number would support the 70-group program, including essential support units. Military personnel returning to the United States for discharge or hospitalization would be charged to the War Department's troop basis.[91]

With Eisenhower's concurrence in the 70-group, 400,000-man program, the AAF Special Planning Division (part of Assistant Chief of Air Staff, Plans), published on December 26, 1945, a definitive plan for the peacetime force. Titled "Assumptions and Ground Rules Pertaining to the Interim and Peacetime Air Forces Plans," it superseded the September 19,1945, plan called "Revision of the Assumptions and Ground Rules of the AAF VJ Plan of 15 July 1945." Distributed throughout the AAF, the new plan pointed out that the Army Air Forces was chiefly concerned with occupation activities in Germany and Japan, with demobilization, and with readjustment from war to peacetime requirements. The Interim Period would be the time during which these needs were being met, with the Air Force being known as the Interim Air Force.[92]

The December 1945 plan defined the postwar military establishment as the organization in being when the military returned to full peacetime status. This establishment was therefore not designed to meet the demands of the transition period from war to peace. But when the interim period ended and Congress passed legislation to put the Air Force on a peacetime footing, it would be known as the Peacetime or Permanent Air Force. And in time it would be termed the Air Force and would comprise the Regular Air Force, Air Reserve, and the Air National Guard.[93]

This plan described the Regular Air Force as the "professional component of the Air Force." In addition to the Regular Air Force, a volunteer Reserve Officer Training Corps system in civilian schools would produce a qualified reserve of air officers. Universal Military Training, once in force, would furnish a trained reserve of enlisted men. The so-called General Reserve was depicted as that part of the interim or peacetime Air Force "available for immediate reinforcement of units which may be committed to action in any part of the world."[94] The M–day Air Force consisted of combat units ready for action on the first day of mobilization. These units included the peacetime Regular Air Force (including Reserves on active duty, and that portion of the Air National Guard (ANG) available for immediate action.*

What became known as the Mobilized Air Force was the Air Force to be created within one year after a future M–day. As of December 1945, it was presumed that with a system of UMT and the resulting million-man reserve in the Peacetime Air Force, the Mobilized Air Force would total 1,500,000 organized into 131 groups (not including antiaircraft artillery). The 131 groups would be formed by 70 Regular groups, 27 from the Air National Guard, and 34 from the Organized Air Reserve.[95]

According to the December 1945 plan, the mission of the Air Force was

> to develop, train and maintain a military force. . .capable at any time, through the immediate sustained, and increasing exercise of air power, of defending the integrity of the United States and its strategic areas, of supporting US international obligations, and of cooperating with ground and naval forces similarly engaged.[96]

The same troop basis and group strength applied to both the Interim and Peacetime Air Forces: 400,000 military personnel and 70 combat groups. With Eisenhower's acceptance of the Peacetime Air Force, the "training overhead" of UMT would require another 70,000 Reserves on extended active duty. Composition of 70 combat groups would be 25 very heavy bomb groups, 25 fighter groups, 5 medium and light bomber groups, 10 transport groups, and 5 tactical reconnaissance groups. The plan also specified a Department of the Armed Forces with three branches—Army, Navy, and Air Force. Also in the postwar Air Force or-

---

*The December 26, 1945, plan presupposed that twenty of twenty-seven Air National Guard groups would be on hand for instant action.

ganization was a Deputy Chief of Air Staff for Scientific Research and Development.[97] In November 1945, Maj. Gen. Curtis E. LeMay had been appointed Deputy Chief of Staff for Research and Development.

The plan additionally called for an "Air Force School" offering Tactical, Command and Staff, and Air War courses, and for creating an Air Force Institute of Technology under the Air Technical Service Command. Antiaircraft artillery and Arms and Services with the Army Air Forces would be integral parts of the Peacetime Air Force. The ratio of rated to nonrated officers in this force was put at 70 to 30.[98]

Final Approval for 70 Groups

Definitive AAF postwar planning forced General Bessell in December 1945 to once again revise his committee's report. This time it afforded an Army Air Forces of 70 groups and 419,355 personnel (53,584 officers and 365,771 enlisted men). Eisenhower approved these figures in the War Department's Tentative Plan for a Permanent Peacetime Army, endorsed by the JCS in late January 1946.[99] As previously directed by President Truman, this plan would have to be integrated with the Navy's program. Hence, after nearly two and a half years of planning, a postwar of Air Force 70 groups and 400,000 men was finally approved by the War Department and the Joint Chiefs of Staff. Although some scholars* have written that 70 groups was basically an arbitrary figure, this objective should he considered as a culmination of two and a half years of intensive work. As we have seen, the Army Air Forces had at first asked for numbers far exceeding 70 groups and 400,000 men.† The 70-group program had evolved in the face of War Department disapproval of the 105-group proposal. Recommendations for the AAF peacetime force structure had reached as low as 120,000 men, a suggestion of the Bessell Committee. Between the summer of 1943 and August 1945, when the AAF set 70 groups as the goal, several postwar air plans had been drafted. As noted, the 70-group figure was set by the AAF only after the War Department had compelled the Army Air Forces to shape its group program to a 574,000 force.

The Army Air Forces took a firm stand on the 70 groups as the minimum force structure. General Norstad argued that the AAF had been under "great pres-

---

*For example, Samuel P. Huntington, *The Common Defense: Strategic Programs in National Politics* (New York, 1961)

†Group Strength during World War II peaked at 232 in early 1945. By September 1945 the group figure stood at 201; in October, 178; November, 128; December, 109. By January 1946 the AAF was down to 89 groups and in August 1946 to 52 groups.

sure" from the War Department to accede to a figure less than 400,000. As to the idea that voluntary recruitment could not support a force of 400,000, Norstad countered:

> We believe that we can maintain a voluntary force of 400,000 at no sacrifice to the other services if we have certain conditions such as an autonomous Air Force, a separate Air Force recruiting program, extra Air Force inducements such as education programs and increased incentives which would be common throughout all services.[100]

In essence, the AAF's rigid position for 70 groups revolved around the concept that this was the least number that could administer active duty training for Reserves to achieve the final mobilization target of one and a half million men within one year after M–day. Fewer than 70 groups could not keep aircraft production at a sufficient rate to meet mobilization needs.[101] The AAF further contended that it would take 70 groups to man the key bases "for protection of the country's interests."[102]

The rationale for the 25 very heavy bomb groups, as part of the 70-group program, was that "the western hemisphere and the Pacific are directly our responsibility and the VHB offers the only strategic coverage." A proposed mobile striking force would be built around the 25 VHB groups. Army Air Forces planners reasoned that in the event of war, attrition of heavy bombers would be substantial during the first year. The planners said that fighter, medium, and light bombers were supplied "in proportion to the requirement for short range responsibilities, tactical operations, and escort of the VHB force."[103]

Besides, the 70-group proposal recognized that it would be necessary to contribute to an air force under international auspices. The foremost factor, however, was the AAF's conviction that air power was now dominant. The United States needed an Air Force in being that could retaliate at once in case of a massive surprise attack.

So on December 26, 1945, simultaneously with publication of the plan for the Interim and Peacetime Air Forces, General Arnold directed that 70 groups and 400,000 men (70,000 more for UMT, National Guard, ROTC, and Reserve), be set as goals for both the interim and peacetime or permanent Air Force. From this point on, all AAF planning centered on 70 groups. The Mobilized Air Force would be reached within a year of M–day (first day of mobilization), and would total one and a half million men. Its 131 groups were apportioned as follows: Regular Army, 70; Air National Guard, 27; and Organized Air Reserve, 34.[104]

Of the 25 very heavy bomb groups, 5 were scheduled for deployment to Europe, 13 to the Pacific area, 2 to the Caribbean area, and 5 to be assigned to the Strategic Striking Force (SSF) in the United States. Seven of the 35 fighter groups would be in the European theater, 11 in the Pacific, 2 in the Caribbean, 2 in Zone of Interior (ZI) training, and 3 (long-range escort) in the SSF. Two medium and light bomber groups were earmarked for Europe, 2 for the Pacific, and 1 for the SSF. Four transport groups would go to Europe, 3 to the Pacific, 1 to ZI training, and 2 to the SSF. One tactical reconnaissance group would be in the European theater, 2 in the Pacific, 1 in ZI training, and 1 in the SSF.[105]

The air forces in the Pacific were to discharge the dual mission of what was termed United States security and the occupation of Japan. The AAF would be organized into an occupation air force for Japan and Korea, and a mobile and defensive force for security of the Pacific area. Units of the Fifth Air Force would be responsible for the occupation of Japan and Korea, under the direct command of the Supreme Commander for the Allied Powers. Other AAF units in the Pacific would be based in the Philippines, Ryukyus, Marianas, Bonin Islands, and Hawaii. These forces would be consolidated under the U.S. Army Strategic Air Forces, under the Commanding General, AAF, acting as executive agent for the Joint Chiefs of Staff.[106] The following is a breakdown of the planned 400,000-man Air Force:[107]

Function	Strength
Combat Striking Force	42,188
Technical Service	73,527
Flight Service	43,052
Operational Support Service	19,300
Engineer Service	46,958
Ordnance Service	1,208
Air Transport Service	46,305
Special Services	6,264
Air Defense	14,785
Training	67,143
General Overhead	39,260
Total	399,990

70 Groups vs UMT

By the end of 1945, it had become clear that the Army Air Force's 70-group, 400,000-man program was being seen in Congress as an attractive alternative to Universal Military Training. This was true even though during 1943–45 the War Department, spurred by General Marshall, continued to plan for a citizen army which could be quickly mobilized in the event of war. Moreover, all through the war, postwar planners in the War Department presumed that Congress would enact the UMT program. And of course President Truman was a strong advocate of UMT. He had in fact once told a reporter that he had favored UMT since 1905, upon first joining the National Guard. However, despite the manifest difficulty which UMT encountered in Congress, the Army Air Forces needed to comply with War Department directives to plan for a UMT program since it might be legislated by Congress. Thus, in 1946 the AAF simultaneously planned for a situation with or without a UMT program.

By early 1946 the War Department realized that chances were increasing that UMT legislation might not be enacted. Despite President Truman's having urged Congress to pass UMT legislation quickly, the lawmakers had failed to respond. And General Marshall's entreaties, prior to his retirement as Army Chief of Staff, had proved no more successful. The *New York Times* pointedly noted that Marshall had mounted a "virtual crusade" in behalf of the UMT program, adding that "the Army geared up its entire public relations machinery."[108] Nevertheless, it had become evident that Congress was not disposed to enact the President's program.[109]

In January 1946 the War Department sent a study to Headquarters AAF titled "Mobilization of the 4.5 Million Army without Universal Military Training." This plan was based upon voluntary enlistment for ten years, the first two years being active duty and the remainder to be served in Reserve status. Those in the Reserves from the third to tenth years would create a pool of trainees which could be mobilized in the same fashion as the pool established under a UMT program.[110]

The AAF concluded that this plan was unsound because: (1) Sufficient men to meet requirements could not be enlisted under a ten-year contract; (2) it would be impossible to maintain the proficiency of so many men in their specialities during eight years in the Reserves; and (3) it was highly probable that men separated under this plan would not form a proper distribution of military occupational specialties.[111]

For these reasons, the Army Air Forces proposed that mobilization be based on maximum use of skills directly available from the civilian labor force. During and after the war it was assumed that nearly everyone inducted into the services required training for a specific military occupational specialty. However, if accurate information were available, men could be called to active duty at the time they were needed. The AAF estimated that from fifty to seventy-five percent of initial AAF needs could be filled from men already qualified in the required military occupational specialities as a result of their civilian training and experience.[112]

The AAF believed that mobilization planning should he extended to civilian war industry, to the extent of detailing production schedules for critical items to plants so that contractors could prepare estimates of manpower needs by occupational specialty. Government agencies would supplement these with industry-wide estimates of manpower requirements for production of less critical items. The AAF recommended a selective service system under which registration would include information on occupational specialty, certified to local selective service boards by employers. In addition an enlisted Reserve technician training program should be started, similar to the presently planned program for rated officers, in which men would be separately recruited for training in specific technical fields, trained in a special status similar to aviation cadets, serve a short period in the military service, and return to civilian life with an obligation to continue in a reserve status and maintain technical proficiency through short periods of active duty and extension courses. It is believed that such a program can be conducted entirely on a voluntary basis, and together with the proposed plan for advance mobilization planning, will meet all mobilization requirements.[113]

In the summer of 1946 the War Department published a draft UMT plan stipulating the trainees be given six months training, and spend the remaining six months obligation in the UMT corps or by selecting one of the options which would furnish the equivalent of another six months training.[114]

Later, the AAF issued a supplement to this plan affording the Air Force 186,000 trainees a year. There would be 46,500 trainees inducted quarterly, each to be sent to one of these training courses: administration; airplanes, engines, and accessories; armament, ordnance, chemical; communications; nonspecialist; manual trades; medical; photography; or special equipment.[115]

With the AAF's planning for a permanent postwar Air Force having finally reached the 70-group, 400,000-man goal, the time had come to translate these figures into a permanent organization. While air planners had been struggling with the complexities of force structure, they had likewise been tackling the problems of deciding on the composition of postwar Air Force headquarters and the major field commands. The question of organization was closely tied to the paramount objective of an independent Air Force, coequal with the Army and Navy. General Spaatz, who was to become Commanding General of the Army Air Forces in February 1946, believed that this first major postwar reorganization should produce a structure suited to a separate Air Force, once this was established by law.

The movement towards a unified defense establishment and a separate Air Force had gathered impetus in April 1945 with the issuance of a special JCS committee report recommending a single Department of National Defense and an independent Air Force. Once the war ended, congressional hearings were held on unification. By this time, it was apparent that the Navy opposed formation of a single department and a coequal Air Force.

Frustrated by the absence of agreement between the Navy and War Department, and with his patience wearing thin, President Truman in December 1945 told the Congress that the time for action was now. Staking a position opposed to the Navy's, Truman stressed that the JCS committee system, a vehicle for collaboration in strategic planning and operations during the war, would undoubtedly fail to satisfy peacetime defense requirements. The future security needs of the nation would best be ensured by creation of a Department of National Defense, with three coequal services—Army, Navy, and Air Force.

3

Unification and a Separate Air Force

True preparedness now means preparedness not alone in armaments and numbers of men, but preparedness in organization also. It means establishing in peacetime the kind of military organization which will be able to meet the test of sudden attack quickly and without having to improvise radical readjustment in structure and habits.

President Harry S. Truman
December 19, 1945,
Special Message to the Congress

In 1944–45, while the Army Air Forces was planning postwar organization and force structure that set the 70-group objective, the debate over armed forces unification and the desirability of a separate Air Force grew more intense. During the spring of 1944, the Woodrum Committee held hearings on the question of unification.* In April 1945, a report of the Joint Chiefs of Staff Special Committee for Reorganization of National Defense touched off heated discussion about postwar reorganization and in October and November 1945 unification hearings were convened before the Senate Military Affairs Committee. Meanwhile, the War Department had created boards (first under Lt. Gen. Alexander M. Patch, Jr., subsequently headed by Lt. Gen. William H. Simpson) to propose an appropriate peacetime organization until such time as unification was achieved. The AAF emphasized that at the least it wanted to preserve what it had gained during the war. Then, in December 1945, President Harry S. Truman's special message

---

*The Select Committee on Post-War Military Policy of the House of Representatives, Clifton A. Woodrum, Democrat, Virginia, Chairman.

to Congress recommended establishment of a Department of National Defense and creation of a separate Air Force, coequal with the Army and Navy.

In the months preceding Truman's message, much of the testimony by military and civilian officials to congressional committees had focused on unity of command. Unified command of land, sea, and air forces had been realized in the various theaters under the impetus of the requirements of war. The matter of an independent Air Force had become linked to unity of command. It was not a question whether unity of command was necessary. All agreed that the war had demonstrated beyond doubt that unified command was indispensable to successful theater operations. The controversy centered on the best way to organize for it. The Navy opposed a separate Air Force and advocated the status quo, coordination being accomplished by the Joint Chiefs of Staff and their committees. The Army favored unification (a Department of National Defense) and an independent Air Force. During the last two years of the war, General Marshall (and also General Arnold) led the War Department's drive for legislation to form a Department of National Defense. Marshall argued that in the future the United States would not have sufficient time to mobilize. Consequently, unification in peacetime was imperative to ensure rapid, effective, unified command in wartime. Once the present war ended, he asserted, unified policies, operations, and command would be much more difficult to attain.

Thus, before the war ended, the AAF and the War Department anticipated a battle over unification and creation of a coequal Air Force. Robert A. Lovett, Assistant Secretary of War for Air, put it this way to General Spaatz:

> There is bound to be tremendous upheaval after the defeat of Germany. . . . our planning has been well done on the whole but we must be prepared for a bitter struggle with the High Command and particularly with the Navy in getting the postwar set-up properly made so that airpower is recognized as a coequal arm.[1]

In November and December 1945, the unification cause received a substantial boost from Gen. Dwight D. Eisenhower who had succeeded Marshall as Army Chief of Staff. Having just returned from Europe where he had led the Allied forces to victory, Eisenhower made clear that, based on the lessons of war, there was no doubt that unification and an independent Air Force were required. He admonished his commanders in this regard and told the Congress that he supported a strong unification bill and a separate Air Force.

First Marshall and then Eisenhower appointed boards in 1945 to shape the War Department's postwar organization prior to unification. Generals Arnold and Spaatz advocated that the AAF be coordinate with the War Department General Staff. In effect this would have created two Chiefs of Staff, one for air and one for the ground forces. To the chagrin of air planners, the Eisenhower-appointed Simpson Board placed the Army Air Forces coordinate with the Army

Ground Forces, under the War Department General Staff. This arrangement, in its main lines, obtained until formation of the United States Air Force in September 1947. However, the Simpson Board recognized the principle of granting more autonomy to the Army Air Forces. It further stated that the Commanding General, AAF, would nominate from the Army Air Forces about fifty percent of the personnel of the War Department General and Special Staff divisions.

In addition the AAF Commander would keep his place on the Joint Chiefs of Staff. The Office of Assistant Secretary of War for Air was retained. Although Arnold and Spaatz failed to receive all they wanted, they realized they had Eisenhower's firm pledge to support establishment of an independent Air Force.

Joint Chiefs of Staff Special Committee Report

In April and May 1944, with the Allies preparing to launch the cross-channel attack, the Woodrum Committee addressed the complex problems of postwar organization. The committee's objective was to study the principle of unity of command to examine its relevance to future military policy and organization. Among those testifying was AAF Brig. Gen. Haywood S. Hansell, Jr., Chief of Staff, Twentieth Air Force. Hansell stressed that, like World War II, future wars would undoubtedly feature combined operations in which ground, sea, and air units would be coordinated by a single staff under one overall command. The Army Air Forces, he said, advocated a single unified organization. As for unity of command:

> In one form or another we have acquired a degree of unity of command in all the theaters of war. . . .However, the achievement of that unity on the field of battle has been reached with great difficulty, and has resulted in delay with its attendant wastage. Furthermore, unity of command on the field of battle is not enough. In order to achieve real unity of effort the foundations for that must stem from unity in basic training doctrine and equipment.[2]

The testimony of War Department officials, including Secretary Stimson and Assistant Secretary of War for Air Lovett, paralleled that of Hansell. Lovett noted that the lessons of the war clearly meant that conflicts in the future would be distinguished by combined operations:

> I assume that airlift for sea forces and ground forces will be allocated and disposed in the interest of national defense by a combined and unified staff consisting of the top ground, sea and air officers in this country, and not on the tortured interpretation of antiquated documents dealing with vague theories and doctrines which have to be thrown away the moment war breaks out.[3]

He also accented long-range bombers, undreamed of years ago, the result of an industrial system peculiarly suited to the American temperament. It was Lovett's opinion that the Navy should maintain its specialized fleet air arm.[4]

Naval leaders refused to support a single department of national defense without considerable additional study. They wanted to keep the Navy strong. The naval air arm was central to their concept of future naval growth and strength. For example, Assistant Secretary of the Navy for Air, Artemus L. Gates, insisted that a strong naval air arm could contribute significantly to keeping the postwar aircraft industry alive. The naval air element, he averred, must be kept the best in the world.[5] With the war nearing a crucial turning point, the Woodrum committee concluded that the time was not right to consider legislation. It recommended that prior to subsequently considering reorganization the Congress should examine the views of military commanders. Under Secretary of War Robert P. Patterson told Secretary of War Stimson that the Woodrum hearings should be shelved because they were distracting from the business of winning the war.[6]

Influenced by the Woodrum Committee's hearings and a desire for some kind of organizational plan, the Joint Chiefs in early May 1944 appointed their own committee. The JCS Special Committee for Reorganization of National Defense conducted a ten-month study, interviewing commanders in the major theaters of operations and in Washington. Issued on April 11, 1945, the committee's majority report was signed by Maj. Gens. William F. Tompkins (WDGS) and Harold L. George (AAF); Rear Adm. Malcolm F. Schoeffel; and Col. F. Trubee Davison (AAF). Although the report was accompanied by a dissenting opinion by the committee's chairman and senior naval member, Adm. James O. Richardson,* its recommendations had wide impact and determined the basis for future discussion and debate. The emphasis would be on an organization designed to ensure integration of land, sea, and air forces.[7]

Of course, how best to organize military air forces had been the subject of controversy since World War I.† In the intervening years, congressional committees debated reorganization and the military produced numerous organizational studies. Deliberations of the JCS committee adhered to several basic assump-

---

*Adm. James O. Richardson was Commander in Chief of the United States Pacific Fleet from January 1940 until his relief in January 1941. He had angered President Roosevelt in September 1940 by telling him that "the senior officers of the Navy did not have the trust and confidence in the civilian leadership of this country that is essential for the successful prosecution of a war in the Pacific." Richardson was replaced by Adm. Husband E. Kimmel. Admiral Richardson had argued the case for basing the fleet on the west coast rather than in Hawaii. See Adm. James O. Richardson (as told to Vice Adm. George C. Dyer), *On the Treadmill to Pearl Harbor: The Memoirs of Admiral James O. Richardson* (Washington, 1973), especially, Chapters XV, XX.

†See Chapter 1.

Key War Department officials addressed the Woodrum Committee. Assistant Secretary of War for Air, Robert A. Lovett *(right)* and Brig. Gen. Haywood S. Hansell, Jr., Twentieth Air Force Chief of Staff, *(below)* testified that future wars would require a unified command on the field of battle.

tions. Committee members concluded that the Navy should retain its air element and that the Marines would remain as part of the Navy Department. The Army would keep its own "integral" aviation units which were essential to the ground forces. And the committee stated the premise that a United States Air Force should be created, coequal with the Army and Navy.[8] A separate Air Force would include aviation which was not inherent to the land or sea forces. Naval aviation would remain integral to the sea forces. Liaison, tactical reconnaissance, and artillery-spotting, aircraft would be a necessary part of the ground forces.[9]

Save for Admiral Richardson, members of the committee endorsed a single Department of National Defense headed by a civilian Secretary, backed by an Under Secretary responsible for departmental business matters. This single department would not merge the services. It would place the Army, Navy and Air Force under a Secretary of the Armed Forces and a single Commander of the Armed Forces. The Army and the Air Force would each be headed by a Commanding General and the Navy would be commanded by an Admiral of the Navy. Excepting Richardson, members believed that the Secretary of the Armed Forces would have more influence as a member of the cabinet than two or three independent secretaries representing the services with their conflicting intersts.[10] The Commander of the Armed Forces would also serve as Chief of Staff to the President, a position held during the war by Adm. William D. Leahy. It was reasoned that this position would overcome the defects of the JCS organization which functioned by unanimous agreement.[11] Further, the committee was concerned lest the President's war powers expire before implementation of a statutory reorganization. Expiration would have caused the War and Navy Departments to revert to their prewar organization. Consequently, the committee endorsed preparation of enabling legislation to be sent to the Congress to create a single department of defense.[12]

Thus, the pressure for statutory change in military organization was increased by the Woodrum hearings, by the ongoing experience of World War II, and by the fact that the President's war powers would expire six months after war's end. The JCS committee commented that the United States entry into the war had forced reorganization in Washington and in the field. War powers granted the President by Congress in December 1941 had permitted swift changes. The Joint Chiefs of Staff was established and the War and Navy Departments were reorganized (AAF became coequal with Army Ground Forces and the Services of Supply in March 1942). The principle of unity of command was adopted. Supreme commanders were appointed. The Joint Chiefs structured a broad strategic and operational framework within which operations could be effectively conducted. The JCS special committee referred to this as "enforced teamwork."[13] The services came to understand that success stemmed from integration of land, sea, and air operations. Nonetheless, the committee warned of potential retrogression once the war ended: "If peace should find the armed forces still operating under the present system, with no wartime compulsion to get together, even the existing degree of cooperation can be expected to disappear. This situation will be aggravated by the forced readjustment to peace-time conditions."[14] As Marshall often underlined, the postwar period would undoubtedly be marked by austerity. The military budget would become very tight. Under these conditions, parochialism tended to increase, teamwork to lessen.

According to the committee, the required integration had not been realized because each Army and Navy component within a specific theater belonged and owed allegiance to a separate department. Hence, the theater commander could not carry out his command decisions as efficiently as he wanted. Significant additional progress was impossible under the existing system. A single Department of Defense at the outset of war would have fostered much better coordination and teamwork between the services. The present system would not work nearly as well in peacetime as in war.

The Navy's View of the Report

Admiral Richardson, senior Navy member of the committee, filed a minority report opposing the recommendation for a single Department of National Defense. He argued that the plan was "theoretically better than any yet proposed, but from a practical point of view it is unacceptable."[15] Richardson favored the status quo, arguing that the lessons of war were not yet clear. After the war the military would face the monumental task of demobilization, and for this reason it would also be inappropriate to reorganize prematurely.[16]

Richardson contended that the effectiveness of combat forces in the field bore no direct relation to the existence of a single department in Washington. Nor did he support the proposals for a Secretary of the Armed Forces and a Commander of the Armed Forces. He was wary of such powerful positions, fearful of their adversely affecting the Navy. Richardson likewise found himself in opposition to an Air Force coequal with the Army and Navy.[17] He freely admitted that his chief concern was that the Navy would lose its air arm to the Air Force.

Though against the creation of a single department, Admiral Richardson advocated that the organization of the Joint Chiefs of Staff (along with wartime organizational changes by the War and Navy Departments) be perpetuated by statute. A joint secretariat should be set up and the subject of reorganization given further study. This reflected the Navy's view that for coordination the services should rely on the Joint Chiefs of Staff and the various JCS committees. Other members of the special committee disagreed with the Navy, observing that matters referred to the Joint Chiefs or to a joint secretariat would then be sent to subcommittees and to groups within the departments. The committee doubted that efficiency could be attained by this kind of group action.[18] Also, it had weighed and discarded the idea of having the Chairman, JCS, act as the Chief of Staff to the President, to decide controversial issues. Under this system, the committee felt that the Chief of Staff to the President would have authority to decide matters but not be charged with their execution. Furthermore, the Chief of Staff would not have to report to the Secretary of National Defense, thus infringing upon the responsibilities and powers of the service secretaries.[19]

Admiral Leahy, Chief of Staff to the President, Adm. Ernest J. King, Chief of Naval Operations, and Adm. Chester W. Nimitz, Commander in Chief, Pacific Fleet, all thought that the committee's recommendations were radical. They resisted the concept of a "super-secretary" claiming that one man could not effectively administer the Army and Navy. Neither economy nor enhanced efficiency would accrue under a single department system. Besides, in their view the Navy's power and influence would suffer under such a reorganization.[20] They recalled that in 1918 Britain's Royal Naval Air Service had been fused into the Royal Air Force. The reorganization put forth by the special committee would subject the Navy's requirements to review by officials who had no responsibility for their initiation. Ultimately, sea power would be weakened by people who did not understand its potentialities.[21]

Appointment of a Commander of the Armed Services—who would double as Chief of Staff to the President—would be a serious mistake. Leahy and King asserted that single command of land, sea, and air forces would be beyond the capacity of one man. They raised anew the specter of "the man on horseback." Instituting this position rested on the premise that unity in the field came from unity of command in Washington—an incorrect assumption.* The Joint Chiefs had proved themselves able to ensure unified command in the field. Field commanders had said they were satisfied with interservice cooperation.[22] On the

---

*After the war, Lt. Gen. James H. Doolittle, former commander of the 12th, 15th, and 8th Air Forces, testified before the Senate Military Affairs Committee. Doolittle stressed unity of command: "I have seen the contention made that you can have effective unity of command in the field in wartime without having unity of control in peacetime. I believe this is wrong. . . . When a war is over the commands in theaters of operation are, of course, liquidated and nothing remains except the home organization. If there is no unity there, there is no unity at all. It is the form of the home organization that will control the training, the tactics, the doctrine, the thinking and the habits of the men who we will train to fight the next war. . . . If they are trained in two departments, we will have the same makeshifts and fumblings in attempting to get a required unity of command in theaters of operations that we had at the outset of the war just past; and we will have commanders who still do not understand the two arms of the service in which they were not fundamentally trained." [Hearings before the Committee on Military Affairs, Senate, *Departments of Armed Forces and Military Security: Hearings on S. 84 and S. 1482,* Statement by Lt. Gen. James H. Doolittle, on Nov 9, 1945, 79th Cong, 1st sess (Washington, 1945), pp 294-95 (hereafter cited as *Hearings on S. 84 and S. 1482).*]

other hand, single command of forces from all the services for a specified operation (task forces) was appropriate. However, should a Commander of the Armed Services be appointed, he should not simultaneously be Chief of Staff to the President. The latter position should be held by a member of the JCS so that the advice of the Joint Chiefs could routinely be passed to the President.[23]

King and Nimitz claimed that the burden of proof rested with the proponents of change. It had not been shown that a single department would provide a military establishment that could meet the test of war.* Procurement problems would not be solved by a single department. To the contrary, the Navy thought it possible that establishment of three departments could lead to even more waste in procurement. As Nimitz saw it: "Should the Strategic Air Force be set up as a separate entity, with its own administrative and supply systems, the duplication in services and facilities which is frequently advanced as a reason for merging the Army and Navy, would become a possibility of triplication."[24] Admiral Nimitz argued that the Army Air Forces should stay part of the War Department, where the AAF could be smoothly integrated into the administration and supply of the department.[25] As for strategic air power, he said the Navy's submarine forces operated strategically; yet submarine units were merged into the Navy's logistic and administrative network. The submarine force had not been made independent, noted Nimitz.[26]

King objected to what he believed to be a lack of objectivity in the proposal for a coequal Air Force. This recommendation should not have been assumed as a starting point, King emphasized, because it was a major point "to be proved or disproved and which is perhaps the matter on which there is the greatest question."[27] The reasons advanced for and against a coequal Air Force should have been presented and debated. He disagreed with the view that there had been grave concern about organization, and that previous studies had been judged less than comprehensive because they had not proposed formation of a separate Air Force.[28]

King pressed for decentralization, pointing out that placing the Army, Navy, and Air Force into a single department would, paradoxically, further separate them because it would inevitably breed friction.[29] Moreover, a single department could lead to what he called the "dangers of orthodoxy." The methods currently

---

*Naval leaders all along stressed the success of wartime operations. For example, Vice Adm. Charles M. Cooke, Jr., Deputy Chief of Naval Operations, told the Senate Military Affairs Committee on November 8, 1945: "The joint amphibious operations conducted under the existing arrangement in this war have surpassed in extent and success those of all previous wars. . . .It is my view that this success can be continued in the future without strait-jacketing the Navy into the status of an Army Auxiliary and thus destroy its effective role in support of our national policy and in the preservation of national security." [Hearings on S. 84 and S. 1482, p 279.]

(Right) JCS Special Committee member, Admiral James O. Richardson reflected the Navy's opposition to organizing a single Department of National Defense. He opposed creating an independent Air Force.

(Below) Adm. Ernest J. King, Chief of Naval Operations, *(center)* with Adm. Chester W. Nimitz, Commander-in-Chief, Pacific Fleet *(left)*, and Adm. Raymond A. Spruance, Commander, Fifth Fleet, *(right)*, aboard the USS *Indianapolis*, July 1944. King and Nimitz cited the naval successes in the Pacific as grounds for opposing unification. The naval establishment, they asserted, was meeting the test of war.

being used in World War II could well be considered sacrosanct long after their usefulness was over. He thought that somehow the job of countering this kind of orthodoxy would be harder to do in a single department organization.[30] Both Leahy and King advocated retention of the two-department system, with each department having a civilian secretary. The Marines could continue to be part of the Navy and among other elements, the Navy would retain ship and land-based aviation to operate against targets at sea, to reconnoiter, and to support landing attacks.[31] Admiral King summed up to the Military Affairs Committee: "if the Navy's welfare is one of the prerequisites to the nation's welfare—and I sincerely believe that to be the case—any step that is not good for the Navy is not good for the nation."[32]

Views of Arnold and Marshall

In contrast to Leahy and King, General Arnold of course supported unification under a single department and favored an Air Force coequal to the Army and Navy. His major thrust was that "fundamental" air power should become coequal with land and sea power. Fundamental air power did not encompass all forms of air power: "certain manifestations of air power will continue as auxiliaries of land and sea power. But I do mean emphatically that development of primary and fundamental air power must be carried out—under supreme overall direction—by a service having this as its major responsibility."[33]

Arnold noted that in the 1920s and 1930s the Air Corps had been denied autonomy because of two obsolete concepts: First, that unity of command could only mean either unified Army command on land or unified Navy command on sea; hence coordinate status for the air would cut across essential unity of command. Second, that the inherent limitations of the airplane made the air arm merely an auxiliary to land power and naval power.[34]

The importance of the March 1942 reorganization of the War Department, Arnold asserted, lay in the air arm's becoming coequal with the Ground Forces.* In every theater during the war, an autonomous, coequal air force emerged under supreme command: "Only with coequal status could the air commander authoritatively present before the Supreme Commander what he could accomplish, assume the responsibility for its accomplishment and be free to carry out that responsibility with full appreciation of air capabilities and limitations."[35] Once again he underscored the need for the air arm to present its budget on an equal footing with the land and sea forces. He felt that substantial coordination had been achieved in wartime through the Joint Chiefs of Staff and other joint boards

---

*See Chapter 1.

and committees. But he believed there were many basic matters on which agreement had not been reached.[36]

Arnold took issue with King's charge that the committee published a report lacking in thought and depth. The report was an interservice effort, the AAF Commander observed, backed by interviews with leading field commanders and staff officers in Washington. All knew the organizational limitations of the War and Navy Departments and of the Joint Chiefs of Staff. Whereas King saw the proposed Secretary of the Armed Forces as a barrier between the President and the military services, General Arnold viewed the Secretary as precisely the authority required below the President to foster economy and efficiency. This was far preferable to the committee system which slowed agreement on important issues of consequence to more than one service.[37] Arnold's view, supportive of a strong Secretary of the Armed Forces, would later be echoed during the unification battle by General Spaatz and Assistant Secretary of War for Air Stuart Symington.

Arnold emphasized that throughout the war the Army Air Forces had proved the destructive power of air attacks and in general had gained recognition as being equal to the ground and naval forces. Postwar aircraft and weapons development would add to the importance of the air forces. In order to perform its mission, the Air Force needed to be coequal with the Army and Navy.[38] According to Arnold, this entailed equal access to and standing before Congress; an equal opportunity to present the air view to the top policy level; and an equal chance to tender the Air Force's funding requirements.[39]

Mindful of naval leaders' fear of an attempt to merge the fleet air arm into the Air Force, General Arnold made clear that he was against any move to bring carrier aviation under the Air Force. As for land-based aviation, Arnold admitted the existence of "twilight zones," areas where the Navy and the Air Force disagreed as to functions and control. This was exactly the type of issue that a single armed forces secretary should decide. The alternative was jurisdictional discord and duplication of equipment.[40]

General Marshall had long advocated a single Department of National Defense. He noted that the Navy had clearly stated its view that coordination could be accomplished by the JCS and other joint committees without unification. Marshall did not support this proposal, saying it was no substitute for unification.[41] The Army Chief of Staff thought that the Joint Chiefs of Staff by itself could not be effective as a peacetime coordinating agency. Even during wartime, Marshall felt that agreement had been reached in the JCS only by numerous compromises and after long delays.[42] However, should the services be integrated into a single department, he desired that the Joint Chiefs continue as a planning staff. Divorced from administrative and operating responsibilities, the JCS would formulate military policy, strategy, and budgetary requirements. The Joint Chiefs would submit these recommendations through the Secretary of National Defense.[43]

Marshall accented the importance of the unification principle: "My own experience in resolving difficulties of unity or direction and of unity of command in this war has been that the problem of the details at first obscured the fundamental principles, but once a favorable decision was reached regarding the latter the difficulties could usually be quickly resolved."[44] There had always been a penchant in each military department for self-sufficiency. He said that under the present setup the Navy had presented its postwar plan without coordinating it. This procedure, the Army Chief asserted, was not in the national interest.[45] The result was certain duplication. During the war, he avowed, time not money was the governing factor. In peacetime, money would be the controlling element.[46] The military must conduct its affairs on a sound, businesslike basis. A single department was needed to resolve complex issues and to work out a comprehensive plan prior to forwarding requirements to the Bureau of the Budget and to the Congress. This was a point which Secretary of War Robert P. Patterson also underlined. Unification would enable the armed forces to furnish Congress a single, comprehensive budget request:

Courtesy U.S. Army

Army Air Forces Commanding General H. H. Arnold was convinced that the proposed Secretary of the Armed Forces would foster more efficient use of costly resources among the services.

The Army and Navy took opposing positions on the issue of creating a single Department of Defense. Adm. Ernest J. King *(left)* believed that unifying the Army, Navy, and Air Force would breed friction among the services. Gen. George C. Marshall *(right)*, however, argued that unification would be necessary for comprehensive planning in peacetime.

> We ought not to tolerate in our military budget overlarge sums for one purpose and insufficient sums for another which inevitably result from a lack of single direction over the planning of all the constituent service elements. The combination of the armed forces in a single department is business-like and will bring economy. The savings will not perhaps be realized at once.[47]

Respected segments of the press reinforced Patterson's opinion. Terming parity of the Air Force with the land and sea forces as "imperative," *The New York Times* dwelt on the possible economies under unification.[48]

Forrestal on Autonomy

Meantime, the Navy in the summer of 1945 had commissioned a special report on defense reorganization. Upon the suggestion of Senator David I. Walsh (Democrat, Mass.), chairman of the Senate Committee on Naval Affairs, Secretary of the Navy Forrestal had asked his friend Ferdinand Eberstadt* to study whether a coordinating agency would be preferable to a single Department of National Defense. Eberstadt sent his study to Forrestal on September 25, 1945. Although proposing Departments of War, Navy, and Air, Eberstadt recommended against a single Department of National Defense: "It seems highly doubtful that one civilian Secretary, with limited tenure of office, could successfully administer the huge and complex structure resulting from a unification of our military services."[49] The Navy would retain its Fleet Air Arm and the Army would keep air units integral to its mission. The three coordinate departments would be tied together by committees, under the Joint Chiefs of Staff.[50]

Testifying in October 1945 before the Senate Committee on Military Affairs, which was considering unification legislation, Forrestal said he had not accepted the recommendations of the Eberstadt report.[†] Unification proposals, including Eberstadt's, had given insufficient attention to effective coordination between departments. They were simplistic approaches to a complex problem.[51]

Forrestal suggested formation of a National Security Council with the President as ex officio chairman. Such a group would assure coordination between the State, War, and Navy Departments. He also proposed creation of a National Security Resources Board (NSRB)—to coordinate planning for industrial mobilization—a Central Intelligence Agency (CIA), and a Military Munitions Board. This was part of his concept of "new organizational forms." Like King and Leahy, he wanted the duties and responsibilities of the Joint Chiefs delineated by statute. As for an independent Air Force, Forrestal said the Eberstadt report had advocated a separate Department of Air, coequal with the Army and Navy. Forrestal stressed that he was opposed to a separate Air Force, but that steps must be taken to prevent the AAF from reverting automatically to its prewar status.[52]

Forrestal was worried that Congress would pass unification legislation without adequately studying ramifications of such a sweeping reorganization. He therefore recommended that a blue ribbon commission study the problem. Like other naval officials, Forrestal charged that the JCS special committee report was simplistic and devoid of the kind of searching inquiry the matter required.[53]

---

*Eberstadt had been chairman of the Army and Navy Munitions Board and vice chairman of the War Production Board.

[†]Stuart Symington has recalled that in early 1946, after he was appointed Assistant Secretary of War for Air, he asked Forrestal whether he would support the Eberstadt report, which called for a separate Air Force. Symington had called it a Navy report. Forrestal had replied that it was not a Navy report, it was the Eberstadt report. Eberstadt himself told Symington that if the Army Air Forces would agree to coordination as against administration, then Eberstadt would persuade Forrestal to support the report. According to Symington, he turned Eberstadt down cold. [Intvw, Hugh A. Ahmann, AFSHRC, and author with Stuart Symington, Washington, D.C., May 2, 1978.]

Moreover, he firmly opposed having a Secretary of the Armed Forces because it would concentrate excessive power in the hands of one man. This super secretary would bring superficial knowledge to the department he was supposed to administer: "He would have authority without knowledge, and authority without knowledge must inevitably become impotent."[54] Forrestal also argued that civilian control of the military would be compromised. The influence of the President, the contemplated civilian secretaries, and the Congress would be diluted. Unification would amount to a revolutionary change, a drastic revision of the American system of defense.[55] He favored a deliberate and orderly transition over a longer time.

Forrestal then turned to a point that proponents had been pushing with marked success—unification would save money and promote efficiency.* Not so, insisted the Secretary of the Navy. When organizing naval procurement, he had found it necessary to disperse procurement through the bureaus instead of consolidating. This resulted in savings. "If you put the Army, Navy and Air Force procurement under one head," asserted Forrestal, "it cannot possibly work, except by the immediate splitting and resplitting of functions."[56] The most telling organizational trend had not been in the direction of merger, but toward breaking down large activities into one manageable and relatively autonomous one. Forrestal said the best example of this had been the "separation" of the Army Air Forces from the Army. He added that the AAF had created its own Air Judge Advocate, Air Surgeon, and Air Inspector General.[57]

At the same time, General Marshall had appointed a committee headed by Lt. Gen. J. Lawton Collins (Deputy Commanding General and Chief of Staff, Army Ground Forces) to come up with a comprehensive plan for organizing a single Department of the Armed Forces. In mid-October 1945, Collins handed the committee's report to General Marshall and on the thirtieth he explained the plan to the Senate Committee on Military Affairs. Based on the April 1945 report of the JCS committee on reorganization of national defense, the Collins Committee's plan specified an independent Air Force, a Joint Chiefs of Staff, a single Secretary of the Armed Forces, an Under Secretary, and a single Chief of Staff of the Armed Forces in lieu of a Commander of the Armed Forces.[†] Also, the Collins

---

*Gen. George C. Kenney testified on November 2, 1945, to the Military Affairs Committee: "I do not hold with those who maintain that inter-service rivalry. . . .is a necessary prerequisite for excellence in equipment and training. . . .It would be as logical as trying to build a winning football team by fostering rivalry between the backs and the line. I feel that tremendous economies can be accomplished by eliminating parallel agencies with a gain rather than a loss in operational efficiency in war and peace." [*Hearings on S. 84 and S. 1482*, p 232]

†The Collins Committee observed that the President was the commander of the U.S. armed forces.

Committee recommended Chiefs of Staff for the Army, Navy, and Air Force, as well as a Director of Common Supply and Hospitalization. Budget recommendations of the JCS would pass through the Secretary of the Armed Forces to the President, the secretary appending his comments.[58]

The Air Force would control all land-based air forces, save those allocated to the Army and Navy for reconnaissance, gunfire spotting, and command and messenger service. The Air Force would likewise supervise all air transport. The Army would comprise all ground forces, except the Marine Corps, and would coordinate all land transportation. The Navy would consist of all sea forces including the Fleet Air Arm, the Marines, and sea transport. The Collins Committee rejected the idea that the Navy be divested of the Marines.* The committee advocated that theater commanders should operate directly under the Chief of Staff of the Armed Forces.[59]

Eisenhower Supports a Separate Air Force

Just returned from commanding the victorious allied forces in Europe, General Eisenhower reinforced the opinions of Marshall and Arnold, and the Collins report. He strongly supported a single Department of Defense with three coequal services, telling the Military Affairs Committee that it would foster economy and unity of command. Though not easily achieved, unified command (as opposed to joint command) was absolutely vital to success. Eisenhower believed the difficulty in achieving unity of command was due to the traditional separation of the Army and Navy. Unified command had to be generated from the top down, beginning at the Washington command level.[60]

According to his own retrospective account, General Eisenhower was surprised and disappointed upon his return to discover that not all military leaders thought the way he did. To the contrary, he found that unification of the services had become a subject of intense controversy. To Eisenhower, these conflicting views had burgeoned beyond reasonable proportion.[61]

In his support of a single defense establishment and a separate Air Force, Eisenhower recognized the need for postwar economy. He strongly believed in what

---

*As Lt. Gen. J. Lawton Collins put it: "There is no question but that the Navy has set up a little army within the Navy. The Marines now consist of six divisions, which is a sizable force, and the Navy right now is advocating a Marine Corps almost as big as the prewar Army and Air Force combined. . . .we feel that any needless duplication would be resolved as soon as we got this single Secretary of the Armed Forces. The Marine Corps has done a magnificent job, it has a hold on the public, and it would be silly if we tried to take it away from the Navy." [Presentation of the Collins Committee Report to the Army Staff and the Chief of Staff, in RG 165, Decimal File 320, Sep–Dec 46, MMB.]

Naval leaders stood united in their opposition to unification legislation. Secretary of the Navy James Forrestal *(center)* favored the formation of a National Security Council to enhance coordination among the separate departments. Fleet Admirals Ernest J. King *(left)* and Chester W. Nimitz *(right)* also warned of the dangers of proceeding too quickly with a sweeping reorganization of the military establishment.

he called the principle of "the three-legged stool," each service mutually dependent upon the other. It was no longer feasible, Eisenhower emphasized, "to arrive at the size and composition of each arm without simultaneously considering the others. Each arm supplements the other and no single service can be independently considered."* A single department of defense was required presiding over three coequal military services. The concept of the three-legged stool was tied to the need for strict economy during peacetime. Should the War and Navy Departments stay under separate administration from the top, duplication would persist. Requirements of the services could no longer be treated separately. While admitting that competition between the services to develop weapons was a good

---

*Testimony before the Senate Military Affairs Committee, Nov 16, 1945.

PROPOSED REORGANIZED ARMED FORCES
COLLINS COMMITTEE, OCTOBER 1945

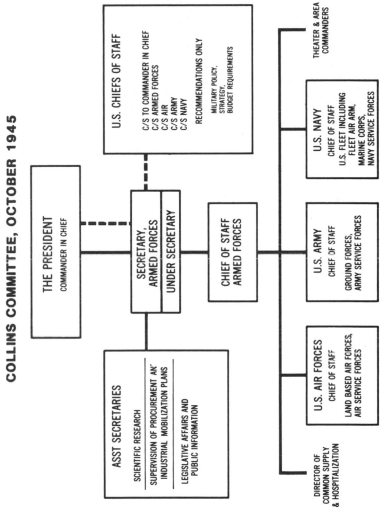

thing, Eisenhower commented that "competition is like some of the habits we have—in small amounts they are very, very desirable; carried too far they are ruinous."[62] Without unification, the military services would continue to compete for money before the various congressional committees. With integration, the nation could buy more security for less.

One of General Eisenhower's strongest convictions was that an independent Air Force should be created. "No sane officer of any arm," he said, "would contest that thinking."[63] He added:

> The Normandy invasion was based on a deep-seated faith in the power of the Air Forces in overwhelming numbers to intervene in the land battle, i.e., that the Air Forces by their own action could have the effect on the ground of making it possible for a small force of land troops to invade a continent . . .Without that Air Force; without its independent power, entirely aside from its ability to sweep the enemy air forces out of the sky, without its power to intervene in the ground battle, that invasion would have been fantastic. . . .unless we had faith in air power as a fighting arm to intervene and make safe that landing, it would have been more than fantastic, it would have been criminal.[64]

Eisenhower in December 1945 convened, and impressed his deeply felt opinion on, the Army staff. He said the air arm had shown beyond any doubt it was equal to the other arms. He reiterated his view that an independent Air Force should be formed. Even if the requisite laws were not passed, within the Army the air arm should be largely independent. In other words, the Chief of Staff stated:

> the Air Commander and his staff are an organization coordinate with and co-equal to the land forces and the Navy. I realize that there can be other individual opinions. . . . But that seems to me to be so logical from all of our experiences in this war—such an inescapable conclusion that I for one can't even entertain any longer any doubt as to its wisdom.[65]

In the interim, he enjoined his staff to vigorously support forthcoming directives, anticipated from the Simpson Board, which would give the AAF as much autonomy as possible short of complete coequality.[66]

As to the contention of naval leaders that the job of the proposed civilian secretary was beyond the capacity of one man. General Eisenhower told the Military Affairs Committee that if that were the case, then no one should become President of the United States.[67] Regarding the Navy's fear that reorganization would subordinate one service to another, he said that experiences in Africa and Europe had proved such fears groundless.[68]

The testimony of War Department and Navy officials revealed that a wide gap still remained on unification. This was reflected in the failure of the Senate Military Affairs Committee to agree on potential legislation.

Truman Advocates a Coequal Air Force

Before the end of the war, President Harry S. Truman had made up his mind that the military had to be reorganized. He wanted the services unified and the air arm to have parity with the Army and Navy. "One of the strongest convictions which I brought to the Presidency," Truman recalled,"was that the antiquated defense setup. . . .had to he reorganized quickly as a step toward insuring our future safety and preserving world peace."*[69] From the Pearl Harbor hearings, the Chief Executive concluded that the December 7, 1941 tragedy had been "as much the result of the inadequate military system which provided for no unified command, either in the field or in Washington, as it was any personal failure of Army or Navy commanders."†[70] So the United States needed a national security organization, the President emphasized, ready to operate instantly in an emergency. Truman's view attracted wide support. An editorial in *The New York Times,* for example, attributed the disaster at Pearl Harbor chiefly to a system not geared to cope with a surprise attack. The answer, according to the *Times.* was a "set-up to simplify and speed up procedure, eliminate rivalry and assure the same kind of coordination in peace which necessity compelled in war."[71]

Truman was well aware that the conflict had bared serious flaws in the ability of the United States to react to total war. At the start of the war, no satisfactory system existed to mobilize manpower, materiel, and production. Logistical shortages hampered execution of strategic plans. There was substandard planning for materiel, requirements, duplication in procurement, and inadequate Army-Navy coordination.

Absence of a Navy–War Department agreement on unification and failure of the Military Affairs Committee to report a bill convinced the President to act. In his special message to the Congress of December 19, 1945, Truman said he had previously recommended to Congress a Universal Military Training program. UMT would give the nation citizen-soldiers who could be mobilized when needed to support a small professional military establishment. Besides UMT, it would be necessary to create a single Department of National Defense. He

---

*In retrospect, Navy officials speculated on the twist of fate that brought Harry S. Truman to the presidency. Truman it was well known, favored unification and had written an article for *Collier's* magazine on this subject. Naval leaders thought that Truman's accession to the presidency set in motion "a set of consequences for the postwar Navy different from what might have been anticipated under a postwar Roosevelt." [Vincent Davis, *Postwar Defense Policy and the U.S. Navy, 1943–1946* (Chapel Hill, N.C., 1962), p 118.]

†It should also be noted that during World War II Truman served as chairman of the Special Committee to Investigate the National Defense Program. This experience gave him a close view of military inefficiency and duplication.

Demonstrating his commitments to U. S. air power, President Truman signs the proclamation designating August 1, 1946, as Air Force Day. The date marked the 39th Anniversary of military aviation. On hand for the occasion are Gen. Carl A. Spaatz, AAF Commanding General, *(center)* and Lt. Gen. Ira C. Eaker, Deputy Commander.

stressed that lessons of the war demanded unified direction of land, sea, and air forces.[72]

Truman remained especially sensitive that on December 7, 1941, the United States had been without a system of unified command. The Japanese success left an indelible blot on the American conscience, and he was determined there would be no more Pearl Harbors. In 1941 the War and Navy Departments had lacked a tradition of collaboration. Also, at that time air power was not organized coequal with the ground and sea forces. The Chief Executive observed that formation of the Joint Chiefs of Staff was meant to correct these defects. Although coordination of strategic planning and operations had been carried out through joint committees under the JCS, this could not be considered a form of unification.[73]

In the theaters, unified commands were set up. "We came to the conclusion, soon confirmed by experience." Truman said, "that any extended military effort required over-all coordinated control in order to get the most out of the three armed forces. Had we not early in the war adopted this principle of a unified command for operations, our efforts, no matter how heroic, might have failed."[74] Nevertheless, leadership in Washington stayed divided. And even in the field, there were differences in doctrine, training, communication, and in supply and distribution systems.

Basically it was a matter of organization. The President sided with the Army (and the JCS Special Committee for Reorganization of National Defense) and against the Navy on the question of whether the JCS system would suffice for postwar organization. He emphatically thought it was not good enough. The Joint Chiefs of Staff was a committee—not a unified command. While the Joint Chiefs cooperated during the war, this would not be the case in peacetime. The Commander in Chief decided there had been sufficient studies of military organization. It was time for action. In his eyes, there was simply no question about the need for unification. He was not going to stand for each of the services continuing to plan programs in their own splendid isolation. The divisive competition for funds must cease.[75] And Truman favored parity of air power:

> Air power has been developed to a point where its responsibilities are equal to those of land and sea power, and its contribution to our strategic planning is as great. In operation, air power receives its separate assignment in the execution of the over-all plan. These facts were finally recognized in this war in the organizational parity which was granted to air power within our principal unified commands.[76]

Despite the success engendered by unified command, it was just as clear there had been shortcomings. These were essentially due to a lack of understanding between the services.

In proposing a Department of National Defense headed by a civilian Secretary of National Defense (and also an Office of Chief of Staff of the Department of National Defense), Truman stressed that unification would be a long-term task. Many difficulties lay ahead. "Unification is much more than a matter of organization," the President said: "It will require new viewpoints, new doctrine, and new habits of thinking throughout the departmental structure."[77]

The AAF Plans for Unification

As we have seen, Arnold had assigned a high priority to planning for postwar organization and to drafting legislation for an independent Air Force. By the end of the war, Col. Reuben C. Moffat's Post War Division (under Maj. Gen. Lauris Norstad, Assistant Chief of Air Staff, Plans), had written a potential bill to create a Department of the Air Force and a United States Air Force. The Post War Division had also began to study various possible organizational forms for a separate Air Force. On September 18, 1945, Col. Jacob E. Smart, Secretary of the Air Staff, concerned over intensified interest in defense organization and with the absence of concrete AAF plans, recommended to General Eaker that the AAF begin to prepare comprehensive draft legislation for formation of a separate Air Force. Such legislation should guarantee that an independent Air Force would from its inception "receive all of the benefits that now accrue as an agency of the War Department, and none of the disadvantages that result from the entangled masses of laws which now affect all components of the War Department."[78] This endeavor, Smart observed, would demand scrutiny of existing legislation and careful planning by many of the AAF's most capable officers. He urged that action be taken immediately so that legislation would be ready if and when a separate Air Force became a reality.[79]

Smart advocated that the Army Air Forces start drafting legislation to create a single Department of National Defense unshackled by restrictions which had been imposed upon the War Department. Even though this matter would eventually undergo joint study, Colonel Smart thought by promulgating the original proposal the AAF would seize the initiative. The War and Navy Departments would then have to start with the AAF's recommendation as a basis for their own.[80]

After receiving Smart's memorandum, General Eaker suggested that Norstad frame at once legislation for a separate Air Force, if he were not already doing so.[81] Norstad replied that the Post War Division had finished a draft bill, but the required legislation stipulating the makeup of the Air Force (termed a "consolidated code") had not yet been prepared. He recommended that the Air Judge Advocate's office draw up the appropriate legislation, monitored by the Post War Division.[82] Eaker agreed, instructing the Air Judge Advocate to study existing legislation in order to draft a law creating an autonomous Air Force and a single Department of National Defense. The Post War Division would oversee this work.[83]

As the Congress deliberated on unification legislation and the Air Judge Advocate commenced his task, Headquarters Army Air Forces kept its major field commanders informed of "the fight that is brewing" on postwar organization. A number of general officers in AAF headquarters wrote to these commanders. They explained that the Navy opposed a single Department of National Defense. Navy leaders feared that unification and a separate Air Force would deprive them of their air arm. These AAF officers also said that the recommendations of the majority report of the JCS special committee were the best the AAF could expect from any such board. If implemented, these proposals would afford the AAF coequal status and achieve unification. Success in the unification fight would extend to the Air Force "the same opportunity as the other components to present our financial requirements. We will be subject to only that administrative control that is applicable to all three components and we will have the same standings as the other services in Congress"[84]

In the face of determined Navy opposition, General Arnold in October 1945 felt confident that an independent Air Force would ensue. He reminded Eaker

(Right) Secretary of the Air Staff, Col. Jacob E. Smart urged General Eaker to take the initiative in drafting legislation setting up a single Department of National Defense and an Air Force coequal with the Army and Navy.

(Below) Anticipating the birth of the Air Force, General Arnold *(right)* directed General Eaker *(left)* to prepare plans for the organization of the new department.

that as Commanding General, AAF he had publicly expressed strong approval of the JCS committee's majority report and its recommendation for unification and a coequal Air Force. Assuming this eventual turn of events, Arnold wanted plans prepared so the AAF would be ready to meet its responsibilities. He directed Eaker to appoint a board of officers to make a comprehensive study, setting forth required AAF actions when defense reorganization occurred. At that time, Arnold said, it would be necessary to determine the Air Force's mission, functions, and organization, as well as its relationship with land and naval forces. Moreover, since the Air Force would be breaking away from the War Department, it would be imperative to fix precise responsibility in personnel, intelligence, supply, and other areas.[85]

During November and December the Office of the Air Judge Advocate worked on reorganization legislation, with General Norstad approving each step. Three plans emerged, in order of priority: (1) a separate Air Force coequal with the Army and Navy and represented in the cabinet by a Secretary of the Air Force; (2) a single and completely unified department; and (3) status quo, with a two-department organization.[86]

Meanwhile, as Congress weighed unification and a separate Air Force, the Army Air Forces strove to preserve the substantial autonomy it had accumulated during the war. Arnold of course appreciated the freedom that Marshall allowed him as Commanding General, AAF. In 1942 the Army Air Forces had won stature equal to that of Army Ground Forces and Army Service Forces. Also, as a member of the Joint Chiefs and the Combined Chiefs of Staff, the AAF commander had a voice in matters of grand strategy. In general he had been given a free hand in shaping the AAF. At Arnold's direction, the AAF had built its own formidable support forces in such vital areas as research and development, logistics, and engineering.

Consequently, immediately after the war, General Arnold turned his attention to preserving the AAF's freedom and at the same time waging the battle for AAF autonomy. Arnold's immediate worry was that the War Department's organization, under which the AAF had gained quasi-autonomy, would automatically expire six months after the end of the war. This structure had originally been authorized by President Roosevelt's executive order, issued under the War Powers Act of December 18, 1941.

Thus, on August 28, 1945 (the same day that Eaker set 70 groups as the AAF's goal),* Arnold recommended to Marshall that a bill be introduced in the forthcoming Congress to extend the War Department organization until permanent legislation could be secured for the postwar military establishment. Arnold supported his proposal by emphasizing that the present structure was a great im-

---

*See Chapter 2.

provement over the prewar one—especially insofar as the AAF was concerned. A return to the postwar setup would result in chaos.[87]

Marshall disagreed with Arnold's proposal, noting that the War Department had not yet defined its views on postwar organization. Introduction of a legislative proposal at this time would therefore be premature. Besides, if time permitted, it would be preferable to submit legislation for the desired War Department structure affording the AAF increased autonomy, rather than Arnold's so-called "interim" bill which would have frozen the current organization.[88] Accordingly, on August 30, 1945, Marshall appointed a board of officers under Lt. Gen. Alexander M. Patch, Jr.,* to examine the War Department organization and to recommend an appropriate peacetime structure.

General Arnold continued to advocate continuation of the wartime structure pending submission of permanent legislation. Keeping the present organization would avoid changing now and even again later. There was also the question of duplication. As before, Arnold pointed to separate facilities, procurement, hospitals, and depots. The country could not stand the expense. In addition, he wanted to remove the command function from Army Service Forces and to make it a procurement agency for common items. The ASF, in Arnold's view, had arrogated excessive prerogatives.[89] The board appointed by Marshall—first chaired by Patch and, after his death, by Lt. Gen. William H. Simpson†—was deliberately weighted against the Army Service Forces.** The members were drawn chiefly from technical services and from General Eisenhower's staff. They opposed continuance of ASF because they felt it had become far too large and had wielded excessive power. Further, they believed a separate supply command violated the principle of unity of command. Realizing Eisenhower would be the next Chief of Staff, the Patch Board paid special attention to his opinions.[90]

Eisenhower's reorganization idea featured a plan to divide a small planning group at the top and functional operating directorates for technical supervi-

---

*Patch was a combat veteran without General Staff experience.

†General Simpson commanded the U.S. Ninth Army during World War II. He formally received four-star rank in 1954.

** The Patch Board was constituted "to examine into the present organization of the War Department and to propose an organization appropriate for peacetime adoption....The organization proposed will be based upon the continuance of the present overall organization of the Armed Services into two departments—the War and Navy—however, the Board should have in mind the practicability of fitting the proposed organization into a single Department of National Defense." [Stmt of Gen. Patch to the Bd, Sep 10, 1945, prior to intvw of Maj. Gen. Laurence S. Kuter, in RG 165, Rcrds of the WD Gen and Sp Stfs, Army C/S, Patch/Simpson Bd File, MMB, NA.]

sion.*[91] Below these, AAF, AGF, and technical services would exercise command functions. Eisenhower had long thought that the War Department General Staff needed reorganization:

> As I see it, our General Staff has gotten into a very bad state for this reason: we set up a General Staff to be thinkers, advisers and coordinators, but not operators. But we found under our system that following up and the issuing of detailed orders were necessary, and that is "operations," so the General Staff enters into it. So I said; "How can I remove from the General Staff what it is doing now in the way of operations?" Then we could have a small General Staff in its original conception and still have the power somewhere to do this following up in detailed operation on a pretty high level, and we know we have to do it.[92]

In their testimony before the Patch Board, Spaatz and Eaker echoed Arnold's view that the War Department should be organized towards eventual creation of a Department of National Defense. Otherwise, noted Spaatz, it would be necessary to reorganize twice.[93] General Spaatz wanted the AAF formed with its own promotion and personnel systems.[94] The AAF advocated a separate promotion system to compensate for the "dissimilar personnel requirements of flying personnel as compared to non-flying personnel."[95] The average useful life of the flying officer was shorter than that of the nonflyer. Flying officers must be younger to meet the physical and mental requirements of piloting modern aircraft. Furthermore, flyers had other important responsibilities. For example, a B–29 group commander who

---

*Eisenhower also informed the Patch Board that it was time to use a "sledge hammer on the empire builders." Eisenhower had reference to "this spirit of bureaucracy [which] has manifested itself too long in the governmental services, and I think it is high time that we in the Army and the Air just set our faces against it and ruthlessly uproot it; the spirit of never letting go of anything that you have ever had hold of." This thought had also been stressed to the Patch Board by Assistant Secretary of War for Air Robert A. Lovett. According to Lovett, one of the major problems in the War Department was the existence of "little armies within the Army—isolated activities or empires which were being sponsored by their Chief without regard to the overall good of the Army." On the other hand, another of his concerns was that safeguards should be set up against "vegetation" of senior officers. Many of these officers in the War Department, Lovett said, espoused a philosophy that had evolved from the years when economy was the watchwork. These officers were unreceptive to the advanced methods of big business which would be required to operate the postwar Army. [Stmt of Gen. Dwight D. Eisenhower to Patch Bd, Sep 23, 1945, in RG 165, Rcrds of the WD Gen and Sp Stfs, Army C/S. Patch-Simpson Bd File , Box 927, MMB, NA; testimony of Robert A. Lovett, Asst Secy of War for Air, to Patch Bd, Sep 6, 1945, in RG 65, Rcrds of the WD Gen and Spl Stfs, Army C/S, Patch-Simpson Bd File, MMB, NA.]

habitually leads 18 to 72 airplanes (and frequently a whole air force)....He commands in his group approximately 300 officers and 150 enlisted men, and in addition to normal equipment found in ground units of similar size, he is responsible for 20 million dollars worth of aircraft. Also he is very often base commander in addition to his duties as group commander.[96]

In consequence, the case for a separate Air Force promotion system rested squarely on flying itself. Overall, the AAF wanted control of its own personnel policies.

When asked for his opinion on the General Staff, Spaatz replied that the General Staff should be a policymaking and coordinating agency, "with the smartest Air, Ground and Service Forces men we can find to put on it."[97] As far as anti-aircraft artillery (AAA) was concerned, he thought it should be operated and controlled by the Air Force so long as integration between fighter aircraft and AAA remained. Combined training of AAA and fighters

should come under the operation and control of the Air and also when it comes to war and the enemy Air is the threat, but when that threat is done away with and you reduce the number of antiaircraft outfits that cover you against air attacks, they should be able to go into the Ground Army and be set up and used as artillery.[98]

Lt. Gen. Alexander M. Patch, Jr., headed a board of officers charged with examining the current organization of the War Department and recommending a structure suitable for peacetime defense.

On October 18, 1945, the Patch Board sent its report to General Marshall who routed it through the War Department staff for comment. General Arnold was disappointed with the Patch report because it ignored his recommendation that the Air Staff should be coequal with the War Department General Staff until the unification question was decided. In effect, the AAF Commander wanted two chiefs of staff in the postwar period, one for the Ground Forces and the other for the Air Forces. Spaatz, at Arnold's direction, had told the Patch Board that reorganization should be sufficiently complete so little reorganization would be needed when the time came for the Air Force to assume coequal status.[99]

The report suggested expanding the size, functions, and responsibilities of the War Department General Staff, and making the Army Air Forces coequal with Army Ground Forces under the Chief of Staff and the War Department General Staff. The Board's plan divided the War Department and Army into four echelons: Office of the Secretary of War; General and Special Staffs for planning and direction; administrative and technical services restored to their prewar autonomy; and on the operating level, the AAF, AGF, and Overseas Departments.[100]

Arnold apprised Marshall that the Army Air Forces would not respond in detail to the Patch report. He said its recommendations could not be reconciled with the War Department's proposals for a single Department of the Armed Forces, nor with the need for coequal status of the Army Air Forces.[101] The AAF Commander emphasized the special relationship that he and his staff enjoyed during the war with General Marshall and the War Department General Staff. Marshall had recognized the special difficulties faced by the Army Air Forces and delegated many responsibilities to Arnold. Naturally, General Arnold wanted the head of the Air Force to stay a member of the Joint Chiefs.[102] The Patch report, by positioning the AAF under the General and Special Staffs, would have kept the AAF from formal (organizational) participation in General Staff planning. Throughout the war, the Air Staff had taken part in such planning. The structure recommended by the Patch Board should "perpetuate this participation by the Army Air Forces organizationally in order that the terms of the reorganization can not be used to demonstrate that such a relationship no longer exists."[103] Air Staff participation at all planning levels must be confirmed. Hence, the current structure should be kept until the unification question was resolved.[104]

When General Patch died on November 21, 1945, General Eisenhower—who had succeeded Marshall as Army Chief of Staff on November 19—appointed a new board headed by Lt. Gen. William H. Simpson. The Simpson Board's task was to review comments on the Patch report, to make revisions, and to draft executive orders to put a reorganization into effect which would permit the AAF subsequently to separate from the Army. General Arnold named Norstad as liaison between the Simpson board and Army Air Forces Headquarters. General Norstad emphasized to the board that the Air Staff should coordinate with the War Department General Staff and that the AAF responsibility for anti-aircraft

116

artillery should be recognized. In December Arnold made his argument to General Simpson: that the Patch Board, by proposing that AAF be coequal with AGF, had failed to see the need for the Air Staff to be on a coordinate level with the War Department General Staff. Moreover, the board's recommendations would make more difficult an eventual transition to a single department. Also, the board wanted to abolish the Office of Assistant Secretary of War for Air, a position established by the Air Corps Act of 1926 (and first held by F. Trubee Davison).* Arnold opposed this and in addition objected strongly to the recommendation to assign antiaircraft artillery to the Army Ground Forces.[105]

Previously, in December 1944, Spaatz had informed Arnold:

> The development of all the weapons for coordinated defense should be pushed. Antiaircraft artillery is making rapid strides in effectiveness. Radar equipment. . .is proving extremely effective not only in defense, but as a method of offense and control. All measures for defense should be coordinated under our control including radar and counter-radar, interceptors. . . .as well as antiaircraft in order that we can get behind research and development in the field.[106]

Postwar planners under Kuter and Davison in 1944 had recommended that the postwar Air Force include an antiaircraft artillery force of 140,000 men. Although the War Department made no reply to this proposal, Arnold proceeded on the assumption that it would be approved. Moreover, the AAF Commander wanted to place nonrated AAA personnel in command of postwar air defenses worldwide. He wished to guarantee the artillerymen the same opportunity to reach high rank as given to flyers.

The Patch–Simpson Board's decision not to integrate antiaircraft artillery into the Army Air Forces mirrored the Army Ground Forces' view. That is, the AAA mission was defense of ground troops and installations, a mission more relevant to ground and service forces than to the Air Forces. If AAA should be integrated into the AAF, War Department and AGF leaders feared its principal development would tend toward defense of Air Force installations. Ground leaders advanced the idea that the Air Force "faces a tremendous future task of its own in the development of new aircraft for offensive and other purposes. The problem faced

---

*High-ranking members of the War Department also desired to keep the position of Assistant Secretary of War for Air. According to Lt. Gen. John E. Hull, Assistant Chief of Staff, Operations Plans Division, the Navy had an Assistant Secretary of War for Air and thus it would be a "very retrogressive step for the War Department to eliminate the Assistant Secretary of War for Air." Besides, civil aviation required a conduit to military aviation and this had been handled by an Assistant Secretary of War for Air. Finally, public criticism would be directed at the War Department should this office be done away with. [Memo for DCSA fr Lt. Gen. John E. Hull, ACS/OPD, USA, subj: Report of Board of Officers on Organization of the War Department, Nov 5, 1945.]

by the AAA of the future is in itself too great in magnitude to be thrust upon the Air Force as an additional problem."[107]

Ground generals pointed to the effective use of AAA in the war, achieved by a coordinated area defense organization under a single commander. During the war, assignment of chief responsibility for air defense to an Air Force sector commander was based on the employment of defensive fighter aircraft. The advent of atomic weapons and long-range rockets would render fighter aircraft obsolete as instruments of defense. Vital installations would depend on well-organized ground defenses using radar and radar-controlled defensive weapons.[108] AAA personnel should be trained as part of the ground forces:

> AAA troops should be trained with a view of their ultimate assimilation for combat or other roles in the Ground Forces. . . .they should be considered and trained from the outset as a part of the Ground Forces. In the development of their weapons consideration should be given to their use, when not required for defense, for offensive purposes in support of ground operations. This desirable versatility was well demonstrated in World War II.[109]

As noted, General Arnold's major objective between the end of the war and passage of unification legislation was to solidify Army Air Forces' gains. The Patch Board proposals could not be reconciled with this goal nor with the War Department's own recommendation for a single Department of the Armed Forces.[110] In December 1945, Spaatz—in the process of taking over from Arnold—also made clear to General Simpson that the Patch Board, by not making the Air Staff coordinate with the War Department General Staff, had slowed the transition of the AAF from a part of a two-department system to a single-department one.[111] Spaatz wanted the current War Department structure, based on presidential executive order, to be continued in the interim by legislation as Arnold had first advocated in August 1945.

The Simpson Board gave General Eisenhower its report on December 28, 1945. It was revised on January 18, 1946, and promptly approved by the Army Chief for planning purposes. On February 1, just before succeeding Arnold, Spaatz expressed his doubts on the Simpson report to Eisenhower. Like Arnold, Spaatz deemed the suggested organization inconsistent with unification proposals. Its adoption would "place in question, in the public mind and in the minds of opponents of unification, the War Department's adherence to these basic principles and will, in my view, seriously jeopardize the unification program."[112] Spaatz said that in general the unification proposals envisioned a small policy-making and planning staff for the proposed Chief of Staff of the Armed Forces. The Simpson report indicated that policy and planning formulation at the staff level could not be divorced from operations. It recommended a General Staff composed of Directors having authority throughout the establishment.[113]

Thus, General Spaatz asserted that the board's report—despite espousing an autonomous Air Force—subjected the AAF to a General Staff consisting of Di-

AAF Commanding General Henry H. Arnold *(left)* **rides with his successor, Gen. Carl A. Spaatz** *(center)*, **and Ninth Air Force Commander Hoyt S. Vandenberg.**

rectors with "directive authority." Among them was a Director of Service, Supply, and Procurement, who besides staff duties would direct the functions of the Army Service Forces. Spaatz urged a full reconsideration of the report and its recommendations.[114]

Previous to the actual reorganization, the War Department issued a memorandum on April 4, 1946, explaining the Simpson Board's proposals. Then Executive Order 9722, May 13, 1946 (amending Executive Order 9082, February 28, 1942) authorized reorganization of the War Department, effective June 11, 1946. On May 14, 1946, War Department Circular 138 promulgated reorganization of the War Department effective June 11 (subsequently termed the "Eisenhower Reorganization").

Though the Simpson report retained the Patch Board recommendation that the Air Staff should be coordinate with the Army Ground Forces staff (rather than with the War Department General Staff), it assented to the principle of granting the AAF more autonomy and set forth proposals favored by the Army Air Forces. For example, the report stated that the Commanding General, AAF, would nominate about fifty percent of the members of the War Department General and Special Staff divisions from Army Air Forces personnel, a point long sought by the AAF. The report additionally stipulated that this goal would be reached as soon as practicable.[115]

According to the report, AAF officers could be required to serve in the Offices of the War Department Chiefs of Technical and Administrative Services, as desired by the Commanding General, AAF, and by arrangement with the chiefs of these services. Ideally, the Simpson Board said, the War Department should be regarded as neither "Ground" nor "Air," but as an agency which serves both. Officers with the General Staff, Special Staff, and technical and administrative staffs and services, should deal with broad War Department functions, not with the interests of a particular branch.[116]

Turning to another point of AAF interest, the Simpson report stated that as Army Service Forces functions were transferred to AAF, a commensurate proportion of personnel (performing these duties) would be moved to the Army Air Forces. Which functions and how many troops would be decided by the War Department after reviewing AAF requirements. The report added that Eisenhower wanted the AAF to have just those technical and administrative services needed for servicing troops. Hospitals and ports, for example, would be run by the Army. So long as the AAF stayed under the War Department, the bulk of administrative and technical officers would be furnished to the AAF by the technical and administrative services. When the AAF became a separate service, there would have to be a specific quota of technical and administrative officers who would be permanent members of the Air Force. Further, according to the Simpson Board,

> additional increments of Regular Officers which may in the future be authorized by Congress will include a proportion, to be later determined, of promotion-list technical and administrative officers commissioned in the Air Corps, to provide in part for eventual complete autonomy. Also, at such time as complete autonomy is achieved, it will be proper and necessary to transfer an appropriate proportion of the officers of the Technical and Administrative Services of the Army to the autonomous Army Air Forces.[117]

Transfers of nonrated officers to the Air Corps—if mutually agreed upon by the Commanding General, AAF, the Chiefs of Technical and Administrative Services, and the individual officers—would still be approved. Prior to Air Force autonomy, officers of the technical and administrative services on duty with the AAF would remain under command of the AAF Commander. The Chiefs of Technical and Administrative Services would handle the long-range career planning of these officers. For proper schooling they would be returned periodically to control of the chiefs of services. Also, the Simpson Board authorized the Commanding General, AAF, membership on the technical committees of the technical services in numbers the AAF Commander felt necessary to represent the interests of the Army Air Forces.[118]

The AAF attempt to win control of antiaircraft artillery was thwarted.* The Simpson Board recommended that artillery be combined under Army Ground Forces, but AAA units could be trained and attached to AAF units. Together the Commanding Generals, Army Ground Forces and Army Air Forces, would develop tactics for AAA when used by the AAF. They would also determine the "technique of fire at aerial targets," military characteristics of weapons and equipment, and tables of organization and equipment for AAA units.[119]

In advance of the Simpson report's actual publication in April, General Spaatz (having replaced Arnold) officially forwarded his comments to the War Department Deputy Chief of Staff. Spaatz knew the paramount issue was whether AAF would be coordinate with the War Department General Staff or Army Ground Forces. However, since Eisenhower had approved the AAF's being placed co-equal with AGF, Spaatz commented on other issues. He was also aware of statements by General Staff officers during meetings with Air Staff members. They had clearly said that if the AAF failed to achieve independence, the Air Force would be made equal to the General Staff and be given its own promotion list.[120]

Perhaps foremost in Spaatz' mind was the status of the AAF's medical service, which he thought would be weakened by the Simpson recommendations. He objected to the wording in the report that The Surgeon General would exercise technical and administrative supervision and inspection of subordinate units of the medical service not commanded by him and not under his immediate control. Spaatz wanted this changed to read that the Commanding General, AAF, would exercise "command responsibility for all medical installations and units of the AAF and for all medical personnel assigned to the AAF."[121]

The board agreed with Spaatz and defined The Surgeon General's major task—as a technical officer of the War Department and chief medical officer of the Army—as setting Army policies for hospitalization, evacuation, and care of the sick and wounded. Moreover, based on Spaatz' comment, the Simpson Board stated that directives would be issued to major subordinate commanders under the War Department "through the proper channels of command, and not directly from the Surgeon General to the corresponding Medical Staff Officer in a subordinate major command."[122]

---

*However, the AAF had not made an all-out attempt to secure control of the antiaircraft artillery mission because it "did not want to antagonize an element of the War Department. . .when we need every friend we can possible get to assist in pushing over unification." [Fourth Meeting of Air Board, Dec 3–4, 946, in RG 340 (SAF), Air Bd Interim Rprts and working Papers, Box 15, MMRB, NA.]

The Surgeon General would command all general hospitals. The Commanding General AAF, would be charged with determining the strength, organization, composition, equipment, and training of medical units assigned to the AAF. Also as General Spaatz suggested, the regional hospital at Coral Gables, Fla., would be redesignated a general hospital and would be an exempted station. This would make the hospital a "specialized hospital," for admission of Air Corps personnel needing hospitalization and convalescent care incident to their tactical mission.[123]

There were additional advances for the AAF in the Simpson report. The Commanding General, AAF, would be responsible for preparing budget estimates and justifying these estimates before the Budget Advisory Committee of the War Department and other appropriate agencies.* Money for operation of Army Air Forces and for procurement of special items for the AAF would be allocated directly to AAF headquarters by the War Department budget officer. The AAF would also be represented on the Communications Advisory Board. Installation, maintenance, and operation of the Army Airways Communications System would be the responsibility of the AAF Commander.[124]

The Simpson Board, appointed by Army Chief of Staff Eisenhower to succeed the Patch Board, established the basic War Department structure under which the AAF would remain until it became a separate service in September 1947.

---

*The AAF had desired to be represented on the Budget Advisory Committee itself. This committee (under the War Department budget office) reviewed estimates of War Department agencies before submitting them to the Bureau of the Budget. Without a representative on this committee, the AAF had no assurance that its needs would be properly considered. Nor could it make direct contact with congressional appropriations committees, several of which had made decisions adverse to AAF programs. [Memo to Lt. Gen. Ira C. Eaker, by Brig. Gen. L. W. Miller, Ch, Budget and Fiscal Ofc, AAF, subj: Air Force Representation Budget Advisory Committee and Committee of Congress, Nov 29, 1945.]

4

Organizing the Postwar Air Force

*To reorganize now in one form and then reorganize
again would be just an awful lot of wasted effort
and time.*

Gen. Carl A. Spaatz,
before the Patch Board,
September 1945

For the Army Air Forces, the period between the end of the war and the
March 1946 major reorganization was extremely hectic, even confusing. The
AAF leaders simultaneously confronted many crucial issues. These included redeployment; demobilization; determination of postwar force structure; potential
impact of the atomic bomb on forces and organization; planning future research
and development; probable reorganization of the defense establishment; and finally, creation of the AAF's own postwar organization.

General Spaatz identified three significant steps that were necessary to make
the postwar Air Force an effective reality. A Department of National Defense had
to be established, in which the Air Force would achieve parity with the Army and
Navy. The AAF's major commands required reorganization. And AAF headquarters needed recasting to facilitate policymaking.

As with the planning for 70 groups, the events leading to the March 1946 reorganization began before the war ended. With the successful invasion of the
European continent in June 1944 and the surrender of Germany in May 1945, Air
Staff planners had to consider organizational changes in the light of redeployment to the Pacific and conversion to B–29 very heavy bomb units. Also, they
had constantly to bear in mind and plan for the eventuality of a separate Air
Force.

The major decision to be made concerned the most effective way to organize the three primary missions—strategic, tactical, and air defense.* In June 1945 the newly created Headquarters Continental Air Forces (CAF) began to assume its responsibilities. Continental Air Forces was engaged in redeployment planning and was assigned the mission of air defense of the continental United States. In addition, CAF concentrated on postwar plans to form a strategic air reserve and to provide tactical air support to Army Ground Forces as well as directing units to participate in potential joint training with the Navy.

During 1945, Headquarters Army Air Forces was intensely involved in postwar organizational planning. Various plans were studied. Among them was a proposal for a separate Training Command along with the formation of an Air Force Combat Command. Another plan specified that Continental Air Forces retain the Training Command and that the Combat Command consist of long-range heavy bombers, escort fighters, and long-range reconnaissance aircraft. This plan contained the concept of a global striking force. This idea came to fruition in January 1946 when Lt. Gen. Hoyt S. Vandenberg proposed a global atomic striking force. Vandenberg stressed that such a force should be based in the United States, ready for instant deployment. This recommendation was approved by General Eaker.

Moreover, General Spaatz made several landmark decisions. In January 1946, after discussions with Army Chief of Staff General Eisenhower, Spaatz decided to create three major combat commands (Strategic Air Command, Tactical Air Command, and Air Defense Command) as part of the AAF's postwar reorganization. This move was influenced by Eisenhower's opinion that the Army required a separate tactical air force to support its ground armies. Also, air leaders held the view that if the AAF failed to furnish tactical air support, the Army would try to secure its own "integral" air units. In February 1946, Spaatz ordered the founding of an Air Board to set long-range policy. By the middle of 1946, the Army Air Forces' postwar reorganization had been codified by War Department Circular 138. Likewise in 1946, Spaatz directed the planning in the newly-formed Air Board, that would eventually bring a Deputy Chief of Staff system to Air Force headquarters.

Continental Air Forces

Following the Allied invasion in June 1944, in which air power played a crucial role, the war in Europe entered its final phases. Simultaneously, the United States pressed the drive against the Japanese in the Pacific. In 1944, U.S. forces

---

*These missions had been described in 1943 in War Department Field Manual 100–20. See Chapter 1.

landed in the Mariana Islands. The AAF anticipated having bases from which B–29 very long range bombers could strike the heart of Japan. By late summer of 1944, the Marianas were being prepared for the arrival of the first B–29s. These events demanded organizational changes.

In August 1944, Kuter and Maj. Gen. Howard A. Craig, Assistant Chief of Air Staff for Operations, Commitments, and Requirements (ACAS–3), stressed that developments in Europe and the Pacific dictated reorganization of continental (home) air forces to resolve expected redeployment problems and to capitalize on the evolving cutback in training. Changes were also essential to facilitate conversion of heavy bomb groups (B–17, B–24) to very heavy bomb groups (B–29). General Craig recommended creation of a Headquarters Continental Air Command to be responsible for all training, distribution, and redeployment and that Headquarters Training Command be abolished with its personnel being used to staff Headquarters Continental Air Command. Also, the First, Second, Third, and Fourth Air Forces, the Troop Carrier Command, Eastern Training Command, Central Training Command, Western Training Command, and Personnel Distribution Command should be placed under Headquarters Continental Air Command.*[1]

One of the principal problems had been the absence of training standardization in the home air forces; this could be remedied by putting these air forces under a continental command. Other chief concerns were conversion and redeployment. Craig thought that his recommendations were flexible enough to meet redeployment needs. His plan called for the First Air Force to receive and organize all units arriving from the European theater. The Second Air Force would administer the requisite training for conversion of heavy bomb groups to very heavy bomb groups. The Fourth Air Force would process and dispatch units to the Pacific theater. The Third Air Force would be charged with all replacement training which, after the war, would be at a low level.[2]

General Arnold agreed with his staff that changes were required. He informed Marshall that the Air Staff was laboring under a heavy load which would grow even more burdensome with redeployment and commencement of the complex task of conversion. He therefore advocated to Marshall creation of a Headquarters Continental Air Forces at Camp Springs, Md. (near Washington, D.C.), to

---

*During the war, the continental or home air forces were primarily responsible for training and air defense. At the start of the conflict, the First Air Force was assigned to the Eastern Defense Command and the Fourth Air Force to the Western Defense Command. The Second and Third Air Forces were responsible for unit training. By September 1943 the training forces were better than twice the size, in men and planes, of the air forces engaged in air defense. On September 10, 1943, the AAF gained complete control of the First and Fourth Air Forces. Later on, training became the main activity of the four air forces.

have command over the four continental air forces and the Troop Carrier Command. Arnold proposed that Headquarters CAF be responsible for the organization and training of units for deployment (or redeployment) overseas; for the establishment of a continental strategic air reserve; for the supervision of joint air-ground training; and for the air defense of the continental United States.[3]

After conferring with General Marshall, Lt. Gen. Thomas T. Handy, Army Deputy Chief of Staff, replied to Arnold. He concurred in the Army Air Forces' setting its own organization and thought decentralization was a good idea. Handy suggested, however, that Training Command be combined with the proposed Continental Air Forces ("the primary mission of the Air Forces in the United States at this time is training"). And in light of General Marshall's desire to move personnel out of Washington, Headquarters CAF should be located outside of the nation's capital. The Army Deputy Chief further questioned the future relationship of Headquarters AAF with Headquarters Continental Air Forces: "I have the impression that considerable difficulty was encountered when we had the Army Air Forces Combat Command with headquarters at Bolling Field."[4] Handy stressed that no increase in the troop basis would be approved for this reorganization.

Arnold admitted that he had seriously considered assigning Training Command to the Continental Air Forces. Nevertheless, Training Command had the mission of training individuals, whereas CAF needed to integrate these people into combat crews and units. Besides, Continental Air Forces would have to retrain and reequip units for redeployment or for assignment to the strategic reserve. Regarding Handy's point about a potential rise in personnel, Arnold responded that Headquarters Continental Air Forces would be organized at Camp Springs, Md. without enlarging the military strength of the Washington area.[5] This could be done by trimming the size of Headquarters Army Air Forces and by transferring the Fighter Replacement Training Unit at Camp Springs out of the Washington area. Command relationships would be sound. Headquarters AAF would deal directly with Headquarters CAF, Training Command, the AAF Personnel Distribution Command, Air Transport Command (ATC), and the Air Technical Service Command. Headquarters Continental Air Forces would have authority over the four continental air forces and the Troop Carrier Command.[6]

On November 17, 1944, General Marshall approved a continental Air Forces and on December 15 the Headquarters Continental Air Forces was activated.[7] Its responsibilities were: command of the four continental air forces, I Troop Carrier Command, and all units assigned to them; air defense of the continental United States; joint air-ground training; organization and training of service and combat units and crews for deployment or redeployment to overseas theaters; supervision of redeployment, including scheduling, determination of aircraft requirements, and movement of units to staging areas; and on completion of redeployment, formation, and command of the continental strategic reserve.[8]

As mentioned, among Arnold's reasons for setting up Headquarters Continental Air Forces was to assist in redeployment of forces.* It was likewise probable that for postwar organization the Commanding General, AAF, envisioned Continental Air Forces on the same command line as the Army Ground Forces. The Air Staff could then be placed on a par with the War Department General Staff, all under the Chief of Staff. In April 1945 the four home air forces and the Troop Carrier Command were formally assigned to Headquarters CAF, although the latter did not assume its full responsibilities until June.[9] As with Twentieth Air Force, Arnold himself retained control of Continental Air Force, appointing Maj. Gen. St. Clair Streett as Deputy Commanding General, CAF. So in reality General Arnold now had two major entities doing postwar planning, the Air Staff and Headquarters Continental Air Forces.

Nonetheless, at war's end, CAF found itself confronted with the immediate and tremendous task of demobilization. After V–J Day, it became apparent in August 1945 that the separation centers operated by Army Service Forces could not handle the volume of personnel waiting to be processed. Consequently, at Arnold's direction, the Continental Air Forces in September 1945 built a network of twenty-seven separation centers. In late October this number rose to forty-three. By December 1945, 500,000 personnel had been separated. In the middle of January 1946, the number of centers was reduced to nine, processing 2,800 daily. A total of 734,715 had been separated when the AAF's demobilization program terminated on February 20, 1946.[10] Brig. Gen. Leon W. Johnson, Chief, Personnel Services Division, noted in late 1945: "We didn't demobilize; we merely fell apart. . . .we lost many records of all the groups and units that operated during the war because there was no one to take care of them. So, it was not an orderly demobilization at all. It was just a riot, really."†[11]

In June 1945, Maj. Gen. Donald Wilson and Brig. Gen. Byron E. Gates of the Air Staff had proposed that Continental Air Forces activate two air defense commands with the same boundaries as the two remaining wartime defense commands. These would act as receiving and training agencies for fighter groups, aircraft warning and control units, and antiaircraft artillery units returning from

---

*Between May and August 1945, under the so-called "White Plan," more than 5,400 aircraft were flown to the United States from the European and Mediterranean theaters. Also, between May and July, the AAF's "Green Project" returned over 100,000 military and civilian passengers from Europe and the Mediterranean by Air Transport Command aircraft. [Chauncey E. Sanders, *Redeployment and Demobilization* (USAF Hist Study 77, Maxwell AFB, Ala., 1953), pp 46–57.]

†General Johnson won the Medal of Honor for his exploits in the Ploesti raid. As for demobilization, the AAF reached a peak of 2,411,294 military personnel in March 1944. By December 31, 1945, this had been reduced to 888,769. In March 1946 the figure had shrunk to 500,472 and to a postwar low of 303,614 in May 1947.

AAF Personnel Services Chief, Brig. Gen. Leon W. Johnson criticized the demobilization as inefficient and disorderly.

Europe. They would train National Guard and Reserve troops in AAA and aircraft control and warning.[12] Wilson and Gates asserted that, since the Air Staff now regarded air defense as relatively unimportant compared to early in the war, the emphasis within the two commands would be rescue and flight control.

Continental Air Forces rejected this plan as being premature. It opposed investing in World War II air defense equipment, recommending that the AAF concentrate on developing equipment to locate and track missiles like those the Germans launched against Britain. In addition, CAF questioned the idea of establishing commands which would be subordinated to ground commanders.[13] In lieu of focusing on air defense restructuring, CAF was chiefly concerned with creating a strategic reserve to, among other missions, furnish tactical air units to support the Army Ground Forces. Meanwhile, General Streett knew that General Arnold was weighing an Air Staff proposal to set up a strategic air force separate from and on line with Continental Air Forces.

Strategic Striking Force

In the summer of 1945, the War Department directed the AAF to form a strategic or General Reserve of air units to support the Army's overall strategic re-

In the aftermath of V–J Day, Army separation centers were flooded with personnel anxious to return home *(below)*. To meet the demand, the Continental Air Forces set up additional separation centers around the country *(right)*.

serve consisting of ground and air units. Based in the United States, these air forces in the General Reserve would move overseas quickly in an emergency. They would reinforce occupation forces in Europe and Asia, form a combat force overseas if required, and help maintain internal security in the United States and its possessions.[14] Thus, the General Reserve would largely be used for tactical support of the Army Ground Forces. By mid-September 1946 these mobile Reserve units and their support elements would be trained and equipped to high combat efficiency. The commanders of the AAF's major combat commands would inform the AAF Commander of the units designated for the General Reserve.[15]

The size of the strategic reserve had fluctuated. In early 1945 the Joint Chiefs had authorized a continental United States strategic reserve of as many as twenty-nine AAF groups and additional separate squadrons. During late July 1945, General Arnold sanctioned an AAF Continental United States (CONUS) reserve of thirteen groups—two heavy bomb, two medium bomb, five fighter, three troop carrier, and one reconnaissance.[16] The AAF troop basis was amended in early August to reflect this thirteen-group strategic reserve.

Shortly thereafter, on September 8, 1945, the War Department approved a Strategic Striking Force to be kept in the United States as part of the General Reserve. Units would be picked for this force. Besides the SSF, Army Air Forces would specify units to be deployed overseas and others to be retained in the United States for training.[17] From September 1945 on, the AAF constantly changed the composition of the striking force, adding and deleting units as required depending on which ones were being returned from overseas or were being inactivated. Also in September, additional tactical units were moved to the SSF since two armies would be retained in the CONUS and the AAF would have to furnish a tactical air command for each.[18] On November 17 the War Department ordered that units of the Strategic Striking Force should henceforth be considered and designated as General Reserve.[19] By the close of 1945, five very heavy bomb groups had been assigned to the General Reserve, including the 40th, 444th, and 509th, comprising the 58th Very Heavy Bomb Wing.*[20]

Plans had also been devised to put the striking force under an Air Force Combat Command. In December 1945, Col. Robert O. Cork, Office of the Assistant Chief of Air Staff, Plans (ACAS–5), presented two plans to the newly appointed Ad Hoc Committee on Reorganization of the Army Air Forces. The first suggested a separate Training Command with an Air Force Combat Command replacing the Continental Air Forces. The second recommended that CAF keep the Training Command with the AFCC having long-range heavy bombers, escort fighters, and long-range reconnaissance.[21]

---

*Each group consisted of four squadrons.

Another proposal put forward for the Air Force Combat Command reflected the concept of Col. Reuben C. Moffat, now head of the Special Planning Division and a member of the ad hoc committee. In presenting his plan for a Combat Command, he said that "such an organization must be prepared to move. . . .tactical organizations to bases throughout the continental United States, the territories and possessions in order that the responsible commander under a system of unified command may have a striking force competent to meet the trend of international relations."[22]

Colonel Moffat pointed out that if all long-range very heavy bombers were permanently assigned to continental U.S. commands and the theaters, there would be insufficient flexibility for the AAF to carry out its mission. The theaters and Continental Air Forces should have ample units to assure the air defense of these areas. These units would be equipped with interceptor and night fighters, perimeter reconnaissance aircraft, and planes to support ground and naval forces. The Air Force Combat Command, reporting directly to the AAF Commander, could move a striking force of sufficient size anywhere to assist units in specific regions.[23]

The AFCC would encompass all units of the Strategic or General Reserve in the continental United States. Movement of these units would be the task of the Combat Command. In peacetime, this striking force would be controlled by the area or theater commander (after movement) for training or in anticipation of hostilities. During war, this force would become an integral part of the theater commander's forces. This, said Moffat, was the concept of unified command as developed during the war. He urged that Continental Air Forces take in the Air Force Training Command and be charged with training National Guard, Reserve, and tactical units to support ground and naval forces, air defense, and perimeter reconnaissance.[24]*

Meantime, following the end of the war, the AAF leadership at once began concerted thinking about the potential effects of the atomic bomb on strategy, organization, and force structure. To look into this matter, General Arnold directed formation of the Spaatz Board (comprising Spaatz, Vandenberg, and Norstad). The board's report of October 1945 recommended that the AAF exploit atomic technology to the utmost, and that "an officer of the caliber of Maj. Gen. Curtis E. LeMay" be made Deputy Chief of Staff for Research and Development. The board concluded that the atomic bomb did not call for a change in the current size, organization, and composition of the postwar Air Force.[25]

Coincident with issuance of the Spaatz Board report, a study by the Joint Strategic Survey Committee of the JCS concluded that, when other nations got the atomic bomb, United States security would be greatly impaired. The Soviet Un-

---

*Colonel Moffat, long active in postwar planning, died on May 18, 1946.

ion was identified as a potential enemy. Inasmuch as its industrial and population centers were strung out over vast areas, the United States needed a network of overseas bases. The committee set the American atomic lead at about five years. To keep this advantage, it recommended American or allied control of the major sources of uranium and acceleration of U.S. scientific research and development. Further, the committee advocated accrual of an adequate atomic stockpile and a policy of the strictest secrecy in the atomic bomb program. This meant refusal to give atomic information to any nation or international organization. Finally, conventional weapons would still be needed. The committee saw no reason for major modification of the military organization.[26]

General LeMay, Deputy Chief of Air Staff for Research and Development, had also been thinking about the A-bomb. In January 1946, the War Department Equipment Board, pondering the results of the atomic revolution, called LeMay to testify. Atomic weapons, he said, changed basic military concepts. The nation would not have time to mobilize once war began. An atomic attack would be impossible to stop. "Our only defense," he stressed, "is a striking power in being of such size that it is capable of delivering a stronger blow than any of our potential enemies."[27] He was certain that conventional bombs would be needed against dispersed industrial targets.

At the same time, General Vandenberg advised maintaining in the United States a global atomic striking force in constant readiness, poised for instant deployment. In early January 1946, Vandenberg drafted a detailed plan, approved by Eaker, for a force, "sufficient in size, to fully exploit the expected availability and effectiveness of new bombardment weapons including the atomic bomb."[28] Manned by the best personnel, this striking force would employ the most advanced aircraft and equipment. Moreover, elements of the force should be located near the Manhattan Engineer District's (MED's) assembly and storage area at Albuquerque, N. Mex., to ensure close coordination with the bomb manufacturing, development, and assembly center.[29]

General Vandenberg wanted the 509th Bomb Group to be the nucleus of the Atomic Air Force. Having returned from the Pacific, the 509th was now at Roswell Army Air Field, N. Mex. There should be a single agency, said Vandenberg, to direct the AAF's atomic units and to establish and maintain the strategic striking force. He accordingly pressed for a wing organization consisting of Headquarters 58th Wing and three VHB groups, the 40th, 444th, and 509th. This organization should be a standard very heavy bomb wing, augmented by personnel and units for handling atomic bombs. It could deploy one or more of its groups. The wing headquarters would take care of training, technical support, and liaison with the Manhattan Engineer District.[30]

General Norstad, Assistant Chief of Air Staff, Plans, believed that ideally the atomic force should include the AAF's standard units supplemented by special personnel and equipment. Still, it would be impossible to move personnel and

132

equipment among all of the VHB units. He agreed with Vandenberg that one basic unit should exploit the atomic bomb. Such a unit demanded highly trained people. Norstad underscored the importance of communicating to the War Department and the Congress that the existence of the atomic bomb did not mean that whole portions of the AAF could be abolished. The single atomic wing, Norstad insisted, was chiefly a mobile striking force. Its personnel would be rotated for training. "The individual components," he said, "would be used as part of the VHB striking force."[31] Vandenberg added that the limited projected troop basis would allow just three groups of four squadrons each, one squadron having atomic modified B-29s. Conceivably, each VHB group might ultimately contain at least one squadron that could deliver the atomic bomb.[32]

Col. John G. Moore, Deputy Assistant Chief of Air Staff, Materiel, recommended to Eaker that solely a single standard wing, without a special atomic designator, be organized at this time. He deemed it easier to obtain funds for equipping a small unit and keeping it ready, than to try to equip all units. When atomic bombs became more plentiful, more units could be converted.[33] Moore suggested there were many targets not calling for the atomic bomb. Therefore, the AAF would still have to stockpile the standard bombs that had been so effective during the war.[34]

Brig. Gen. John A. Samford, Deputy Assistant Chief of Air Staff for Intelligence, agreed that a specific wing should be made the atomic wing. He cautioned, however, that a term like "atomic bombing force" should be avoided: "The missions of the wing should include the development of practices and organization that will permit the easiest possible adaptation of any similar bombardment wing to the task of atomic bombing."[35]Should a wing be designated as "atomic," Samford thought it would be "vulnerable to control by interests whose proper authority over atomic matters may be completely foreign to the use of atomic energy as a weapon."[36] The best tactic, then, would be to designate this wing as a Bomb Wing (Special).[37]

In June 1946, Headquarters AAF approved the role of the 58th Bomb Wing as the first unit of the atomic strike force. The wing's mission, adopted from SAC's, was "to be capable of immediate and sustained very long range offensive operations in any part of the world, either independently or in cooperation with land and naval forces, utilizing the latest and most advanced weapons."[38] In addition the 58th Wing would help the Manhattan Engineer District conduct tests, when appropriate, as well as handle AAF liaison with MED on atomic matters.*

---

*Liaison on policies pertaining to potential use of the atomic bomb and to atomic information would in time be transferred to the Air Materiel Command. This would be done after SAC had elicited sufficient atomic information to enable it eventually to employ the bomb, if need be.

B–29 in flight. General Norstad advocated that one unit or wing of these aircraft should be capable of delivering the atomic bomb.

In general the AAF's atomic program had been slow to evolve due to redeployment and demobilization problems after the war. The Air Staff had been occupied with postwar organization planning, while the 58th Bomb Wing (Brig. Gen. Roger M. Ramey, Commander) was caught up in the "Crossroads" atomic tests.[39]

At the same time that the AAF planned its atomic striking force, Maj. Gen. Leslie R. Groves, MED head, wrote a memorandum clarifying his thinking about the impact of the atomic bomb on military organization and strategy. Groves thought it unlikely that the world's major nations would reach an arms control agreement. Should this prediction materialize, the United States must keep its supremacy in atomic weapons for immediate use in the event of an atomic attack.[40] Like many military leaders and governmental officials, Groves played up the importance of the United States having a worldwide intelligence network.

Groves was skeptical of the War Department's postwar mobilization planning. He wrote that in an all-out war, with atomic weapons used on one or both sides, there would not be time to mobilize, train, and equip a large army. Yet, he argued that the atomic bomb was not an all-purpose weapon: "One would not use a piledriver for driving tacks when a tack hammer would do a better and cheaper job."[41] He opposed relying exclusively on the atomic bomb. Balanced military forces were required, able to react instantaneously.[42]

Meanwhile, the Army Air Forces was unhappy over its arrangements with the Manhattan Engineer District. General LeMay wished to take from MED the responsibility for procurement, storage, assembly, and transportation of the atomic bomb. This would leave the district with the missions of research and development and fabrication and delivery to the AAF of components manufactured by MED.[43] In LeMay's view, the split responsibility between the AAF and MED violated the principle of unity of command. This issue would become more troublesome in the future as the AAF gained even more autonomy.[44]

Postwar Organization of Major Commands

The previously mentioned Ad Hoc Committee on Reorganization of the Army Air Forces was established by Eaker on December 11, 1945, to examine postwar organization and missions.* At the start the committee members differed, among other things, on the proposed functions of the Combat Command, Strategic Striking Force, Continental Air Forces, and Training Command.[45] Committee members also disagreed on how to set up the technical services. The Assistant Chief of Air Staff, Supply, advocated a functional staff structure with little visibility for the technical services, such as ordnance, engineers, quartermaster, and chemical warfare. On the other hand, the Assistant Chief of Air Staff, Personnel, recommended a semicorps or service-type structure in which specialized activities would be represented by special staff agencies through the command up to the top. The Assistant Chief of Air Staff, Plans, also favored representation by special staff agencies.[46] Unable to concur on command structure, the committee forwarded several alternatives to Eaker for possible approval.[47]

In early January 1946, General Spaatz approved one of the recommended organizations for planning purposes. With minor revisions, this plan could have been appropriate to any of the conceivable plans for reorganizing the national defense structure, including a single department with coequal Army, Navy, and Air Force. General Norstad saw the plan as a compromise between the views of Air

---

*Members of the committee were: Col. Reuben C. Moffat, Plans (A–5), steering member; Col. Bourne Adkison, Training and Operations (A–3); Col. Robert E. L. Eaton, Personnel (A–1); Col. Harris B. Hull, Intelligence (A–2); Col. John G. Salsman, Supply (A–4); Col. J. B. Hill, Air Judge Advocate's Office; Lt. Col. William P. Berkeley, Plans; Col. Keith K. Compton, Continental Air Forces; Brig. Gen. Glen C. Jamison, Deputy Assistant Chief of Air Staff, Plans, monitoring the study's development; and Maj. C. F. Byars, Plans, recorder.

Staff members. Designed for 70 groups, it could be adapted to any size force if the major missions remained the same.[48] Under this suggested compromise, there were the Air Force Combat Command, comprising the strategic, tactical, and air defense forces; the Air Technical Service Command; the Air Transport Command; and the Training Command.[49] Norstad said the relationship between theater air commands and AAF headquarters "is designated by a dotted line to indicate the administrative, logistical, training, and tactical supervision exercised by the Commanding General, AAF. Dependent upon the organization of the military service, this line may in some cases be solid to indicate command and complete control."[50]

Despite the recommendations of the ad hoc committee, Eisenhower and Spaatz convened definitive discussions on the subject of tactical air support. As mentioned, General Eisenhower had become Army Chief of Staff in November 1945. Even though General Arnold would not retire until February 1946, Spaatz

The development of the atomic force raised many issues for postwar planners. In the early stages of atomic testing, AAF observers (*left to right*) Brig. Gen. William F. McKee, Maj. General Curtis LeMay and Maj. Gen. Earle E. Partridge confer over a scale model of Bikini Atoll. The AAF participated in the tests as part of the Joint Army–Navy Task Force.

(Right) Stressing the importance of tactical operations in future operations, Brig. Gen. William F. McKee recommended forming two tactical air commands, one to service the Army Ground Forces and a second to train AAF personnel.

Maj. Gen. Samuel A. Anderson *(left)* with Brig. Gen. Edwin J. Backus in France, 1945. After the war, General Anderson served as Chief of Staff for Continental Air Forces and became a strong advocate for strengthening tactical air support capabilities within Army Air Forces.

had shouldered important portions of Arnold's workload since November, when the AAF Commander, in ill health, announced to the Air Staff that he would be retiring. In fact, between November 1945 and February 1946, Spaatz spearheaded the AAF drive for unification and a separate Air Force. On November 14, 1945, Arnold had directed Eaker to give Spaatz the job of determining the permanent status of the Army Air Forces.[51] Thus, until Spaatz succeeded Arnold in February, he would function officially as his deputy. As architect of AAF plans pointing to permanent status, Spaatz would keep in close touch with the War Department and of course could call on any Air Staff office for assistance.[52]

Tactical air support of Army Ground Forces was one of the most important and pressing postwar issues facing the Army Air Forces. As noted, the ad hoc committee in December 1945 was studying formation of an Air Force Combat Command, embracing the AAF's strategic, tactical, and air defense forces. Also, a proposal to lodge all combat air power in the Continental Air Forces had been weighed. General Arnold knew that the Army's ground forces would conduct postwar training maneuvers in which tactical air support would be required. When Eaker had set the 70-group goal in late August 1945, he had also approved for planning purposes an Air Staff proposal that light and medium bomber and certain fighter groups be formed into a model tactical air force acceptable to the Army Ground Forces.[53] Army ground commanders deemed air superiority crucial to the success of the ground forces.[54] Leaders of the AAF of course agreed with AGF commanders that tactical experience in World War II had shown that ground troops must move under the cover of air superiority.

In the meantime, CAF headquarters recommended to Arnold that the First Air Force be made into an "operational" air force composed of two tactical air commands. The First's training function would then be split among the other three continental air forces.[55] Aware of the proven importance of tactical air support, Maj. Gen. Samuel E. Anderson, Chief of Staff, Continental Air Forces, pointed out to Arnold that the Army Ground Forces had advocated support aviation within their own units. The AGF had argued that Army Air Forces had given low priority to equipping and training units designed to support ground operations. Hence, to preserve its tactical mission, Anderson emphasized, the AAF should create a headquarters at Air Force level to administer air-ground and joint training operations.[56]

In August 1945, General Vandenberg endorsed the proposition that one of the four numbered air forces be redesignated and consist of two tactical air commands. Brig. Gen. William F. McKee, Deputy Assistant Chief of Air Staff for Operations, proposed in late October that this tactical air force be integrated in the AAF's postwar plan. The AAF view was that "new developments may change the employment of Tactical Air Forces, but cannot diminish its necessity. Whenever AGF units are employed, cooperating tactical air units are necessary."[57] However, the Army Air Forces expressed concern lest the AGF establish organic air units. The AAF therefore acted on the assumption that, if AGF postwar tactical air requirements were not met, the AGF would try to satisfy them on its own.* The proposed tactical air force would meet AGF needs. McKee recommended that the first or "model" Tactical Air Command be organized at full strength. It would support the AGF's proposed mobile striking army and would be ready for immediate action in event of an emergency. The second or "skeleton" command should be formed at reduced strength. The skeleton command would be a training TAC, to relieve the model TAC from the responsibility for training with the AGF in joint Army-Navy exercises.[58]

Agreeing in principle with McKee, Colonel Moffat said that his Post War Division had included a tactical Air Force headquarters in its plan for organization of a permanent Air Force. Moffat assumed that such a headquarters would be sufficiently flexible to accommodate one or more "skeletonized" Tactical Air Commands.[59] Nevertheless, he noted that the plan for a 70-group Air Force with 400,000 men would force all units to be only at half-strength at best.[60]

But McKee believed the model Tactical Air Command would be organized at full strength with all the requisite elements for air-ground operations. McKee's idea was to make the model TAC highly mobile to meet the Army's ground force needs. The model command would be a fully trained striking force set for instant action. The skeleton TAC would be organized at reduced strength to be used chiefly as a training command. It would in addition give technical training to aircraft control and warning personnel.[61] Though approved in August 1945, this plan was not implemented. The surrender of Japan caused the Air Staff to forego

---

*Maj. Gen. Elwood R. Quesada, commanding general of the IX Tactical Air Command during World War II (who would become CG, Tactical Air Command, in March 1946), held what was a common view among the AAF leadership in the postwar period: "There is a strong tendency within the Army—in my mind, the Army and Ground Forces are the same—to gain control and command of tactical forces. . . .I've learned that through my close association with Devers [Gen. Jacob L. Devers, CG, Army Ground Forces] and his Army commanders, corps commanders and division commanders. They have picked up very cleverly our own suggestions. The Navy should continue control of its carrier-based aircraft to support fleet operations. So they, likewise, say that the Army should have control of its tactical air forces to support land operations." [Fourth Meeting of the Air Board, Dec 3–4, 1946, p 185, in RG 340, SAF, Air Bd Mtgs, Box 16, MMB.] Interestingly, General Kenney (to be CG, Strategic Air Command), did not even like to use the words "tactical" and "strategic." He thought that all types of aircraft and air organizations would do both kinds of missions. He felt that to divide AAF organizations into tactical and strategic was to help the Army in its attempts to obtain an "integral" air force. Kenney noted that some ground officers compared tactical air to artillery. [Memo for Gen. Arnold fr Lt. Gen. Hoyt S. Vandenberg, ACAS-3, subj: Daily Activity Report of the AC/AS-3, Aug 27, 1945, in RG 18, AAG 319.1, OC&R, 1945, ox 369; Fourth Meeting of Air Board, Dec 3–4, 1946, p 179.]

immediate organizational changes and, along with the War Department's planners to attempt to chart even more intensely the permanent postwar structure.

Maj. Gen. Samuel E. Anderson proposed in September 1945 that Continental Air Forces be responsible for a global striking force, tactical air units for all training conducted with Army and Navy forces, planning for the air defense of the continental United States, and training combat units and crews for overseas.[62] Then in mid-November, Maj. Gen. St. Clair Streett, CAF deputy commander recommended that Continental Air Forces be organized into Eastern and Western Air Commands for air defense, a Central Air Command for training, and a Tactical Air Command. Streett stressed that strategic forces would operate under the Commanding General, Army Air Forces, in an M-day Strategic Air Task Force.[63] Even before the war ended, General Norstad, Assistant Chief of Air Staff for Plans, had pressed for a postwar Strategic Air Force that would include all the very heavy bomb units.[64] And in December, the ad hoc committee on reorganization advocated that four air forces (one strategic, one tactical, and two air defense) be created under Continental Air Forces. One thing was certain—the eventual postwar organization of the Air Force would include units to carry out training maneuvers with the ground forces and to undertake tactical operations in case of emergency.[65]

However, as noted, General Eisenhower had made a strong point to Spaatz on the importance of a separate tactical air organization to support the Army Ground Forces.[66] The Army Chief had long held firm views on tactical air support of ground forces. The Army, said Eisenhower, had always accepted without reservation the idea of mutual dependence between the services. World War II had attested to the effectiveness of the unified command principle. The concept of complementary roles—air, ground, and sea—meant that no single service should have the forces or equipment to carry out joint missions by itself, if these forces or equipment duplicated those in the other services.[67] The war confirmed the need for air superiority over the battlefield if ground operations were to be successful. Control of the air, Eisenhower argued, was most economically gained by employment of air forces operating under a single command. He was emphatic in his conviction that the Army's dependence on tactical air support had been matched by the AAF's effectiveness in furnishing it. Nonetheless, the Army Chief's position did not rest solely upon the manifested efficiency of such support:

> Basically, the Army does not belong in the air — it belongs on the ground . . . . Control of the tactical Air Force means responsibility. . .for the entire operating establishment required to support these planes. This includes the requisite basic air research and development program necessary to maintain a vital arm and the additional specialized service forces to support the army . . . . assumption of this task by the Army would duplicate in great measure the primary and continuing responsibilities of the Air Force and, in effect, would result in the creation of another air establishment.[68]

Spaatz, now Arnold's deputy but actually operating for him, agreed with Eisenhower on the need for a separate tactical air structure. In mid-January 1946, Spaatz thus turned away from the idea of having the combat air forces under CAF. He directed the demise of CAF and instead formed three major combat air commands—the Strategic Air Command, Tactical Air Command, and the Air Defense Command.[69] General Spaatz would later recall that "Eisenhower and I thought along the same lines about this thing. I certainly would not call it pressure."[70] Lt. Gen. Elwood R. Quesada, named TAC commander in March 1946, recalled:

> Bradley and Eisenhower were assured by Spaatz that the Air Force would always honor and always meet its commitments to the Army and provide strong tactical air forces. Spaatz made that commitment to Eisenhower and it was a very strong commitment. Eisenhower was persuaded by it; Spaatz meant it. . . .He made strong promises to Eisenhower to the effect that the tactical air forces would remain intact. . . .They would honor their commitment and their obligation to provide that service to the Army. It was to a large extent that that commitment by Spaatz permitted Eisenhower to support a separate air force. I think without it he wouldn't have.[71]

The other AAF commands would be the Air Materiel Command (formerly the Air Technical Service Command), Air Training Command, Air University, the Air Proving Ground Command, Air Transport Command, and the theater commands. The ad hoc committee on reorganization commented that the restructuring was not arrived at by the committee's deliberations, but rather by a command decision: "as such, the Ad Hoc Committee has no bone to pick with the command organization."[72] By January 29, 1946, Eisenhower and Spaatz had formally approved this reorganization plan and it was distributed within the Air Staff. It was originally to become effective on February 15, 1946.[73]

With dissemination of the plan to the Air Staff, the objectives of the ad hoc committee changed. The first priority became distribution of materials to realize the new organization. The second priority was to adjust the implemental plans to the Simpson Board's recommendations, which would eventually involve the AAF's assuming additional functions with commensurate personnel.*[74]

The peacetime reorganization implemented by General Spaatz on March 21, 1946, followed functional lines, the AAF forming a major command to conduct each of the air roles specified in Field Manual 100–30. SAC, TAC, and ADC were established as the three major combat commands. This was in line with a previous proposal by Vandenberg and Norstad to form a separate "strategic Air Force." The Army Air Forces really wanted to create just two commands, a Continental Air Forces and a long-range strategic bomber force. The AAF reasoned

---

*For details on the Simpson Board's recommendations, See Chapter 3.

St. Clair Streett (*left*) and Major Banfield on the beach of Los Negros Island. As a major general, Streett proposed reorganizing Continental Air Forces into separate commands for air defense, training, and tactical air support.

Lt. Gen. Elwood R. Quesada headed Tactical Air Command, first in Florida and later at Langley Field, Virginia.

that the CAF would occupy the same command line as the Army Ground Forces. With this arrangement, the Air Staff would then be on the same line with the War Department General Staff, under the Chief of Staff. However, Eisenhower and Gen. Jacob L. Devers' Army Ground Forces desired air forces specifically designated for air-ground operations. Since Eisenhower was such a strong proponent of a separate Air Force, Spaatz was not disposed to contest this issue. Had a Tactical Air Command not been formed, the ground generals would probably have acted in concert to achieve their own tactical aviation. No doubt Eisenhower stressed this last point to General Spaatz.

The March 1946 peacetime reorganization, implemented by an order signed by The Adjutant General of the War Department, placed the major commands directly under the Commanding General, Army Air Forces.[75] This restructuring embodied the principle that numbered air forces would be intermediate headquarters in the chain of command, between the major commands and wings or the equivalent.[76] This type of arrangement, relying on the major commands below the top headquarters, reflected the RAF influence. Headquarters Continental Air Forces was redesignated as Headquarters Strategic Air Command under Gen. George C. Kenney, located at Bolling Field, Washington, D.C., then moved to Andrews Field, Md., in October 1946.* Headquarters Air Defense Command was activated at Mitchel Field, N.Y., under Lt. Gen. George E. Stratemeyer. Headquarters Tactical Air Command was activated at Tampa, Fla., under Maj. Gen. Elwood R. Quesada. Subsequently, Quesada moved TAC headquarters to Langley Field, Va., near the Army Ground Forces headquarters at Fort Monroe, Va., and the Navy's Atlantic Fleet headquarters at Norfolk. Quesada said that TAC would stress mobility and flexibility and would be prepared to cooperate with the AGF.[77] His idea of air support for the ground forces was to do the job so well "that the Army would be the first to admit that the tactical air command forces under the jurisdiction of the United States Air Force was to their benefit."[78]

Locations of the supporting commands and their commanders were: Air Materiel Command (a redesignated Air Technical Service Command), Wright Field,

---

*In August 1946, SAC was issued orders to move to Colorado Springs, Colo. Within a week these orders were canceled because of "lack of funds." [Charles R. Rowdybush, *The History of Bolling Field, Anacostia, D.C., 1917–1948* (Masters Thesis, American University, Mar 57).] Sometimes referred to as "MacArthur's airman," for his ability to get along with Gen. Douglas MacArthur, Kenney had a distinguished record in World War II. Fifty-seven years old, he was appointed a member of the United Nations' Military Staff Committee and thus did not command SAC until October 1946. His deputy, Maj. Gen. St. Clair Streett, commanded until October.

Gathered around AAF Commanding General Carl A. Spaatz are the commanding generals of the reorganized air forces. *Standing, left to right:* Lt. Gen. Nathan F. Twining, Air Materiel Command; Maj. Gen. Donald Wilson, AAF Proving Ground Command; Maj. Gen. Muir S. Fairchild, Air University. *Seated, left to right:* Lt. Gen. John K. Cannon, Air Training Command; Gen. George C. Kenney, Strategic Air Command; General Spaatz; Lt. Gen. Harold L. George, Air Transport Command; Lt. Gen. George E. Stratemeyer, Air Defense Command; and Maj. Gen. Elwood R. Quesada, Tactical Air Command.

Ohio, Lt. Gen. Nathan F. Twining;*[79] Air Transport Command, Washington, D.C., Lt. Gen. Harold L. George; Air Training Command, Barksdale Field, La., Lt. Gen. John K. Cannon; Air University, Maxwell Field, Ala., Maj. Gen. Muir S. Fairchild; AAF Proving Ground Command (formerly the AAF Center), Eglin Field, Fla., Maj. Gen. Donald Wilson.

In this reorganization, eleven of the AAF's wartime air forces were assigned to the three new combat commands: SAC took control of the Eighth and the Fifteenth; TAC received the Third, Ninth, and Twelfth; ADC got the First, Second,

---

*In February 1946, there had been discussions in the Air Staff to change Air Technical Service Command to "Air Service Command." General Twining, the ATSC commander, objected, insisting that the name, Air Materiel Command, "had more appeal." General Spaatz agreed. [Lt. Gen. Nathan F. Twining, CG, ATSC, to Lt. Gen. Ira C. Eaker, Feb 11, 1946, in RG 18/AAG, Eaker Personal and Reading File, ACAS–5, File/6.]

AIR STAFF

MARCH 21, 1946

General Carl A. Spaatz, Commanding General, AAF

Lt. Gen. Ira C. Eaker	Deputy Commander & Chief of Air Staff
Lt. Gen. Harold L. George*	Director of Information
Maj. Gen. Charles C. Chauncey	DCAS, Administration
Maj. Gen. Curtis E. LeMay	DCAS, Research & Development
Maj. Gen. Fred L. Anderson	ACAS–1, Personnel
Brig. Gen. George C. McDonald	ACAS–2, Intelligence
Maj. Gen. Earle E. Partridge	ACAS–3, Operations & Training
Maj. Gen. Edward M. Powers	ACAS–4, Materiel
Maj. Gen. Lauris Norstad	ACAS–5, Plans
Maj. Gen. Hugh J. Knerr	Secretary-General of the Air Board
Maj. Gen. Junius W. Jones	Air Inspector

---

*Also Commanding General, Air Transport Command.

AAF MILITARY PERSONNEL DISTRIBUTION: MARCH 1946*

CONUS

TOTAL	328,079
Strategic Air Command	84,231
Tactical Air Command	25,574
Air Defense Command	7,218
Air Proving Ground Command	7,295
Air Training Command	128,742
Air Materiel Command	25,070
Air Transport Command	21,304
Air University	3,867
Personnel Distribution Command	4,002
Other	20,776

OVERSEAS

TOTAL	172,393
European Theater	47,554
Mediterranean Theater	2,555
Caribbean Air Command	4,279
Pacific Air Command	71,959
China Theater	7,668
Alaskan Air Command	2,740
Air Transport Command	35,015
Other	623

---

*USAF Statistical Digest, 1947, pp 46, 53.

AAF TACTICAL GROUPS AND SEPARATE SQUADRONS*

MARCH 1946

		GROUPS	SQUADRONS
TOTAL:		71	212
Very Heavy Bomber		21	66
Heavy Bomber		7	24
Medium Bomber		2	7
Light Bomber		2	7
Fighter		22	63
Reconnaissance		3	4
Troop Carrier		12	37
Composite		2	4
LOCATION:	At Home	21	64
	Overseas	50	148

		SEPARATE SQUADRONS
TOTAL:		72
Heavy Bomber		5
Fighter		6
Night Fighter		9
Reconnaissance		22
Troop Carrier		8
Liaison		10
Emergency Rescue		7
Geodetic Control		1
Tow Target		4
LOCATION:	At Home	19
	Overseas	53

---

*USAF Statistical Digest, 1946, pp 4–5.

Fourth, Tenth, Eleventh, and Fourteenth, aligned geographically to match the Army's six continental United States army areas.[80]

Overseas air forces were deployed and commanded as follows: Fifth Air Force, Nagoya, Japan, Maj. Gen. Kenneth B. Wolfe; Sixth Air Force (became Caribbean Air Command, July 1946), Albrook Field, Panama, Maj. Gen. Hubert R. Harmon; Seventh Air Force, Hickam Field, Hawaii, Maj. Gen. Thomas D. White; Thirteenth Air Force, Fort McKinley, Luzon, Philippines, Maj. Gen. Eugene L. Eubank; Twentieth Air Force, Harmon Field, Guam, Maj. Gen. Francis H. Griswold. The Fifth, Thirteenth, and Twentieth Air Forces operated under Lt. Gen. Ennis C. Whitehead's Far East Air Forces (Tokyo, Japan). Tactical Air Forces in Europe operated under Maj. Gen. Idwal H. Edwards' United States Air Forces in Europe (Wiesbaden, Germany). The Alaskan Air Command (formerly Eleventh Air Force) was under Brig. Gen. Edmund C. Lynch, at Adak.[*] The chain of control of air units abroad ran from Headquarters AAF to numbered air force headquarters and then to bombardment and fighter groups. The fighter units, with radar and communications furnished by new tactical control groups, would perform the air defense and tactical air missions. This elimination of intermediate headquarters and assignment of dual missions to fighter groups enabled Army Air Forces to meet overseas requirements with a minimum of personnel.[81]

As far as missions were concerned, General Spaatz assigned the Strategic Air Command with the interim mission of being prepared to carry out long-range global operations on their own or with land or naval forces. SAC was also responsible for maximum-range reconnaissance.[82] The Tactical Air Command should be ready to operate jointly with ground or naval forces and, if required, to assist Air Defense Command with air defense operations. And, if necessary, it would help the Army Ground Forces train airborne units.[83]

Air Defense Command's official interim mission was to defend the continental United States, one air force being assigned to each of six air defense areas. In addition ADC would be prepared to cooperate with the Navy against hostile forces or to protect coastal shipping. Besides, it would train the Air National Guard, administer and train the Air Reserve, and instruct and train the Reserve Officers Training Corps.[†84]

---

*There had been discussion in the Air Staff aimed at forming an Arctic theater. This failed to materialize. [R&R Comment, 1, Maj. Gen. Charles C. Chauncey, DCAS–5 (plans), subj: Creation of Arctic Theater, Apr 24, 1946, in RG 18/AAG Eaker Personal and Reading File, ACAS–5, File/6.]

†Air Defense Command would likewise handle AAF's contacts with the civilian community. Lt. Gen. Ira C. Eaker, Deputy Commander, AAF, explained ADC's mission in these words: "In the last war we found that when the emergency developed, the trained commanders and their staffs went away to war and we were left at the most critical period in our history with the necessity of reorganizing the home establishment which had to do

Air Proving Ground Command was responsible for improving operational suitability. The command would further make recommendations on the establishment of military characteristics and requirements for operational systems and materiel.[85] The Air University would supervise and operate the Air War College, the Air Command and Staff School, and other schools and courses as called for.[86]

The Air Transport Command would provide air transport for all War Department agencies (except those served by Troop Carrier Command and local services required by overseas area commands or occupation forces) and for any other governmental agency, as required or directed. Moreover, ATC was responsible for air evacuation of sick and wounded from overseas theaters and between points within the United States, as well as control and operation of aerial ports. Additional responsibilities of this command were: Air Transport Service (new), Air Rescue Service (new), Air Weather Service (old AAF Weather Service), Air Communications Service (old Army Airways Communications Service), Aeronautical Chart Service (old Aeronautical Mapping and Chart Service), Flight Services (old AAF Flight Service), and Flying Safety Service.[87]

The Air Materiel Command would undertake research and development essential to the AAF mission and conduct all required experimental static and flight tests. It would also be charged with quality control and acceptance of materiel procured by the AAF, modification of aircraft, industrial mobilization planning, and depot supply operating functions.[88] The Air Training Command would train all airmen—from recruits to flying officers and technicians, mechanics, and maintenance personnel.[89]

Spaatz asserted that the AAF could accomplish its mission only by maintaining an Air Force of adequate size and proper composition, "strategically deployed and in a high and constant state of readiness." The next war would begin in the air. The AAF could discharge its responsibility most effectively only if granted coequal status with the ground and naval forces. General Spaatz also stressed that nonflying officers would have the chance to hold command and staff positions for the first time.[90]

Despite Spaatz' retention of the sixteen air forces, the AAF lacked the resources to man them. Spaatz therefore allocated personnel as best he could prior to deciding what part of the 70 groups the three new combat commands would receive, when the Army Air Forces reached the 70-group objective. Meantime, the AAF would strive to rebuild as swiftly as possible. The missions of the Strategic Air Command and Tactical Air Command enabled them at once to begin

---

all our procurement and train two million airmen. We believe we have obviated this condition in the establishment of the ADC. Tactically, it is charged with the Air Force portion of the defense of the United States." [Address, Lt. Gen. Ira C. Eaker to National War College, Jun 5, 1947.]

forging combat readiness. The Air Defense Command, on the other hand, had not been authorized to conduct air defense activities in any meaningful sense. Consequently, it focused on Reserve and other geographic duties. As the Simpson Board had recommended, General Stratemeyer changed the wartime boundaries of the First and Fourth Air Forces and adjusted the boundaries of the other air forces to coincide with the six ground armies. Air Force commanders would have their subordinate units administer the Air Reserves in the various areas. General Devers and his six Army commanders, and Spaatz, through Stratemeyer and his six ADC air force commanders, were equally responsible for air defense of the United States.[91]

Planning the Headquarters Organization

As mentioned, with the war apparently entering its final phases, General Arnold began to lay the foundation for the transition from war to peace. In January 1945, he promulgated three principles to govern future activities of the Air Staff and the major commands. The first was that operating functions would be decentralized. Amid the wartime expansion, Headquarters AAF had devised operating procedures leaving little room for the unfettered exercise of command by subordinate levels. This system of "rigid control," as Arnold called it, was necessary in the early years of the war. Maximum decentralization was now in order. Too many people in AAF headquarters were spending time and effort on command matters. These tasks should be done by the Continental Air Forces and the major commands. The Air Staff must be divorced from daily operating duties.[92]

Arnold's second principle specified that the Air Staff become more deeply involved in planning and policy development. He felt strongly about this concept. Although not possible earlier in the war, ideally he had thought of the Air Staff as a compact organization, devoting most of its time to planning. Moreover, the Army Air Forces had already started postwar planning. To the Air Staff, Arnold emphasized the importance of this work. It would determine the organization and deployment of the postwar Air Force, and could only be successful if done by an Air Staff free from the pressures of daily operations.[93]

Third, Arnold observed that technology in the future would be more important than ever to the air arm's success. The evolution of radar and guided missiles was a harbinger pointing to entirely new modes of warfare. Hence, no longer need officers be rated to hold key positions in the Air Force. Regulations restricting the responsibilities and careers of nonrated officers must be changed. As directed by General Arnold, these three principles would be carried out by each Air Staff agency. They would be adhered to in manning the Continental Air Forces and in decentralizing operating functions to field commands.[94]

Gen. Hap Arnold, Assistant Secretary of War for Air Robert A. Lovett, and Brig. Gen. Grandison Gardner on an inspection tour at Eglin Field, Florida. In 1945, Mr. Lovett advised General Arnold to create an Office of the Air Comptroller, which would apply sound business practices to the defense mission. General Gardner became the first comptroller general in June 1946.

After the end of the war, on September 15, 1945, Arnold ordered a revamping of the headquarters structure, the first major realignment since March 1943.* This reordering would last until October 1947, following establishment of the United States Air Force.

The March 1943 organization had provided for six assistant chiefs of air staff, including an Assistant Chief for Training and also one for Operations, Commitments, and Requirements. The September 1945 restructuring combined Training and Operations under a single Assistant Chief of Staff. This reorganization—analogous to the War Department General Staff system—included five assistant chiefs of air staff: Personnel (ACAS–1), Intelligence (ACAS–2), Training and Operations (ACAS–3), Supply (ACAS–4), and Plans (ACAS–5). The Air Sur-

---

*Though created on August 23, 1945, this new organization did not become effective until September 15, 1945.

geon and Air Judge Advocate were transferred to ACAS–1. Special Assistants for Air Communications and for Antiaircraft Artillery were eliminated and instead subordinated to ACAS–3.

Also, the Special Staff was abolished. The Air Inspector and the Budget and Fiscal Officer were assigned to the Commanding General, AAF. Special Projects, Legislative Services, Headquarters Commandant, and the Office of the Historian were transferred to Statistical Control and Program Monitoring in the Office of the Secretary of Air Staff.[95]

Research and Development, which had been under Operations, Commitments, and Requirements, was put under ACAS–3. In December 1945, Arnold, concerned about future weapons development, and acting on recommendations made in October by the Spaatz Board, directed formation of the Office of the Deputy Chief of Air Staff, Research and Development. Maj. Gen. Curtis E. LeMay was assigned to head this new office which would handle the AAF's overall research and development program. Earlier, in September 1945, Arnold had made $10 million available over the next three years to Douglas Aircraft Corporation to study future warfare. This marked the beginning of the Research and Development (RAND) Corporation.[96]

More changes were being planned in late 1945. After creation of the new Headquarters structure, Robert A. Lovett, Assistant Secretary of War for Air, suggested that General Arnold form a new office, which ultimately became the Office of the Air Comptroller. A banker prior to entering the War Department in 1940, Lovett during the war had been interested in applying advanced management practices to AAF production. He played an important role in solving many complex production problems and thereby gained Arnold's confidence.

Lovett warned Arnold in October 1945 that the evolving and inevitable reduction of defense funds ("the cycle of sharp contraction"), combined with keener competition between the services, might in time place the AAF at a disadvantage. He reminded Arnold that the AAF had made outstanding progress in adapting business principles to the needs of wartime operations. These principles and procedures had to be refined during the coming peacetime austerity. The AAF demanded the best possible business management. Every dollar would count.[97]

Such sound business practices called for a system to produce a completely organized, coordinated, and budgeted program. The AAF leadership should be prepared to successfully justify its requests for appropriations. Lovett consequently emphasized that the AAF was a large business which demanded corporate support systems. The Commanding General needed systematically developed and coordinated information. Lovett recommended that an Office of Air Comptroller General be organized under a senior officer who would report directly to the Commanding General, Army Air Forces.[98]

The Office of Air Comptroller General would absorb the functions of the Office of Program Monitoring, the Office of Statistical Control, and the Budget and

Fiscal Office. As Lovett envisioned it, the new office would have these responsibilities:

> To organize and to unify the operational plans of other staff sections into a single coordinated program; to check the phasing and proper balance of all components of that program; and to analyze actual AAF performance against the scheduled standards;
>
> To operate a reporting system and to analyze the status and operational data of personnel, supplies, facilities and activities, making continuing studies of the relationships among these various factors;
>
> To reduce the physical programs to monetary terms; to allocate the funds among various activities; to supervise all budget functions. including representation of the AAF on all matters pertaining to appropriations and expenditures;
>
> To act as liaison with industry, educational institutions, and research foundations on new developments in business methods applicable to Air Force operations; and to aid in organizing the curriculum for institutions participating in post war AAF officer training in these specialties.

In Lovett's view, this office would ensure a more orderly evolution of postwar programs, a more persuasive presentation of AAF requirements, and thus greater confidence in these programs on the part of the Commanding General and the Chief of the Air Staff. The Assistant Secretary of War for Air termed the overall objective of the Air Comptroller General's office as "continuous business control."[99] He stressed that this position demanded an officer of the highest caliber. To Arnold he said that the AAF, among the services, had set the pace in advanced business practices. He felt that creation of an Air Comptroller would merely anticipate what the other services would someday do under the twin pressures of economy and efficiency.[100]

Arnold discussed Lovett's proposal with Eaker and Spaatz. They agreed that this agency should be set up as soon as possible. They also agreed that, although activities like the Statistical Control Unit and the Program Monitoring Unit would be affected by the loss of wartime officers, the AAF should send young officers to specialized schools to replace such losses. Eaker in early November apprised Lovett that Maj. Gen. Curtis E. LeMay would be selected to organize and head the Office of Air Comptroller General.[101]

However, by November 29 Arnold had changed his mind about LeMay and, in line with the Spaatz Board report, made LeMay the first Deputy Chief of Air Staff for Research and Development.[102] Not until June 15, 1946, was the Office of the Air Comptroller established,* headed by Brig. Gen. Grandison Gardner

---

*In January 1946, Lovett was replaced as Assistant Secretary of War for Air by Stuart Symington, who actually arrived on the job in February. In February 1946, Spaatz succeeded Arnold as Commanding General, Army Air Forces.

who reported directly to the Commanding General, AAF. He was replaced in November by Brig. Gen. Edwin W. Rawlings.* As initially conceived by Lovett, the Office of the Air Comptroller combined the functions of the Offices of Budget and Fiscal, Statistical Control, and Program Monitoring.

Establishment of the Air Board

Between the end of the war and organization of Headquarters USAF in October 1947 (following creation of the Department of the Air Force and the United States Air Force), General Spaatz made one of his most significant decisions. He announced his intent to form an Air Board with Maj. Gen. Hugh J. Knerr as its first Secretary-General.[103] This board was to play an important part in shaping the organizational structure adopted by the Air Force in October 1947. Also, in 1946–47, it would help frame the AAF's position on unification as eventually reflected in evolution of the National Security Act of 1947.[104]

Spaatz intended to create this Air Board in order to have "somebody off in a cloistered cell doing a little thinking and not doing the routine of the Air Staff."[105] Spaatz conferred with General Eisenhower who thought an Air Board was a good idea, so on March 5, 1946, the board was formally established (the old AAF Board was inactivated on July 1, 1946). Eisenhower had told Spaatz that the Army might create a similar group (with representatives from the Ground Forces, Air Forces, and Service Forces) to concentrate on formulating overall Army policy.[106] Based on his own experience at the pinnacle of command, the Army Chief had long felt that the Army badly needed a group that did nothing but think and frame potential policy. Eisenhower thought the Army had been weak in one aspect of organization: "We have not kept a body free for thinking. Everybody is an operator with us. . . .and we have had no body which is compelled by the very nature of its organization and function to do nothing but think."[107]

Spaatz' long experience convinced him that policy should be deliberately considered and made at the top of the organization. Thus, the Air Board should have some of the best minds, complemented with operational commanders and should have direct access to the AAF Commander. Spaatz was determined to avoid de-

---

*Born in 1892, Gardner earned a Master of Science degree from the Massachusetts Institute of Technology in 1928. He was one of the AAF's observers in England in 1940. He progressed through several positions as an armament expert and then headed the AAF Proving Ground Command, 1942–45. Before becoming the Air Comptroller, he had been deputy to the chairman of the U.S. Strategic Bombing Survey. Rawlings was born in 1904 and won a Master of Business Administration degree from Harvard in 1939. He was regarded as one of the AAF's foremost production and procurement experts.

veloping policy at lower levels where it later tended to rise to the top for approval—a mass of evidence to be weighed by the AAF Commander. He had carefully considered these views and had talked to Eisenhower about them. He knew that General Knerr, to be Secretary-General of the Air Board, supported and encouraged them.*[108]

Since February 1946, Knerr had been Spaatz' special assistant for reorganization. Knerr's own view proceeded from his judgment, similar to Lovett's, that the AAF was in essence a big business. Policy could not be formed by one person, no matter how able.[109] Corporations, for example, had their boards of directors. Knerr said that some officers mistakenly regarded the staff as kind of a board of directors. The staff, he noted:

> actually occupies the status of vice-presidents, charged with specialties. The staff, if given command responsibility as well as the authority inherent in their positions should operate the military business within the bounds of announced policies created by the Air Board, which then functions as a Board of Directors.[110]

The Air Board reported to the Commanding General, AAF, who in turn answered to the Assistant Secretary of War for Air. The Commanding General, of course, could not delegate to the Air Board his responsibility to the assistant secretary. He would accept or reject policies proposed by the board, which of necessity needed his full confidence.[111] The board would interpret policy, secure its approval, and disseminate it to the staff without the fear of having it diluted or changed by other echelons or agencies. Policy should be broad and avoid detail.[112] As an integral part of his office, the Air Board would spare the Commanding General time and effort. The board could not be a staff agency and survive.[113]

General Knerr saw the Air Board providing continuity, competence, and broad vision. "Modern war," he said "is an industrial cataclysm. It had passed beyond the capacity of the military-trained mind to manage, just as certainly as it had passed beyond the capacity of the industrially trained mind to technically control."[114] Knerr and Spaatz conceived the board as affording perspective and

---

*Knerr, born in 1887, graduated from the U.S. Naval Academy in 1908. He commanded the 2d Bomb Group at Langley Field (1927–30). He was Chief of Staff, GHQ Air Force, under Frank Andrews from 1935–38. A strong outspoken advocate of autonomy for the air arm, he was ostracized by the War Department to the post of Air Officer, VIII Corps Area, Fort Sam Houston, Tex. Knerr was thus given the same job, and even the same office, that Billy Mitchell had received when exiled. Retired in March 1939, Knerr was recalled to active duty in October 1942, appointed Deputy Commander, Air Service Command, and subsequently, Deputy Commander, Eighth Air Force Service Command.

General of the Army Dwight D. Eisenhower *(left)* **with the top AAF leaders, Gen. Carl A. Spaatz** *(right)* **and Lt. Gen. Ira C. Eaker, June 1947.**

eschewing dogma—an idea rooted in the board's composition. From the beginning, General Spaatz insisted that the board include commanders of the major commands. As active commanders, they would understand command problems and could anticipate the potential consequences of various policies. Others on the Air Board were the Secretary-General (Knerr),* retired and Reserve officers, and civilians as appropriate.[115]

Architects of the Air Board hoped to circumvent the eventual time-consuming resolution by higher authority of conflicting policies established at lower levels. Frequently, a higher commander found that policies were not in line with his own or even with those of commanders above him.[116] General Spaatz also created this board to deal with the unique and thorny problems of the immediate postwar years. Foremost among these were the evolving struggle over unification; establishing the Air Force as a separate service; and identifying and forming the proper organization for what was to become the United States Air Force.

Spaatz's memorandum of April 1946 described the board's purpose:

> I take it we are of the common belief that war ought to be avoided if possible, but we must plan in such a way that if war comes, we shall meet the en-

---

*With a rank corresponding to that of the head of the Navy General Board.

emy with maximum effectiveness, with the least possible injury and violence to our people and in a manner which will avoid waste. To this end, I have created the Air Board. . .to assist me in establishment of top air policy.[117]

At its first meeting he directed the board to give top priority to post-unification organization of the Air Force, air defense policy, and research into the history and lessons of the war. The AAF Commander urged the board to examine major defects in the existing AAF structure and make recommendations to improve it.[118]

War Department Circular 138

The War Department formally reflected the Spaatz reorganization, as part of the Department structure, in Circular 138, May 14, 1946. This circular reorganized the department, effective June 11, 1946, in accordance with the Simpson Board proposals. In general, it enlarged the size and responsibility of the General Staff. The Army Air Forces was made coordinate with Army Ground Forces under the Army Chief of Staff and the War Department General Staff. Headquarters Army Service Forces and the service commands were abolished. The Chief of

Maj. Gen. Hugh J. Knerr served as the Secretary– General of the Air Board.

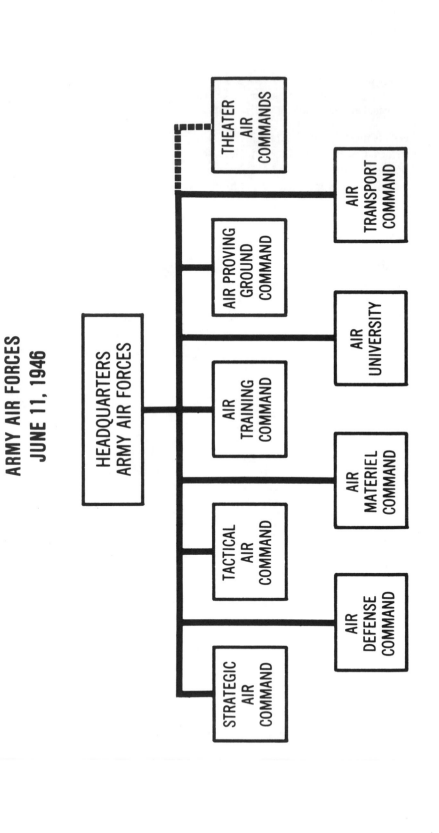

ARMY AIR FORCES
JUNE 11, 1946

HEADQUARTERS
ARMY AIR FORCES

THEATER
AIR
COMMANDS

AIR PROVING
GROUND
COMMAND

AIR
TRANSPORT
COMMAND

AIR
TRAINING
COMMAND

AIR
UNIVERSITY

TACTICAL
AIR
COMMAND

AIR
MATERIEL
COMMAND

STRATEGIC
AIR
COMMAND

AIR
DEFENSE
COMMAND

Staff would serve directly under the Secretary of War. Directly under the Chief of Staff were the General Staff with its directorates (Personnel and Administration; Intelligence; Organization and Training; Plans and Operations; Service, Supply, and Procurement and Research and Development), the Special Staff (support divisions, e.g., Legislative Liaison, Information and Education, Historical, Budget, etc.), and the Technical and Administrative Staffs and Services (Quartermaster, Engineers, Medical, etc.).[119]

Basically, this restructuring under Circular 138 followed the ideas of General Eisenhower. These concepts reflected Eisenhower's convictions as they had been refined in the war. The major tenets were economy and efficiency. The War Department staff should implement the Chief of Staff's directives quickly and effectively. According to Circular 138, the War Department General Staff would deal primarily with policy and planning. The staff must be kept simple with as few people as possible answering directly to the Chief of Staff or his Deputy.[120]

Decentralization would be rigorously applied: "No functions should be performed at the staff level of the War Department which can be decentralized to the major commands, the Army areas, or the administrative and technical service without loss of adequate control by the General and Special Staffs."[121] Circular 138 stressed that the General Staff should delegate sufficient authority to commanders and the heads of the administrative and technical services. While accenting decentralization, the focus would also be on minimizing duplication and overlapping between commands and services. This would become increasingly important as the Army Air Forces was progressively given more autonomy within the War Department structure.[122]

Based on the Simpson Board report and the Eisenhower-Spaatz agreement, Circular 138 stated that the AAF "must be provided with the maximum degree of autonomy permitted by law without permitting the creation of unwarranted duplication in service, supply and administration."[123] The circular recognized the AAF reorganization of March 21, 1946, forming the three major combat air commands. It noted that the Commanding General, AAF, would establish Headquarters Strategic Air Command at Andrews Field, Md.; Headquarters Tactical Air Command at Langley Field, Va.; Headquarters Air Defense Command at Mitchel Field, N.Y.; and other commands as necessary.[124]

The circular said that among the chief responsibilities of the Commanding General, AAF, was to direct operations and training of the continental air commands. In addition, he would determine organization, composition, equipment, and training of the AAF's combat and service units. He would present the AAF's budget estimates to the War Department and would initiate research and development requirements. He would conduct the AAF's part of the UMT program (under War Department directives) and supervise and inspect training of the air components of the ROTC, National Guard, and the Organized Reserve.[125]

THE STRUGGLE FOR AIR FORCE INDEPENDENCE

By late 1946, with President Truman determined to pry unification legislation from the forthcoming Congress, Eisenhower and Spaatz believed that reorganization should largely adhere to Circular 138 until unification. In mid-November 1946, the War Department's General and Special Staff Divisions recommended significant reorganization. However, Eisenhower rejected this report. He favored the proposals in Circular 138, with some revisions to eliminate duplication. He opposed substantive amendments while unification legislation was pending in Congress.[126] The Army Chief of Staff felt that Circular 138 was flexible enough to accommodate any possible unification bill. If unification legislation failed, he made clear that he would then support a reorganization of the War Department. Since returning from Europe after the war, Eisenhower had emphasized to the War Department General Staff that the Army air arm had proved itself in the war and deserved to be a separate service, equal to the Army and Navy. Should the appropriate legislation not be passed by Congress, Eisenhower than favored making the air arm "largely" equal to the land and sea forces, by going "just as far as we can within the legal limits imposed on us."[127] Always concerned about duplication, after unification he wanted the War Department's technical services to continue to procure and distribute supply items common to the air and ground forces.[128] Thus, with minor revisions, Circular 138 remained in effect until passage of the National Security Act and formation of the National Military Establishment.

As mentioned, the air planners were disappointed with the result of the Simpson Board report which reorganized the AAF on the same level with Army Ground Forces. Nevertheless, General Spaatz had not vociferously protested to Eisenhower. The major goal was an independent Air Force. Although the AAF had been placed on a line coordinate with the Ground Forces (there would not be two Chiefs of Staff, one for air and one for ground), Spaatz would be a member of the Joint Chiefs of Staff, as Arnold had during the war. Also, there would be an Assistant Secretary of War for Air, a position assumed by Stuart Symington in February 1946. Moreover, the Army Chief assured Arnold of his strong support for a separate Air Force. Spaatz knew very well that, despite Navy opposition, General Eisenhower's backing would virtually assure an independent Air Force.

In the unlikely event that the AAF failed to become a separate service, the War Department General Staff said it would advocate that the Air Staff be put on the same level with the General Staff; that a separate AAF promotion list be created; and that the AAF be granted technical and professional independence by giving it appropriate personnel and functions of the technical and administrative corps and branches of the Army.

The Simpson Board had issued its report and Circular 138 had implemented its recommendations. The AAF, as part of the War Department, had in 1946 settled on and executed its own postwar reorganization, and had already begun assigning and training forces under this new structure.

160

5

Moving Toward Autonomy

A co-equal or autonomous Air Force able to do its own
planning in such wise as to guarantee the security of the
country can be the only primary objective of Air Force
and other enlightened personnel. We do not have such an
Air Force now. . . .Public sentiment, as a force, is such
that we have one more opportunity for success. If we fail
this time it is unlikely that there will ever be another
opportunity so favorable.

> Col. Harold W. Bowman, AAF
> Deputy Director of Information
> September 1946

President Truman's 1945 recommendation to Congress to form a Department of National Defense under a civilian secretary had included establishment of a United States Air Force, coordinate with the Army and Navy.* The Navy would retain its carrier aviation and also the Marines as part of the Navy Department. The President's program received the full support of Army Chief of Staff General Eisenhower. Eisenhower made clear to Congress and to his subordinate commanders that the Army Air Forces' wartime record demanded that the AAF be given parity with the Army and Navy. He argued that such equality was mandatory for the nation's postwar security. Generals Arnold and Spaatz firmly backed the President's position.

The Navy opposed Truman's plan, Secretary of the Navy Forrestal commenting: "As the President knows, I am so opposed to the fundamental concept ex-

---

*See Chapter 3.

pressed in the message that I do not believe there is any very helpful observation that I could make on the draft you referred to me. "[1] Thus, Forrestal had not changed his mind. He continued to believe deeply that unification would hurt the Navy and would damage the best interests of the country. He advocated a gradual approach, deeming effective coordination far preferable to the hasty solution of unification (including formation of a separate Air Force). As would be expected, the leading naval commanders shared Forrestal's opinion.

As January 1946 dragged on, it became even more apparent that irreconcilable differences divided the Army and Navy. There had been no evidence of real progress since Truman had presented his unification plan to Congress. The Navy feared that the Air Force would take over naval aviation and that the Army would grab the Marine Corps. Naval leaders were also apprehensive that the Army and Air Force would frequently work together on major issues at the expense of the Navy's interests. In the final analysis, they thought that decisions on naval requirements would be made by those unfamiliar with the Navy's needs.

Meanwhile, Congress reacted to Truman's unification message. In January 1946 Senator Elbert D. Thomas, chairman of the Senate Military Affairs Committee, created a subcommittee to write a unification bill. Besides himself, he appointed Senators Warren R. Austin and Joseph Lister Hill to the subcommittee. Maj. Gen. Lauris Norstad, Assistant Chief of Air Staff, Plans, and Vice Adm. Arthur W. Radford, newly appointed Deputy Chief of Naval Operations (Air), were named as advisers to assist the subcommittee in writing the legislation. In early April the subcommittee reported a bill (S. 2044) to the Military Affairs Committee combining features of the Eberstadt report and the Collins plan.* In May 1946, the committee recommended to the Senate that S. 2044 be approved.

This proposed Common Defense Act of 1946 called for a Department of Common Defense with three coequal services. There would be a civilian Secretary of Common Defense, an Under Secretary, and three service secretaries. The bill further recommended a Chief of Staff of Common Defense to be military adviser to the President. Norstad was generally pleased with S. 2044 (it satisfied the fundamental principle of a single department of national defense with three coequal services). While he expected the Navy to mount delaying tactics during subsequent congressional hearings, Norstad was confident of ultimate passage of the legislation.[2]

_____

*See Chapter 3.

Truman Increases the Pressure

During subsequent hearings on S. 2044, naval officials opposed the provisions for a Secretary of Common Defense, a Chief of Staff of Common Defense, and an independent Air Force. They reiterated that enactment of such a bill would open the way for the loss of the naval air arm and the Marine Corps. Naval leaders, including Forrestal, repeatedly pointed to the experience of the British Navy which had lost its fleet air arm to the Royal Air Force.*

President Truman became more and more impatient at what seemed to be an evolving impasse. In mid-May he invited Patterson and Forrestal, together with military leaders, to the White House. Truman underscored the urgency of passing unification legislation saying he was not disposed to wait indefinitely while the Army and Navy consistently failed to resolve their differences. He asserted that the time had come to stop this controversy. He told Patterson and Forrestal that he had decided against a single Chief of Staff. He then directed them to break the impasse and to have on his desk by May 31 a satisfactory compromise solution.[3] The Commander in Chief informed Admiral Leahy that he was tired of the Navy's criticism of his stand on unification. He asked Leahy to try at once to silence this carping by naval officers.[4] In view of Truman's desire to resolve the issue, General Spaatz instructed AAF officers to make no remarks "critical of the Navy or its personnel or accomplishments."[5] He also ordered a ban on statements referring to the eventual possibility of an AAF integration of administrative and technical services, guided missiles, or antiaircraft artillery.[6] A sustained effort must be made to reach agreement.

Spaatz and Symington realized that unification negotiations were entering a crucial and most sensitive phase. They thought that the AAF should avoid doing anything to heat the atmosphere. Subsequently, Symington admonished General Kenney, SAC commander, that everything possible should be done to keep opponents of the bill from believing that the Air Force was attempting to prove that strategic bombing was the way to win a war.[7] It was a fact, said Symington, that people in high positions felt that the Air Force often "popped off."[8]

Following Truman's direction, Patterson and Forrestal went to work, helped by Symington and Eberstadt. While the two sides concurred on a number of noncontroversial issues, they failed to agree on air organization and on the amount of authority to be afforded the Secretary of National Defense. It was apparent to Patterson that the Navy would not "face up to the issue." The Navy was reluctant to give up any of its authority to a single administrator. Conversely, Patterson, Spaatz and Symington wanted someone to operate, supervise, and control the Department of National Defense.[9] On May 31, Patterson and Forrestal submitted

---

*See Chapter 1.

Frustrated by the impasse on the unification legislation, President Truman *(left)* asked the Chief of Staff to the President, Adm. William D. Leahy *(below)* to quell the opposition among naval officers.

their report to the President. In relation to S. 2044, they agreed on eight points and disagreed on three crucial areas. Points of agreement were: no single military Chief of Staff; formation of a Joint Chiefs of Staff; a National Security Resources Board; a Council of Common Defense; a Central Intelligence Agency; an agency for Procurement and Supply; an agency for Research; and an agency for Military Education and Training. The areas of disagreement were long-standing, major items of contention: creation of a single Department of National Defense; organization of the Army and Navy air arms; and status of the Marine Corps.[10]

In their letter to the Chief Executive, the two service secretaries detailed their major differences. The War Department wanted a single department headed by a civilian with the power of decision. The Navy wished a system of strengthened coordination that preserved "sound administrative autonomy and essential service morale." The Navy resisted a single department of national defense with three coequal services, asserting that naval aviation had been completely integrated into the Navy. Naval officials advocated that the Army similarly integrate its air and ground components.[11]

Forrestal contended that no one knew the Navy's aviation needs better than the naval leaders themselves. A principal reason why the Navy stoutly contested a single department was what it considered to be the AAF's constant chipping

Courtesy National Archives

Vice Adm. Arthur W. Radford was the Navy's representative to the Senate subcommittee preparing defense unification legislation.

away at naval aviation. Naval leaders felt that this would ultimately impair sea power.[12]

The Army Air Forces, on the other hand, clearly stated that the Navy should control water-based aircraft for training and for essential internal administration and air transport "over routes of sole interest" to the Navy. It was the War Department's view, held by Eisenhower, that the military services should not be self-sufficient. They ought to be mutually supporting.[13] In general, the Navy persisted in the fear of losing its freedom of operation. Naval leaders were also upset over the AAF position that the Army Air Forces could conduct long-range reconnaissance for the Navy as well as for the Army. Moreover, the AAF argued that it could take care of the air mission for antisubmarine warfare.[14] The air leaders were convinced that AAF aircraft possessed the characteristics to accomplish search and antisubmarine operations. Equipped with the most modern radar and electronic devices, these aircraft could deliver the necessary munitions. According to Spaatz:

> The primary function of the Strategic Air Force is to destroy the enemy's munitions making capability, as well as his will to wage war. Any or all of it can be diverted, at the will of the Supreme Commander, to the anti-submarine problem, which must include attacking the submarines at their home bases, as well as where they are manufactured, this just as the Strategic Force was diverted to support the land campaign in France on many occasions in the course of the Second World War.[15]

Covetous of its traditional roles and missions, and bent on holding them, the Navy stayed distrustful of a single department and a single civilian secretary ("the man on horseback," as King and Leahy put it). The Navy held that it required whatever personnel and equipment were necessary to carry out its mission, including long-range reconnaissance, antisubmarine warfare, and support of amphibious operations.[16] The Army, led by Eisenhower, countered that such self-sufficiency fostered tremendous duplication at prohibitive cost. Spaatz claimed that using Navy aircraft for long-range reconnaissance, protection of shipping, and antisubmarine operations would duplicate the AAF's land-based air forces. Divided command responsibility would result.[17]

Between January and May 1946, this roles and missions debate went on in the Joint Chiefs of Staff. Even though the JCS directed the Joint Strategic Survey Committee to prepare a missions statement, the issue could not be resolved. Eisenhower concluded that further paperwork would be fruitless. He believed that the matter would have to be confronted and settled at a higher level, namely by the President.[18] By late May 1946, he firmly agreed with Admiral Nimitz, Chief of Naval Operations, that the roles and missions question should be shelved by the Joint Chiefs without further action.[19] Norstad also thought that roles and missions would not be decided short of intervention by Truman. Showing some pique himself, General Norstad wrote the recently retired Arnold that whereas the Navy usually did not hesitate to criticize the Army, even during the war, naval officials always seemed to be offended at the criticism of their own service.[20]

At the same time, Truman welcomed as a significant achievement the agreement of Patterson and Forrestal on eight points, though they were plainly not crucial ones. [21] The three areas of disagreement had proved especially contentious and would be extremely difficult to solve. After receiving the May 31 letter, Truman met with Patterson, Forrestal, and other Army and Navy officials. On June 15, 1946, he told Patterson and Forrestal that he was sure the remaining points of contention could be worked out. He reiterated that a Department of National Defense should be created as set forth in S. 2044, headed by a civilian who would be a cabinet member as well as a member of the Council of Common Defense. Each of the military services would be controlled by a civilian secretary (not a cabinet member) who would be in charge of administering his own department. The services would be "coordinated," Truman emphasized, and they would be coequal. Each would retain its autonomy subject to the overall direction of the Secretary of National Defense. As to the appointment of four Assistant Secretaries (research, intelligence, procurement, and training), as specified in S. 2044, this would not be necessary. [22]

He thought the Air Force should have responsibility for development, procurement, maintenance, and operation of military air. These, however, would be the Navy's responsibility: ship, carrier, and water-based aircraft essential for naval operations, including Marine Corps aircraft; land-type aircraft needed for internal and transport purposes over routes of sole interest to naval forces and where the requirements could not be met by normal air transport facilities; and land-type aircraft required for training. The President additionally decided that land-based planes for naval reconnaissance, antisubmarine operations, and the protection of shipping should be under Air Force control. The Marines would be kept as part of the Navy Department.[23]

In Truman's mind, the main lines of the unification question had now been settled. Legislation could be drafted. The framework for an integrated national security program could be erected. There was no intention, he observed, to erode the integrity of the services: "They should perform their separate functions under the unifying direction, authority and control of the Secretary of National Defense. The internal administration of the three services should be preserved in order that the high morale and esprit de corps of each service can be retained."[24]

Norstad and Sherman Draft a Plan

Yet the Navy still objected. Even though S. 2044 was amended to correspond with Truman's views, naval officials testifying before Congress opposed this revised version. Ever since the Commander in Chief had announced his unification plan in December 1945, naval officials considered him, in Admiral Radford's

(Above) Maj. Gen. Carl Spaatz and Air Chief Marshal Sir Arthur Tedder after having attended the Roosevelt-Churchill conference at Casablanca. After the war, Tedder lent Spaatz his support in the struggle for an independent air force.

(Left) Viscount Trenchard with Maj. Gen. William E. Kepner, Commanding General of the VIII Fighter Command in England. Known as the father of the RAF, Trenchard helped AAF leaders develop a strong case for an autonomous air arm.

words, to be "a hard-line Army man" who "had put us in a very difficult position."[25] Basically, Admiral Leahy and other naval officers believed that Truman was now trying to compromise and primarily wanted the cabinet-level Secretary of National Defense. On the other hand, naval authorities readily admitted that, as Leahy observed, "the War and Navy Departments remained in essential disagreement because each is suspicious of the other's motives."*[26]

In the meantime, the AAF solicited opinions on appropriate strategy and tactics to be used in seeking eventual passage of satisfactory unification legislation. Leaders of the Royal Air Force proved helpful. In late 1946 and early 1947, responding to the request of Symington and Spaatz, Lord Trenchard, Lord Tedder, Lord Portal, and Sir John Slessor sent material regarding the RAF's historical fight for independence. They also offered suggestions to aid the AAF in its struggle. Trenchard underlined the importance of making the case in easily understandable language. He cautioned Spaatz that the AAF should know exceptionally well the arguments of the opposition.[27] Secretary of War for Air Symington had been concerned about the statements of unification opponents that the Coastal Command's success during the war was due to its controlling its own operations. However, Tedder and Slessor pointed out that the RAF actually controlled the Coastal Command's plans and operations.[28]

An analysis by Norstad's staff showed that the crux of Tedder's position was that "only by employing a unified Air Force can the Air Force attain the flexibility so vital to the successful employment of air power."[29] Air Marshal Tedder listed the chief elements of this flexibility as simplicity of command, close cooperation among lower commanders, and economy of force. The War Department found that Tedder's observations and conclusions accorded with the concepts it had advocated in the drive for unification and which were embodied in S. 2044.[30]

Norstad's staff warned that proponents of S. 2044 should guard against two possible "violations" of Tedder's principles—allowing the Navy to keep a large land-based force for antisubmarine warfare and reconnaissance, and acceding to a large tactical air force for support of the Marines.[31]

The British were likewise engaged in creating a Ministry of Defence. The Minister of Defence would report to the Cabinet and to the Parliament. He would

---

*Adm. Marc A. Mitscher, a World War II carrier and task force commander (he commanded the carrier *Hornet* for Doolittle's Tokyo raid in April 1942), told Forrestal that naval air had been attempting to protect itself from within and without for twenty-five years. The Army's air element had been trying to take over the Navy's air arm since Billy Mitchell's time. The AAF's ultimate objective, Mitscher said, was complete control of all military air forces. [Diary, Vol VI, Oct 46–Mar 47, entry, Dec 5, 1946, Forrestal Papers, in OSD Hist Ofc.]

monitor preparation of a unified defense policy and distribution of resources between the services. The Chiefs of Staff Committee would frame strategic policy. Some U.S. naval officers had stated that the British reorganization would be along the lines of the Eberstadt plan. But Spaatz and Symington saw the potential new British system as a move towards unified control, modeled more on the defense reorganization pending before the U.S. Congress.[32]

In this connection, Secretary Patterson said he could accept legislation that confined the Secretary of National Defense to carrying out broad policy. Eisenhower agreed with Patterson that such an approach would be more acceptable to the Navy. The Army Chief of Staff noted that the Navy would have nothing to fear from a Secretary of National Defense: "I believe that intelligent men can make almost any organization work as time goes on, if your law isn't too rigid."[33] Patterson and Forrestal therefore met once again with their military leaders. As a result, the JCS in July 1946 appointed Maj. Gen. Lauris Norstad (now Director of Plans and Operations for the War Department General Staff) and Vice Adm. Forrest P. Sherman (Nimitz' Deputy for Operations) to draft a unification plan upon which the Army and Navy could agree. Sherman replaced Admiral Radford, considered a "hard liner" even in the Navy. Forrestal and Nimitz had come to agree that Sherman, who was not opposed to establishment of an independent Air Force, could work more effectively with Norstad. Radford would subsequently admit that Sherman and Norstad broke the impasse between the services.

In the meantime, Norstad and Symington continued to work, checking with Patterson and meeting with Forrestal, Ferdinand Eberstadt, and Radford. Norstad enjoyed a close working relationship with Symington: "I have put my heart and my lungs in your hands," Symington told him.[34] To Norstad, speaking of Symington and Vandenberg, "there was a long time when we had reason to believe perhaps the only people we could really trust were each other."[35]

Norstad's move from AAF Headquarters to Director of Plans and Operations for the War Department gave him more leverage in the unification talks and a clear mandate to represent the views of Patterson and Eisenhower. Moreover, General Eisenhower had specifically requested Norstad, showing his confidence in the airman and also indicating to the Army staff the maturity, as Ike saw it, of the air arm.

Meeting in the summer of 1946, Norstad and Sherman divided their deliberations into three categories:* national security organization, service functions, and

---

*Also participating in these discussions were Symington, Vice Adm. Arthur W. Radford, and Maj. Gen. Otto P. Weyland, Assistant Chief of Air Staff, Plans, who had replaced Norstad in this position. Norstad wrote the retired Arnold in July 1946 that Admiral Radford had a tendency to "work himself up" on the subject of land-based air.

Vice Adm. Forrest P. Sherman was chosen to help draft a defense unification plan, which would address the problems of combined operations, among other issues.

Sherman's partner in developing a unification plan was Maj. Gen. Lauris Norstad.

the matter of unified commands. Organization of unified commands in overseas theaters was of some urgency. This was due to the press of occupation responsibilities and the fact that unified command in the Pacific had never been worked out. Command arrangements in the Pacific was the major hurdle to be surmounted. Representing the War Department, Norstad argued that command arrangements should be made on the basis of functions. The Navy preferred to keep its flexibility by emphasizing geographical areas.[36] During the war, clashing service interests had ruled out unified command in the Pacific. In preparing for the invasion of Japan, the JCS in April 1945 had designated General MacArthur as Commander in Chief, Army Forces, Pacific. At the same time, Admiral Nimitz was named Commander in Chief, Pacific Fleet. After the war, the Army and Navy took differing views of command responsibility in the Pacific. In general, the Army wished to emphasize unity of command of forces while the Navy stressed unity of command according to specific areas. This arrangement, which the Navy insisted upon, allowed it to maintain control of its own forces over an entire geographical area.

The Joint Chiefs approved the command plan drafted by Norstad and Sherman, forwarding it to President Truman on December 12. The plan envisioned a system of unified command in which a single commander would control land, naval, and air operations within a given area.[37] This so-called "Outline Command Plan," actually the first of its kind, was based on the war experience in which unified command had evolved by necessity. Both Army and Navy leaders agreed that unified command was central to successful combined operations. General Norstad described unified command organization as "an idea whose time had come." He recalled that he and Sherman sought a solution which seemed reasonable to themselves and therefore to the services they represented.[38] For the most part, they concurred in a system of unified command for all theaters. They defined it as a theater commander responsible to the Joint Chiefs of Staff, with a joint staff and three service commanders under him. The fact was that prior to the end of the war the Joint Chiefs had decided to have a peacetime unified command structure. Also taking note of occupation requirements, the JCS resolved to establish these unified commands: Far East Command; Pacific Command; Alaskan Command; Northeast Command; Atlantic Fleet; Caribbean Command; and European Command. The Joint Chiefs further observed that a Strategic Air Command had been created, composed of strategic air forces not otherwise assigned.[39]

Norstad said he thought that Truman appreciated the AAF's not getting caught up in a running argument on this matter. [Ltr, Maj. Gen. Lauris Norstad, WD Dir, Plans & Ops, to H. H. Arnold, Jul 21, 1946 in H. H. Arnold Collection, Box 33, Norstad folder, LC.]

Normally, there would be two or more service components assigned to each unified command, each commanded by an officer of that particular component. The joint staff of each unified commander would be drawn from the service components under his jurisdiction. The JCS would exercise strategic direction over the unified commands and assign them missions and tasks. The component commander would deal directly with his own service on matters of administration, supply, training, finance, and construction. For each command operating under missions prescribed by the JCS, either the Army Chief of Staff, Chief of Naval Operations, or the Commanding General, AAF, would be made executive agent for the Joint Chiefs.[40]

With President Truman's approval of this command plan on December 14, 1946, the Norstad-Sherman conferences bore their first fruit.[41] Acceptance of the plan, however, did not mean automatic creation of the above commands. By March 1947 the Far East Command, Pacific Command, Alaskan Command, and the European Command had been set up. By December 1947, all of the commands had been formed except Northeast Command, which would not be established until October 1950.

The Joint Chiefs of Staff Unified Command Plan of December 1946, as approved by the President, stated: "There is established a Strategic Air Command composed of strategic air forces not otherwise assigned. These forces are normally based in the United States. The commander of the Strategic Air Command is responsible to the Joint Chiefs of Staff as are other commanders provided for in this plan."[42] Admiral Nimitz had at first assumed that strategic air forces based overseas would be under the unified commands. He had in mind what he deemed to have been the organizationally confusing experience of the Twentieth Air Force, controlled by General Arnold in Washington rather than by Nimitz on Guam. This kind of organization was anathema to Nimitz' philosophy of unified command. Even so, General Spaatz took the position that SAC should be under the control of a single commander, worldwide. Spaatz suggested a statement that SAC would operate independently or in cooperation with other components as ordered by the Commanding General, AAF, acting as executive agent for the Joint Chiefs. After 1946 the Commanding General, AAF and later the Air Force Chief of Staff acted as executive agent for the JCS. Nevertheless, not until January 4, 1949, did the Joint Chiefs officially designate the Air Force Chief of Staff as executive agent for the Strategic Air Command.[43] And not until April 13, 1949, did the SAC commander receive a directive from the JCS. It noted that the Commanding General, SAC, would "exercise command over all forces allocated to him by the Joint Chiefs of Staff or other authority."[44] Missions would include strategic or other air operations as instructed by the Joint Chiefs, with the support of other commanders under the JCS.[45] Actually the December 1946 plan made the Strategic Air Command a specified command, i.e., reporting directly to the Joint Chiefs of Staff.*

Agreement between Patterson and Forrestal

Following approval of the Unified Command plan, Norstad and Sherman worked with the Senate Military Affairs Committee to craft legislation for a new national security organization. Their strategy called for them always to appear together before the committee. "We agreed," Norstad recalled, "that if one of us was called. . . .one would notify the other and would also suggest to the committee that they call the other member . . . . Sherman and I were invited every time . . . .It was clear that there were differences between us, certainly in degree, but they never really split us on the the principles."[46] Norstad emphasized: "It was characteristic of our relationship, due more to him than to me perhaps, that we never wasted time rearguing established differences between the services. We outlined the issues."[47] Working with the committee, they were able to agree on service functions and on a draft of military organization.

Secretary of War Patterson and Secretary of the Navy Forrestal sent a joint letter to Truman on January 16, 1947. It said they had resolved the problems of draft legislation and of a proposed executive order spelling out service functions. The letter added that differences still existed on specifics of the proposed unification bill. A compromise was therefore required to achieve a structure that could eliminate unnecessary duplication, afford a nucleus for integrated action, and secure the support of the three services. It was not a perfect draft. As with all compromises, it failed to satisfy completely any of the services or their advocates. Nonetheless, it was probably the best bill attainable at the time.

Patterson and Forrestal agreed to support legislation to include a general framework for a complete national security organization.[48] There would be a Council of National Defense, a National Security Resources Board, and a Central Intelligence Agency. Also envisioned were an Office of the Secretary of National

---

*In a memorandum of November 10, 1948, to the Joint Chiefs, General Vandenberg observed: "Paragraph 4 of J.C.S. 1259/27 (December 11, 1946) establishes the Strategic Air Command as a Specified Command under the Joint Chiefs of Staff." However, formal designation of SAC as a specified command did not appear in the unified command plan until March 9, 1955. The term "specified command" was defined in Joint Action Armed Forces, September 19, 1951: "A JCS Specified Command is a uni-Service command which has a broad continuing mission which is specified as a command operating under JCS direction." [Joint Action Armed Forces, JCS, Sep 51; paper on SAC as a specified command, Feb 79, sent to Wolk by Sheldon A. Goldberg, SAC archivist.]

Defense, and Secretaries of the Army, Navy (including the Marine Corps and naval aviation), and Air Force, each with a military chief, under Departments of the Army, Navy, and Air Force. Each military service would be headed by a Secretary and, under overall direction of the Secretary of National Defense, would be administered as a separate entity. After informing the Secretary of National Defense, a service secretary could at any time present to the President a report or recommendation relating to his department. In addition, a War Council would be created consisting of the Secretary of National Defense as Chairman (with power of decision), the service secretaries, and the military heads of the three services. The council would handle matters of broad policy pertaining to the armed forces.

Provision was made for a Joint Chiefs of Staff, comprising the military heads of the services. A Chief of Staff to the President would be appointed, if this should prove desirable. Subject to the authority and direction of the Secretary of National Defense, the JCS would give strategic direction to the armed forces and would formulate strategic plans, assign logistic responsibilities to the services, integrate military requirements, and as directed advise on integration of the military budget. Moreover, a full-time Joint Staff would be formed, consisting initially of not over a hundred officers to be furnished in equitable numbers by the services. Operating under a Director, the Joint Staff would carry out policies and directives of the Joint Chiefs of Staff. As head of the armed forces establishment, the Secretary of National Defense would be vested with the authority, under the President, to establish common policies and common programs for integrated operation of the three departments.

Patterson and Forrestal acknowledged that the proper way to chart roles and missions (functions) was by presidential executive order, to be issued concurrently with Truman's approval of unification legislation. Their letter to the President enclosed a draft executive order specifying roles and missions (eventually to become Executive Order 9877, signed by the Chief Executive on July 26, 1947). Truman replied that he was very pleased with the resolution of issues by Patterson and Forrestal. Noting that each of the services had compromised, he was convinced that the agreement would work.[49]

Subsequent to the Patterson-Forrestal agreement, General Eisenhower requested and the War Department approved the convening of a board of officers in January 1947. The board was to identify and then to recommend solutions to major unification problems facing the Army in light of the joint agreement and the evolving unification bill in Congress.[50] Members of the board were Maj. Gen. William E. Hall, Chief of Staff, War Department Advisory Group, and president of the board; Maj. Gen. Hugh J. Knerr, AAF; Maj. Gen. Charles L. Bolte, AGF; and Brig. Gen. Stanley L. Scott of the War Department's Directorate of Service, Supply, and Procurement.

The board believed that World War II had revealed major weaknesses in military organization. Also, serious deficiencies were evident in the relationships between the military and other agencies concerned with national security. These were chiefly defects of communication and coordination. Further, there were gaps between strategic planning and logistic implementation, between JCS planning and the military and civilian agencies responsible for industrial mobilization. Additional gaps existed

> between and within the military services, principally in the field of procurement and logistics. [There were] gaps in information and intelligence, between the executive and legislative branches of the Government, between the several departments and between government and the people. These. . . defects of coordination were the result of inadequate direction and control below the level of the President.[51]

In the board's view, the evolving unification bill reflected an organization capable of coping with the problems facing the military establishment. Naturally influenced by the Patterson-Forrestal agreement, the report concluded that an organization featuring unified control over a coordinate structure with three departments, each headed by a civilian secretary, promised to foster efficiency and

Army Maj. Gen. William E. Hall chaired a War Department board whose findings supported the Patterson-Forrestal compromise, in the light of organizational problems encountered during World War II.

economy within the services.[52] Moreover, this potential legislation had a chance at least to ameliorate the roles and missions struggle.

The principal problem was preparedness. The board felt that the next war would probably start with little or no warning, almost immediately achieving a high level of destruction. Combined with the longer time needed to prepare the defense establishment for a major war, this meant that a country not completely ready would be at a critical disadvantage. The board's report called for preparedness, not only to react after being attacked, but more important to deter attack. The deterrent value of preparedness was underscored.[53]

Passage of the unification bill would be but a first, yet necessary step, in revamping the defense structure. As to the Patterson-Forrestal compromise agreement, the board found its terms the best attainable. The War and Navy Departments saw this legislation serving the country's best interests.

Both departments presumed that the agreement and the proposed unification bill would open a way to rid duplication and other inefficiencies from planning, logistics, and operations. Mirroring Eisenhower's thinking, the War Department contended that the unification bill should contain broad powers to allow the Secretary of National Defense to enhance economy and efficiency:

> In any new organization the administrator (Secretary of National Defense and the Secretaries of the Army, Navy and Air Force) must be given a free hand in the determination of existing faults and their corrections. It is impracticable and unsound administratively to attempt to fix by statute the details as to how an administrator is to accomplish this task.[54]

The War Department avoided advocating instant, drastic action which would have upset present procedures and thrown the military into confusion. It judged the details of reorganization so complex that the process would develop gradually with functions and personnel falling in place. Thus, the bill would prescribe two years from date of passage as the time during which personnel, property, records, installations, agencies, activities, and projects would be transferred between the Army and the Air Force.

A major part of the rationale for unification was that, over a period of years, tremendous savings would accrue by doing away with duplication in personnel, procurement, intelligence, training facilities, storage, communications, and other common services. These economies would not be forthcoming, however, until functions had been assigned through specific agreement or by direction of the Secretary of National Defense.

THE STRUGGLE FOR AIR FORCE INDEPENDENCE

Struggle over Roles and Missions

On February 27, 1947, while the Hall Board was in session, President Truman sent to Congress a draft of the National Security Act of 1947. Truman noted that the draft had been approved by Patterson, Forrestal, and the Joint Chiefs of Staff. It was introduced into the Senate as S. 758.* This legislation would create a National Defense Establishment comprising the Department of the Army, Department of the Navy, and the Department of the Air Force. A Secretary of National Defense would preside over the National Defense Establishment. With the birth of the Department of the Air Force, the Department of the Army would of course lose the functions of the Commanding General, Army Air Forces. The draft let the Navy keep its aviation units and the Marine Corps. As recommended in the Patterson-Forrestal draft executive order, the Navy's aviation forces would be responsible for naval reconnaissance, antisubmarine warfare, and protection of shipping. As previously noted, Forrestal was prepared to accept legislation only if it stipulated that the military departments would retain their individual autonomy insofar as administration was concerned, a point agreed to by Truman and Eisenhower.

Still, the AAF basically wanted a strong unification bill. This entailed not only an independent Air Force, but substantial authority vested in the secretary who would head the military establishment. AAF leaders thought they could rely on a strong Secretary of Defense to support, among other interests, the Air Force's strategic mission. To the air leaders, this mission held the key to the Air Force's receiving the largest slice of the defense budget. Spaatz and Symington felt they could count on the President as Commander in Chief to make decisions in the nation's best interests. In March 1947, during unification hearings before the Senate Armed Services Committee, General Spaatz sought to counter the charge that a "Super-Secretary" would arrogate excessive power:

> The Secretary will be appointed by the President with the advice and consent of Congress and further, the President prescribes the roles and missions of the Army, Navy and Air Forces. The Secretary cannot change those roles and missions without going to the President. There is another check on the Secretary when he comes to Congress with his budget. Congress controls the armed forces through the budget.[55]

General Spaatz was asked what might happen if the Air Force Secretary testified to Congress contrary to the so-called "Super-Secretary." Spaatz replied that "if he was right and the Secretary of National Defense was wrong, he would last; if he was wrong and the Secretary of National Defense was right, he would not

---

*The designation in the House of Representatives was H.R. 2319.

last." The decision, he said, would depend on the merits of the case. The Air Force would get what it needed if the requirements were justified.[56]

Spaatz' strong support for unification stemmed from the lessons he learned in the war. The United States did not want another Pearl Harbor. An organization affording unified action was needed. The war taught that a separate Air Force must be created. Spaatz said that all major nations had accepted this conclusion and put their air forces on a parity with their armies and navies. Unification legislation should be supported because it would aid badly needed integrated planning and unified action. It would provide an efficient and economical organization. Spaatz conceded that carrier planes belonged to the Navy, but he opposed duplicating the Air Force's land-based planes, a point stipulated in the draft executive order on roles and missions.[57]

The AAF Commander had long been concerned over the Navy's land-based aircraft, some of which he considered to be strategic bombers. He wanted the Navy to have land-based planes which "formed a part of the Auxiliary Air Force which travels with, fights with, and protects the fleet."[58] Spaatz said the Air Force looked on naval aviation as a secondary arm of the Navy organized to fight with the fleet. The Army Air Forces furnished the Strategic Air Force of the United States. He held that the Navy's patrol bombers had characteristics similar to the AAF's long-range bombers. He did not object to the Navy having land-based planes so long as this did not require duplication of aircraft and their support complexes. Such support included building the necessary operating bases.[59] The Navy nevertheless pointed to its policy since World War I of striving to develop all the aircraft necessary for naval warfare. A paper prepared for the Chief of Naval Operations in June 1946 said that during World War II the Navy had discharged its responsibilities for defeating the German submarines, destroying Japanese shipping, and conducting amphibious operations. This paper asserted that land-based patrol planes remained indispensable for these kinds of activities. The Navy, to fulfill future responsibilities, must provide for its own needs.[60]

Symington expressed his concern directly to Forrestal. From the moment he had taken over as Assistant Secretary of War for Air he had attempted to blunt apparent Navy encroachment on the Air Force's strategic bombing mission. He explained to Forrestal that the AAF thought that the Navy might form its own Strategic Air Force.[61] Symington had made a point to Patterson that the Navy's "die-hard attitude" over unification grew out of its conviction that strategic air was the key to future defense funding. Consequently, he claimed, the Navy would do anything except relinquish the right to build a strategic air force.*

---

*It is difficult to find direct statements about the AAF's alleged desire to gather all air elements, including the Navy's, under its aegis. At a meeting of the Air Board in December 1946, Gen. George C. Kenney, commander of the Strategic Air Command, talked

A strong voice for unification, AAF Commanding General Carl A. Spaatz told the Senate Armed Services Committee that the proposed Secretary of Defense would promote efficiency and integrated planning among the services.

Symington, emphasizing the AAF as part of the War Department, warned Patterson:

> if the War Department loses strategic air, the days of the War Department may well be limited under the conception of the new warfare and therefore, it's of just as much importance to the War Department to maintain a solid position against two strategic air forces—which would probably break the American people—as it is to that component part of the War Department— the Air Forces.[62]

As if to illustrate this point, Adm. John D. Price, commander of naval air forces in the Pacific, was quoted in the press as having said that the Navy's patrol bombers (PV–2s) were being modified to carry atomic bombs on long-range mis-

---

about having all strategic air elements under one group—the Strategic Air Command. Kenney argued that the Navy was building large carriers and long-range reconnaissance aircraft as part of an effort to structure a strategic air force. Kenney made clear his view that after unification the Air Force should make a strong bid to gain control of all strategic air elements. [Fourth Meeting of Air Board, Dec 3–4, 1946, p 184, in RG 340, (SAF), Air Bd Interim Reports and working Papers, MMB, NA.]

sions. Symington protested to Clark M. Clifford, President Truman's special counsel, that there was grave danger that the Navy was building a duplicate strategic air force. If this issue could not be worked out, Symington said, the result would be a battle in the Congress during which both services and the administration would suffer.[63]

The Navy, desirous of keeping land-based reconnaissance and antisubmarine missions, and despite the Forrestal-Patterson agreement, wanted roles and missions written into the unification legislation.* Spaatz and Army Chief of Staff Eisenhower opposed the idea. Spaatz and other AAF leaders took the position that roles and missions should be approved by the executive branch as a function of the Commander in Chief. Should the legislative branch take responsibility, this would withhold the means by which the authority of the Commander in Chief could be executed. The AAF view was that the legislative branch obviously could not command military forces. Therefore, it could not withhold power necessary to the function of the Commander in Chief. General Knerr, Secretary-General of the Air Board, echoed the prevailing AAF opinion that proper war planning demanded that decisionmaking be highly centralized and feature flexibility in the assignment of military tasks and responsibility.[64] Proper flexibility could be achieved by executive order realigning roles and missions as circumstances required. This flexibility could not be had by resort to legislation. National security should take precedence over the desire of a single service.[65]

Eisenhower agreed. The question of roles and missions, he said, could not be solved by promulgating a statement or plan governing every phase of common effort and dictating rules by which each service would operate. Legislation should not be designed to resolve every intensely debated detail. Instead, it should establish sound, fundamental principles. Eisenhower feared that attempts by the Navy and its supporters to write functions into the bill would succeed

---

*A succinct appraisal of the Navy's view on roles and missions is in Lulejian & Associates, *History of the Strategic Arms Competition, 1945–1972: U.S. Aircraft Carriers in the Strategic Role* (Supporting Study, Contract N00014–75–C–0237, Washington, 1975): "The central issue in this conflict, as most naval officers saw it, was whether the unification of the armed services should be allowed to restrict what they perceived to be the traditional, professional military prerogatives of the Navy in preparing for and conducting combat operations. The Navy. . .with the Marine Corps and naval aviation, was capable of conducting warfare operations in 'three dimensions—sea, land, and air.' Such operations . . .did not rival the Army's wartime responsibilities, but rather complemented them. These conclusions had been reached after years of consideration and combat experience, and the Navy was not about to give up the freedom to use its capabilities as it saw fit within the general concept of future war plans. Unification threatened this freedom" (p I–61).

(Left) Secretary of the Navy James Forrestal received Mr. Symington's warning about the dangers of forming a separate strategic force.

(Below) W. Stuart Symington and Air Vice Marshal Sir Arthur Tedder. As Assistant Secretary of War for Air, Mr. Symington opposed the Navy's developing its own strategic bombing capabilities.

solely in arousing resentment.[66] He opposed this Navy ploy to structure a detailed "legislative pattern" for unification.[67]

While the Army Chief of Staff wanted a single civilian head of military forces, he was convinced that progress in coordinating functions should be permitted to evolve gradually. He knew coordination was difficult, each service covetous of its traditional organization and missions. Even so, the services could present their problems to the Secretary of National Defense, whom

> each service will learn to know and understand, one to whom they can go to present their aspects of a problem, their point of view; I believe it will provide one who will bring to you [Congress] his recommendations. . . .then and only then can you get a true complete picture of the National Defense set-up on which, possibly, you could base detailed legislative study.[68]

Eisenhower presumed the services could accept decisions of a single Secretary of National Defense who would be concerned solely with the security of the country.[69] He saw nothing to fear from a Secretary of National Defense. There were sufficient checks by the Congress and the Chief Executive. So in March 1947, Eisenhower and Spaatz signed a Memorandum of Understanding saying they desired to grant substantial power to a Secretary of Defense. In contrast, Forrestal continued to espouse the concept of a Secretary as more of a coordinator than a figure with authority. This was the key issue. Forrestal insisted that the Secretary could do an effective job of coordination—but that he should do no more. Forrestal visualized a Secretary of National Defense acting through the heads of the three departments. His assistants should be few.[70] Forrestal thought in terms of ten to fifteen top civilian assistants and twenty to twenty-five officers. Symington advocated that the single Secretary be empowered to remove any of the service secretaries. Forrestal dissented, saying that in the first place the Secretary should have the decisive voice in selecting the three secretaries.[71]

The Secretary of the Navy clung to his belief that the National Defense Establishment would be too large to be successfully administered by one man. Eisenhower resisted having a coordinator because it ran counter to his experience and firm conviction. In preparing for global war, the United States needed a Secretary with a great deal of authority to get things done. Although the services had cooperated fairly well during the war, there had been "plenty of division below and above the surface and only a fool would suppose that everything was great and that now no changes were necessary for peacetime, in the atomic era."[72] Striking a prophetic note, General Eisenhower averred that, as the services worked with the Secretary over the years, the flow of centralization toward his office would undoubtedly increase.

Hearings before the Senate and House committees went on, with leading military and civilian officials testifying. Then on June 5, 1947, the Senate Committee on Armed Services approved S. 758 with amendments. Both the Senate and the

House approved the bill in July by voice vote. A conference committee worked out the differences and on July 26, 1947, the President approved the unification legislation known as the National Security Act of 1947. Among its provisions, the act established the Office of the Secretary of National Defense and a United States Air Force. On the same day, Truman signed Executive Order 9877 which outlined the functions of the armed forces.

Executive Order 9877

This executive order was identical to the draft order that Patterson and Forrestal had sent to the Chief Executive in January 1947. Truman described it as an assignment of primary functions and responsibilities. The order noted that the Navy would retain naval aviation and the Marine Corps. Among the Navy's functions were naval reconnaissance, antisubmarine warfare, and protection of shipping. The air aspects of these activities would be coordinated with the Air Force including aircraft development and procurement. Air Force personnel, equipment, and facilities would be used "in all cases where economy and effectiveness will thereby be increased."[73] Subject to this proviso, the Navy would not be restricted as to aircraft maintained and operated for these purposes. Regarding air transport, the Navy would have the aircraft necessary for internal administration and for flying routes of sole interest to the Navy where requirements could not be met by normal air transport.[74]

Air Force functions encompassed all military aviation, combat and service, not otherwise assigned. Specific USAF functions were: air operations including joint operations; gaining general air supremacy; establishing local air superiority; responsibility for the strategic air force and strategic air reconnaissance; airlift and support for airborne operations; air support to land and naval forces, including support of occupation forces; and air transport except for that furnished by the Navy.[75] The order further charged the Air Force with supplying the means to coordinate air defense among the services.[76]

The functions of the Army were to organize, train, and equip land forces for operations on land, including joint operations; seizure or defense of land areas, including airborne and joint amphibious operations; and occupation of land areas. In addition the Army was to develop weapons, tactics, and equipment for combat and service forces, working with the Navy and the Air Force in areas of joint concern to include amphibious and airborne operations.[77] The Army would also assist the Navy and Air Force to accomplish their missions, including the provision of common services and supplies.[78]

The Air Force detected conflict in some cases between Executive Order 9877 and the National Security Act. For example, the act said that naval aviation would embrace air transport essential for naval operations. The executive order, however, authorized the Navy to provide the air transport necessary for only internal administration and for travel over routes of sole interest to naval forces.[79] The Navy held that the act was the appropriate authority whenever it and the executive order conflicted. The Navy accordingly argued that air transport essential for naval operations was actually that which the Navy already had.[80]

On the other hand, the Air Force deemed the executive order preeminent where missions were in question. Congressional committees deliberating over the act had stressed that the reason for injecting statements on naval aviation and the Marine Corps into the act was to preserve the integrity of these elements of the Navy. Delineation of roles and missions was properly a function of the executive branch. The Air Force argued that differences over interpretation of the executive order and the act should be resolved "through command channels provided by the Act itself," namely by decision of the Secretary of National Defense or by the President himself.[81]

National Security Act of 1947

In the National Security Act of 1947 (Public Law 253), Congress declared its intent to provide

> a comprehensive program for the future security of the United States; to provide for the establishment of integrated policies and procedures for the departments, agencies and functions of the Government relating to the national security; to provide three military departments for the operation and administration of the Army, the Navy (including naval aviation and the. . . .Marine Corps), and the Air Force, with their assigned combat and service components; to provide for their authoritative coordination and unified direction under civilian control but not to merge them; to provide for the effective strategic direction of the armed forces and for their operation under unified control and for their integration into an efficient team of land, naval and air forces.[82]

The act created a National Military Establishment, to include the Departments of the Army, Navy, and Air Force (to be administered as individual executive departments) and to provide for coordination and direction by the civilian secretaries of these departments. The law stipulated that the Secretary of Defense would be a civilian appointed by the President as his principal assistant for national security.[83]

The powers of the Secretary of Defense were to establish general policies and programs for the military establishment; to exercise general direction and control over the three departments; to abolish duplication in procurement, supply, transportation, storage, health, and research; and to supervise and coordinate the defense budget. These broad powers appeared to deliver on President Truman's desire for firm civilian direction of the armed forces. Nevertheless, the following proviso considerably negated the control and powers of the Secretary of Defense:

> nothing herein contained shall prevent the Secretary of the Army, the Secretary of the Navy or the Secretary of the Air Force from presenting to the President or to the Director of the Budget after first so informing the Secretary of Defense, any report or recommendation relating to the Department which he may deem necessary.[84]

Since the law in effect made the President the arbiter of last resort, the final appeal became not only the right but the duty of the incumbent service secretary. Nor could the President, in turn, refuse to hear such an appeal. By permitting appeal, the act implied the duty of the Chief Executive seriously to entertain it.*

Besides, the law circumscribed the powers themselves. It did this by stating that powers and duties not specifically conferred on the Secretary of Defense should be retained by the service secretaries. Having no residual power of his own, the secretary was severely limited in the authority he had. The secretary's charter to exercise "general direction" placed him at the start in a weak position. The words reflected the Navy's idea of the secretary as a coordinator rather than as an administrator. It revealed the naval leadership's fear of the secretary as a potential man on horseback.

The act specified that the Navy took in the Marine Corps and naval aviation. Naval aviation consisted of combat, service, and training forces, and embraced "land-based naval aviation, air transport essential for naval operations, all air weapons and air techniques involved in the operations and activities of the . . . Navy."[85] Too, the Navy would be "generally" responsible for naval reconnais-

---

*Following passage of the National Security Act of 1947, Clark M. Clifford, presidential adviser, informed Truman that a question had been raised as to whether the President was Commander in Chief of the Air Force in the same way that he was Commander in Chief of the Army and Navy. Clifford instantly asked the Department of Justice for an opinion. On August 27, 1947, Clifford quoted the Justice Department's reply to the President: "It is clear that the President is Commander in Chief of all the armed forces of the United States comprised within the National Military Establishment. . . .The phrase "Army and Navy" is used in the Constitution as a means of describing all the armed forces of the United States. The fact that one branch of the armed forces is called the 'Air Force,' a name not known when the Constitution was adopted, and the fact that the Congress has seen fit to separate the air arm of our armed forces from the land and sea arms cannot detract from the President's authority as Commander in Chief of all the armed forces." [Memo for the President fr Clark M. Clifford, subj: Scope of the President's Authority as Commander in Chief, Aug 27, 1947, in RG 218, Rcrds of the US JCS, Chmn's File 123, "Memos to and from the President," MMB, NA.]

sance, antisubmarine warfare, and protection of shipping. The National Security Act required the Navy to develop aircraft, weapons, and tactics of naval combat and service forces. Matters of joint concern would be coordinated between the services. Like the Army and Navy, the Marine Corps would be allowed "such aviation as may be organic therein."[86]

According to the act, the United States Air Force

> shall include aviation forces both combat and service not otherwise assigned. It shall be organized, trained and equipped primarily for prompt and sustained offensive and defensive air operations. The Air Force shall be responsible for the preparation of the air forces necessary for the effective prosecution of war except as otherwise assigned and, in accordance with integrated joint mobilization plans, for the expansion of the peacetime components of the Air Force to meet the needs of war.[87]

Hence, the National Security Act used broad terms in setting up the United States Air Force, affording the Air Force latitude in organizing its headquarters and field structure. As mentioned, the Air Force—like the Army and Navy—would be constituted as an executive department called the Department of the Air Force and be headed by the Secretary of the Air Force. The Secretary would be a civilian, appointed by the President and confirmed by the Senate. The Department of the Air Force was further authorized an Under Secretary and two Assistant Secretaries, to be civilians appointed by the President with the consent of the Senate. As to USAF personnel and functions, formerly under the Department of the Army or "as are deemed by the Secretary of Defense to be necessary or desirable for the operations of the Department of the Air Force or the United States Air Force, these shall be transferred to and vested in the Secretary of the Air Force and the Department of the Air Force."[88] For two years the Secretary of Defense should direct the movement of personnel, property, and installations from the Army to the Air Force.

The United States Air Force was established under the Department of the Air Force. The act specifically directed that the Army Air Forces, the Air Corps, and the General Headquarters Air Force (Air Force Combat Command) be transferred to the Air Force. A Chief of Staff, USAF, would be appointed by the President for a four-year term. The functions of the Commanding General, GHQ Air Force, of the Chief of the Air Corps, and of the Commanding General, AAF, would be transferred to the Chief of Staff, USAF.[89]

All officers, warrant officers, and enlisted men of the Air Corps or Army Air Forces would be transferred to the United States Air Force. Others serving in the Army components, but under the authority or command of the Commanding General, AAF, would be transferred to the control of the Chief of Staff, USAF.[90]

Under the act, the principal responsibilities of the Joint Chiefs of Staff were to prepare strategic plans and give strategic direction to military forces, to prepare joint logistic plans and to assign to the services logistic tasks in accord with such

National Security Organization

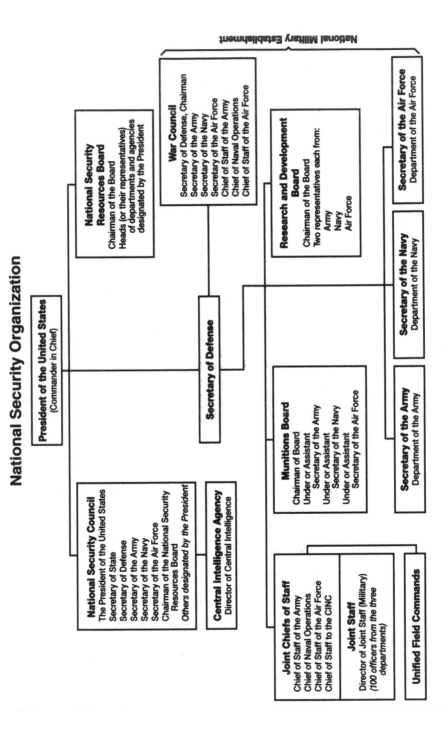

National Military Establishment

President of the United States
(Commander in Chief)

National Security Council
The President of the United States
Secretary of State
Secretary of Defense
Secretary of the Army
Secretary of the Navy
Secretary of the Air Force
Chairman of the National Security
Resources Board
Others designated by the President

Central Intelligence Agency
Director of Central Intelligence

National Security Resources Board
Chairman of the Board
Heads (or their representatives)
of departments and agencies
designated by the President

Secretary of Defense

War Council
Secretary of Defense, Chairman
Secretary of the Army
Secretary of the Navy
Secretary of the Air Force
Chief of Staff of the Army
Chief of Naval Operations
Chief of Staff of the Air Force

Research and Development Board
Chairman of the Board
Two representatives each from:
Army
Navy
Air Force

Munitions Board
Chairman of Board
Under or Assistant
Secretary of the Army
Under or Assistant
Secretary of the Navy
Under or Assistant
Secretary of the Air Force

Secretary of the Army
Department of the Army

Secretary of the Navy
Department of the Navy

Secretary of the Air Force
Department of the Air Force

Joint Chiefs of Staff
Chief of Staff of the Army
Chief of Naval Operations
Chief of Staff of the Air Force
Chief of Staff to the CINC

Joint Staff
Director of Joint Staff (Military)
*(100 officers from the three
departments)*

Unified Field Commands

plans, and when in the interest of national security to set up unified commands in strategic areas. The Joint Chiefs would additionally act as the key military advisers to the President and the Secretary of Defense.[91]

Aside from the military departments and the JCS, a War Council was formed, consisting of the Secretary of Defense (chairman), the service secretaries, and the military heads of the services. The council would advise the Secretary of Defense on broad policy matters.[92]

The act also created a National Security Council (NSC) to advise the President on national security and a Central Intelligence Agency to report to the NSC. Also organized were a Munitions Board, a Research and Development Board, and a National Security Resources Board. The NSRB would advise the President on coordination of military, industrial, and civilian mobilization. Members of the NSC included the President, the Secretary of State, the Secretary of Defense, the Secretaries of the Army, Navy, and Air Force, and the Chairman, National Security Resources Board. The NSC had the duty, under the President, to make sure the United States had a military establishment strong enough to support the country's foreign policy. Thus, the NSC advised the President on the integration of domestic, foreign, and military policies. Under the NSC the CIA coordinated all intelligence activities and evaluated the intelligence collected.

The National Security Act of 1947 gave the Army Air Forces independence, but it was not exactly what any of the services had originally wanted. Lt. Gen. Ira C. Eaker said the act really "legitimized four military air forces."[93] However, the architects of Public Law 253 had to maneuver within the realm of the possible— which meant compromise. In February 1947, Symington (to become Secretary of the Air Force in September) had written James E. Webb, Director of the Bureau of the Budget, that a better bill could have been drawn, but "a bill which was considered better could not have gotten everybody's approval; and therefore would not have given the President the opportunity to show agreement to the Congress and the people. I don't say this is a good book, but I do say it is a good chapter."[94] It was a starting point, a first step toward a truly integrated establishment. To gain passage it had taken a long time, a great deal of effort, and much give-and-take by all concerned. Symington differed with those critics who believed that the Navy had succeeded in structuring the unification bill expressly to suit its own purposes. Nor did he share the feeling of those who felt that Norstad had capitulated to the Navy's desires, regarding the fact that the post of Secretary of Defense was structured as a coordinator. Symington argued that under the circumstances Norstad had done an outstanding job.[95] It had not been easy. Of all the Air Force participants, Symington said, "Norstad should get the most credit for unification. In the days when it looked grim, he stuck to it."[96]

In their deliberations on functions and organization, Norstad and Sherman faced some hard realities. They realized that President Truman had laid out the major tenets of unification organization, namely a single department of national

James Forrestal, the nation's first Secretary of Defense, in his office at the Pentagon, September 1947.

defense and three coequal services including a separate Air Force. The Navy lost on the issue of Air Force independence but won its point on the individual services maintaining their "integrity" and thereby their flexibility of action and administration. Under the National Security Act, the Secretary of Defense would be a coordinator as the Navy wanted, not a strong administrator as desired by the Army and the Air Force.

As War Department representative negotiating with the Navy, General Norstad found himself in the middle of sensitive and emotional issues. He and Sherman could not have completely satisfied both the War Department and the Navy. Norstad's especially good relations with Sherman did not extend to the rest of the naval hierarchy. In general the Navy fought unification legislation up to the final bill and enactment.

Not surprisingly, Norstad came under fire within the War Department for his unification role. It had been necessary for him to sometimes reject what he considered to be selfish interests within the War Department.[97] Norstad recalled that just prior to passage of unification legislation, General Devers, AGF commander, told him that the Army thought he was deliberately compromising its best interests.[98] There was some similar feeling within the Army Air Forces itself.

Failure of this antipathy to disappear after enactment of the legislation impelled General Norstad to ask Spaatz for a transfer out of Washington. Specifically, Norstad suggested that he leave Washington, preferably with a reduction of

President Truman's Defense Department appointments: Secretary of the Air Force W. Stuart Symington *(above, left)*; Secretary of the Army Kenneth C. Royall *(above, right)*; and Secretary of the Navy John L. Sullivan *(below, right)* being sworn in by Chief Justice Fred Vinson.

one grade; or if kept on the Air Staff, that he not be promoted in grade or position.[99] Spaatz and Symington turned down Norstad's recommendations. Even General Arnold, now retired, expressed dissatisfaction to Norstad about the National Security Act; subsequently however, Arnold personally indicated to Norstad that he appreciated the difficult work and negotiations that General Norstad had completed.

While the National Security Act was a major achievement, it was likewise an obvious compromise in which the services yielded on matters of principle to achieve a common goal. Neither the Army, the Army Air Forces, nor the Navy was entirely satisfied with the legislation. The outcome left unsolved basic points of disagreement between the services—roles and missions and the absence of requisite authority in the Office of the Secretary of Defense. Admiral Leahy wrote in July 1947 after the unification bill cleared Congress: "if the history of the British Royal Air Force is valid evidence, the removal of our Air Arm from control by the Army will result in a definite reduction in the efficiency of our national defense establishment."[100] Still, the 1947 act was probably the best legislation that could have been secured at that time. It was clear to Spaatz, Symington, and Eisenhower, among others, that in the future the defense establishment would continue to evolve toward unification.

President Truman's first pick as Secretary of Defense was Robert P. Patterson, the Secretary of War, a man highly respected in the defense community and in the government. Patterson declined, explaining that his financial condition dictated that he leave the government. The President then named Forrestal to the position even though the Secretary of the Navy had fought determinedly against unification and a separate Air Force. In certain important respects, however, Forrestal was a logical selection. He had headed the Navy Department, and as Secretary of Defense he might be expected not only to get along with the naval leaders—men he knew and had worked with—but to enlist them as supporters of unification. Having championed legislation featuring coordination as opposed to administration, Forrestal now had the chance to head a National Defense Establishment in the major role of coordinator. *The New York Times* commented that Forrestal was the logical choice and "the happiest one that could he made." Forrestal's selection

> is the best guarantee that could be given that unification of the services will be carried out intelligently and efficiently. . . . Selection of any other man than the former Secretary of the Navy would have sent unification on its way with a handicap. It has been painfully evident that all through the long hearings and debate in Congress that there are many in the Navy who still distrust the whole idea. With Mr. Forrestal as the Secretary, the Navy opponents of unification will know that there is at the top a man who has an intimate knowledge of their branch of the service and one to whom it will not be necessary to spell out in detail their side of the case when difficulties arise.[101]

As Forrestal and the naval leaders desired, the services had managed not only to preserve their integrity, but to hold in effect a veto power over the Secretary of Defense. On the issue of defense itself, Forrestal had warned of the perils of instant demobilization. He believed deeply in a strong national defense.

After appointing Forrestal, Truman named Symington to be Secretary of the Air Force; John L. Sullivan, Secretary of the Navy; and Kenneth C. Royall, Secretary of the Army.* Having been Assistant Secretary of War for Air since January 1946, Symington brought topflight management credentials to his new post. He had also shown uncommon ability to work effectively with the Congress. Moreover, he nurtured an excellent working relationship with General Spaatz. This combination of Symington and Spaatz held the promise of affording the new independent Air Force unusually fine leadership.

---

*Symington had known Forrestal personally for years. Interestingly, Truman had asked Forrestal about Symington. Forrestal told the President that frequently friends found it hard to work with one another. [Walter Millis, ed. *The Forrestal Diaries* (New York, 1951).]

6

Independence and Organization

No Air Force can be created by legislative action alone. All the National Security Act of 1947 has done is to give us the green light. It must be considered an opportunity and not an accomplishment. . . .We cannot pass the buck—to the War Department or to the Navy, or to the Congress, or to the people. We certainly cannot afford to rest on our laurels.

Secretary-Designate of the Air Force
Stuart Symington
to the First Annual Convention of the
Air Force Association
Columbus, Ohio
September 15, 1947.

The creation of the United States Air Force in September 1947 was both an end and a beginning. It marked the end of the long fight for independence. It signaled the beginning of the effort to bring the Air Force to true parity with the Army and the Navy. This meant that over several years the Air Force would have to take on the functions and personnel that would enable it to operate completely as an independent service.[1] Certainly as of September 1947 the Air Force was a long way from commanding the kind of critical support services needed for true independence. Consequently, the Air Force began immediately to plan for the transfer of various functions and for establishing and expanding certain necessary technical services. Of immediate concern, Secretary of the Air Force Symington and Chief of Staff Spaatz had to organize and staff the Department of the Air Force and the Headquarters United States Air Force. In October 1947 the headquarters was reorganized under a Deputy Chief of Staff system.

195

Organization and transfer of functions and personnel were not the only critical matters facing Symington and Spaatz. They viewed the ongoing struggle with the Navy over roles and missions as a vital part of the drive for equality with the other services. What some air leaders called the "liberal construction" of the National Security Act enabled the Air Force generally to organize as it wished.[2] Also, the act neither delineated functions nor gave the Secretary of Defense statutory power to control the National Military Establishment. As a result, the roles and missions controversy not only continued, but was exacerbated by the administration's austerity program. Besides, the Air Force was especially sensitive to the need to bring its forces to the 70-group goal. It seemed all too clear to the air leadership that as an interim objective it would have to settle for considerably less than 70 groups. Though not underestimating the magnitude of the tasks ahead, the airmen did enjoy the realization that the long-sought goal of independence had been achieved.

"At Long Last"

Establishment of the Department of the Air Force and the United States Air Force on September 18, 1947, elicited a wave of exultation from USAF leaders. These men—Arnold, Spaatz, Eaker, Vandenberg, and all the rest—had fought for an independent service prior to World War II, had led the AAF during the war, and had brought the unification struggle to a successful conclusion. Now, after many years and many battles, their faith, vision, and plain hard work had paid off.

It was this belief in the idea of independence that brought out the best in the airmen. They were struggling toward an objective of commanding importance. In the sense that the air weapon was new and untested before the war, these men were sometimes perceived as "revolutionaries."[3] Basically pragmatic, they were sure the development of better military aircraft would solidify the Air Force's position as the predominant service. They were apolitical in that they thought primarily in terms of advancing technology. The battle they waged over many years was carried on by a relatively small band of men. Symington described them as "a tight-knit group of activists." He added: "We were determined. It was a hard fight and it was a good fight. We survived."[4]

The war had afforded them the opportunity to prove their theories and they made the most of it. They alleged that the effectiveness of air operations during the war proved the case for independence. Air power could best be developed by a separate Air Force, a point made by General Eisenhower himself. And the air leaders were convinced they had earned the support of the public and Congress. They accented the AAF's vital contribution to victory. Moreover, they asserted that air power was now the most significant part of the nation's defense. National security demanded a strong Air Force in being.

Not only airmen harbored these views. On the eve of the Air Force's creation, the final report of the War Department Policies and Programs Review Board underscored that air power had become "the first line of defense."[5] The nation would support only a small peacetime Army. Traditions, the board noted, must give way to facts. Foremost among these traditions was the emphasis on the importance of ocean barriers. In arriving at the size of the peacetime Air Force, "the favorable psychological effect of air power in being and the adverse psychological effect of lack of air power are factors of much greater importance before the initiation of hostilities than are the state of readiness or existence of other types of forces."[6] Similarly, the President's Advisory Commission on Universal Training concluded that the long range of aircraft and the existence of atomic weapons made it imperative that the United States maintain a "counterattacking force." This force should be able to retaliate instantly with the most powerful weapons.[7] When Truman's UMT program bogged down in Congress, part of the reluctance to accept UMT stemmed from the recognition of air power's value.

In the drive for independence, the airmen had received considerable help from many military and civilian leaders. Foremost among these was General Eisenhower, whose thinking on the Air Force had remained constant since the end of the war:

> I am particularly anxious that the existing pleasant and friendly relations between ground and air personnel continue, and that every possible means be adopted to insure that legal recognition of the autonomy of the Air Force will serve only to bring us closer together in friendship and in performance of duty.[8]

Complementing Arnold, Spaatz, and the other leading airmen, Lovett and Symington made sizable contributions. Both brought to the Air Force a sensitive, intelligent appreciation of the business practices of American corporations. They were certain that the Air Force could be operated like a large corporation. During the war Lovett had worked on production problems. He assisted Arnold in his attempt to make the AAF autonomous and he maintained a sound working relationship with Marshall. Late in the war, due in no small part to the efforts of Arnold and Lovett, the Army Air Forces was in large measure operating as an autonomous entity. General Marshall had assented to this arrangement. Lovett's views on independence generally accorded with Arnold's and Spaatz's. Lovett thought that the War and Navy Departments had been unable to orchestrate a maximum war effort in terms of efficiency and effectiveness.[9] He firmly believed that the AAF deserved to be separate and to enjoy equal consideration in the sharing of the defense budget. In his relations with the War Department and other agencies, Lovett, like Arnold, felt that a certain amount of trust should exist between friends and among the established departments.[10] These relationships formed the cement with which to build solid programs.

Most men who had in one way or another participated in the negotiations over the National Security Act believed with Lovett and Symington that it was a clear compromise.* Here, too, these people concluded that the successful outcome of the negotiations had hinged on trust between men in positions of leadership. This was part of the collective frame of mind of the air leaders upon the creation of a separate Air Force. In their own minds it had been a long, grueling struggle. On September 18, Symington and Spaatz wired Arnold: "At long last the U.S. Air Force came into being at noon today."[11] General Vandenberg noted that the airmen were now the "masters of our destiny."[12] The air leaders savored the satisfaction resulting from so many years of hard work and belief in themselves. In a real sense, the arduous striving had been an act of faith.

The majority of AAF leaders, Vandenberg included, realized it would take several years for the Air Force to secure the requisite men and functions to be on equal footing with the Army and the Navy.[13] General Knerr told the Air Board in September 1947: "As with any vigorous organization freed from onerous restraint there is danger of its feeling its oats and lashing out at all obstacles at the very beginning. Such action would be a great mistake, for we simply do not have the muscle on our bones to carry through with such desires."[14]

Spaatz and Symington also sounded a cautionary note before the first meeting of the Aircraft and Weapons Board in August 1947. With the advent of air independence, the major problem for the Air Force had changed. Though it had served the AAF well in the past, publicity was not now to be the main ingredient. Caution was a must. First, the Air Force must make a record of accomplishment for itself. The byword was action, deeds. The airmen had won the opportunity to prove they deserved the independence they had so long fought for.[15] The chief objective now was to build a strong, effective Air Force during a period of austerity. This would not be easy. The Hall Board had shown the way toward a potentially orderly transition from Army Air Forces to United States Air Force. This meant using the two years allotted for the actual transfer of necessary functions. The National Security Act of 1947 did not confer instant parity on the Air Force.

---

*There were also some in the Air Force and the War Department who thought too much had been compromised away to the Navy as the price for the Navy's approval of the National Security Act. Norstad was well aware of this feeling.

Establishing the Air Force

Together with General Spaatz, Secretary Symington epitomized the effective transition between the fight over unification and the actual formation of an independent Air Force. It will be recalled that Secretary of War Patterson had given Symington the job of shaping and driving through Congress the War Department's position on unification. Patterson had instructed all members of the War Department's higher echelons to coordinate unification matters with Assistant Secretary of War for Air Symington.[16] Symington proved especially adept at dealing with congressmen and in communicating AAF and War Department thinking to the public. He maintained a heavy speaking schedule throughout the country and lost no opportunity to voice his views in the halls of Congress.

Favorably impressed with Symington's administrative and business talents, Truman in January 1946 proffered to him three possible positions: Assistant Secretary of the Navy, Assistant Secretary of State, or Assistant Secretary of War for Air. Based on his background and interest in logistics, Symington chose the air post and set about securing passage of unification legislation through Congress. Symington's skilled and sensitive hand at logistics and procurement was sorely needed by the new service. Being under the War Department, the AAF in World War II had no opportunity to draw contracts and follow them through to fruition. It was in this aspect of procurement that Symington knew he could make a contribution. After appointment, he plunged into the unification fray with characteristic energy and determination. Norstad, who worked closely with Symington, wrote Arnold: "Symington has entered into this game, particularly unification, with an inspiring enthusiasm. . . .He is doing a swell job. . . .He is very definitely a leader and has the intelligence and experience to make it count. His peculiar qualities make him an ideal man for the Air Forces at this time."[17]

While not Forrestal's first selection, Symington was the natural choice to be Secretary of the Air Force. Before the war they had been friends, but after the war Forrestal and Symington clashed as they promoted the policies and views of their respective services. In addition to Symington's experience as Assistant Secretary of War for Air, he and Spaatz had developed a close working and personal relationship. As Secretary of the Air Force, Symington immediately began an intensive campaign to secure 70 air groups. The role of advocate fitted him well. A deep believer in air power who knew logistics, procurement, managerial techniques, and congressional relations, he spearheaded the drive to steer Air Force requirements through Congress. "My theory in functioning as a good secretary," he recalled,

> was for them [the military] to make the balls and I'd roll them. . . .I had a Chief of Staff, and it wasn't my duty to get into everything. He built the picture and I presented the picture because that was my job. I concentrated on two things: on the logistics, to be sure the taxpayer got a good return on his

investment and on the presentation to Congress, so we could get what we hoped to get.[18]

Secretary Symington was determined "to get as much of the pie as I could for the Air Force."[19]

Beyond strictly Air Force needs, but nonetheless related to them, Symington saw the postwar years as posing a stiff challenge to the United States. The nation had assumed a position of world leadership—in itself unique in American history—which required of the American people "a responsibility for strength, and for sacrifice; and for the same resolute determination in peace that you displayed in war."[20] The atomic age demanded a new concept of preparedness reflecting an acceptance of this responsibility. However, Symington also knew that ultimately the military would have to scale down its requirements:

> we must face the constant compromise between what military authority considers necessary on the basis of maximum security and what is finally decided as the minimum requirement on the basis of a calculated risk. . . .This must be the case, because the maintenance year after year of armed forces certain to be adequate to handle any emergency would be such a constant drain upon the American economy as to destroy the American way of life just as surely as would conquest from without.[21]

Hon. W. Stuart Symington, Secretary of the Air Force, and Gen. Carl Spaatz, Air Force Chief of Staff, announcing the new organization set-up for the Department of the Air Force, October 1, 1947.

Nevertheless, there remained a reasonable minimum below which national security would be endangered. Air needs had to be stated in terms of the task at hand. To the Air Force this meant 70 air groups in being, capable of retaliatory attack to deter potential aggressors. The United States would have to maintain an atomic deterrent force to prevent general war.[22] This called for an aircraft industry that could produce advanced aircraft at a satisfactory rate, and for an adequate training establishment to turn out sufficient manpower.

As the first Secretary of the Air Force, Symington was given a recess appointment by President Truman and was sworn into office on September 18, 1947, by Chief Justice Fred M. Vinson. Recess appointments were also received by Under Secretary Arthur S. Barrows and by Assistant Secretaries of the Air Force Cornelius V. Whitney and Eugene M. Zuckert. They assumed their positions on September 25, 1947. The Senate confirmed these appointments on December 8, 1947, and Truman approved permanent commissions the next day.[23]

Under Secretary Barrows was a former president of Sears, Roebuck, and Company. His duties would embrace procurement and production, research and development, liaison with the Atomic Energy Commission, and industrial mobilization. Whitney would work with government agencies on civil and diplomatic affairs. Zuckert would concentrate on programming, cost control, and organizational and budget planning.[24] Selection of Barrows, Whitney, and Zuckert showed Symington's penchant for picking experienced and highly qualified executives to serve in the Department of the Air Force. Symington also brought with him personnel from the Office of the Assistant Secretary of War for Air. At the beginning, the Office of the Secretary of the Air Force had 121 personnel, 68 civilian and 53 military.[25]

Other services in the department were supplied by the Office of the Administrative Assistant, under the direct supervision of the Air Force Secretary. The appointment of John J. McLaughlin as Administrative Assistant was made permanent on December 14, 1947.[26] Symington also appointed a Director of Information, a General Counsel, and a Director of Legislation and Liaison. He later set up a Secretary of the Air Force Personnel Council.[27]

General Spaatz became the first Chief of Staff of the United States Air Force. Lt. Gen. Hoyt S. Vandenberg, Deputy Commanding General, AAF, and Chief of the Air Staff, became Vice Chief of Staff, USAF. During the war, he had been chief of staff of the Twelfth Air Force and the North African Strategic Air Forces, and commanding general of the Ninth Air Force. After the war, he had been Assistant Chief of Air Staff for Operations, Commitments, and Requirements, had sat on intelligence committees of the Joint Chiefs of Staff and the Secretary of War, and subsequently headed the Central Intelligence Board. Brig. Gen. William F. McKee was made Assistant Vice Chief of Staff. In 1943–45, he had been Deputy to the Assistant Chief of Air Staff for Operations, Commitments, and Requirements.

DEPARTMENT OF THE AIR FORCE

Secretary of the Air Force

Stuart Symington

Under Secretary of the Air Force

Arthur S. Barrows

Assistant Secretary of the Air Force

Cornelius V. Whitney

Assistant Secretary of the Air Force

Eugene M. Zuckert

Administrative Assistant

John J. McLaughlin

General Counsel

Brackley Shaw

Director of Legislation and Liaison

Brig. Gen. Ralph F. Stearley

Director of Information

Stephen F. Leo

With the Air Force now an independent service, General Spaatz instantly gave high priority to personnel policies. A separate promotion list, one of the AAF's major objectives of long standing, was finally achieved with passage of the Officer Personnel Act of 1947 (Public Law 381). Also called the "Promotion Bill," this law created a promotion system for career officers of all the services. Putting the Air Force and the medical services on separate lists, promotion was by qualification and selection rather than by strict seniority.[28] The Officer Personnel Act permitted the Secretary of the Air Force to promote officers (Regular and Reserve) on active duty, to higher temporary grades. At the time of independence, the Air Force was authorized twenty thousand Regular officers, not counting the Regular officers serving in Arms and Services with the Army Air Forces. This act let the Air Force Secretary fill vacancies in each grade permanently regardless of length of service.[29]

As Arnold before him, General Spaatz was bent on building a strong postwar officer corps. Training highly qualified officers in various specialties would be the key. An integrated system of officer training would be developed, centered at the Air University at Maxwell Field.[30] Nonrated officers would have every chance to climb the career promotional ladder. Air Force leaders for some time had been convinced that nonrated officers needed to be assured that they could make decent careers for themselves in the Air Force. General Arnold emphasized this often during the final phase of the war and also immediately prior to his retirement.[31] In April 1947, Maj. Gen. Fred L. Anderson, Assistant Chief of Air Staff, Personnel, said:

> There is nothing in our present career planning which aims at guaranteeing rated officers exclusive opportunities in the Air Force of tomorrow, yet we know that the rated officer is less anxious as to his future than the non-rated officer. I believe that the confidence of the latter group can only be enhanced with time through the impartial implementation, when appropriate, of our present plans and through the gradual elimination of unwarranted prejudice barriers.[32]

The AAF also wanted to be able to attract United States Military Academy cadets who might be thinking about electing the Air Force upon graduation. Of course, cadets who wished to fly would be attracted to the Air Force for that reason alone. Logically, an autonomous Air Force would offer more opportunities for nonrated people than the Air Corps had in the prewar period. The end of World War II witnessed a shift in the AAF's training emphasis. During the war the major consideration was to bring each combat unit to high operational efficiency. Post-war, and in the United States Air Force, one of the primary objectives would be training individual officers to become important members of the Air Force. Hence, the value of career development to these officers. In the future, technology would dictate a trend toward specialization, especially in the higher echelons of command and staff.[33]

In addition, the Air Force desired to forge strong career incentives for enlisted airmen. Air leaders were aware they would have to compete with industry for able young men. To keep competent airmen the Air Force would have to give them the chance to advance. Professional and technical training courses would be available at various Air Training Command schools. Spaatz was persuaded that airman would have to be educated and trained beyond traditional military concepts. Airmen should be encouraged to make the Air Force a career.[34]

General Spaatz likewise directed plans to organize the AAF's civilian components. As noted, after World War II the War Department's basic plan for the postwar military establishment included the Regular Army, the National Guard, and the Organized Reserve Corps. The Active Reserve was part of the Organized Reserve Corps. The War Department assumed that Congress would enact UMT legislation.

Established after the second World War, the Air National Guard from the start was deemed a significant element of the postwar Air Force. Before the war, twenty-nine National Guard aviation observation squadrons had been activated, manned by about forty-eight hundred personnel. The plan for a postwar Air National Guard essentially reflected General Marshall's conviction that the postwar Army would have to depend upon a system of universal training.*

The original postwar ANG program specified 514 units—tactical, service, engineering, and communications. In April 1946 the 120th Fighter Squadron (Denver, Colo.) became the first ANG unit to be activated. It gained federal recognition on June 30, 1946.[†] By the end of June 1947, the Air Guard's assigned strength totaled 10,341: 257 units had earned federal recognition. Although this seemed to be a reasonably good beginning, the ANG was far from able to play its intended role. This was due partly to a reduced training program, resulting from the Air Guard's budget having been slashed in February 1947.**[35]

The Air Defense Command, established in March 1946, had responsibility for the organization and training of the Air Reserve.[‡] The first objective of the initial plan was to activate 40 of 130 planned Reserve training bases. The aim was to

---

*See Charles Joseph Gross, *Prelude to the Total Force: The Air National Guard, 1943–1969* (Washington, D.C., 1985).

[†]Federal recognition required twenty-five percent of officers and ten percent of airmen present for duty.

**By May 1949 the ANG had organized the 514 units. Tactical organizations included 72 fighter and 12 light bomber squadrons. By February 1950 the Air Guard possessed 2,400 aircraft, 211 of them jet fighters. By the start of the Korean War in June 1950, the Air National Guard had 44,728 personnel including 3,600 pilots. [Gross, pp 36–37.]

[‡]See Chapter 4.

conduct a program which at the start might be described as "a flying club with no objective or training other than pilot proficiency."[36]

This program was revised by Air Defense Command in September 1946 to encompass nonrated officers and enlisted men organized into combat and service units. It called for 147,500 men (17,500 rated officers; 5,000 staff, administrative and technical officers; and 120,000 enlisted men) to be trained at 70 bases. Also others might be affiliated with the Inactive Reserve. However, as mentioned, the February 1947 budget cuts forced a reduction in these plans and thus the elimination of 29 bases. But by June 30,1947, over 400,000 air reservists were enrolled in the Inactive Reserve. Seventy of a planned 306 combat wings, groups. and squadrons had been organized along with 15 of 278 service units. Following the February 1947 reductions, 2,883 pilots and 1,330 aircraft comprised the Air Reserve program.[37]

Organizing the Headquarters

One of Spaatz's first principal decisions as Chief of Staff was to reorder the headquarters under the Deputy Chief of Staff system. So in its main lines the AAF headquarters reorganization of September 1945* lasted until October 1947. Between these dates, Spaatz, the Air Staff, and the Air Board mounted a major study of postwar organization. The five Assistant Chiefs of Air Staff (A–Staff), or so called General Staff system, had generally served the AAF adequately—but no better than that. Anticipating unification, Spaatz in April 1946 ordered General Knerr, Secretary-General of the Air Board, to have the board begin a detailed study of Air Force headquarters organization. It it should then be decided that a different structure would be more effective, reorganization at the time of unification would be directed.[38]

The board's natural point of departure was the AAF experience in World War II.[†] During the war, the absence of clear lines of authority handicapped the command of air forces. The difficulty of eliciting decisions from AAF headquarters impeded the smooth functioning of subordinate commands. Because this traditional staff system was not flexible enough, attempts were made during the war to delegate authority to lower units.[39]

At the AAF headquarters level, a sharp delineation of function and responsibility was required, with sufficient delegation of authority. During April 1946 the Air Board began moving to the conclusion that a Deputy Chief of Staff system

---

*See Chapter 4.

†The AAF expanded from 25,000 men and 1,200 aircraft in 1930 to over 2,400,000 men and 80,000 planes in 1943.

best met these needs. The deputy system achieved this (at Headquarters Air Materiel Command, for example) by adopting vertical control as the basic principle of organization as opposed to the traditional General Staff system that led to lateral dispersion of responsibility. Hence, the deputy arrangement would tend to eliminate the appended position of the special staff.[40]

In AAF headquarters, the staff structure gradually evolved toward a functional division of responsibility. Within their own specialties, deputies and directors emerged from the status of staff advisers and participated directly in the command function. The war, for example, stressed the significance of support services (supply, medical, weather) and in Europe these were elevated to directorates. Supply and maintenance were eventually united on a vertical command basis, cutting through all echelons.[41]

This concern about authority and responsibility was another way of noting that under the staff system AAF leaders were anxious about how much time it took to get a top-level decision. In March 1946, immediately after creation of the Air Board, General Knerr wrote Spaatz. He said that, when the French general staff structure had been adopted by the U.S. War Department, land armies were decisive in warfare. Wars were fought at a slower tempo. Usually time was of secondary significance. With the tremendous increase in the speed and destructive power of modern weapons, air leaders wanted a post-unification organization that would sharply reduce the time required to make decisions. Among time-consuming factors were no clear policy, split responsibility and authority, excessive coordination, and reluctance to accept responsibility.[42]

Knerr indicated that military organizations might be structured in one of three ways: a "one-man show," a general staff system, or a deputy system. He quickly discarded the idea of an organization completely controlled by one man. And he asserted to Spaatz that the deputy system would be more adept at filling a policy vacuum because a deputy holding responsibility and authority would "not remain in jeopardy through lack of a policy to cover his actions. A general staff, on the other hand, having no command responsibility, is too often content to let the matter slide."[43] Addressing the possibility of split responsibility and authority, again Knerr suggested the deputy structure because the staff system required cross-coordination through a central point—the Chief of Staff, which usually became a chokepoint. The deputy system combined responsibility and authority in one person. From top to bottom, each commander had to deal with only two or three people to have something executed promptly. Regarding reluctance to accept responsibility, Knerr observed that the staff structure nurtured people

> who like to "pass the buck". . . it is a source of despair to those who are not
> so constructed but who find themselves in staff positions. The deputy system
> is a barren prospect for "do it tomorrow" people. Caught in such a system
> they stand out as the choke-points causing delay, self-labeled for elimination.[44]

The staff system also suffered from jurisdictional confusion. This would not be a problem under the deputy structure wherein each deputy operated under a charter clearly delineating his jurisdiction.

Deputies would have the authority to decide promptly which matters should be considered by the Chief of Staff. Experience with deputies during World War II in the European theater and at Wright Field revealed that three deputies—Personnel, Materiel, and Operations—might provide the basic organization. Fundamental to this system was the idea that no intermediary be established between the Commanding General and his deputies. The function of directing the flow of business to and from the Commanding General should be done by an administrative assistant, assigned to the commander's office and without command responsibility or authority.[45] Thus, in 1946 the Air Board and Air Staff agreed that operation of the Air Staff was unsatisfactory "in speed and efficiency to fight the next war."[46] General Knerr and Lt. Gen. Nathan F. Twining, Commanding General, Air Materiel Command, advocated the Deputy Chief of Staff system. Knerr had also made his views known to Maj. Gen. Muir S. Fairchild, Air University commander, who then organized a major study of this subject (under Maj. Gen. Orvil A. Anderson) by faculty and students of the Air War College.

Study findings were first presented to Knerr and on December 3, 1946, formally to the Air Board. The report concluded that reorganization should be guided by the principles of big business. Foremost among these principles was simplicity—everyone should be able to understand their position in the organization. The structure should have unity of command ("there must be one commander and one boss") and must be compatible with the mission, featuring delegation of authority coequal with responsibility.[47]

The Air War College study recommended three deputies: Deputy for Personnel and Administration, Deputy for Materiel and Logistics, and Deputy for Plans and Operations. It further proposed creation of an Air Combat Command, comprising SAC, TAC, and ADC, emphasizing that these three commands should be controlled by one individual. The report suggested that conceivably air defense forces might be used for tactical purposes and that tactical units might be employed in air defense or strategic operations.[48] This recommendation stood counter to the existing organization, featuring SAC, TAC, and ADC. Since Spaatz and Eisenhower had come to concur in this structure, there was little likelihood it would be changed.

General Knerr supported that portion of the report calling for three deputies under the Commanding General. He said the commander should delegate a certain amount of his responsibility, "because one man is not capable of taking care of all of the command functions. . .above the air force level without killing him."[49] The Commanding General and his three deputies represented the command function. Under the general staff system, this function had been divided among members of the staff. As mentioned, this parceling out was unsatisfactory

Maj. Gen. Hugh Knerr, Secretary General of the Air Board, recommended structuring Air Force headquarters under a deputy system, in which a commander would delegate authority to two or three individuals.

As a major general, Muir S. Fairchild conducted a major study of the proposed deputy system. The Air War College study advocated establishing three deputies under the Air Force Commanding General.

because many people worked on the same problem without arriving at a solution.[50] The deputy system was an attempt to free the Commanding General from a substantial part of his workload. Ideally, the commander and his deputies should know each other well enough so that the deputy might implement what he knew to be the commander's wishes.[51]

After the Air War College's presentation, the Air Board agreed in December that three deputies would be the best system to adopt under unification. The board informed General Spaatz of this conclusion. While there was no consensus of the Air Staff, most of the staff favored the status quo—a lateral staff structure. Once more Knerr pointed out that the A–Staff was adequate for the leisurely study of problems, but it could not handle what would be required of it in the future.[52]

General Kenney, SAC commander, General Twining, and others backed Knerr's stand. They underscored the need to delegate authority. What Kenney liked best was that the deputy system placed control at the top; it decentralized operations: "too often we see the top crowd trying to operate as well as do the primary job of organizing. . . .This organization [deputies] . . .decentralizes operations to the operator."*[53] Twining said the deputy structure (which he commanded at Air Materiel Command and which Spaatz had set up in Europe during World War II) proved especially sound because it produced decisions. On the other hand, the A-Staff system slowed decisions.[54]

The Air Board saw the three-deputy system as most suitable for a large headquarters. These deputies in effect should be commanders, issuing orders in the name of the Commanding General. Each deputy should have directors under him, on a "staff" level. In this way, the staff function would be put directly below the command level. Unlike the numbered A–Staff, these deputies would have functional titles such as Personnel, Operations, and Materiel. As General Knerr put it: "When we come to the autonomous air force. . .we are not going to keep our hands tied to the old archaic system of numbering and lettering they have in the War Department staff; we are only doing it now because it is expedient."[55]

By using three deputies, the Air Board and the Air War College aimed to avoid a purely advisory staff whereby the Commanding General made nearly all decisions. In contrast, the deputies would be delegated considerable authority. Consequently, on December 4, 1946, the Air Board proposed to General Spaatz "that the organization of the autonomous Air Force be based upon the principle of decentralized operation as set forth in the study submitted by the Air War Col-

---

*Lt. Gen. George E. Stratemeyer, ADC commander, agreed with Kenney: The deputy organization would "get these people out of this operating business, and we are annoyed with it every day of the world." [Fourth Meeting of Air Board, Dec 3–4, 1946.]

lege. The essence of this principle is the delegation of command authority through deputies."[56]

Subsequently, after Forrestal and Patterson had reached agreement on potential unification legislation, Spaatz in June 1947 directed General Vandenberg, Acting Deputy Commanding General and Deputy Chief of Air Staff, to form a team to integrate the recommendations of the Air Board, the Air War College, and Air Staff. It was Vandenberg's idea—having accepted the deputy concept—to combine Operations and Plans at the director level. He also advocated that the Air Comptroller be placed on line with the deputies. The Commanding General would be called the "Chief of Staff of the Air Force" and he would have a "Vice Chief of Staff." Under them would be the deputies, supported below by directors.[57]

Based for the most part on work done by the Air Board and the Air War College, Vandenberg's report to Spaatz bore fruit on October 10, 1947, when the headquarters reorganized. As planned, this new structure relieved the Chief of Staff of much work. The number of officers reporting directly to the Chief of Staff, USAF, was reduced from thirteen to seven,* as follows: Vice Chief of Staff (Vandenberg); Deputy Chief of Staff, Materiel (Lt. Gen. Howard A. Craig); Deputy Chief of Staff, Operations (Lt. Gen. Lauris Norstad); Deputy Chief of Staff, Personnel and Administration (Lt. Gen. Idwal H. Edwards); Air Comptroller (Lt. Gen. Edwin W. Rawlings); Air Inspector[†] (Maj. Gen. Junius W. Jones); and Secretary-General of the Air Board (Maj. Gen. Hugh J. Knerr). The last two were not directly in the chain of command. Thus, this reduction of the number of people reporting directly to General Spaatz fulfilled the idea of giving these few deputies authority as well as responsibility.**

In their own spheres of specialization, the Deputy Chiefs of Staff actually spoke for the Chief of Staff. The Deputy Chiefs made policy and supervised their directorates. Under the Deputy Chiefs and the Air Comptroller, there were twelve directorate offices and four special offices (see Chart).[‡] In the several years after the October 1947 reorganization, the headquarters structure would

---

*Eight, if the Chairman of the Scientific Advisory Board was included.

[†]Redesignated the Office of the Inspector General on January 6, 1948.

**Brig. Gen. Reuben C. Hood, Jr., described the new headquarters organization as a consolidation and streamlining "into a business like organization designed for efficiency of operation according to the highest standards of American business." [Address, Brig. Gen. Reuben C. Hood, Jr., Ch/Orgn Div, Dir/tng & Rqmts, DCAS/Ops, "Organization of the Headquarters U.S. Air Force," to Industrial College of the Armed Forces, Dec 15, 1947.]

[‡]The Air Comptroller would be redesignated as the Office of the Comptroller on December 30, 1947.

Air Staff
Headquarters United States Air Force

10 October 1947

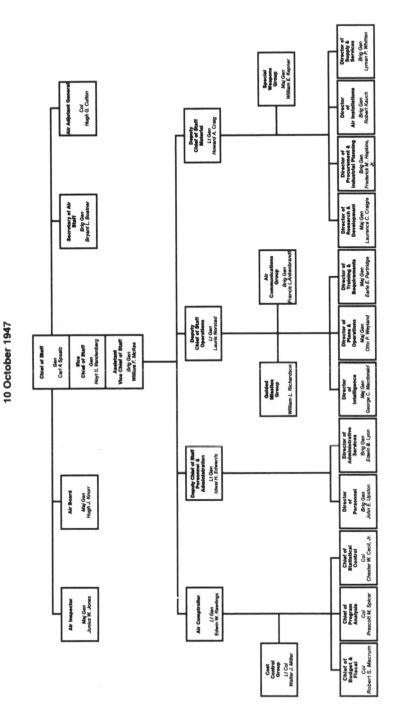

change considerably as more functions, some of them new, needed access to the Chief of Staff.

Planning the Technical Services

While occupied with organizing the headquarters, Spaatz laid plans to assure the Air Force adequate special service support. The War Department's Hall Board, which had convened in January 1947, took pains to stress that an independent Air Force would not set up separate special services. e.g., its own medical corps.* This point had been previously accepted by Eisenhower and Spaatz. The board's report stated that the War Department would continue to support the Air Force logistically after unification. Subsequently, the Secretary of Defense would be in the best position to make any desirable changes.[58]

The Hall Board suggested that each department should have a chaplain organization and the minimum medical service for basic needs, i.e., organic medical service for troop units and installations. There would be no duplication in the general hospital or medical supply system, both to be operated by one department for the others.[59]

Some in the AAF, like General Knerr, were wary that the War Department's technical services were trying to keep the Air Force dependent upon them after unification.[60] Hearing of the AAF's fear of not having proper support from the War Department, General Eisenhower reminded Spaatz of their agreement on separate services for the Air Force:

> I have repeatedly stated that if there develops an intention, either in Congress or elsewhere, to set up such completely separate special services, I will oppose the whole plan with all the emphasis I can possibly develop. In this you have agreed with me unreservedly, and yet it appears that many others interpret certain features of the Hall board report as announcing such an intention.[61]

The Army Chief of Staff was particularly disturbed about the medical corps. He endorsed the consolidation of medical organizations and he opposed the specialization of aviation medicine. Regulations to assign specialized personnel to the Air Force should come from the Secretary of National Defense, who Eisenhower emphasized—would be solely guided by national security and not by any special interest.[62] In talks with Eisenhower on March 24, 1947, Spaatz reaffirmed that he had every intention of adhering to their agreement on separate

---

*See Chapter 5.

services. He then reminded the Air Staff that the Hall Board report called for unification, not duplication.[63]

Meanwhile, Secretary of War Patterson was perturbed over a statement in the report that "the proposed legislation neither specifically prohibits nor authorizes the creation of common supply, procurement, or distribution of services." The report also underscored that if common staff agencies were created, they should be established by contributions from the Departments of the Army, Navy, and Air Force, and not by creation of independent or common departmental logistic entities to support the three service departments. Furthermore, the Patterson-Forrestal agreement made clear that each department should use personnel, equipment, facilities, and services of other departments in cases where economy and effectiveness would be enhanced. Patterson reiterated to Eisenhower that the War Department was committed to common services. Any service, he feared, might build and control all resources required for a specific mission, instead of relying on resources and means already available in another service. Opposing duplication, he recommended to Eisenhower that the Hall Board reconsider its report.[64]

General Hall told Eisenhower he was in accord with Patterson's views. The board had not intended to propose organizing more supply and technical services. What it meant to advocate was cross-procurement and cross-servicing. It had advised organic medical service for troop units and installations while one department operated the general hospital and medical supply systems. As to quartermaster service, it urged that common quartermaster activities above base level be performed by one department for the others. However, it did call for each department to have its own chaplain. After unification, the Air Force would still handle the logistic functions it now performed. Air Force officers, or officers transferred to the Air Force, would continue to discharge their logistic duties in the new Department of the Air Force. But the board also intended that the Air Force would not duplicate organizations now in the Army providing services for both the Army and Air Force. This applied to construction, real estate, operation of ports, general hospitalization, and depots.[65]

Nevertheless, Patterson did not think that separate chaplains were needed or even such quartermaster services as the board suggested. Besides, he thought the board should be reminded that doing away with competing services and facilities was the common aim. "It is not enough," the Secretary of War said, "to declare an intention as a matter of policy. It must be supported by specific recommendations without equivocation."[66] He insisted to Eisenhower that the report's wording be changed.

General Hall accordingly wrote Eisenhower that, while the board knew its report rested on the principle of abolishing duplication, there were statements which had been interpreted as violating this principle. He therefore recommended that the Office of the Chief of Staff send this statement to recipients of the report:

MAJOR AIR COMMANDS

October 10, 1947

Air Defense Command
Lt. Gen. George E. Stratemeyer

Air Proving Ground Command
Brig. Gen. Carl A. Brandt

Air Materiel Command
Gen. Joseph T. McNarney

Air Training Command
Lt. Gen. John K. Cannon

Air Transport Command
Maj. Gen. Robert W. Harper

7th Air Force
Maj. Gen. Ralph H. Wooten

Air University
Maj. Gen. Muir S. Fairchild

Alaskan Air Command
Maj. Gen. Joseph H. Atkinson

Bolling Field Command
Brig. Gen. Burton M. Hovey

Caribbean Air Command
Maj. Gen. Hubert R. Harmon

Strategic Air Command
Gen. George C. Kenney

Far East Air Forces
Lt. Gen. Ennis C. Whitehead

Tactical Air Command
Lt. Gen. Elwood R. Quesada

United States Air Forces in Europe
Lt. Gen. Curtis E. LeMay

In no case will this report be interpreted to violate either of these basic provisions: (1) The Air Force will not set up additional technical services as an
immediate result of Unification and (2) Service support of the Air Force by
the Army will continue following unification with the understanding that the
Secretary of National Defense will effect such changes in services as later
prove desirable.[67]

The key word was "immediate." In time the Air Force expected to establish its
own services.[68] General Hall's statement was disseminated and in June 1947
General Spaatz directed that the structuring of the Air Force upon unification
should adhere to the principles of the Hall Board report.[69]

The 70-group, 400,000-man postwar Air Force had been approved by Eisenhower and the Joint Chiefs.* Even so, Spaatz knew there could not be complete
autonomy until the Air Force gained additional functions and personnel. Entailed
were all kinds of functions, embracing such basics as laundry, salvage and repair,
and commissary. At the end of 1946, the War Department's major components
had been broken down as follows: Army Air Forces—400,000 troop basis of
which over 28,000 were ASWAAF; Army Ground Forces—340,000 with 64,000
personnel of the arms and services.[70] Army Air Forces leaders wanted the postwar total of service personnel to be counted above the 400,000 figure rather than
as part of it. If not then in effect the Air Force would be required to accept a reduction from its 400,000-man force.

In the words of Maj. Gen. Earle E. Partridge, Director of Operations: "We do
not feel that we are now autonomous because we can't support ourselves. . . .The
number of people transferred to us determines the state of our independence. If
we get the functions without the people we are lost. We can't perform these functions without reducing something else."[71] Partridge said that in the last analysis
the AAF would have to work with the War Department to transfer entire functions along with personnel. The problem from the AAF standpoint was that the
War Department remained reluctant to transfer military and civilian spaces to the
AAF concurrent with the transfer of certain functions. The War Department controlled the technical and administrative personnel assigned to the Army Air
Forces. The progression of these career officers was managed by the technical
and administrative services. The AAF's objective was of course to have its support personnel actually serving in the Air Force.[72] But prior to the achievement
of independence, the AAF avoided pressing this matter so as not to antagonize
Eisenhower and the War Department toward the paramount issue of autonomy.[73]

Historically, control of the technical services had varied. Before March 1942,
when War Department Circular 59 established the Army Ground Forces, Army
Service Forces (Services of Supply), and the Army Air Forces, all units of the

---

*See Chapter 2.

As Director of Operations, Maj. Gen. Earle E. Partridge realized that to be truly independent, the AAF needed to gain both the basic support functions and the personnel to perform them.

technical services were governed by these services themselves. They were responsible for tables of organization and equipment, troop basis, activation, and training. From March 1942 to July 1943, divided responsibility existed. Frequently, the AGF, ASF, and AAF activated identical service units. In some cases, service units allocated in the troop basis to Army Ground Forces and Army Air Forces were activated by Army Service Forces and the technical services. These units were trained by the technical services of ASF.[74]

With very few exceptions, split responsibility for identical service units ended in July 1943 for AGF and ASF. Tables of organization and equipment, troop basis, and activation and training responsibility were assigned to either the Army Ground Forces or the Army Service Forces. The AAF went on duplicating a number of units allotted each of the other forces. Technical services and ASF continued to train AGF and AAF units on request. Where such units were not trained for AGF and AAF, cadres were furnished by the technical service, and the Army Service Forces. In addition to training units and providing cadre, the technical services and ASF supplied or trained many technical specialists. Officer procurement and training for administrative and technical services were also done by the technical services and the Army Service Forces.[75]

216

Prior to creation of the United States Air Force, one of the major goals of General Spaatz and the Air Staff was to keep officers of the administrative and technical services who had been serving with the AAF and had been included in the AAF troop basis. These ASWAAF officers worked in such specialties as adjutant general, chemical, finance, medical, engineers, and transportation. The AAF also wanted to absorb functions being performed for Army Air Forces by the administrative and technical services.[76]

Spaatz in early 1947 repeated that ASWAAF officers should be considered an integral part of the AAF (and eventually, the USAF). He did not want anyone to feel that these officers were not members of the Air Force:

> This feeling, if it becomes general, will be a serious blow to the Air Force. It will insure that we do not get the best officers from other branches of the service to serve with us and it will further insure that such officers will not join up with the Air Forces as permanent personnel if unification, with full autonomy for the Air Forces, becomes a reality.[77]

Spaatz also wanted to be sure officers from other branches were used in their specialty. With the advent of an independent Air Force, Spaatz noted that his agreement with General Eisenhower specified that no officer would be transferred from the Army to the Air Force without authorization of his branch chief and the approval of General Spaatz. In the event of disagreement, the Army Chief of Staff would make the decision.[78]

As mentioned, Spaatz agreed unreservedly with General Eisenhower that, upon separation from the Army, the Air Force would not at once duplicate many of the Army's support services or corps. However, the Air Force did intend in time to man its technical segments with its own personnel. The Air Force would, for example, have its own engineer, logistical, and air communications career fields.[79] General Knerr commented that under the present arrangement the Air Force continued to be the "poor relative of the War Department."[80]

The Air Force as an independent service, coequal with the Army and Navy, planned after two years to organize its own technical and professional services. Before September 1947 the Army Air Forces had set forth the policy that technical and professional services in the autonomous Air Force were needed for the "high morale essential to an efficient Air Force."[81] A proper percentage in grades of colonel and above on the single promotion list would be given to each segment to ensure command careers for officers in the technical and professional fields. The fields ultimately to be created and their manning should be determined as circumstances dictated.[82]

The question of which technical and professional segments the Air Force would eventually have was sensitive and controversial. Air Staff members held divergent views. Historically, the Army had formed corps and by September 1947 there were twenty-eight. The oldest corps were the Signal Corps and the

Medical Corps. Several new corps came into being during World War I and its aftermath, including the Air Corps. Over the years, new corps sprang up when a need existed to accelerate development of a specialty whose growth was being inhibited by absorption into the command staff structure. The tendency to neglect an ongoing function seemed to justify a new corps. Special boards investigating Army problems often recommended more corps as the solution.

The War Department General Staff had tried both to eliminate and consolidate corps. It had little success. The Army's technical and administrative services desired to keep their corps, which had gained considerable influence. Throughout World War II, however, the AAF had made a determined—and for the most part successful—effort to integrate these services into functional organizations. Thus, with creation of the United States Air Force, air leaders confronted a familiar problem, laced with the unique aspect of the Air Force as an independent service:

> It is not difficult to understand the sincerity which motivates recommenda-
> tions of the specialists in each field of the Air Forces for the establishment of
> segments representing their specialty with adequate authority and responsi-
> bility to insure the effective and efficient accomplishment of their special-
> ized missions as members of the Air Force team. . . .however it must be
> remembered that war experience has repeatedly taught the necessity of com-
> pletely integrated and coordinate action.[83]

Air leaders realized that, without corps, special functions were apt to be sub-merged. Career progression of technical and professional officers was impeded. Moreover, cross-training had jeopardized the development of skilled specialists. Even so, air officials judged the case against specialized segments persuasive. It was based on the conviction that personnel were likely to become overly special-ized and therefore not sufficiently qualified to perform general duties during na-tional emergencies. Then, too, corps spawned duplication of functions and frequently "empire-building"; allegiance to the unit was diluted by loyalty to corps; corps tended to make services fail adequately to support overall opera-tions; and the entire organization became vulnerable by allowing it to become weaker than its elements.[84]

Consequently, the Air Force in October 1947 decided on utmost integration of its personnel while assuring some recognition of specialized functions. The Air Force consensus was that there could be no question about placing the "control-ling reins in the command structure where they belong rather than in separate corps. The delegation of authority to a specialized segment should be the pre-rogative of the commander in each echelon whose operations its services are sup-porting."[85] On the other hand, though normal operation of segments should be through the staff structure, agencies in the staff representing specialized functions should have direct access to the commander in each echelon.[86]

Also, training activities should emphasize that technical and professional serv-ices be given every consideration. A specialty's unsatisfactory performance might be traced to its receiving too little support. For example, General Spaatz felt that, when a new specialized activity had achieved recognition in the highest but not in the lower command echelons, a temporary corps should be set up until the specialty had reached proper stature. He thought it might be desirable for guided missiles to be given corps status even though its personnel requirements were still limited. He further contended that segments whose distinctive characteristics precluded cross-training should be delegated more authority than those less specialized. The Medical Service, for example, might be given jurisdiction over all personnel in its field. Career fields that might suffer from limited opportunities should not create unnecessary positions, but rather expand opportunities to include duties in related segments and in the staff elements.[87]

The Air Force planned for a specific percentage in the grades of colonel and above in each specialized segment.[88] Still, the allocation of senior grades should not be in direct proportion to the number of officers in every field. The allotment of space for colonel and above would be based on the scope of the specific function, amount of responsibility, supervisory positions required and finally the number of officer, enlisted, and civilian personnel in each particular segment. Highest grades should not be the same throughout these specialized fields. For example, if requirements of the communications field justified a lieutenant general, this did not mean that other fields would likewise have lieutenant generals as chiefs. Nor did it signify that chiefs and senior officers would be at least as high rank as comparable officers in the Army and Navy. The Air Force view was that the significance of a function was not the same between the services. The Army Chief of Engineers might be a lieutenant general, but this would not justify a similar grade for the Chief of Air Force Engineers. The weather specialty in the Air Force might well call for a higher rank than in either the Army or Navy.[89]

The Air Force opposed establishment of corps with responsibility for assignment and control of personnel vested in the corps commander. Responsibility would remain in the normal staff structure with special functions subject to the chain of command. In this manner the Air Force sought to avoid the Army's history of proliferation of powerful corps with strong vested interests, to the detriment of the overall organization. The Air Force accordingly organized to assign officers to a command and guide their career growth either within a specialty or broader progression in several fields. To prevent submergence of special functions, specialists would have access to the commander although normal operation would be through the proper staff agency.[90]

The Air Force wished to encourage cross-training to develop personnel with broad command experience. But a minority in each career field would limit their specialty so as to ensure high professionalism in that particular field. In addition, General Spaatz directed that separate corps organizations for physicians, lawyers and chaplains would be authorized in a so-called Air Force Act "in order for them to function under domestic and international law."[91] There would be no other exceptions.

As of October 1947, the Air Force planned to establish twelve major career fields: medical, chaplain, justice, aeronautical engineering, electrical engineering, automotive and armament, construction, personnel and administration, general supply and procurement, information, flying, and nonflying tactical.[92]

The status of the medical service presented a special problem to the Air Force leadership. Spaatz had long thought to upgrade the medical service, once independence was a reality.* Air operations in the war had been to some extent handicapped by the way medical support was set up in the various theaters of operations. Army Air Forces and Ground Forces personnel had been hospitalized and evacuated through the same medical support system. The special needs of the flyers were not considered. While the AAF operated station hospitals in the United States, it did not participate in the management of general hospitals where treatment was prescribed by physicians untrained in the practice of aviation medicine.[93] The AAF believed that unification presented the opportunity to change this system: "It is manifestly undesirable that the organization for Medical Service which so handicapped the Army Air Forces continue to operate to the detriment of the United States Air Force. It is believed that unification affords an opportunity for corrective action."[94] Interestingly, General Eisenhower thought it "absolutely silly" to dwell on aviation medicine, a view reflecting his reluctance to duplicate medical support facilities. As with other functions, he felt that the Secretary of Defense should decide which ones were absolutely necessary for the Air Force.[95]

The military services had presented their medical service plans during congressional hearings on unification. The Army Surgeon General recommended a single medical command to operate a common hospital system for the military. This command would be headed by a Director, responsible to the Secretary of Defense. Conversely, the Navy proposed individual medical services for each of the military services, coordinated through the Joint Chiefs. Like the Navy, Maj. Gen. Malcolm C. Grow, the Air Surgeon, advocated separate medical services. However, he suggested that coordination be done through a Medical Advisory Board consisting of the three Surgeons General and their representatives.[96]

Seeking to reconcile the Army and Air Force plans, the Hall Board report recommended a separate medical service for the Air Force with general hospitals staying under the Army. Yet, the board urged that Air Force medical service personnel take part in the management and in the training programs of general hospitals. The National Security Act of 1947 did not deal with the problem of medical organization. Nonetheless, after assuming office, Secretary of Defense

---

*See Chapter 2.

Serving as Air Surgeon, Maj. Gen. Malcolm C. Grow contended that the Air Force should operate its own medical service. The USAF Medical Service was established in June 1949 and General Grow became the first Air Force Surgeon General.

Forrestal appointed an interdepartmental medical committee to study the organization of the military's medical services. The USAF stand was clear:

> The Air Force has not attained parity so long as an operational veto remains in the hands of the Army, whose failure or inability to provide the medical attendance required by the Air Force in an emergency might jeopardize the mission of the latter arm. . . .it is difficult to minimize the effect of the present organization upon the morale of these medical officers who have served with the Air Force and contributed so much to the advancement of aviation medicine.[97]

Months of study by the Department of Defense, by the interdepartmental committee, and at the service level would finally result in creation of the USAF Medical Service and in the establishment of the Office of the Air Force Surgeon General in June 1949.

Transfer of Functions

As noted, the National Security Act of 1947 established the United States Air Force but did not automatically give the Air Force functions equivalent to the Army and Navy. The Secretary of the Air Force inherited solely those functions of the Secretary of the Army as were then assigned to or under the control of the Commanding General, Army Air Forces. Over two years the Secretary of Defense was authorized to assign to the Department of the Air Force such other responsibilities of the Department of the Army as he deemed necessary or desirable, and to transfer from the Army to the Air Force appropriate installations personnel, property, and records.[98] Thus through August and September 1947, the Air Force had to figure out in each field what it needed in personnel, facilities, and funds to discharge new or enlarged duties.[99] Since necessary business could not be allowed to lapse during the transition period, the Air Force did not intend to take over functions until ready to do so. In research and development, the Army and the Air Force agreed in August that the War Department need no longer approve the development of military characteristics for AAF equipment or the testing of materiel used by the Army Air Forces alone. As in other functional areas, the two services disagreed on the number of military and civilian spaces to be allocated in research and development from the Army to the Air Force.[100]

Since the Army Air Forces had become substantially independent long before passage of the National Security Act, separation of the AAF from the Army was at first largely a matter of realigning departmental control and jurisdiction. Prior to the National Security Act, the Hall Board had suggested solutions to the administrative and organizational difficulties of separating the AAF from the Army. According to the Secretary of the Army, the board report "provided a general blue-print for the divorcement of the Air Force from the Army."[101] Other studies were completed in the Office of the Under Secretary of War. After enactment of unification legislation, these studies guided the Army Chief of Staff and the Commanding General, Army Air Forces, to promulgate policies for separation. These subsequently led to about two hundred agreements between the AAF and the Army. The first, signed by Spaatz and Eisenhower, was published on September 15, 1947.[102]

Based on the Hall Board's work, Spaatz and Eisenhower had directed their staffs to work out specific transfer agreements. Eisenhower assigned his Deputy Chief of Staff, Lt. Gen. J. Lawton Collins, and Spaatz assigned his Deputy Commander and Chief of Air Staff, Lt. Gen. Hoyt S. Vandenberg, to prepare basic agreements by which the Air Force would be established separate from the Army. If problems arose, Collins and Vandenberg were ordered to present them to Eisenhower and Spaatz.[103] Agreements would not be implemented until the Army and Air Force staffs said they were able to transfer a particular function.[104] However, agreements were reached and in mid-September Generals Eisenhower and Spaatz forwarded a number of these to Secretary of War Kenneth C. Royall. He in turn sent them for approval to Secretary-designate of Defense Forrestal. Royall noted that both he and Secretary-designate of the Air Force Symington were in accord with the agreements and believed that this procedure would prove sound and sufficiently flexible.[105]

Among other subjects, Vandenberg and Collins arrived at policy agreements on service support organic services, and Regular Army officers. Regarding support the joint agreement stipulated that the Army would continue its support of the Air Force:

> Each department will make use of the means and facilities of the other department in all cases where economy consistent with operational efficiency will result. Except as otherwise mutually agreed upon cross-servicing and cross-procurement as now in effect will continue until modified by the Secretary of Defense.[106]

The agreement on organic services held that a service unit organic to an Air Force group or wing would be designated as an Air Force unit. One not organic which performed a service common to both the Air Force and Army (e.g., an engineer battalion) would be considered an Army unit attached to the Air Force.[107] Army personnel attached as individuals or as units supporting solely the Air Force would be listed in the USAF troop basis.[108] As for the agreement on Regular commissions, a total of twenty thousand Regular Army commissions would be given the Air Force. Regular commissions for officers attached to the Air Force, or with Army units servicing the Air Force, would be part of the Army's allotment of thirty thousand.[109] The Air Force found that the adjustment of personnel authorizations was one of the most difficult immediate aspects of this separation process:

> In view of personnel ceilings the obvious solution to provide for this increased load and at the same time keep our troop program intact is by allocation of authorizations from the Army to the Air Force. However, in many cases the Army requirement is not decreased in the same amount as our requirement is increased. This leaves a net deficiency that must be made up from Air Force resources. An interim solution is feasible to meet the need for military personnel and the eventual solution must be sought through realistic programming, culminating in the presentation of our needs to the Secretary of Defense and to the Congress.[110]

Civilian authorizations proved an even more critical problem because a low ceiling left little flexibility.

In specific fields, the Air Force and Army concurred that for at least a while the Army would operate central examining and recruiting stations as well as induction stations. The Air Force would furnish a proportional share of personnel for their operation.[111] There was some concern about the Army's operating recruiting stations. Gen. George E. Stratemeyer, ADC commander contended:

> We can get all the recruits we need if we enlist them ourselves and go out and get them. But if we have to do it through the Army I don't know. . . . I'll just issue a warning. . .whenever there is a chance, where they are going to take something over we are entitled to, we have to step out and insist on our rights and recommendations.[112]

In the case of central welfare funds, the Air Force would receive a proportionate share of these funds as determined by the Central Welfare Board, to then be approved by the Chiefs of Staff of the Army and the Air Force. In the field of intelligence, it was agreed that the Air Force would assume responsibility for mapping and photography, over which the War Department previously had final review and control. It was further understood that the Air Force would provide official liaison between military representatives of foreign governments and the new Department of the Air Force. Both the Departments of the Army and Air Force would operate, maintain, supervise, and control separate attache systems. The two departments surveyed the field and decided that the Air Force would operate attache systems in twenty-one countries.[113]

Unless otherwise directed, the Army Audit Agency—with USAF representation—would handle contract and industrial auditing and military property account auditing pertaining to supplies or property for the Department of the Army or Air Force. The Air Force would continue to administer its existing disbursement, paying its own military and civilian personnel through USAF command channels in accordance with accounting directives of the Army Chief of Finance or such higher authority as might subsequently be designated.[114]

The Department of the Air Force would design specialized technical facilities for the Air Force. The Army and Air Force would ascertain their needs for personnel, material, and services and also business requirements within their separate budget estimates for repairs and utilities functions. Each department would administer, direct, and supervise repairs and utilities at its own installations. The Air Force would prepare and defend before Congress those budget estimates covering USAF personnel, services, and material. Where cross-procurement was affected, the using department would provide the procuring department the funds. As to cross-servicing, the department receiving the service would furnish the department supplying the service the funds as mutually agreed upon.[115]

Both departments would figure their own needs for real estate and construction and put them in their budget estimates. The Army would act as agent for the Air Force in acquiring and disposing of real estate. Too, the Army was designated contract construction agent for the Air Force. The latter would fund such construction, collaborate on specifications, and review and approve contracts prior to awards. It was spelled out that if USAF requirements were not being met, the Air Force could do the job itself or contract for the work.[116]

The Army-Air Force agreements by themselves did not transfer functions or personnel. Following creation of the United States Air Force on September 18, 1947, and issuance of the joint agreements worked out by Collins and Vandenberg, Secretary of Defense Forrestal signed and published a series of implemental transfer orders.[117] Forrestal emphasized that these orders would be mutually agreed upon and written by the Army and Air Force. Orders entailing extensive coordination by the Secretary of Defense would be disapproved. Transfers that duplicated organizations would also be turned down unless these functions in each service were absolutely essential (organic). In areas where Forrestal felt that a reallocation of functions was in order, the services would be requested to submit recommendations. Transfer orders would be sent to the Secretary of Defense by a joint memorandum signed by the Secretaries of the Army and Air Force. Funding would be adjusted between the two services until the Air Force produced an appropriations plan approved by the Bureau of the Budget and the proper congressional committees.[118]

In 1947 the first major orders transferred personnel and some primary functions from the Army to the Air Force. The first transfer order was signed by Forrestal on September 26, 1947. It stipulated that functions of the Secretary of the Army and the Department of the Army, which were assigned to or under the control of the Commanding General, AAF, would be transferred to the Secretary of the Air Force and the Department of the Air Force. Also, most units under AAF control were transferred to the United States Air Force.* The initial order stated that the functions of the Commanding General, General Headquarters Air Force (Air Force Combat Command); of the Chief of Air Corps; and of the Commanding General, AAF, were transferred to the Chief of Staff, USAF.[119]

All officers commissioned in the Army Air Corps and officers holding commissions in the Air Corps Reserve were transferred to the Department of the Air Force. All warrant officers and enlisted men under the Commanding General, AAF (with some few exceptions) were transferred to the Department of the Air Force.[120] Officer and enlisted members of the Women's Army Corps, on duty with the AAF, would remain assigned with the Army until enactment of legislation establishing procedures for the appointment and enlistment of women in the United States Air Force.[121] In addition, the property, records, installations, agencies, activities, projects, and civilian personnel under the jurisdiction, control, or command of the Commanding General. AAF, would be continued under the jurisdiction, control, or command of the Chief of Staff, USAF.[122]

---

*The exceptions were chiefly some engineer and medical units.

As mentioned, transfer of functions, units, and individuals commenced with the first transfer order. The last one (Transfer Order 4) was signed on July 22, 1949, by Secretary of Defense Louis A. Johnson. By June 30, 1948, sixty percent of these transfer projects had been completed. They covered nearly every field of military command and administration and included adjustments relevant to personnel administration, fiscal matters, intelligence, organization, training, research and development, supply, procurement, operations, and other fields of special staff and command activity.[123] By June the transfer orders signed by Forrestal had given the Air Force jurisdiction and control over all its military and civilian personnel. All separation projects were finished by the end of the two years stipulated by the National Security Act.

According to Secretary of Defense Johnson, the forty transfer orders fulfilled the intent of the Congress through the National Security Act, to grant a broad legal basis to operations of the Air Force. These orders, observed Johnson, had furnished the Air Force "a legal basis for operations comparable to that of the Departments of the Army and Navy."[124] Provision had also been made for the Army to go on performing common services for the Air Force in finance, hospital facilities, quartermaster administration, and transportation.

Secretary of Defense Louis Johnson *(third from left)* converses with three Secretaries of the Armed Services following his first press conference after taking office, March 1949. *Left to right:* Secretary of the Air Force W. Stuart Symington, Secretary of the Army Kenneth C. Royall, Mr. Johnson, and Secretary of the Navy John L. Sullivan.

7

Epilogue

In this day when a quick powerful counterattack is America's only real answer to aggression, there can be no question that we need the world's first Air Force. It is only through the global, flashing mobility of the Air Force that we can hold our counterattack poised. It is only by continuing to improve and strengthen the Air Force that the counterattack will have sufficiently impressive substances and weight. . . .we feel, with deep conviction, that the destiny of the United States rests on the continued development of our Air Force. The question of whether we shall have adequate American air power may be, in short, the question of survival.

> Secretary of the Air Force
> Stuart Symington
> to the University Club of New York City
> January 10, 1948

The question of how best to organize the Army air arm had been debated as far back as before World War I. Reorganization had become a bone of contention soon after the formation of the Aeronautical Division as part of the Signal Corps. Although air forces failed to play a major role in the first World War, they showed sufficient potential to prompt some airmen, Billy Mitchell among them, to think that the air arm should be reorganized and eventually given independence. For the air arm to develop and prosper, the airmen argued that they should administer and control these forces, supported by adequate funding. Put simply, air forces should be operated and controlled completely by airmen. Significant though its potential may have been, air power had not shown that it

227

could substantially affect the outcome of war. Between World Wars I and II, the War Department leadership remained convinced that the airmen's missions should be direct support of ground troops along with aerial coastal defense.

In the 1930s the Army and the Navy clashed repeatedly over the coast defense mission. The Navy wanted control of all air operations over the water. The Air Corps wished to be responsible for air defense up to three hundred miles out to sea. Aside from this controversy, some airmen reasoned that the Air Corps had an independent role, i.e., the strategic mission, to strike the enemy's war-supporting resources and to cripple his will to carry on military conflict. Nevertheless, in the 1930s the concept of the independent mission was still nothing but theory.

For the Army airmen, World War II was the turning point in the autonomy drive. After building up early in the war, the AAF in 1943-45 successfully demonstrated the effectiveness of air power. Changing doctrine and tactics when called for, the AAF contributed greatly to the Allied victory in World War II. This display of power furnished the air leaders the evidence they felt they needed to win the campaign for an independent air arm. They insisted that, despite setbacks, in the final analysis their basic assumptions about air power had been proved. In the ultimate test, the air arm had showed it could be decisive. Thus, they reiterated a conviction expressed long before the war: decisions on air requirements ought to be made by airmen in total control of their own forces, with their own budget and promotion list. This meant creation of a separate service. Support for the AAF's cause came from several vital quarters. Army Chief of Staff Marshall backed General Arnold, with whom he had worked closely during the war. Marshall's successor, Gen. Dwight D. Eisenhower, fresh from triumph in Europe, threw his strong support to the drive for an Air Force, coequal with the Army and Navy.* The public and the Congress also seemed to favor a separate Air Force.

During World War II, the AAF held in abeyance its major arguments for becoming an independent service. General Arnold had naturally agreed with Marshall and Lovett that winning the war was the top priority. Marshall had promised that once the war was over he would support the drive for a separate Air Force. So although during the war Arnold generally played a waiting game as to the subject of independence, he encouraged and directed the AAF to make plans for autonomy and postwar organization. He put great emphasis on this

---

*Norstad recounted a meeting with Eisenhower in May 1948. According to Norstad, Eisenhower stated that he had been told by people in the Air Force that without his support and advocacy an independent Air Force would not have been possible. Eisenhower was proud of the part that he had played in this effort. [MR, Lt. Gen. Lauris Norstad, DCS/Ops, subj: Conference with General Eisenhower, (1 May 1948), May 7, 1948, Gen. Lauris Norstad Papers, 1945–48, Box 6.]

planning, which proceeded in Washington simultaneously with wartime operations in various theaters. He and his planners thought this activity would culminate the many years of striving for independence. The idea of air independence had driven the air leaders for many years. It had never been absent from their minds. This was true during the war. Arnold never lost sight of what the "lessons" of the war might prove. He was certain they would buttress the cause of an independent United States Air Force.

The air leaders stressed the preeminence of air power as the primary rationale for independence. The advent of the atomic weapon and the achievements of air power during the war meant that the roles of the ground and naval forces had diminished. The Air Force was now the "first line of defense." The oceans no longer insulated America from the rude shocks of war. The advantages of time and space vanished. The character of war had changed. Destruction caused by years of bombing could now occur in a flash. "A world accustomed to thinking it horrible that wars should last four or five years," wrote defense analyst Bernard Brodie, "is now appalled at the prospect that future wars may last only a few days."[1] Now even a few bombers penetrating enemy territory could leave tremendous destruction. It could be argued that the atomic bomb had resurrected Giulio Douhet. War had become total. The United States was vulnerable to the most devastating kind of warfare. There would no longer be sufficient time to mobilize. The era of come-from-behind victories was over. The second World War was the last of its kind. The greatest danger now stemmed from a possible future surprise attack by atomic bombers flying across the northern polar regions to targets in the industrial and population centers of North America.

Even so, military planners and AAF leaders acknowledged that the advent of the atomic weapon had not made all weapons and strategies obsolete. The Army Air Forces accented the importance of conventional weapons and warfare. Spaatz no doubt agreed with the air power advocate Alexander P. deSeversky, who asserted that despite the A–bomb's demonstrated destructiveness, it did have "known limitations." Writing to Secretary of War Patterson, deSeversky said the essential concepts of military strategy still applied: "Human conflict, though more destructive than ever before, will continue to be possible; that the one-hour or one-day war of popular journalism is nonsensical; that those who see the end of the world and the suicide of civilization reflect neither good science, good logic nor good public policy."[2]

Fortunately, General Arnold had foresight, vision. He had known everyone in the prewar Air Corps, and when war erupted, he had his fingers on the buttons. He already had determined whom he wanted in critical command and operational positions. He knew the strengths and weaknesses of his people and, like any superb leader, he did not hesitate to relieve commanders, to move them out when in his judgment they were not performing well. This was a great strength in wartime. As General Ira Eaker put it, Arnold "had the faculty of leading all subordi-

229

nates to their highest possible effort; he picked many subordinates for prominent positions when I well knew that he did not particularly care for them, but he judged that they had the ability to do the job required."

Arnold had always stressed the connection between wartime operations and postwar planning. He had led the vast buildup of the AAF in 1942-44. While commanding worldwide air forces during the last two years of the war, he had set his mind to assuring the success of the drive for independence and to completing plans for the AAF's reorganization. He wanted to be sure that the broad outline for the Air Force of the future was fixed prior to passing the mantle to Spaatz. In his wartime command of the Army Air Forces and in his vision of a postwar Air Force, Arnold displayed his considerable skill at relating the complex parts of a mosaic. Though not a brilliant strategic thinker, he understood the relationship between command and the many crucial support functions without which successful leadership was impossible. He had always kept his lines of communication open with leading American aviation industrialists and with the scientific community. Moreover, he had the gift of recognizing leadership in his subordinates.

To his critics, he seemed an impatient promoter who lacked understanding of the crucial details of operations. But Arnold had a far better grasp of the basics of operations than many gave him credit for. He appreciated how necessary it was for the AAF to show results. He was under tremendous pressure in Washington. President Roosevelt had not only approved but had initiated a huge buildup of air power. Direction of this expansion was an astonishingly difficult and complex task. Results were slow in coming and during 1943 Arnold clearly became frustrated. However, he persevered, changing plans and strategy when necessary, and commanders when in his judgment they failed to produce.

Having finally seen his forces unleash the awesome destructiveness of air power, General Arnold was dead set on seeing that the Air Force would not again be caught unprepared for war. He perceived that a future war might erupt with dramatic suddenness. Hence the immense importance of a sound research and development program. He instructed his friend, Theodore von Karman, to form a scientific group to chart the course of research and development for the Air Force.

Arnold plotted the course for independence and internal reorganization of the Air Force. He depended upon the skills of the unusually competent General Carl A. Spaatz. Wartime commander of the strategic air forces, Spaatz would ensure that the plans developed before the end of the war would bear fruit. Arnold knew that in Spaatz he had a man he could trust and count on. Tooey Spaatz had earned the respect of the new Army Chief of Staff, General Eisenhower, who described him as "the best operational airman in the world."* Spaatz and Eisenhower had

---

*General Kuter wrote Arnold in 1945 that Eisenhower had depicted Spaatz in this

worked extremely well together in the war. Both preferred quiet competence to flamboyance and self-promotion. Their styles suited each other. More important, they had long agreed on the crucial issues. Eisenhower backed air independence. On the matter of tactical support of the ground armies, he and Spaatz could work out a satisfactory organizational solution. After so long, the way would be cleared for creation of the United States Air Force. Arnold and Spaatz appreciated that Eisenhower's strong support would assure success, despite the considerable opposition of the Navy and its congressional allies. This was an era when it was still possible for a relatively few men to make the crucial decisions that would affect military organization and forces for a long time. The process of immediate postwar AAF internal decision-making was a holdover from the war years.

The Army Air Forces postwar planning started in 1943 and much had been done by 1945. The AAF's 70-group program, however, had not been defined until August 1945. General Eaker set the 70-group goal in response to a directive from the War Department. The air planners thought that the best guarantee of preventing general war was a strong standing Air Force, coequal with the Army and Navy. They viewed Marshall's advocacy of Universal Military Training as a direct threat to the 70-group Air Force and the goal of autonomy. Reflecting Marshall's opinion, the War Department felt certain that Congress would enact UMT. The American people would not support large peacetime forces. The standing peacetime Army would consist of volunteers. A system of UMT would be the answer. But to the War Department's chagrin, Congress in effect backed the 70-group Air Force as the best guarantor of peace and as a counterweight to UMT.

The AAF officers engaged in postwar planning faced a tremendously difficult task. Amidst the huge demobilization in 1945–46, they had simultaneously to deploy air forces, build a postwar force structure, reorganize the major commands, and plan for an independent Air Force. They had to ready their plans without knowing with any precision what shape United States foreign policy might take and without knowing specifically what missions the postwar Air Force might have to undertake. As far as American foreign policy was concerned, the immediate post–World War II period in which the Army Air Forces fought for independence was a time of crucial change in the evolution of foreign and military policies. Airmen whose suspicions of the Soviet Union had been fueled by their contacts with the Russians during the war considered that their fears had been

---

manner. Eisenhower had added that although Spaatz was not "a paper man," he could make sound decisions and "he knew exactly what he was doing." [Ltr, Kuter to Arnold, Jan 28, 1945, Gen. H. H. Arnold Collection, LC, Box 38, Folder, Correspondence–Commanders in the Field.]

confirmed by the evolution in eastern Europe of Communist "democratic governments."* Moreover, President Truman's own experience with the Soviets at Potsdam in July-August 1945 convinced him that the Soviets were going to be difficult. Then in October 1946 in London, the first meeting of the Council on Foreign Ministers ended with bitter quarreling after Foreign Minister Vyacheslav Molotov of the USSR insisted that the western powers recognize the Soviet satellites prior to writing peace treaties. Refusal of the USSR to withdraw its troops from Iran at the close of the war also brought a strong reaction from the United States and Great Britain. This issue was brought before the Security Council of the United Nations in early 1946. Soviet troops were then withdrawn.

American policy was also heavily influenced by what had been termed "the Pearl Harbor syndrome." The Japanese surprise attack, bringing the U.S. into World War II, convinced even parsimonious congressmen that the nation must not be caught unprepared again. Thus, the manner in which America entered the war became a postwar counterweight against the tradition that was opposed to large standing peacetime forces. Citizens came to believe that the "cold war" (a term made popular by Walter Lippmann[†]) or what Symington called the "tepid war," was being forced on the country.

Meanwhile, despite the obvious complexity of the planning task, the AAF planners stayed sufficiently sensitive to their paramount objective of independence and also to fluctuations in public opinion. As mentioned, the War Department had early become locked into General Marshall's advocacy of UMT as the sole answer to the structuring of a postwar military establishment that the public and Congress would accept. The Army Air Forces suffered no such constraint. The potential enactment of UMT stood in the way of the AAF's plan for a large standing postwar force, which in turn was the key to air independence. Arnold and Spaatz easily grasped this situation and did not hesitate to confront Marshall and the War Department with it. In this connection, both Arnold and Spaatz kept a keen interest in the AAF's public relations program and its importance to the drive for a separate Air Force. They believed that the war had demonstrated that air power, i.e., the AAF, had become synonymous with national

---

*During the war, the Army Air Forces had more opportunities to deal with the Soviets than the Army or Navy. The AAF's shuttle bombing—Operation FRANTIC—involved missions into eastern Germany in which these bombers would "recover" at Russian bases. The contacts with the Soviets afforded AAF leaders through these missions: through the lend-lease aircraft program; and by negotiations to gain the release of AAF personnel who had landed behind Russian lines, convinced the AAF that the Soviets were especially difficult to deal with. [See Richard Lukas, *Eagles East: The Army Air Forces and the Soviet Union, 1941–1945,* (Tallahassee, Fla., 1970).]

[†]Political columnist and philosopher.

security. The AAF's public relations program was aimed at persuading the American public that "the establishment of adequate air power is the key to victory in war and the maintenance of security in time of peace."[3]

In retrospect, speculation centered on the idea that the Army had supported the AAF in its fight for autonomy because it feared that the airmen would dominate the War Department during the postwar period. While conceivably this may have been a factor, Eisenhower undoubtedly spoke for the prevailing view in the Army hierarchy when he underscored that the AAF deserved independence on its wartime record. As we have seen, Eisenhower himself felt strongly that the War Department should make every effort to help the transition of the Army Air Forces to an independent service. He constantly admonished his commanders and staff to do their utmost to ensure successful implementation of the National Security Act.[4] Symington later recalled that Eisenhower was one hundred percent behind the concept of a separate Air Force.[5] Some observers and historians wondered if the AAF itself would not have been better off to stay as part of the Army, ultimately perhaps gaining closer to one-half of the budget rather than one-third. But this was never a considered alternative in the airmen's postwar scheme of planning. The goal of independence, for so long all-consuming to the air leaders, was preeminent.

Arnold in November 1945 had picked Spaatz to lead the effort to complete the postwar status of the Air Force. Spaatz in early 1946—as Arnold had before him—proposed that a Chief of Staff for Air be established, coequal with the Army Chief of Staff. However, in deciding on the War Department's postwar organization, the Simpson Board made the AAF coequal to the Army Ground Forces, under the Chief of Staff and the War Department General Staff.

Spaatz, in the postwar period, counted on Maj. Gen. Lauris Norstad to help him shape the postwar Air Force. Norstad himself had labored under the guidance of Arnold and Eisenhower. From Arnold, Norstad learned to take a concept, mold it, and make it his own. He also appreciated Arnold's determination to get things done. From Eisenhower, he took eternal optimism, the importance of reason, and the determination not to be defeated by detail. Over-arching principles remained most important. The organization did not solve problems; people resolved problems.

Stuart Symington worked exceedingly well with Norstad. He also maintained an excellent relationship with General Spaatz based on mutual respect and a comfortable division of labor. Symington confessed to the Air Board in December 1946 that "I don't know anything about airplanes and operating them." He made "a deal" with Spaatz that the latter would handle operational and force structure issues and Symington would concentrate on "the business end of it" and "spearheading" the unification program.

The business part of the program included shaping the AAF budget and controlling costs. "The more that we can impress the government that we are not careless, that we're not just a bunch of fliers," Symington emphasized, "that we are business people handling the taxpayers money carefully, that to the extent that we can do that will be the extent to which we can develop our position."

For the Army Air Forces, the years 1945-47 were distinguished by considerable turbulence. After the war ended, demobilization broke out in full sway. The mighty AAF was decimated. Between September 1945 and March 1946, the AAF's combat capability plummeted. Yet 70 groups remained the fixed objective. Nevertheless, it became apparent in 1946-47 that this goal would be very hard to achieve. Although the Truman administration never publicly opposed the Air Force's aim, it imposed a ceiling on the defense budget that postponed the 70-group program.

By the close of 1946, Symington thought that cutbacks in defense funds threatened to wreck the AAF's planned program. The War Department approved a fiscal 1948 budget sufficient only for 55 operational groups. General Spaatz therefore decided to activate 70 groups by mid-1947, but to keep 15 of them at skeleton strength. The 70-group objective would not be abandoned. It should be noted that overall American military strength at this time had been sharply pared. In early 1947 the military numbered 1.56 million, of which 305,774 were in the Army Air Forces. By March 1948 the totals were 1.35 million in the armed forces with 367,332 in the Air Force.[6]

In mid-1947, when a separate Air Force had been assured, Spaatz activated 70 groups: 21 very heavy bomber, 22 fighter, 5 light bomber, 4 tactical reconnaissance. 10 troop carrier, 3 all-weather fighter, 2 long-range photo-reconnaissance, 1 long-range mapping, and 2 long-range weather reconnaissance. Of these 70 groups, 55 were manned, with the remaining 15 on a skeleton basis. Of the 55 manned groups, 36 were operational: 8 very heavy bomber, 15 fighter, 3 light bomber, 2 tactical reconnaissance, 6 troop carrier, 1 long-range photo reconnaissance, and 1 long-range mapping.[7]

In late 1947, Symington continued fervently to explain why the Air Force needed 70 operational groups. As he saw it, the problem was first to consider 70 groups the "bedrock minimum," then to weigh the cost against the possible consequences from not meeting this requirement. In the event of war, Symington contended, "the Air Force must be prepared to carry out the air defense of the United States. . . .it must be prepared to undertake immediate and powerful retaliation, a capacity which is itself the only real deterrent to aggression in the world today."[8] Symington averred that anything under 70 groups would seriously impair the Air Force's capacity to retaliate. Under present and anticipated funding, the Air Force could not make more than 55 groups operational. More money would be needed.[9]

Worse news broke in 1947. The administration's authorized budget estimate for fiscal 1949 made it doubtful that the Air Force could bring even 55 groups to operational status. Symington protested in the strongest terms to the White

234

House, to Forrestal, and to James E. Webb, Director of the Bureau of the Budget. Symington repeated that 55 groups fell far short of national security needs. An Air Force in being could not be assured without adequate aircraft production and without a satisfactory research and development program. Keenly sensitive to the problems of industrial preparedness, he admonished the administration that after the war the nation had "resolved that we would never allow any country to out-strip us in the development of new and superior weapons. . . .not one airplane whose development started after Pearl Harbor was ever used in combat."[10]

Should the administration's authorized budget estimate not be changed, the Air Force would only be able to make something less than 55 groups operational. The 70-group program, supported by the Joint Chiefs, required an estimated $5.2 billion for fiscal 1949. Cognizant of the necessity for economy, the Air Force submitted an estimate for $4.21 billion. The Bureau of the Budget authorized the Air Force only $2.904 billion. Symington's reaction was pointed: "We are more shocked at this decision of the Bureau than at anything that has happened since we came into Government."[11]

Supporting 70 groups were the President's Air Policy Commission (Finletter Commission) and the Congressional Aviation Policy Board (Brewster-Hinshaw Board). Even so, the Air Force in early 1948 saw little hope of reaching its goal.* "We believe," the Finletter Commission declared, "that self-preservation comes ahead of economy."[12] Both reports increased congressional and public support for the Air Force's objective. General Eisenhower, among others, noted this and emphasized the "tremendous obligation" it placed upon the Air Force. This sup-port weakened the backing for Truman's UMT program.† All the military serv-ices were aware of this trend. In a thoughtful memorandum to the Army Chief of

---

*The Air Policy Commission's report was not greeted with praise in all quarters. Wal-ter Millis charged that the commission was "responding mainly to the Air Force's some-what parochial view of problems." Believing the report's mention of naval aviation to be an afterthought, Millis observed: "Given a Navy which was already carrying a large pro-portion of its firepower on wings, it would seem that any study of 'air policy' should have given closer attention to what constituted an 'adequate' naval component. There were many, not only in the Navy but outside it, who were not convinced that all strategic wis-dom resided in the young generals of the Air Force." [Walter Millis, Harvey C. Mansfield, and Harold Stein, *Arms and the State: Civil-Military Elements in National Policy* (New York, 1958), pp 67.]

†The War Department proceeded to update its UMT plan. In June 1947 this plan was revised, as always based on the assumption that Congress would eventually enact UMT into law. [Ltr, Maj. Gen. Edward F. Witsell, TAG to CGs AAF, AGF, et al, subj: WD Plan for UMT, Jun 11, 1947, in RG 340, Air Board Gen File, 1945–48, Box 12.]

Secretary of the Air Force Symington *(left)* with Fred Vinson, Chief Justice of the Supreme Court; John L. Sullivan, Secretary of the Navy; and Kenneth C. Royall, Secretary of the Army, September 1947. In the days of defense austerity, Symington continued to fight for increased funding for the fledgling U. S. Air Force.

Information, Army Col. S. L. A. Marshall commented that increasingly the basis for war planning was "confidence in the decisive character of air power."

Congressional opinion, he said, supported "the belief in stronger air power as a substitute for UMT, as a guarantor of the continuing peace of the country, and equally as a move for preparedness of war."[13] Marshall pointed out that the credibility of UMT was dwindling at the same rate that support for air power was gaining. He suggested that in light of congressional opinion, the Army should consider withdrawing its support of the UMT program.[14]

Meanwhile, even rising cold-war tensions, fueled by the Czechoslovakian coup of February 1948, failed to budge the administration from its austerity program. Not that President Truman failed to acknowledge the threat to peace. In an extraordinary speech to Congress in March 1948 he named the Soviet Union, as the principal threat to world peace.[15] Yet the administration's stringent economies continued seriously to affect the military budget. Truman was quick to detect the difference between a strictly military requirements point of view and the larger, national perspective. He cited the danger of "explosive inflation" should additional, large military procurement programs be tacked to the budget. Therefore, a rise in military expenditures should he carefully weighed. As President, he would not approve any program that he thought would undermine the economy.[16] His UMT program in deep trouble, Truman in early 1948 also evinced growing frustration over service rivalry. He admonished the military to suppress its parochial service preferences. Truman wrote Air Force Chief of Staff Vandenberg that "there are still some of you who are thinking more of representing interests and objectives of your individual service than of interpreting the broad national program and its requirements to your subordinates and to the Congress."[17]

Believing that the expanding importance of air power made it "the first line of defense," the Air Force thought it merited more than the roughly one-third slice of the defense budget it was getting. Both Webb and Forrestal continued to insist on a balanced force program, a defense budget practically split three ways. By December 1947 the Air Force had manned and equipped 47 groups with varying degrees of operational efficiency. It was clear that it would be difficult to reach 55 groups.

Symington saw that the chances for reaching 70 groups had slipped away for the foreseeable future. He kept pressing for an Air Force in being, which he insisted was the opposite of an Air Force that might be ready months after war erupted. By this time, the Secretary of the Air Force preferred the term Four-Year Program to the 70-group program. "I believe," he said, "that this name (70 groups) is undescriptive, and for that reason I consciously avoid its use. It is true

President Truman aboard a new B–36, during a demonstration of the aircraft at Andrews AFB, Maryland, February 1949. Though concerned about the Soviet threat, the president was cautious in approving large military expenditures.

that the program is built around 70 combat groups of aircraft; but the number of groups, while essential, is not its distinctive feature.[18]" Of greater importance, the Four-Year Program provided for replacement of obsolescent aircraft and made possible a dynamic research and development program. Further, it promised an effective long-range striking force and it included plans to sustain the military aircraft industry. The major point according to Symington was that the United States could no longer afford what he termed stop-and-start planning.[19] The key here was a steady flow of orders to enable the industry to modernize plants and train manpower, thus permitting rapid expansion in case of war.[20]

Symington had become increasingly perturbed, not the least of all at Forrestal. In light of the worsening international situation, the Secretary of the Air Force felt that the Office of the Secretary of Defense had not given a solid hearing to the Air Force program. Forrestal stuck to a balanced force program, denying the Air Force's claim to sufficient funds to equip 70 groups. Symington informed Forrestal directly that, regarding the Air Force's requirements, "Spaatz and myself never had a chance to present our position to you or even your staff and this is especially unfortunate in that nobody who ever served a day in the Air Force was. . . .a member of your permanent top staff."[21] Or as Brig. Gen. W. Barton Leach, USAFR, observed:

> These civilian officials are not prejudiced against the Air Force, nor are they unwilling to learn. But an instinctive understanding of Air Force problems is not in their blood; they do not naturally seek the association of Air Force people; and when the chips are down it too often happens that the Air Force gets the short end of those very important decisions that are controlled by the staff of the Secretary of Defense. . . .For the most part OSD has been staffed with able men. But ability is not enough. A Supreme Court comprising the nine ablest lawyers in the country would not be acceptable if it turned out all nine came from Wall Street firms.*[22]

Thus in the spring of 1948, an increasingly contentious atmosphere existed between the Air Force and the Office of the Secretary of Defense. Norstad pointed to a lack of confidence between the two.[23]

Transfer of functions and personnel from the Army, and meeting the 70-group objective, were not the only problems confronting the newly independent Air Force. The roles and missions dispute between the Navy and the Air Force had not been settled in July 1947 by Executive Order 9877.* Before the war ended, the Navy had laid postwar plans to rely on air and undersea forces. Task force commanders were enthusiastic about building carriers larger than the Midway class. Naval air would become the foremost combat element of the fleet. Naval leadership would soon be dominated by airmen bent on commanding forces that

---

*See Chapter 5.

Kenneth C. Royall is sworn in as Secretary of the Army by Robert P. Patterson, the retiring Secretary of War. Mr. Royall shared the Air Force view that the services should be mutually dependent in time of war.

could deliver the atomic bomb. In December 1947, Rear Adm. Daniel V. Gallery (Assistant Chief of Naval Operations, Guided Missiles) proposed "an aggressive campaign aimed at proving that the Navy can deliver the Atomic Bomb more effectively than the Air Force can."[24] The Air Force should be relegated to the primary mission of air defense.

Such a campaign, suggested Gallery, would take the Navy off the defensive where it had been since the end of the war. Gallery said that the Navy had been put in the position of replying to the argument that navies were obsolete. Delivery systems were the key. He noted that the B–29 was restricted by its operational range. It had to operate from oversea bases. The B–36 would have longer range but would be vulnerable to interceptors. In Gallery's opinion, it would continue to be true "that you can build better performance into a short range bomber than you can into a transoceanic bomber, and that is where the Navy will always have the edge over the Air Forces."[25]

Aside from the issue of atomic bomb delivery, the fundamental conceptual difference between the Army-USAF view and the Navy persisted. This difference antedated and accented this roles and missions dispute. Basically, as Eisenhower pointed out, the Navy emerged from the war convinced that it required self-sufficiency in its forces. This was the idea of the World War II balanced task force. On the other hand, the Army believed in three service components mutually dependent upon each other. General Norstad, Director of War Department Plans and Operations in October 1947, put it this way:

> Under the three service concept, the Army does not agree with the thought that each service should have all the resources necessary for a balanced combat task force without assistance from the other services. . . .The experiences of this war have certainly indicated that in many if not the majority, of specific operational missions, the task was of necessity accomplished by contributions from two or three services acting under the principles of unified command.[26]

Secretary of the Army Kenneth C. Royall agreed with the Air Force view. The Navy, he asserted, went on building its integrated striking forces—land, sea, and air. The Navy intended to discharge its mission without relying on the Army or

Gen. Hoyt S. Vandenberg being administered the oath of office as Air Force Chief of Staff by Chief Justice Fred Vinson, April 30, 1948. General Vandenberg succeeded Gen. Carl Spaatz (center). **Also present are James Forrestal, Secretary of Defense,** (left) **and W. Stuart Symington, Secretary of the Air Force.**

Air Force.[27] On his part, Secretary of the Navy John L. Sullivan stressed that the Navy had kept integrated forces for many years and wanted to go on doing so.[28]

By 1948 the auguries were clear that the roles and missions clash would heat up.[29] The Key West conference of March 1948, convened against the backdrop of rising international tension, in retrospect failed to ameliorate the roles and missions disagreement. To the contrary, the controversy escalated. Symington was especially displeased with an attack on the Air Force by Rear Adm. John W. Reeves, Jr., Commander of the Naval Air Transport Service. Testifying before the House Subcommittee on Naval Appropriations in March 1948, Reeves cast doubt on the Air Transport Command's capacity, thereby questioning the viability of the coming merger establishing the Military Air Transport Service. The effect, Symington wrote Forrestal, was to furnish the groundwork for a return of the Naval Air Transport Service to the Navy.[30] This attack, said the Air Force Secretary, undercut efforts at mutual understanding and exemplified "clear and flagrant disloyalty—both to you and our government."[31]

In spite of the continuing controversy, Secretary Forrestal in May 1948 directed the Navy and Air Force to merge their air transport services to create the Military Air Transport Service.[32] This organization was the first of the National

Secretary of Defense James Forrestal with the Joint Chiefs of Staff and other military leaders at the Naval War College, Newport, Rhode Island, August 1948. *Left to right:* **Lt. Gen. Lauris Norstad, USAF; Gen. Hoyt Vandenberg, USAF; Lt. Gen. Albert Wedemeyer, USA; Gen. Omar Bradley, USA; Mr. Forrestal; Adm. Louis Denfeld, USN; VAdm. Arthur W. Radford, USN; and Maj. Gen. Alfred M. Gruenther, USA.**

Military Establishment to combine personnel from two of the services under a unified command. Forrestal ordered that the Military Air Transport Service be commanded by an officer appointed by the Air Force Chief of Staff. Chosen as the first commander was Maj. Gen. Laurence S. Kuter, who had been instrumental in planning the organization of the postwar Air Force, and who afterwards commanded the Atlantic Division of the Air Transport Command. Rear Adm. John P. Whitney was appointed vice commander.[33]

The basis of Forrestal's rationale to combine the Air Transport Command and the Naval Air Transport Service was essentially the pursuit of economy. Forrestal wanted desperately to show that the promise of economy in the defense establishment could be delivered. He also wanted to demonstrate that regardless of the controversy over roles and missions, the services could in fact work together. He knew it would take time for the Navy and Air Force to complete a true consolidation of their transport services.*

Meanwhile, Secretary Symington and General Spaatz (to retire and to be replaced as Chief of Staff by Vandenberg in April 1948) believed that the National Security Act should be changed. "After nine months," Symington informed Clark Clifford, "it is now my considered opinion that the present National Security Act must be changed in order to work."[34] The Air Force had supported the act as a first step although it had advocated stronger legislation. Specifically, to break the deadlocks in the Joint Chiefs of Staff, Symington wanted a military Chief of Staff who "ranked" the three service chiefs. He felt that had such a position been created from the start, there would not have been so great a controversy over the 70 groups.[35] Moreover, the Secretary of Defense himself needed more authority and more personnel to make the National Military Establishment work. The overburdened secretary required clearly delineated responsibilities and a Deputy Secretary. Symington had not changed his opinion that the Navy had succeeded in so weakening the legislation establishing the National Security Act that the Secretary of Defense (the former Navy Secretary) could not do his job. Forrestal was a coordinator but he should be an administrator.[36] Changes to the Na-

---

*As approved by Forrestal, the Military Air Transport Service charter directed this new consolidated command to transport personnel and cargo for all agencies of the National Military Establishment and also for other governmental agencies, as authorized. Forrestal's directive allowed the Navy and Air Force to use their aircraft to evacuate sick and wounded when required. To advise him on transport policy, Forrestal established a Military Air Transport Board comprising one representative from each of the military services. The board would also arbitrate and make recommendations to the Secretary of Defense when any department complained about an alleged failure to receive satisfactory service. [Memo for SA, SAF, and JCS fr James V. Forrestal, May 3, 1948.]

tional Security Act should therefore develop more along the lines of what the Army and the AAF wanted in the first place.

Spaatz endorsed a much stronger Office of the Secretary of Defense, with an Under Secretary and whatever Assistant Secretaries were needed. The Defense Secretary should additionally have a military Chief of Staff and a General Staff. The civilian secretaries heading the three military departments should be abolished. The military heads of the services should be designated Commanders instead of Chiefs of Staff. Spaatz was also for eliminating the Joint Chiefs of Staff.[37]

Belief in a stronger Office of the Secretary of Defense was not uncommon among leaders of the military establishment. Along with Symington, Spaatz, and Forrestal, Eisenhower insisted that the office was far too weak to cope with the problems of the postwar years. Norstad thought that Forrestal should have one senior officer as a military assistant, of the stature of Gen. Omar N. Bradley, who commanded the respect of the three services.

So just as passage of the National Security Act and establishment of the Air Force did not at once solve the basic issues of unification, neither did these events automatically resolve the internal and external problems afflicting the Air Force. While the goal of 70 operational groups had not changed since August 1945, it had not been achieved. Chances to reach this objective in the near future seemed dim. Furthermore, the Air Force continued to remind Congress that without adequate aircraft production, the desired Air Force in being could not be built. At the same time, the Air Force in 1947-48 continued to have functions and personnel transferred from the Army. Even though the Officer Personnel Act of 1947 gave the Air Force a separate promotion list, many personnel policies had yet to be worked out. And over all this hung the roles and missions battle with the Navy.

Yet, the fact remained that a United States Air Force had been created. No matter what crises lay ahead, the central objective had been won. After the war, General Arnold proclaimed a separate Air Force to be the highest priority. He had given Spaatz the responsibility for seeing this mission through to the finish. General Spaatz had not disappointed Arnold, his mentor. Having achieved independence for the Air Force, Spaatz himself retired in April 1948 in favor of General Vandenberg. The concerted AAF postwar planning which had started in the summer of 1943, and which had gone through numerous convolutions under the War Department's lash, had resulted in a 70-group goal and a solid Air Force command organization.

* * *

Nonetheless, Stuart Symington was correct when he emphasized that the National Security Act of 1947 was a good first chapter, but certainly not a book. Symington's frustration focused on the fact that the Secretary of National Defense remained a coordinator rather than an administrator, this having been a contentious issue in 1946–47 between the Army airmen and the Navy prior to enactment of the National Security Act. From the start, the airmen had favored a strong Secretary of National Defense. However, Symington and the AAF leadership understood that compromise was required in order to pass legislation. To the Army airmen, the creation of an independent Air Force was most important. On the negative side, the National Security Act, as General Eaker noted, established four air forces and failed to give the Secretary of National Defense requisite authority over the National Military Establishment.

Recognizing the validity of Symington's point, the Congress passed legislation in 1949 strengthening the hand of the Secretary of Defense and followed this in the 1950s with two reorganizations that also gave the Secretary more power and authority. Yet it is important to note that these changes, made in response to weakness in the nation's top security organization, kept intact the major framework of the 1947 Act. The three service departments remained coequal, each headed by a civilian secretary, under the Department of Defense. The legislative imperative, in the late 1940 and 1950s, that strengthened the Office of the Secretary of Defense at the expense of the service departments, would continue in subsequent decades, and call into question whether this trend had gone too far.

This centralization of authority was in large part a clear response to the evolution of nuclear technology and the concomitant dispute over roles and missions which played a key part during 1945–47 in the unification struggle. In the late 1940s, however, Secretary of Defense James Forrestal himself recognized that he operated from a position of weakness. In his 1948 report on the National Military Establishment, Forrestal called for strengthening the Office of the Secretary by giving it more power over the military services. The result became the 1949 Amendments to the National Security Act. This important legislation downgraded the services to military departments, removed the service secretaries from the National Security Council, and designated the Department of Defense as an executive department. The Secretary of Defense was thus empowered with "direction, authority, and control" over the Defense Department and became the President's primary voice on defense issues. Supported by Secretary of the Air Force Symington, this 1949 legislation marked a turning point in American military organization, starting the inexorable flow of power and centralization from the services to the Office of the Secretary of Defense.

The 1949 amendments became law literally during one of the most bitter and public interservice feuds in American military history—the so-called "Revolt of the Admirals." Triggered by Secretary of Defense Louis Johnson's cancellation of construction of the aircraft carrier, *United States* (Forrestal had resigned in early 1949, in deep mental stress, and subsequently jumped to his death from the sixteenth floor of the Bethesda, Md., Naval Medical Center), at the heart of the confrontation was the struggle between the fledgling Air Force and Navy over the atomic deterrent mission during a period of budgetary cutbacks. Despite two years of experience with the National Military Establishment, the Navy had yet wholeheartedly to accept the concept of unification.

Additional flow of centralized civilian control to OSD occurred in 1953 under President Dwight D. Eisenhower. Reorganization Plan No. 6 of 1953 eliminated the Munitions Board and the Research and Development Board and created six Assistant Secretaries of Defense. This process of placing more power and authority within OSD with the resultant diminution of the authority of the service secretaries greatly accelerated with passage of the 1958 Reorganization Act. This legislation effectively removed the service secretaries from the operational chain of command, which now ran from the President and the Secretary of Defense through the Joint Chiefs of Staff to the unified and specified commanders. As with previous reorganizations, the Air Force supported the 1958 changes. General Thomas D. White, Air Force Chief of Staff, noted that the 1958 reform gave "unequivocal" authority to the Secretary of Defense. This reorganization was the most significant reform since passage of the National Security Act of 1947.

The Army Air Forces in mid-1946 maintained control over training and operations of air forces, within the United States, including the Strategic Air Command (SAC). With promulgation of the Outline Command Plan [later the Unified Command Plan] in December 1946, the JCS were authorized strategic direction over all elements of the armed forces. The primary function of the Army Air Forces became training rather than operations. Unified commands would undertake operations, as well as SAC, all under the control of the Joint Chiefs. This defense organization, shaped in the late 1940s and 1950s, basically remained in place until the mid-1980s. In 1986, the Goldwater-Nichols Reorganization Act marked the first significant defense reorganization since 1958. Similarly, in the realm of Air Force organization, the March 1946 postwar reorganization remained in place for 46 years, until the USAF 1992 reorganization of its combat commands.

Echoes of the roles and missions debate of the late 1940s continued to resonate in the 1980s and 1990s. The major difference was that, unlike the 1940's, the debate in the 1990s was not primarily carried out in the glare of congressional hearing rooms. It would be difficult in the 1990s to contemplate another "Admirals' Revolt." In the almost half-century since the Navy's 1949 challenge to the unification concept, the services have learned generally to fight their budgetary and weapons battles from the inside and formally before the Congress. In the early 1980s, members of Congress and the Chairman of the Joint Chiefs, Air Force General David Jones, thought that changes were required to strengthen the Chairman's position as well as the commanders of the combatant commands.

"We need to spend more time on our warfighting capabilities," Jones emphasized, "and less in intramural squabbles for resources."* Mounting criticism from such powerful figures as Senator Sam Nunn, chairman of the Senate Armed Services Committee, also significantly influenced the debate. The critics charged that service parochialism had gone too far, affecting the authority of the unified commanders. When the final version of Goldwater-Nichols was signed by President Ronald Reagan, in October 1986, Senator Nunn commented that this legislation fulfilled President Eisenhower's vision with the 1958 Reorganization Act.

Goldwater-Nichols designated the Chairman of the Joint Chiefs of Staff as the principal military advisor to the President and the Secretary of Defense. The Chairman of the Joint Chiefs would be responsible for overall strategic planning; assessing service budget requests; forwarding budget recommendations to the Secretary of Defense; and supervising joint staff activities. The law also created a four-star vice chairman's post who could not be from the same service as the chairman. The chairman and vice chairman could serve as many as three terms, a total of six years, as opposed to the prior limit of four years.

Importantly, this legislation strengthened the authority of the combatant commanders. The chain of command ran from the President through the Secretary of Defense to the combatant commanders. The services continued to be responsible for training, equipping, and organizing their forces while the combatant commanders were in charge of directing operations. Goldwater-Nichols directed that the chairman conduct reviews of the mission and force structures of the unified and specified commands and every three years submit a report on the subject of roles and missions.

Chairman of the Joint Chiefs, General Colin Powell, in fact subsequently issued a report that Congressional critics, including Senator Nunn, charged failed to address fundamental roles and missions and had been influenced by parochial service interests. In the wake of General Powell's report, in the spring of 1994, Secretary of Defense Perry appointed a Commission on Roles and Missions of the Armed Forces. In May 1995, the Commission's report called for meeting a proper balance between the competition among the military services and the need for downsizing and reducing costs. This echoed General Eisenhower's 1945 observation that competition between the services generally was productive, but carried too far could be "ruinous." "We must find the best way," the Commission noted, "to provide a fighting force in the future that is not bound by the constraints of the roles and missions outlined in 1948." The Commission emphasized that Army and Marine Corps capabilities were complementary and that "inefficiencies attributed to the so-called 'four air forces' were mostly in the infrastruc-

---

*Drew Middleton, "Army Chief of Staff Urges a Broad Reorganization," *The New York Times*, 31 March 1982, p 19.

ture, not on the battlefield." Fully supporting the Goldwater-Nichols report, the Commission called for its full implementation, including improved joint war-fighting capabilities. Consistent with its findings on "the four air forces," the Commission deemed it appropriate that all of the services perform close air support. No savings could be realized from subtracting any of the services' capabilities without weakening overall warfighting ability.

In the 1990s, the issues of organization and direction of America's military forces, inseparable from the question of roles and missions, again took center stage, accelerated by the collapse of the Soviet Union, the resultant end of the cold war, and by the stunning success of American arms in the war with Iraq.

The collapse of the Soviet Union ushered in a major downsizing of America's military forces. In the decade from the mid-1980s to the mid-1990s, the Air Force budget shrunk 40 percent and personnel declined from 600,000 to about 400,000. This downsizing, coupled with the experience of the Gulf War, which evidenced a blurring of the Air Force's strategic and tactical missions, resulted in a reorganization of air commands. This historic move was the first major combat command reorganization since the post-World War II reorganization of March 1946.

From the end of World War II until the onset of the 1990's, the Strategic Air Command (SAC), had been pre-eminent within the United States Air Force. Formed in March 1946, along with the Tactical Air Command and the Air Defense Command, SAC under General Curtis E. LeMay, evolved into an elite force, the premier nuclear deterrent force of the free world, poised as a ready force in-being to counter any nuclear attack by Soviet long-range forces.*

The experience of the Korean war in the early 1950s and the conflict in Southeast Asia (SEA) in the 1960's, pointed to the increased importance of tactical forces in the cold war era. The success of SAC in the nuclear deterrent role meant that the Air Force's tactical air elements would most likely be the forces engaged in actual conflicts, although in both Korea and Southeast Asia, strategic air power came into play. In Southeast Asia, B-52s struck the enemy in jungle terrain while fighters attacked the enemy's capital. Overall, the Korean, Southeast Asian, and Gulf War conflicts indicated a gray area between tactical and strategic missions, bringing to mind General George Kenney's emphasis in 1946 on the blurring of the strategic and tactical missions.

Congressional and public pressure to downsize, in the wake of the breakup of the Soviet Union and the experience of the Gulf War, was quickly followed in June 1992 by the USAF reorganization. The Air Force combined the Tactical Air Command with most of SAC and a small piece of the Military Airlift Command,

---

*See Walton S. Moody, *Building a Strategic Air Force* (Washington, D.C., 1996).

to create the Air Combat Command with headquarters at Langley AFB, Virginia. At the same time, most of the Military Airlift Command's resources combined with some key SAC resources to form the Air Mobility Command. Also, the Air Force Materiel Command was established, a combination of Air Force Systems Command and the Air Force Logistics Command. This marked the first time since 1946 that the Air Force was bereft of a Combat Command devoted solely to strategic operations. This reorganization was also distinguished by a return in nomenclature, if not totally in functions, to another benchmark of 1946, namely, the Air Materiel Command. Too, the nomenclature of Air Combat Command could be traced to 1942.

Nonetheless, the concept and thrust for this new organization remained clearly future oriented. Underlying the shift in force structures reflected in the organization was the fundamental Air Force concept for the 1990s—*Global Reach— Global Power*. This white paper, published in 1990, charted how the USAF contributed to national security and the ways in which the service would continue dynamically to support American policy through the turn of the century. *Global Reach—Global Power* emphasized that air forces could accomplish both tactical and strategic roles, depending upon the mission, and relying on the unique Air Force attributes of speed, range, flexibility, precision, and lethality.

Although the military services continue their painful downsizing, restructuring, and conceptualization of doctrine for the future, this activity and thinking connect to the legacy of the past. The immediate post–World War II period is the snapshot most evident in the shifting sands of 1990s roles and missions issues. The major questions affecting the military immediately after World War II were downsizing, restructuring, reorganization, competing roles and missions, and the challenge of advancing technology—all in the shadow of strict budget limitations.

Too, the military establishment after the war had completely to revise its thinking towards deterrence and maintaining forces in-being. Ironically, fifty years later, as the end of the century approaches, the American military is once again faced with a major task of rethinking and reorganizing; this time the challenge is to turn away from emphasis upon deterrence in order to stress conventional warfighting capabilities.

Thus, the 1946 experience remains painfully relevant for the new century because it indicates that now, as then, the only certainty is that a continuum of shifting service doctrine and force structure will apply into the foreseeable future. In this regard, it is instructive to consider the words of General George C. Marshall, when he opened the Air Corps Tactical School semester in October 1938 at Maxwell Field, Alabama:

> Military victories are not gained by a single arm. . . .but are achieved through the efforts of all arms and services welded into a team.

The most difficult problem. . . .is the determination of the best organization
. . . .within the limits of the funds available.

. . . .it is literally impossible to find definite answers for such questions as:
who will be our enemy in the next war; in what theater of operations will
that war be fought; and what will be our national objective at the time?

Now it is a very simple matter to say that we need a balanced force, but the
headache develops when we work out the detailed composition of such a
force that is within the financial means available.

There are no series of facts that will lead to the one perfect solution, and
short of war, there is no method for testing a solution.

At the close of World War II, General Henry H. Arnold observed that "today's aircraft are the museum pieces of tomorrow." The challenge for the Air
Force is to keep its doctrine and weapons current, able to best any force in the
world. This is dependent upon leadership. Today's Air Force leaders can do no
better than to study the post–World War II Army Air Forces leadership. The
leaders who founded the Air Force were men of perspective, clear thinkers, and
direct in crafting their objectives. They were in a real sense visionaries and,
above all, true to themselves.

Appendices

Appendix 1

A Study to Determine the Minimum Air Power the United States should have at the Conclusion of the War in Europe*
April 1943

1. *Statement of Problem:*

   "Prepare a secret study very definitely arriving at the minimum air power this country should have in being when an armistice is signed."

   Discussion:

2. *The Armistice.* Neither the present world conflict, nor United States participation therein, will likely be concluded by a single armistice. Japan is not so related to the European Axis that the defeat of either may be expected to force, or induce, the immediate capitulation of the other. And it is entirely possible that an armistice between the United Nations and one or more of the Axis satellite nations may precede, for a substantial period of time, the collapse of German resistance. The United Nations strategy is directed toward a defeat of the European Axis and Japan in the order named. This paper will therefore attempt to reach a logically supported conclusion as to what the strength of the United States Air Forces should be when *Germany* signs an armistice. That point will probably mark the peak of our requirements.

3. *Criteria.* Military forces are justified only as necessary means of implementing national policies for the accomplishment of national objectives. A determination of the desired ultimate strength of our air arm therefore hinges upon a discovery and appreciation of our national objectives related in point of time to (1) the signing of the German armistice, and (2) the immediately succeeding period of treaty conferences, and European postwar readjustments. The latter will probably proceed concurrently with the final phase of the war with Japan, unless unforeseen developments alter our present overall strategic program.

4. *Reference to Tab "A".* In Tab "A" are gathered pertinent extracts from authoritative utterances of the President and Secretary of State, and senatorial comment, relative to our national objectives, the accomplishment of which will be involved at the time of the armistice terminating the war in Europe, and during the formulation of treaties governing postwar reorganization.

---

*Operational Plans Division, Air Staff, Extract.

5. Our National Objectives. On the basis of such official statements as those quoted in Tab "A", our national objectives, after the defeat of our enemies, appear to include:

(a) Avoidance of chaos in Europe.

(b) Restoration of sovereign rights and self-government to those who have been forcibly deprived of them.

(c) Establishment of Western Hemisphere solidarity, and security, under United States leadership.

(d) Insurance of permanent world peace, and a stabilized world economy; to be achieved by use of an international military force.

(e) Accomplishment of an orderly transition of the industrial organization of the United States, and of the world, from a wartime to a peacetime basis. This process should be initiated to the extent necessary to absorb surplus war production and military personnel (if any), concurrently with the prosecution of the final phase of the war in Asia.

6. *Probable Situation in Europe (National Objectives "(a)" and "(b).").* Conditions are ripe for unprecedented chaos to sweep over Axis occupied Europe (centering in Germany) upon the collapse of the German military power. Unless Great Britain and the United States are in position to join her in doing so, Russia may have sufficient provocation to alone occupy and assume control of not only all of Germany, but all of Central and Eastern Europe now under Axis domination. Therefore she might be disposed to amend her recently announced intentions as to territorial expansion. We do not know by what national policies or objectives she may be guided. She has not taken us into her confidence. Having been afforded the least possible information as to her current operations, her present capabilities or her future plans, we have no assurance that she will even participate in our peace negotiations with the Axis powers—in which negotiations the United Nations (with or without Russian cooperation) will doubtless invite the Axis conquered states to participate.

7. *To win the Peace.* To implement its policies, and lend convincing force to its arguments, the United States should be in the strongest practicable military position at the time of the armistice with Germany, and during the period of treaty negotiations. The strength and mobility of our armed forces (relative to those of our allies) with which we are in position to immediately support our views expressed at the peace table, will have much to do with the reception which those views receive. A record of past industrial usefulness (measured by contributions of weapons and supplies) will entitle us to the kindly consideration of our allies, but will no more command attention to our points of view than it has currently won the confidence of Russia. As between the Allied Nations the weight of our counsel will depend upon:

(1) Our current military strength.

(2) The extent to which we have contributed, by combat, to the victory.

(3) The extent to which we at the time share in the military control of areas lately under Axis domination, or key bases for future military control of the world, the disposition of which will be under consideration.

(4) Our probable future economic usefulness.

8. *Control of Controversial Areas.* Russia will likely have borne the brunt of land warfare, will have suffered most, and geographically conquered most. She may have a huge army in central Europe. British Empire ground forces will probably predominate in the army of occupation of Western Europe. Our preoccupation in the Pacific will prevent our supporting a large land army in Europe, or dispersed in North African or Mediterranean areas. With available shipping, we can support a substantial air force in Atlantic, European, North African and Mediterranean areas. An air force, with limited ground security forces, can, like artillery, but with vastly greater range, control large areas without fully occupying them. Its capabilities for massing heavy concentrations of fire, and the range of its threat, will depend upon its strength in heavy bombardment units.

9. *U.S. Air Arm Requirements in Europe and Adjacent Areas.* For the reasons above indicated, the United States should plan not only to conduct the major air offensive operations which will contribute to the ultimate defeat of the European Axis, but should be prepared, at the time of the German armistice, to furnish the major portion of the air component of the armed forces of the United Nations which will occupy or patrol and control, during the peace negotiations, all of presently Axis dominated Europe, and critical adjacent areas. Its air arm should be characterized by a preponderance of heavy bombardment, with adequate range. By preponderant offensive air strength we should offset the preponderant ground forces of Russia and England in position to influence the situation in Europe. For the purpose of minimizing her own bloodletting, Germany may, toward the end, do what she can to favor a conquest and occupation from the West.

10. *Requirements in Western Hemisphere.* In support of our policy for Western Hemisphere solidarity and security it will be desirable that during the period of European peace negotiations the United States, as leader of the Western Hemisphere group of nations, be in possession of and controlling by mobile air forces, as many key island bases as practicable in the Atlantic and Caribbean areas.

11. *To Support Our International Security Force Policy.* If and when an international military force is established, we must be in position to immediately contribute substantially to manning and equipping it; since the extent of our influence in its management and control will probably be in direct proportion to our military investment therein. To be effective, within reasonable bounds as to aggregate strength, it must be highly mobile. To be highly mobile it must be predominantly an air force, with sufficient surface forces to provide local security and logistic support for international bases, and to temporarily garrison recalcitrant areas. Its principal offensive weapon will be the heavy bomber, of medium (present "long range") and long range. At the outset it is believed desirable that

we be in position to provide approximately 50% of the aggregate air component of the international force for Europe and the Western Hemisphere; and to proceed, meanwhile, with operations for the defeat of Japan, with less than equal participation by Great Britain and her dominions. There is no assurance, or present indication, of Russian participation against Japan. If she does participate voluntarily, it will probably be only when Japan is near the point of collapse, or it appears that we and our allies will, unless assisted, be forced to withdraw from the field, short of victory, leaving Japan so powerfully entrenched as to be in position to dominate Eastern Asia. Our air forces required for the purposes stated in paragraphs 6 to 10, inc., above, should become available to serve our purposes in the establishment of an international armed force; first in the Western Hemisphere and Europe—in Asia and the Pacific after our defeat of Japan.

12. To Facilitate Establishment of Post War Air Commerce. In the control of the world trade, following this World War, air transportation will supplement, and to a substantial degree compete with, merchant shipping. It has been the traditional policy of the United States to provide American transportation for the distribution of American industrial products and surplus commodities throughout the world. Lately a policy to emphasize interAmerican trade has been indicated. For these purposes, immediately following the defeat of Germany, the United States will desire to rapidly expand its commercial air transport services, throughout the Western Hemisphere and to Europe and Africa, and to increase its military transport services to the Far East and Pacific Areas. To this end no means is more appropriate than having, at the conclusion of the European war, a large air force, particularly strong in long range bombardment and air transport equipment. Suitably trained pilots, navigators, maintenance, communications and administrative personnel will be available for gradual absorption in commercial activities; also surplus military airplanes suitable for conversion to commercial cargo and transport aircraft. Manufacturing plants not required to provide replacements in the Pacific will be suitably equipped and experienced to support the rapidly expanding air lines.

13. Limiting Factors. Factors limiting the ultimate strength of our air arm are our resources in manpower and raw materials, our plant production capabilities, and the extent to which these may be directed to the support of our air forces without encroaching upon the other requirements of the United States and her allies essential to the successful prosecution of the war and to the maintenance of national economic and social stability. All these factors have been taken into account in developing our present airplane production program. This program, for which our national industry is already geared, is expected to reach its peak at or shortly following the end of 1943, with a capacity to supply to our Air Arm approximately 135,000 airplanes annually. In view of the foregoing discussion, it is believed that it would be unwise and economically unsound to decrease this production program.

14. *Present Air Production Program Should Not be Reduced.* Decisive superiority over our enemies in the air, and a powerful air offensive against vital targets in the heart of Axisoccupied Europe, and the Japanese Empire, successively, afford the most apparent, and for the United States certainly the most practicable, means of winning the war (both wars), at minimum cost in human life, time, and natural resources. These means must of course be used in connection with naval action for which we are rapidly becoming equipped. and land operations by such ground forces as we will be able to transport to and logistically support in the critical theaters. For economy in total expenditure of our national resources, our armed forces, particularly our air arm, should be brought to ultimate strength as early as practicable—not later than 1945. A reduction of our present aircraft production program is therefore not warranted. The remaining paragraphs are to the effect that no increase in the production program is required.

15. *Air Strengths of Allies.* Taking into consideration the present production program of each of the nations involved, airplanes received from other sources, airplanes expected to be allocated to allies, and attrition expected on the basis of accumulated experience, there has been compiled in the office of Statistical Control, of the Air Staff, estimates of the comparative air arm strengths of each of the principal allies of the United States as of the end of each year, 1943 to 1946 inclusive, assuming that the war will continue that long both in Europe and in the Pacific. These estimates are shown in Tab "B".

16. *Japanese Air Strength.* Data with reference to Axis and Japanese air strength are shown in Tab "C".

17. *Desired Air Arm Strength.* On the basis of the entire foregoing discussion, with particular reference to the probable strengths of the air arms of our allies, it is believed that at the time of conclusion of the war in Europe, the strength of the air arm of the armed forces of the United States should be substantially as hereunder indicated, and that this strength should be reached in 1944, or as soon thereafter as practicable:

Desired Ultimate Strength of the Air Arm of the U.S. in Tactical Type Airplanes

Airplane Type	*Number*
Bombers, Heavy (B–17 and B–24 or equivalent) and Very Long Range	6,000
Bombers, Medium, Light, Dive and Torpedo	4,000
Fighters	7,000
Troop Carriers	1,500
Cargo-Transports	7,500
Total Tactical Unit Initial Issue Strength	26,000
For Operational Reserve, "Pipe Line" Requirements, Modification Center and Depot Repair "Back Log"	13,000
For Combat Crew Training Establishments	6,000
Aggregate	45,000

18. *Comparison of Allied Nations Air Forces.* A comparison of the desired strength of the air arm of the United States, with the strengths of the air arms of its principal allies predicted as of December 31. 1945, appears in Tab "D". It is believed that an increased tempo of offensive operations, and an increased rate of attrition, will likely produce a leveling off of the air strengths of our allies, as well as our own, not later than the end of 1945.

19. *Naval Air Strength Not Involved.* Neither in Tab "D", nor elsewhere in this paper, is there taken into consideration the requirements of our Navy for carrier-borne or such other aircraft as it may need to support its surface forces, in the performance of the Navy's mission. It is believed best to leave a discussion of such needs to appropriate Naval authorities.

20. *The 273 Group Program.* The Army Air Forces "273 Group Program" has been fitted into our present war production program, and is well under way toward accomplishment with completely trained and equipped units in 1944. Its unit equipment implications are shown in Tab "E". Given some augmentation of group strength, and an appropriate operational reserve of combat aircraft, the "273 Group Program" can absorb the entire tactical air strength indicated in paragraph 17 (above) to be desired. The extent, if any, to which this strength can not be built up and maintained by our aircraft production program without curtailment of the minimum needs of the Navy for its own air coverage, may be met by reduction of the operational, pipe line and depot reserves to a figure lower than the desired 50% minimum.

21. *Post-Armistice Deployment of Air Arm.* It is believed that 50% to 60% of the projected strength of the principal air arm of the United States would be sufficient, at and after the conclusion of the war in Europe, for the control of key bases in the Western Hemisphere, and to represent the United States in the combined United Nations armies of occupation to control hostile, turbulent, controversial and key areas in Europe, Africa and the Mediterranean region, during the period of the armistice. The remaining 40% to 50% would be adequate, in cooperation with our land and naval forces then available, to complete the defeat of Japan.

22. *Lend-Lease Allocations.* The estimates shown in Tab "D" contemplate a continuation of lend-lease allocation on substantially the present scale. From U.S. aircraft production in 1943 we are allocating to our allies 18,146 airplanes, of which 12,450 are combat types. (See Tab "F" for further detail.) Under this program, Great Britain, after fully utilizing her personnel resources for air force expansion, has been enabled to build up and maintain a greater percentage of reserve combat aircraft than we have as yet even planned. Russia is receiving a very substantial flow of combat aircraft of types suitable for the close support of her heavily engaged ground forces. Under present conditions China has not the facilities or organization to produce an effective Air Force of substantial strength. It is believed that we should retain for our own use our heavy bomber and sub-

stantially all our air transport production; and that we should not at this time commit ourselves to any material increase in lendlease allocations of any types. Some increase of our allocation of air support type airplanes to Russia and China should be anticipated if and when actual increase in our production has made it clear that it can be done without detriment to our own air forces program.

23. *Conclusion and Recommendation:*

That the United States should have in being when an armistice is signed signifying the defeat of Germany, a principal air arm of the strength of approximately 45,000 tactical airplanes, with a relative composition by types, as indicated in paragraph 17, above.

s/O. A. ANDERSON
Brig. General, U.S.A.
Asst. Chief of the Air Staff, Operational Plans

Appendix 2

War Department Basic Plan
for the Post-War Military Establishment*
March 29, 1945

Introduction

A. *Purpose of this plan.* The War Department Basic Plan is designed to furnish such general plans, policies and concepts relating to the postwar military establishment as are essential to permit further and more detailed planning. In final form the completed plan will furnish a comprehensive presentation of the character of the contemplated postwar military establishment. The War Department Basic Plan will be followed by the plans of the Army Air, Ground and Service Forces. When the latter plans are approved, they will be combined with the War Department Basic Plan to form the War Department Plan for the Post-War Army.

B. *Use.* Implementation of this War Department Basic Plan will mean significant changes from the pre-war military establishment, with resulting changes in existing laws and regulations. Also, unless such legislation is secured, the Army will revert to its pre-war organization generally. Consequently, it will be assumed that such alterations of or additions to present legislation and regulations as may be necessary to carry into the peacetime establishment the general structure of the existing establishment and to implement this plan will be secured. However, while this War Department Basic Plan will be used for all post-war planning, care must be exercised that no commitment. either actual or implied, is made to an individual or group except by express authority of the War Department. Legislation which will be necessary to implement planning is under study by appropriate staff agencies.

C. *Definition of Post-War Military Establishment.* The post-war military establishment is that organization which will be in existence when the Armed Forces of the United States return to a full peacetime status. In keeping with the foregoing, the post-war military establishment is designed to meet the requirements of peacetime, including preparation for future possible emergencies. It is not designed to meet the requirements of the transition period from war to peace.

---

*Extract.

THE STRUGGLE FOR AIR FORCE INDEPENDENCE

Part I

Section I—General Concepts

1. The security of the United States requires the establishment and maintenance of adequate military forces. "Adequacy" must depend basically upon the nature of the postwar world which will result from the present conflict. The exact form of international organization, and the specific international commitments which may be entered into by the United States following the present conflict cannot be anticipated in detail at this time. It may be assumed, however, that the conclusion of peace will require an American military establishment capable of:

    a. Maintaining the security of the continental United States during the initial phases of mobilization;

    b. Supporting such international obligations as the United States may assume;

    c. Holding strategic bases to ensure our use of vital sea and air routes;

    d. Expanding rapidly through partial to complete mobilization.

2. *Basis of Composition of Post-War Military Establishment.* National tradition and the demands of economy unite to require that the post-war military establishment conform to that type of military institution through which the national manpower can be developed, based upon the conception of a professional peace establishment (no larger than necessary to meet normal peacetime requirements), to be reinforced in time of emergency by organized units drawn from a citizen Army Reserve, effectively organized for this purpose in time of peace; with full opportunity for competent citizen soldiers to acquire practical experience through temporary active service and to rise by successive steps to any rank for which they can definitely qualify; and with specific facilities for such practical experience, qualification and advancement definitely organized as essential and predominating characteristics of the peace establishment.

3. The Congress will authorize and direct the employment of the entire naval and military forces of the United States and the resources of the government to carry on war against an enemy government; and to bring the conflict to a successful termination, the Congress will pledge all of the resources of the country. In this connection, the War Department will support a Universal Military Training Act in order to establish the principle that every able-bodied American is subject to military training and in order to provide a reservoir of trained Reserves.

Section II—Basic Principles and Assumptions

1. *Post-War Relationship Among the Principal Nations.* For planning purposes it may be assumed that the following relationship will exist among the principal nations:*

    a. An international organization for the maintenance of world-wide peace and security and for regulation of armament is in full and effective operation.

    b. Such international organization to be controlled by major powers, one of these being the United States.

    c. Other nations to contribute to such organization to the extent found necessary and/or desirable by the major powers.

    d. Control of the sea and air throughout the world to be a primary responsibility of the major powers, each power having primary control in its own strategic areas.

    e. Total power of such world organization to be adequate to ensure peace against any potential aggressor, including one of the major powers.

    f. The strategic area over which the United States is to exercise primary control will be as covered in J.C.S. 570/2 and succeeding documents. Control of the rest of the world is to be divided between other major powers.

2. *Nature of the Next War.* For purposes of planning, it will be assumed that for the next war, the actual attack will be launched upon the United States without any declaration of war; that the attack will represent an all out effort on the part of the enemy; that the war will develop into a total war; that the United States will be the initial objective of aggressors in such a war and will have no major allies for at least 18 months. However, it will be further assumed that the United States will have recognizance of the possibility of war for at least one year, and during this year preparatory measures will be inaugurated.

3. *Universal Military Training.* It is assumed for purposes of planning that the Congress will enact, (as the essential foundation of an effective national military organization), that every able-bodied young American shall be trained to defend his country; and that for a reasonable period after his training, (unless he volunteers for service in the regular establishments of the Armed Forces), he shall be incorporated in a reserve, all of any necessary part of which shall be subject to active military duty in the event of an emergency requiring reinforcement of the Regular Army. (See para. 3.a.(4) below)

    a. The Army and Navy have agreed to a set of principles in the following terms to be applied in connection with a program of Universal Military Training:

---

*In this connection, the time of transition to the post-war military establishment will be assumed to be contingent upon these relationships being firmly established.

General Principles

(1) Every citizen owes to his country the duty to defend it.

(2) Because of the scope and speed of modern war, defense of the United States will require a reserve of young men trained in military practices. In the considered judgment of the Army and Navy an adequate reserve can be created only by adoption of universal training for all able-bodied male citizens.

(3) The Army and Navy assume that the peacetime professional Army and Navy will be no larger than necessary to discharge peacetime responsibilities. Therefore, in emergencies. they must be reinforced promptly by previously trained civilian reserves.

(4) Young men should enter universal military training for training only. During their training they should not be an integral part of the Armed Forces. Neither should they be available for combat or other operational requirements which may arise during peace. After their prescribed training they should not be subject to call for service or for further training except during a national emergency expressly declared by Congress.

Principles Governing Training

(5) Training should be truly universal. It should be applied impartially so that no young man capable of contributing to the nation's defense will be exempt, except for bona fide religious scruples.

(6) This training should occur in youth. The age most favorable for military training is from 17 to 20 years. In determining when an individual begins his training, consideration should be given to his educational status. (For example, young men who will be graduated in the 18 and 19-year age groups should start military training on the first induction date following graduation. High school and preparatory school graduates in the 17-year age group should be accepted for training only if they volunteer and have their parental consent. Trainees who have not entered a preparatory or high school upon reaching 18 years should start their training on the first induction date after they reach 18.)

(7) Registration, examination and selection of trainees should be administered by civilian agencies. After induction the program should be administered by the military and naval services.

(8) The program should be undertaken solely to provide adequate military training and should not be diluted by training for other purposes.

(9) Training should be for one continuous year. This is the minimum time required to develop the skills demanded of fighting men in modern warfare.

(10) Men eligible for training in the Armed Services should, within quota limitations, receive training in the Service of their choice. Otherwise, trainees should be allotted to the Army and Navy, (including Marine Corps), in proportion to the approved strength of these Services.

(11) Standards governing acceptance of trainees should be the same for both the Army and Navy.

(12) Qualified young men may enlist in the Regular Army, Navy and Marine Corps and in the Coast Guard either before or during training. Trainees completing the prescribed year of training may apply for further training leading to promotion in all grades to and including a commission in the Armed Services or their Reserves. After completing the prescribed year of training, each trainee should become a member of the Army's Enlisted Reserve Corps or the U. S. Naval Reserve remaining in this status for five years but being subject to call only as outlined in par. 4.a.(4) above. In lieu of these five years in a special reserve, trainee might voluntarily enroll in the National Guard, the Organized Naval or Marine Corps Reserve, or the Regular Army, Navy or Coast Guard.

4. *Basic Composition of Post-War Military Establishment*. The post-war military establishment will consist of the Regular establishment, one-year trainees, the National Guard of the United States. and the Organized Reserve Corps. All components of the establishment will be liable for entry into the Army of the United States and for overseas service upon the declaration of an emergency.

5. *Peacetime Industrial Organization for an Emergency*.

a. *Research and Development:* An adequate program of military scientific research and development in the post-war period will be of large importance to the future military security of this nation and must form an integral part of the broad plans for the post-war military establishments of the Armed Forces. There must be an intimate relationship between the Armed Services and industry, university laboratories and general government laboratories.

b. *General Materiel Mobilization Scheme*. The general materiel mobilization plan of the post-war military establishment must be designed to meet the anticipated demands of the next war. The following requirements and assumptions are furnished therefore and for planning purposes:

(1) The next war will be a "total" war.

(2) Preparation for materiel mobilization for the next emergency will require retention in pilot production, or in standby reserve, of such government-owned facilities and equipment for the production of

non-commercial items as may be necessary to provide for continued development of techniques and for the availability of adequate production capacity to ensure future military security.

(3) Detailed plans will be developed and revised from time to time by the War Department agencies concerned to integrate private industry with the materiel mobilization scheme for the next emergency. Close liaison of research and development programs will be required and experimental and development contracts issued.

(4) The War Department War Reserve is to consist of those items of military supply and equipment of commercial and non-commercial types which are essential to equip, supply and maintain the armed forces either in training or in active operations, and which cannot be obtained from normal civilian industry or from government-owned manufacturing facilities of all types of sufficient quantities upon mobilization and during the period required for industry to make sufficient deliveries. Equipment will be maintained in the hands of permanent forces and in war reserve so that a total of 4,500,000 men can be mobilized effectively within one year following M–day.

6. *Time Factors.*

a. *Initiation of Post-War Military Establishment.*

(1) Three years will be the duration of the period between the defeat of Japan and the return of United States to a full peacetime status. Personnel and materiel provision for the post-war military establishment will be planned accordingly.

b. *Length of Next Emergency.* It is assumed for planning purposes that the next war will be of five years duration.

c. *Rate of Expansion from Post-War Military Establishment to Emergency Establishment.* The prescribed expansion of the Army of the United States by activation of its then authorized Reserves subsequent to M–day in any future emergency will be assumed to occur over a period of one year in equal monthly increments.

7. *Targets of Expansion for Next Emergency.*

a. *Personnel.* It shall be assumed that following Mday the personnel of the active military establishment will be capable of rapid expansion to 4,500,000 trained and equipped troops.

b. *Industrial.* It shall be assumed that the maximum required annual rate of production in the next war will be equivalent to the rate of production in the year 1943.

Section III—Missions

General Statement

The post-war military establishment must be prepared at all times to protect the vital interest of the United States by successful implementation of national policies with such Armed Forces as may be required. Specifically, it must prepare to carry out the national will for the first year of a major war.

1. *Combat*

a. *Offensive.* The post-war military establishment must be capable both of assuming the strategic and tactical offensive in time to prevent any sustained attack on our vital bases and lines of communication, thereby shielding completion of the full military and industrial mobilization of the country, and of subsequently maintaining that offensive.

b. *Defensive.* In conjunction with assuming the offensive, the post-war military establishment must be prepared at all times to protect outlying bases, lines of communication and the continental United States against any sustained and unpredicted attack.

c. The post-war military establishment must be capable of complementing the efforts of our Naval Forces in upholding the interest of the United States by carrying the war to the enemy for a conclusive victory in a minimum of time.

2. *Training.* In conformity with the combat mission, the training doctrine of the postwar military establishment must stress, both in the immediate and in the long-run employment of forces, preparation to assume the offensive at the earliest possible moment and maintain it to final victory.

Section IV—General Deployment

1. *Overseas Forces.* The peacetime military establishment will be organized to provide overseas forces at peace strength. These forces will be composed of Regular enlisted personnel. A proportion of the officer personnel may consist of Reserves on temporary active duty. In an emergency, overseas forces will be brought to war strength as required by movement of fillers.

2. *Home Forces.* These forces will be composed of:

a. Administrative, supply, development and instructional overhead not assigned to units, composed of Regular personnel reinforced as necessary and practicable by Reserve officers on temporary active duty. A proportion of officer candidates on temporary active duty may be included.

(1) *Air Forces.* For planning purposes, it will be assumed that the permanent Air Forces will be organized administratively into a headquarters and such Air Forces, Commands and other elements as may be provided within the established troop ceiling.

(2) *Ground Forces.* For planning purposes it will be assumed that the permanent Ground Forces will be organized administratively into a

headquarters and such Army Corps headquarters and separate Commands as may be provided within the established troop ceiling.

(3) *Service Forces.* For planning purposes it will be assumed that the permanent Service Forces will be organized administratively to support the requirements of the Ground and Air Forces.

b. *Strategic Reserves, (immediate action force).* During the transition stage from war to peace or peace to war, the maintenance of strategic reserves in the United States will be desirable. For this purpose, Regular officers and non-commissioned officers at cadre strength will be provided for in the permanent establishment. Normally, there will be at least a few mobile tactical units available for reinforcement of overseas forces or other emergency uses.

c. *Training Forces.* Each unit in the training forces will consist of an overhead, (administrative, supply and instructional), and the trainees. Each unit will be maintained at war strength plus one cadre. Regular personnel will be limited to cadre strength and reinforced as necessary by Reserve officers, officer candidates, and Reserve noncommissioned officers on temporary active duty. Where "on-the-job" training is indicated, it may be conducted within regularly constituted units within the United States; this will apply even though such units are earmarked for overseas deployment.

Appendix 3

Report of the
Joint Chiefs of Staff
Special Committee for
Reorganization of National Defense*
April 1945

Statement of the Problem

1. To recommend the best practicable organization of the Armed Forces of the United States for their most effective employment in time of war and their most efficient preparation for war, in time of peace.

Facts Bearing on the Problem

2. This problem has been a matter of grave concern since World War I. During this period a number of bills to effect some major reorganization of our Armed Forces have been considered by Congressional committees and more than twenty-six departmental studies have been submitted, all without any comprehensive result. The Select Committee of the House of Representatives on Post-War Military Policy is now actively concerned with this problem and looks to the War and Navy Departments for a solution. The Joint Chiefs of Staff Special Committee has studied this problem for ten months. It has visited the major commands in the field and obtained their views.

Summary of Conclusions

3. The Special Committee, excepting the senior Naval member, is unanimously in favor of a single department system of organization of the Armed Forces of the United States. This view is supported by Generals of the Army MacArthur and Eisenhower, Fleet Admiral Nimitz, Admiral Halsey, a substantial number of other commanders in the field, and many officers in Washington.

4. After carefully weighing many conflicting considerations, the Special Committee agreed upon the organization shown in the attached Chart, Enclosure "A."

---

*Extract.

The organization proposed is along the lines upon which the independent colonies were united into a federal union. Strong differences of opinion will exist with respect to details of the organization. Therefore, the Special Committee, in the analysis of the proposed organization, Enclosure "B," discusses alternative solutions of specific issues and the reasons for its conclusions in each case. The Special Committee urges that the proposed organization be viewed as a whole and that its basic principle be approved regardless of differences of opinion of individual provisions.

5. The Special Committee adopted certain basic agreements, as set forth in Enclosure "B." It believes that the inclusion of these agreements in the proposed legislation will clarify the position of aviation, and of the Marine Corps, and will secure the support of the services of this legislation.

6. Before the expiration of the war powers of the President, there must be a thorough statutory internal reorganization of both the War and Navy Departments in order to retain the improvements effected by executive orders and administrative action. Almost without exception, the "witnesses voiced deep concern lest, through inaction, we revert to the departmental organizations and to the inter-service relationships that existed before Pearl Harbor." The Special Committee believes that any further organizational changes made in either department prior to the enactment of legislation should be designed to facilitate the creation of a single department.

7. The Special Committee believes that enabling legislation for the creation of a single department should be enacted without delay and that overall reorganization should be effected by direction of the President not later than six months after the end of the war.

8. The Special Committee believes that a council composed of representatives of the Department of the Armed Forces and Department of State should be established, as set forth in Enclosure "B," in order to correlate national policies and military preparedness.

Recommendations

9. The Special Committee recommends:

a. That the single department system of organization of the Armed Forces, as shown in Enclosure "A," be adopted, and that the preparation of the enabling legislation for presentation to the Congress be undertaken under the general direction of the Special Committee.

b. That this legislation include the Special Committee's agreements with respect to the position of aviation, and the Marine Corps, set forth in Enclosure "B."

c. That any further organizational changes made in either department, prior to the enactment of legislation, have in view the creation of a single department.

d. That the council described in Paragraph 8 above be created.

s/M. F. SCHOEFFEL
Rear Admiral, U.S. Navy
Member

s/H. L. GEORGE
Major General, U.S. Army
Member

s/W. F. TOMPKINS
Major General, U.S. Army
Member

s/F. TRUBEE DAVISON
Colonel, AUS
Alternate

The dissenting views of Admiral J. O. Richards n are attached hereto marked Minority Report.

s/J. O. RICHARDSON
Admiral, U S Navy (Ret.)
Senior Member

Joint Chiefs of Staff
Special Committee for
Reorganization of National Defense

Minority Report of
Admiral J. O. Richardson, U.S. Navy (Ret.)

1. I do not concur in the recommendations contained on page two of this report.

2. After considerable objective study, and after careful consideration of the views of many officers, I am convinced that it is not now in the best interests of the Nation to adopt a single department system of organization of the Armed Forces.

3. If those in authority decide to establish a single department system I can at this time, conceive of no better plan than that proposed by the Special Committee. It is theoretically better than any yet proposed, but from a practical point of view it is unacceptable.

4. Among the considerations which have led me to dissent, the following are briefly noted:

In General

a. The present organization of the War and the Navy Department are the result of over one hundred and fifty years experience. Existing organizations of such magnitude should be changed only as a result of the most indisputable evidence that the proposed change is desirable and will accomplish the ends sought. I believe that the two department system under the Joint Chiefs of Staff, with the addition of a Joint Secretaryship, will provide a satisfactory organization of the Armed Forces in the foreseeable future.

b. The lessons of this war must be thoroughly digested before they can be applied properly to postwar organization. Some of these lessons are now well understood; others are only indicated; many are yet to be learned.

c. At the present, the nature and size of our post-war Armed Forces required to preserve the peace and prepare for war is not known. It is too early to design an organization to meet the needs of the post-war Armed Forces whose characteristics are so indistinct.

d. At the termination of the war the Army and Navy will be faced with tremendous problems of demobilization. It would be unwise at that time to undertake major reorganization. I believe that the present organization is best suited to demobilize successfully and to deploy our forces to meet the needs of the postwar world order.

e. Many of the officers whose opinions should be of most value in seeking a solution to this problem stated that they were so fully occupied in the prosecution of the war that they had been unable to give the subject the study which its importance merited.

Regarding the Single Department.

f. I am not convinced as to the validity of many reasons advanced to support the thesis that there should be a single department. For example, I do not agree that the effectiveness of the effort of the forces in the field depends upon the existence of a single department in Washington.

g. Many proponents of the single department system assert that if a single department is not created, then the only solution is to create a three department system. This might be true if it were necessary to create a coordinate Air Force.

h. Because the interests and activities of the Army and Navy are so divergent, so great in magnitude, and so distinct in mission, I believe that a single department system would inevitably hamper the full and free development of each.

Regarding the Form of the Single Department Proposed.

i. I believe it unwise to give power proposed herein to one Secretary and one Commander of the Armed Forces. Aside from the difficulty in finding men capable of discharging those vast duties acceptably, there is real danger that one component will be seriously affected by the decisions of one man to the detriment of the effectiveness of the Armed Forces as a whole.

j. I am far from convinced that there will be an increase in the effectiveness or the economy of the Armed Forces by the adoption of this proposal. The components are granted such autonomy as is consistent with teamwork. This is vague and may result in three separate services being farther apart than are the Army and Navy today; especially in the field of logistics.

k. I am not convinced that an Air Force should be set up on a basis coordinate with the Army and Navy. Proponents of this idea assert that this is necessary for full development of air power. Naval air power has developed within the Navy. I fear that the creation of an Air Force on a basis coordinate with the Army and Navy would inevitably draw the Naval Aeronautical Organization out of the fabric of the Navy into which it is now intimately woven. Such disintegration of the Navy would be prejudicial to the effectiveness of the Armed Forces as a whole.

l. I foresee practical difficulties in the functioning of the Staff of the Commander of the Armed Forces. The Commander will desire a staff which, in his judgment, will best assist him in discharging his duties. Throughout the years, the Army and Navy have differed fundamentally on the composition and duties of major staffs. Initially, at least, the staff which would be suitable for a Naval officer in command of the Armed Forces could not be expected to be acceptable to an Army officer in the same capacity. Thus, when the Commander drawn from one component is succeeded by a Commander drawn from another, the successor will be forced either to carry on with an unfamiliar staff organization or upset the whole department by reorganizing his staff.

m. I would expect the staff to be very large and inevitably operate three components. This would surely develop if one or more of the components had, in being, a force capable of conducting operations while the other component, due to the lack of such a force, was primarily concerned with education and planning.

n. The Commander and his staff will be required to resolve with the Under Secretary and his Office so many problems concerning the military aspects of business matters that they may be fully occupied with material things to the prejudice of their higher responsibilities of thinking and planning on the highest level. The same will be largely true with respect to the Commanders of the three components.

o. In time, the Office of the Under Secretary will either be the master rather than the servant of the Armed Forces, or become impotent. If the former, each component will lose control of its logistic support and be unable to demand and receive munitions of war it deems best for its own peculiar needs. If the latter, a major claimed advantage for the single department will disappear.

5. I propose, instead of reorganization of the Armed Forces,

a. That the present Joint Chiefs of Staff organization be continued after the war by statute.

b. That the reorganizational gains of the War and Navy Departments made possible by Executive Order and administrative action be continued after the war by statute.

c. That study of reorganization of the Armed Forces be continued in the light of our war experiences.

That the advisability of establishing a Joint Secretaryship in the present organization be fully explored.

s/J. O. RICHARDSON
Admiral, U S. Navy (Ret)

Enclosure "B"
Joint Chiefs of Staff Special Committee for
Reorganization of National Defense*

Section I
Introduction

Studies Since World War I.

101. The problem of overall reorganization of the armed forces has been of concern for many years. Since World War I, numerous bills which would either merge the War and Navy Departments or create a separate Air Force have been introduced in Congress and considered by Congressional committees. During that time no less than twenty-six Departmental reorganization studies have been made. Not one of these bills or studies has produced comprehensive results.

Congressional Activity.

102. The Congress is again actively concerned with this problem and looks to the military profession for definite proposals. Unless an acceptable solution is developed by the Armed Services, Congress may take the initiative and adopt its own. Bills for reorganization were introduced in the present Congress before it had been in session for one month.

103. In April and May of 1944 the House of Representatives Select Committee on Post-War Military Policy, under the chairmanship of Representative Woodrum, held hearings on a proposal to establish a single Department of the Armed Forces. Senior officers and officials of the War and Navy Departments testified. In general, the Army witnesses favored the establishment of a single Department of the Armed Forces. Practically every Navy witness either definitely expressed the view or conveyed the impression that his mind was not made up; that the matter should be seriously studied; that the lessons of the war largely remained to be learned, and that no decisions should be reached until the views of the commanders in the field had been considered. The Woodrum Committee was in accord with the almost unanimous view of the witnesses that no comprehensive or revolutionary changes should be made at that critical period in the war. In its report, (House Report No. 1645, 78th Congress, 2nd Session) it commented favorably upon the action of the Joint Chiefs of Staff in establishing this Special Committee to study and make recommendations concerning the reorganization of national defense.

---

*Extract.

THE STRUGGLE FOR AIR FORCE INDEPENDENCE

The Situation.

104. *At the outset of the war* the Army and Navy were far apart in their thinking and planning. Initial operations were conducted on a basis of cooperation. Because each knew so little of the capabilities and limitations of the other, adequate mutual understanding which is so essential to unity of effort was lacking to an alarming degree. Moreover, the War and Navy Departments were organized along cumbersome and inefficient lines which hindered rather than facilitated cooperation. It became evident immediately that radical reorganization, both in Washington and in the field was necessary. Fortunately. the broad war powers granted the President by Congress permitted immediate action. The Joint Chiefs of Staff came into being as an agency to direct the broader phases of the conduct of the war. The War and Navy Departments were substantially reorganized by Executive Orders. The principle of unity of command in the field was adopted and supreme commanders were appointed in the combat area; but this did not produce complete integration of effort within theaters of operations.

105. *During the progress of the war* great strides have been made in bringing the services closer together. Within the framework of Executive Orders, improvements continue in departmental organization; and, under the Joint Chiefs of Staff our armies, air forces, and fleets have vastly improved in effectiveness. The broad strategy of the war and the logistic support of our Armed Forces are now sufficiently effective for the successful prosecution of the war. Great progress has been made toward satisfactory relationships between the civilian parts of our government and the Armed Forces. And, most important of all, and because war has compelled it, the services are beginning to understand each other and as a team. This enforced teamwork, in operations on a scale hitherto not attempted, has convinced them that no service is sufficient in itself. They know that success results from the effective integration of the efforts of land, sea, and air forces.

106. *At the end of three years of war* the Special Committee has observed that even in areas where unity of command has been established, complete integration of effort has not yet been achieved because we are still struggling with inconsistencies, lack of understanding, jealousies and duplications which exist in all theaters of operations. That these handicaps have been overcome in any degree is due to the stature of our leaders at home and abroad. It is not to be expected that any reorganization will automatically cure the defects which continue to hamper the Army and Navy. The first step is to set up that form of organization whose framework is such as to be most conducive to the development of complete integration of effort. Then there must follow joint education and training of the Armed Forces aimed to develop in all ranks and ratings a knowledge and understanding of the capabilities and limitations of each other, without which no form of organization can be effective. Without exception all officers heard placed great emphasis on this point.

War Powers.

107. The major changes in the organizations of the War and Navy Departments since December 1941 were made under the war powers of the President. Those powers lapse six months after the war. Unless comprehensive statutory changes are made before those powers lapse, the Departments will revert to their pre-war organizational status and the services will lose the gains in efficiency and cooperation which these changes made possible. Almost without exception. the witnesses voiced deep concern lest, through inaction, we revert to the departmental organizations and to the interservice relationships that existed before Pearl Harbor.

Joint Chiefs of Staff Directives

108. Pertinent parts of the Joint Chiefs of Staff directive to the Special Committee as contained in paragraph 12 of J.C.S. 749/7 are quoted below for convenience:

"12 *b.* That a Special Committee consisting of two officers of the Navy and two officers of the Army be constituted to make a detailed study and recommendations to the Joint Chiefs of Staff as to the most efficient practicable organization of those parts of the executive branch of our government which are primarily concerned with national defense. . . .

"c. That the Committee, in carrying out the above directive be guided by the concept that the basic organization must be designed primarily to insure the efficiency and overall integration of effort of the land, sea and air forces; secondly, to obtain effective integration of land-sea, land-air, and sea-air combinations of forces; and thirdly, to provide land, sea, and air forces, each organized, manned and equipped to perform most effectively its part as an essential component of the overall military organization.

"d. That in its studies the Committee include a thorough examination of the relative advantages, disadvantages, and practicability of the following basic systems of organization:

(1) Two departments—War and Navy.

(2) Three departments—War, Navy, Air.

(3) One Department of War (or of Defense).

"e. That particular emphasis be placed on eliminating unwarranted duplications.

"f. That conclusions reached on a theoretical basis can be adjusted to practical considerations, as may appear necessary.

"g. That in any plan involving a change. consideration be given to a period of transition in which the Joint Chiefs of Staff in so far as practicable, would be in a position to guide the development from the present to the new military organization.

"*k*. That in its final recommendations, it will indicate what legislation if any is considered necessary, together with particular comment on the practicability of supporting such legislation on the basis of efficiency and economy."

Agreements

109. In order to establish workable points of departure the Special Committee agreed upon the following fundamentals which would be applicable in the consideration of a Single Department System of organization:

First; there shall be maintained as an integral part of the Navy an aeronautical organization commensurate with its needs, including requisite numbers and types of aircraft.

Second; there shall be maintained as an integral part of the Navy the Marine Corps, including the Fleet Marine Force.

Third; there shall be maintained as an integral part of the Army such specialized aviation as forms an integral and essential part of its ground forces.

Fourth; there shall be maintained as the United States Air Force, coordinate with the Army and the Navy, that part of the aeronautical organization of the Armed Forces of the United States which does not form an integral part of the Army or of the Navy.

110. These agreements are basic in that they fix the position of aviation and of the Marine Corps in accordance with the beliefs of the Special Committee as to their proper roles in the organization of the Armed Forces. As the lessons of the war are more fully digested, as teamwork is more completely realized, as technological development progresses, modification of these agreements may be advisable. In order to settle these questions which have been the subject of controversy for years, it is deemed essential that these agreements be incorporated in the enabling legislation for reorganization, with the proviso that during the ten years subsequent to the enactment of the legislation, the United States Chiefs of Staff by unanimous action may modify these agreements with the approval of the President. The legislation should permit modification of the agreements thereafter by the Commander of the Armed Forces, with the approval of the Secretary of the Armed Forces.

Appendix 4

Minority Report of AAF Member of Special War Department Committee on the Permanent Military Establishment (Bessell Committee)
28 Nov 45

1. Plans for the composition and deployment of the 203,600 man regular Air Force have been furnished the Special War Department Committee on the Permanent Military Establishment under directive from the Committee. However, it is desired to emphasize that the Army Air Forces does not in any sense concur with the concept that limits the AAF to the figures shown therein. Submitted at this time are the considered recommendations of the Army Air Forces for the minimum size Air Force that will, in conjunction with other components of the armed forces, provide national security for the United States during the foreseeable future.

2. At this time, after the second major war in this century and the costliest ever suffered by this nation, it is desperately necessary that we lay well-conceived plans for a military security force that will effectively guarantee the peace and safety of the U.S. It is with this in view that these proposals are submitted. In these, the first and governing consideration has been the national security; the next consideration has been the national economy and minimum interference with civil life.

3. Each attempt of the Army Air Forces to portray its strength requirements for accomplishment of its post-war mission has been met with an artificial allocation in the neighborhood of 200,000 personnel, considerably lower than the minimum considered adequate. It is the belief of the AAF that insufficient time has elapsed since the initiation of the Army Forces Voluntary Recruitment Act of 1945 to determine definitely the capabilities of voluntary recruitment and it is held entirely possible that further exploration in this field may show a larger yield forthcoming. While the AAF agrees that an Army of greater size will certainly increase the share of the Federal Budget normally allotted to national defense, it nevertheless feels that the nation, given the awareness of the real threat to its security, will approve and find the means to meet such a threat. This headquarters at least would feel remiss in its duty if it failed because of arbitrary estimates in budgetary terms to make realistic plans. And to be realistic these plans

must envision accurately the character of future warfare. V–1 and V–2 type missiles, atomic power, and 5,000 mile bombers—in enemy hands—would leave us no time for even miraculous manpower and materiel mobilizations.

4. Even under the broad assumptions of the report, a standing regular Air Force of 203,600 is inadequate to meet its first responsibility, namely, to meet aggression with immediate destruction of the aggressor's vitals. The destructiveness of strategic air warfare which transcends front lines with conventional or atomic explosives is a matter of minutes and hours rather than weeks and months. The assumption of superior intelligence in the report is not based upon a practical assurance, nor does it provide the actual will to build up the Air Force in time, even though the assumed Universal Military Training may provide part of the air crews within a few months of the initial warning.

5. Reference is made to the attached chart (Appendix D) which indicates the lapse of time of some two to four years between decision to expand and effective application of air units in combat (expressed in bomb tonnage). It is reiterated that a sudden strike against the U.S. requires immediate action by an Air Force in being. A year's warning does not provide means for building up the tiny Air Force allocated in this study to an Air Force effective against any major power or combination of major powers. With Universal Military Training we would be assured of obtaining in time the enlisted specialists only.

6. Two years of planning in the Air Staff have resulted in the firm conviction that the 70-Group Air Force (which, excluding overhead for training civilian components, has been squeezed into a 400,000 tentative Troop Basis) is the bedrock minimum with which the Air Force can accomplish its peacetime mission. This mission includes the following factors:

a. Need for a ready striking force to operate immediately anywhere in the world, and capable of sufficient sustained effort to protect mobilization at home.

b. Need for overseas bases with intermediate fields and flight services to provide mobility for our forces and denial of an enemy to our vital routes and to our homeland.

c. For a minimum sized thoroughly trained force of first line combat units to provide development of new equipment and techniques, and to maintain the ability of the aircraft industry to rapidly improve, modify, and expand.

d. Need for a sufficient number of units to give reserve personnel, especially air crews, experience in operating units at home and overseas to enable rapid reinforcement in an emergency. The output of military pilots, who must have operating experience in combat units before going into the Reserve, must be balanced with the output of Universal Military Training.

7. In connection with the factor pertaining to overseas bases, it is noted that the Committee Report does not differentiate between air and other types on a "caretaking status." Air bases die on the vine if not used by aircraft. When used, even on a caretaking status, they involve more than a few plumbers, electricians,

and guards. They involve additional personnel and equipment for airdrome maintenance, communications, navigational aids, crash fire fighting, and fuel servicing. In addition, whether these bases are maintained operationally as recommended herein, or on a caretaking status, their advanced location makes them more vulnerable to destruction than their allocation of defensive antiaircraft by the Committee Report would seem to indicate. To justify their yearbyyear expense it is to be expected that these bases should withstand the first blow and permit our immediate employment. Therefore, regardless of whether antiaircraft remains as part of the AGF or is integrated with the AAF it is recommended that antiaircraft allotments to advanced bases be further strengthened in consonance with their vulnerability.

8. Reduction of Air Force strength from the recommended 400,000 to 203,600 means largely a reduction of the striking force of the Air Forces. Certain fixed functions of an Air Force having global responsibilities cannot be reduced in manpower requirements proportionate to the reduction in total strength. It should be noted that reduction of air striking forces below 70 groups in effect denies the units necessary to maintain the base facilities required for and essential to the national interest. Also, stripping the Air Force of the units needed for its mission will be an admission that this country must rely for security in the air on the Naval Air Forces, which is a more expensive and less effective way of attacking the problem of air security.

9. Therefore, the AAF Member of the Committee recommends:

a. That portions of the interim plan contained in Inclosure A as pertain to the Army Air Forces be disapproved for War Department planning purposes and that it not be furnished the Army and Army Air Forces members of the Joint agencies charged with preparation for the President of a comprehensive plan for the peacetime establishment of the Armed Forces of the United States.

b. That the AAF plan for the permanent military establishment attached hereto be approved for War Department planning purposes and that it be furnished the Army and Army Air Forces members of the Joint agencies charged with the preparation for the consideration of the President of the comprehensive plan for the peacetime establishment of the Armed Forces of the United States.

s/G. C. JAMISON
Brigadier General, USA
AAF Member, Special War Department
Committee on Permanent Military
Establishment

Appendix 5

War Department
The Adjutant General's Office
Washington 25, D.C.

AG 322 (21 Mar 46)
OB–I –AFCOR–(971 (d))–M

SUBJECT: Establishment of Air Defense, Strategic Air and Tactical Air Commands; Redesignation of the Headquarters, Continental Air Forces and Certain Other Army Air Forces Units; Activation, Inactivation and Assignment of Certain Army Air Forces Units.

TO: Commanding Generals,
        Army Air Forces
        Continental Air Forces

   1. Letter, this office, AG 322 (11 Mar 46) OD–I–AFOOR–(930(d))–M, 13 March 1946, subject as above, is revoked. (Distribution withheld).

   2. Effective this date:

     a. The following Commands are established under the Commanding General, Army Air Forces:

       Strategic Air Command
       Tactical Air Command
       Air Defense Command

     b. The Headquarters, Continental Air Forces is redesignated as the Headquarters, Strategic Air Command, with station at Bolling Field, Washington, D.C. This Headquarters will move from its present station to Andrews Field, Maryland, on or about 1 July 1946, as directed by the Commanding General, Army Air Forces.

     c. The Headquarters, Tactical Air Command is constituted, assigned to the Army Air Forces and will be activated at Tampa, Florida, on or before 31 March 1946.

       (1) The Commanding General, Tactical Air Command is authorized to designate, organize and discontinue Army Air Forces Base Units within the block of numbers 300 to 399, inclusive, and within the bulk allotment of personnel authorized his command.

d. The Headquarters, Air Defense Command is constituted. assigned to the Army Air Forces and will be activated at Mitchel Field, New York, on or before 31 March 1946.

(1) The Commanding General, Air Defense Command is authorized to designate, organize and discontinue Army Air Forces Base Units within the block of numbers 100 to 199, inclusive, and within the bulk allotment of personnel authorized his command.

e. Personnel will be authorized in accordance with bulk allotment of personnel as published in Army Air Forces letters of the 150-series.

f. Administrative and housekeeping equipment is authorized in accordance with T/A 201, as amended.

g. The Headquarters, Ninth Air Force is assigned to the Tactical Air Command and will be activated by the Commanding General thereof at Biggs Field, El Paso, Texas, on or before 31 March 1946.

(1) Personnel for manning the Headquarters, Ninth Air Force will be furnished from the bulk allotment of personnel authorized the Tactical Air Command and as directed by the Commanding General thereof.

(2) Administrative and housekeeping equipment is authorized in accordance with T/A 201, as amended.

h. The Headquarters, Fifteenth Air Force is assigned to the Strategic Air Command and will be activated by the Commanding General thereof, at Colorado Springs, Colorado, on or before March 1946.

(1) Personnel for manning the Headquarters, Fifteenth Air Force will be furnished from the bulk allotment of personnel authorized the Strategic Air Command, and as directed by the Commanding General thereof.

(2) Administrative and housekeeping equipment is authorized in accordance with T/A 201, as amended.

3. Effective this date:

a. The Headquarters, Second Air Force is relieved from its present assignment, assigned without change of station to the Strategic Air Command, and will be inactivated by the Commanding General thereof on or before 31 March 1946. Concurrently with its inactivation, this unit is assigned in an inactive status to the Air Defense Command.

(1) Personnel and equipment will be utilized to the fullest extent practicable in manning and equipping the Headquarters, Fifteenth Air Force.

(2) Records of the inactivated unit will be disposed of and reported in accordance with provisions of AR 15-15, 20 September 1945 and TM 12-259.

b. The Headquarters and Headquarters Squadron, XIX Tactical Air Command is relieved from its present assignment, assigned without change of station to the Tactical Air Command, and will be inactivated by the Commanding General thereof on or before 31 March 1946.

(1) Personnel and equipment will be utilized to the fullest extent practicable in manning and equipping the Headquarters, Ninth Air Force.

(2) Records of the inactivated unit will be disposed of and reported in accordance with provisions of AR 1515, dated 20 September 1945, and TM 12259.

c. The Headquarters, Third Air Force is relieved from its present assignment and assigned to the Tactical Air Command, and will be transferred, less personnel and equipment, from its present station to the Greenville Army Air Base, Greenville, South Carolina, on or before 31 March 1946, as directed by the Commanding General, Tactical Air Command.

(1) Personnel for remanning the Headquarters Third Air Force will be furnished from the bulk allotment of personnel authorized the Tactical Air Command and as directed by the Commanding General thereof.

(2) Administrative and housekeeping equipment is authorized in accordance with T/A 201, as amended.

d. The Headquarters and Headquarters Squadron, IX Troop Carrier Command is relieved from its present assignment, assigned to the Tactical Air Command without change of station, and will be inactivated by the Commanding General thereof on or before 31 March 1946

(1) Personnel and equipment will be utilized to the fullest extent practicable in remanning and reequipping the Headquarters Third Air Force.

(2) Records of the inactivated unit will be disposed of and reported in accordance with provisions of AR 1515, 20 September 1945, and TM 12259.

4. Effective this date:

a. The following units are relieved from the control of the War Department and assigned in an inactive status to the Commands indicated below:

Unit	Command
Hq & Hq Sq, Tenth Air Force	Air Defense Command
Hq & Hq Sq, Twelfth Air Force	Tactical Air Command
Hq & Hq Sq, Fourteenth Air Force	Air Defense Command
Hq & Hq Sq, 53d Troop Carrier Wing	Tactical Air Command (for further assignment to Third Air Force)

b. The following units are relieved from their present assignments and assigned without change of station to the Commands indicated below:

Unit	Command
Hq, First Air Force	Air Defense Command
Hq, Fourth Air Force	Air Defense Command

c. The units listed in the attached inclosure are relieved from their present assignments and assigned to the Tactical Air Command without change of station:

(1) The current group assignments of the units listed in inclosure 1 are not affected by this action.

d. All units currently assigned to the Continental Air Forces and not specifically assigned by this letter are assigned to the Strategic Air Command without change of station.

5. The funds of the Continental Air Forces will be assumed by the Strategic Air Command until suitable distribution between the Air Defense Command, Tactical Air Command and the Strategic Air Command can be provided under the provisions of AAF Letter 3025, 4 August 1945.

6. Twenty (20) copies of the order issued pursuant to this letter will be forwarded to the Commanding General, Army Air Forces (Attention: Publication Division, Air Adjutant General); *in addition* to the distribution directed in paragraph 17c, AR 31050. No other distribution will be made to offices of Headquarters, Army Air Forces.

7. When the actions directed herein have been accomplished a report will be submitted to this office by letter and copies furnished the Service Commander concerned.

8. Obligate the appropriate allotment published in Section III, Circular No 178, War Department, 1945, as amended, to the extent necessary.

BY ORDER OF THE SECRETARY OF WAR:

> /s/ Edward F. Witsell
> Major General
> The Adjutant General

Appendix 6

War Department Office of the Chief of Staff
Washington 25, D.C.

4 April 1946

MEMORANDUM FOR: PRESIDENT, BOARD OF OFFICERS ON ORGANI-
ZATION OF THE WAR DEPARTMENT (LIEUT.
GENERAL W. H SIMPSON)
CHIEFS OF WAR DEPARTMENT GENERAL
AND SPECIAL STAFF DIVISIONS
COMMANDING GENERAL, ARMY AIR
FORCES
COMMANDING GENERAL, ARMY GROUND
FORCES
COMMANDING GENERAL, ARMY SERVICE
FORCES
CHIEFS OF ALL ADMINISTRATIVE AND TECH-
NICAL SERVICES.

SUBJECT: Statement of Approved Policies to Effect Increased Autonomy of the
Army Air Forces within the War Department Structure.

1. The following approved policies, designed to effect increased autonomy for
the Army Air Forces within the structure of the War Department, in accordance
with the recommendations of the Simpson Board Report, are published for the
information and guidance of all concerned. They will be implemented to the fullest degree possible, beginning with the effective date of the reorganization of the
War Department contemplated in that report.

2. *Representation on War Department Staffs.*

a. The Commanding General, Army Air Forces, will nominate approximately 50 per cent of the members of War Department General and Special Staff
Divisions from Army Air Forces personnel. This goal will be reached as soon as
practicable. The officers nominated will be qualified to perform the duties of the
Division for which nominated, and will be acceptable to the Director or Chief
thereof.

b. Army Air Forces officers may be detailed to duty in the offices of Chiefs of Technical and Administrative Services as desired by the Commanding General, Army Air Forces, and by arrangement with the Chiefs of these Services in each instance.

c. It is to be emphasized that the War Department, including the General Staff, Special Staff and the Technical and Administrative Staffs and Services, should be looked upon as neither "Ground" nor "Air" but as an overall agency which controls and serves both. All officers on duty with these staffs should deal with broad functions at the War Department level, rather than with the interests of a particular force or branch.

3. *Allocation of Service Troops.*

a. The War Department recognizes the interests of the Army Air Forces in that part of the War Department troop basis now indicated as Army Service Forces and Army-wide activities.

b. As functions now performed by the Army Service Forces are transferred to the Army Air Forces, a proper proportion of personnel performing these functions will also be transferred to the Army Air Forces troop basis.

c. The determination of functions and troops to be transferred will be worked out over a period of time by the War Department, with full consideration being given to the needs of the Army Air Forces.

d. In making such adjustment, the general principle will be followed that services which are required with the field armies or the Air Forces are included in the Ground Force and Air Force portion of the troop basis respectively, and that those elements which perform functions in support of both ground and Air will be provided in a separate War Department section of the troop basis. *It is the Chief of Staff's conviction that both now and in the future, the Army Air Forces should have only those amounts of ordinary technical and administrative services needed for actual servicing of troops; hospital systems, ports, etc., to be run by the Army.*

4. *Supply of Officers of The Technical and Administrative Services.*

a. While the Army Air Forces remain within the War Department, and under the ceiling on commissioned personnel and methods of commissioning by branch imposed by existing law, considerations of avoidance of duplications and economy in personnel dictate that the bulk of administrative and technical officer personnel continue to be furnished to the Army Air Forces by the Technical and Administrative Services.

b. It is recognized that when the Army Air Forces become completely autonomous, they will require a quota, to be later determined, of Technical and Administrative Officers who will be permanent members of the autonomous Air Forces.

Additional increments of Regular Officers which may in the future be authorized by Congress will include a proportion, to be later determined, of promotion list technical and administrative officers commissioned in the Air Corps, to provide in part for eventual complete autonomy. Also, at such time as complete autonomy is achieved, it will be proper and necessary to transfer an appropriate proportion of the officers of the Technical and Administrative Services of the Army to the autonomous Army Air Forces.

During the present period of preparation of the Army Air Forces for autonomy, the transfers of individual nonrated officers of the promotion-list services to the Air Corps, as mutually agreed upon by the Commanding General, Army Air Forces, the Chiefs of Technical and Administrative Services and the individual officers concerned, will, in general, continue to be approved.

c. During the present period, officers of the Technical and Administrative Services assigned to duty in the Army Air Forces will continue to be under the command of the Commanding General, Army Air Forces. The Chiefs of Technical and Administrative Services will continue to be responsible for the long range career planning of these officers over the entire period of their commissioned service. In order that their schooling and proper rotation of duties may be provided for, they will be returned to the control of the Chiefs of Services from time to time, in accordance with policies to be determined by the War Department.

5. *Representation on Technical Committees.* The Commanding General, Army Air Forces, is authorized membership on the Technical Committees of the Technical Services in such numbers as he deems necessary to represent the interests of the Army Air Forces.

6. *Command Communication System.*

a. The Chief Signal Officer of the Army under the direction of the Chief of Staff and the General Staff is responsible for the installation, maintenance and operation of a single domestic and overseas integrated military communications system known as the Army Command and Administration Network. The size of this system will be based on military traffic requirements and individual circuits will be allocated to the using services for control and use as required. Where established facilities to meet specific emergency operational requirements do not exist, the Chief Signal Officer, upon the recommendation of the Communications Advisory Board, may authorize the installation, operation and maintenance of additional facilities by the agencies having primary interest. The Chief Signal Officer is responsible for the movement of all command and administrative traffic over this system except the movement of such traffic over allocated facilities which is a responsibility of the using service.

The Communications Advisory Board to the Chief Signal Officer will consist of the Chief, Army Communications Service and the Air Communications Officer of the Army Air Forces.

In the interest of economy, the Chief Signal Officer, upon the recommendation of the Communications Advisory Board, will delegate to the Commanding General, Army Air Forces, responsibility for the operation of any designated system station.

The installation, maintenance and operation of the Army Airways Communication System will be the responsibility of the Commanding General, Army Air Forces. Traffic handled over this system will be operational and weather traffic pertaining to the movement of aircraft and such administrative traffic as is authorized by the Chief Signal Officer upon the recommendation of the Communications Advisory Board. Such administrative traffic originating on the Army Airways Communication System will be routed into the Army Command Administrative network at designated gateways.

b. The provisions of Circular 388, War Department, 1944, in respect to communications, will remain in effect. All questions involving the application of the provisions of this Circular on the lease of communications services not covered therein will be resolved by the Chief Signal Officer upon the recommendation of the Communications Advisory Board.

c. There will be one contracting agency for the War Department for obtaining commercial communications services. The Chief Signal Officer has already been designated this function and will apply this authority in accordance with Circular 388, War Department, 1944, and recommendations of the Communications Advisory Board.

d. Based on the requirements as stated by the Commanding General, Army Air Forces, the Chief Signal Officer will be responsible for the defense of all funds and for the procurement of all common items of communications equipment.

e. All funds for the procurement of communications services for the Army Air Forces will be obtained and obligated by the Chief Signal Officer based on requirements submitted by the Commanding General, Army Air Forces.

f. Pertinent Army Regulations and War Department Circulars will be reviewed by the Army Air Forces and Signal Corps and amended to reflect the above approved principles.

7. *Determination of Items of Communications and Radar Equipment Peculiar to the Army Air Forces.* War Department Circular 429, dated 3 November 1944, will be the general guide in determining communication and radar equipment peculiar to the Army Air Forces. The application of the general principles set up in this circular to specific items will be decided by the Director of Service, Supply and Procurement, after consultation with the Commanding General, Army Air Forces, and the Chief Signal Officer.

8. *Responsibilities of the Army Air Forces in Connection with Anti-Aircraft Artillery.*

a. The Commanding General. Army Ground Forces, is charged with the development and determination of the tactics of antiaircraft artillery when employed by the Ground Forces.

b. The Commanding General. Army Ground Forces, in cooperation with the Commanding General, Army Air Forces, is charged with the development and determination of special tactics as are necessary for antiaircraft artillery when employed by the Air Forces.

c. The Commanding General, Army Ground Forces, in cooperation with the Commanding General, Army Air Forces, is charged with the development and determination of the technique of fire at aerial targets, with prescribing military characteristics of weapons and equipment, and with the preparation of tables of organization and equipment for units of antiaircraft artillery.

The Army Ground Forces will continue the assignment of three battalions of antiaircraft artillery for employment at Army Air Forces Schools, so long as the troop basis continues to make this assignment possible.

9. *Responsibilities of the Army Air Forces in Connection with Research and Development.*

a. The Army Air Forces are responsible for the conduct of research and development of aeronautical materials, associated equipment, accessories and supplies procured by the AAF, and of such other materials as may be allocated to the AAF for research and development.

b. The Army Air Forces will conduct all experimental, static and flight tests necessary to the development of such material.

10. *Responsibility of the Army Air Forces in Connection with Supply and Procurement.* The Army Air Forces are responsible for:

a. Determination of qualitative and quantitative requirements of items peculiar to the Army Air Forces and items assigned to the Army Air Forces for procurement, and for recommendations or requirements for common items.

b. Procurement of all items peculiar to the Army Air Forces or which are assigned to the Army Air Forces for procurement.

c. Storage, and distribution to all Army Air Forces units, facilities and personnel of AAF procured material, and such other items as are assigned by the War Department to the Army Air Forces for storage, maintenance and issue.

d. Preparation of all Army Air Forces logistical planning factors.

11. *Responsibility of Army Air Forces in Connection with Repairs and Utilities Functions.*

a. Repair and maintenance of Army Air Forces real property and the operation of the Army Air Forces utilities is a command responsibility of the Commanding General, Army Air Forces.

b. As a Technical Staff Officer of the War Department, the Chief of Engineers is responsible for:

(1) Preparation and submission to the Director of Service, Supply and Procurement, for the latter's approval and publication, or uniform technical procedures, policies and standards of Army-wide application for the performance of

repair and utility functions. Such action will be coordinated with the Major Commands concerned prior to publication.

(2) The conduct of technical inspections on the War Department level to assure that prescribed standards, procedures and policies are being followed.

(3) Prescription of Army-wide cost and accounting methods, the review of estimates and rendering of technical advice thereon.

c. The Chief of Engineers will make available to the Commanding General, Army Air Forces, qualified officers of the Corps of Engineers for the performance of repair of utilities duties, subject to their availability in the Corps of Engineers, and subject to their being requested by the Commanding General, Army Air Forces.

12. *Responsibilities of the Army Air Forces in Connection with Estimation, Defense and Control of Funds.* The Commanding General, Army Air Forces, will be responsible for the preparation of budget estimates for the appropriation "Air Corps, Army" and the justification of such estimates before the Budget Advisory Committee of the War Department and other appropriate agencies. Funds for the operation of the Army Air Forces and for the procurement of the items peculiar to the Air Forces will be allocated directly to Headquarters, Army Air Forces, by the Budget Officer for the War Department.

Activities at Army Air Forces installations, not peculiar to the Air Forces, but, which are under the Air Force's command jurisdiction, will be financed by an allocation of funds from the Budget Officer for the War Department to Headquarters, Army Air Forces. Requirements of funds for these activities will be included in the estimates of the various appropriate War Department appropriations. An example of this type of activity is: Repair and Utilities at Army Air Forces installations.

13. *Army Air Forces Responsibilities in Connection with Hospitalization, Evacuation and Care of the Sick and Wounded.*

a. The Commanding General, AAF has *command* responsibility for all medical installations and units of the AAF, and for all Medical personnel assigned to the AAF.

b. The Surgeon General, in his capacity as a Technical Staff Officer of the War Department, is Chief Medical Officer of the U.S. Army and Medical advisor to the Secretary of War, Chief of Staff, and War Department General and Special Staffs. As such he has primary responsibility for the formulation of Army-wide policies of hospitalization, evacuation, and care of the sick and wounded, which policies are reviewed. revised as necessary, and promulgated by appropriate General Staff Divisions.

Directions or instructions will habitually be issued to major subordinate commands under the War Department through the proper channels of command, and not directly from the Surgeon General to the corresponding Medical Staff Officer in a subordinate major command. However, the duties of the Surgeon

General, acting in his capacity as a Technical Staff Officer of the War Department, will include such technical supervision and inspections of Armywide medical activities as the Chief of Staff may prescribe.

In his capacity as a Chief of a Technical Service, the Surgeon General will command all General Hospitals. The Surgeon General performs these duties in the interests of the Army as a whole, and not in the interests of a particular force or branch (See pare 2c above).

c. (1) The Commanding General, Army Air Forces, will be responsible for the determination of the strength, organization, composition, equipment, and training of Medical Units assigned to the Army Air Forces. The Commanding General, Army Air Forces, will continue to exercise technical supervision and control over research and training in all matters that have to do with flying personnel.

(2) The Surgeon General will be responsible for all technical training of Medical Department personnel, including Flight Surgeons, except for training at the Flight Surgeon School which is the responsibility of the Commanding General, Army Air Forces.

d. Upon completion of the task of caring for overseas patients in general hospitals, it will again become possible to transfer Zone of the Interior patients from station hospitals to general hospitals. At that time, it is desired that regional hospitals be eliminated from the system of hospitalization. Accordingly, the regional hospital at Coral Gables, Florida, now operated by the Army Air Forces will be redesignated a general hospital, and this installation will be classified as an exempted station operating under the command of the Surgeon General. An adequate number of Flight Surgeons will be detailed to the staff of this hospital. This hospital will be considered a specialized hospital, particularly for the admission of Air Corps personnel requiring hospitalization and convalescent care incident to their tactical mission, as Fitzsimmons General Hospital at Denver, Colorado, is a specialized center for tubercular cases.

e. (1) The Surgeon General will have command responsibility to include responsibility for assignment and reassignment, for Medical personnel on duty in installations under command of the Surgeon General.

(2) Assignment to and relief from major forces or overseas commands of Medical officers will be the responsibility of the Central Officers Assignment Division, operating under the direction of the Director of Personnel and Administration, after coordination with the Major Commands. The primary interest of the Surgeon General in the overall career planning of Medical officers, including Flight Surgeons, will be recognized by the Director of Personnel and Administration, and Medical officers will be returned to the control of the Surgeon General as required by consideration bearing on the advancement of their professional education and experience. The peculiar requirements of the Army Air Forces with respect to Medical officers, including Flight Surgeons, will be recognized

by the Director of Personnel and Administration and the Surgeon General in all career planning affecting Medical personnel.

14. *Responsibilities of the Army Air Forces in Connection with Air Transport.*

a. The Army Air Forces are responsible for control and operation of all Air Transport and related facilities.

b. Determination of policies pertaining to movement and priorities of passengers and freight on transport aircraft of the ATC, and commercial transport aircraft in conformity with the overall transportation program prepared by the General Staff is a function of the War Department.

15. *Communications in the Field with Navy Commanders.* Direct communication between field commanders of the Army Air Forces and the Navy, as required on operational matters requiring coordinated action of both forces is authorized.

BY DIRECTION OF THE DEPUTY CHIEF OF STAFF:

/s/ H. I. HODES
Brigadier General, GSC
Assistant Deputy Chief of Staff

Appendix 7

Report to Chief of Staff, United States Army on Army and Air Force Organizational Matters Under Unification* March 14, 1947

(Report submitted by: Maj. Gen. William E. Hall, GSC; Maj. Gen. Hugh J. Knerr, USA; Maj. Gen. Charles L. Bolte, GSC; Brig. Gen. S. L. Scott, GSC.)

Why A Unification Measure is Necessary

World War II has been fought and won by the superior performance of our military forces. The superb home front support provided by labor, industry, agriculture—in fact, by every important element of our civilian life—was a glowing testimony to the vitality of democracy.

We hope never again to become involved in a great war. Should we be compelled to fight another war, we must enter that war well prepared to marshal our national resources promptly and effectively in our defense. We are engaged in considering the measures necessary to secure the peace and to provide most effectively for our national security. In order to plan wisely for our future security, we must measure our proposals against two standards:

What weaknesses revealed by World War II should be corrected?

What new dangers must we anticipate and guard against? It is no reflection upon the character or the ability of the men who directed the prosecution of the recent war to acknowledge that mistakes were made. Rather, it is evidence of their integrity that they should promptly call attention to those errors and propose corrective measures.

Defects in our security structure revealed by World War II were:

Our foreign policy and military policy were not always closely integrated.

There was no adequate machinery for the adjustment of our civilian economic life to meet the military requirements of total war.

---

*Extract.

When the war started, there was no adequate machinery for the mobilization of our material resources, productive capacity and manpower.

There were gaps in the translation of strategic plans into plans for material and personnel.

There were weaknesses in planning of material requirements and duplication in procurement both within and between the military departments.

The coordination and integration of military and other war budgets were not as thorough and detailed as desirable.

Coordination between the Army and Navy was inadequate. The first test of any plan for national security is the extent to which it applies the lessons of the past in the development and execution of corrective measures for the future. A plan which neglects this requirement is misconceived, and a plan which fails to fulfill this requirement must be judged inadequate. We must determine the answers to the following questions:

WHAT CHANGES IN THE PRESENT RELATIONSHIPS OF THE MILITARY SERVICES AND OTHER GOVERNMENT DEPARTMENTS HAS OUR WAR EXPERIENCE INDICATED AS DESIRABLE TO OUR NATIONAL SECURITY AND ELIMINATE THE DEFECTS OUT LINED ABOVE?

WHAT FORM OF ORGANIZATION SHOULD BE ESTABLISHED AND MAINTAINED TO ENABLE THE MILITARY SERVICES AND OTHER GOVERNMENT DEPARTMENTS AND AGENCIES EFFECTIVELY TO PROVIDE FOR AND PROTECT OUR NATIONAL SECURITY?

With reference to the first question: Experience in the last war has revealed serious weaknesses in our present organizational setup—weaknesses between and within the services, as well as in their relationships to other important elements concerned with our national security.

For the most part, they were defects of direction, control and coordination. Gaps between foreign and military policy—between the State Department and the Military Establishments. Gaps between strategic planning and its logistic implementation—between the Joint Chiefs of Staff and the military and civilian agencies responsible for industrial mobilization. Gaps between and within the military services—principally in the field of procurement and logistics. Gaps in information and intelligence—between the executive and legislative branches of our Government, between the several departments and between Government and the people. These gaps and defects of coordination were the result of inadequate direction and control below the level of the President.

We have concluded that these faults were also due to lack of appropriate and seasoned mechanisms and of adequate plans, policies, and procedures for coordination; lack of clear understanding and appreciation by one group or individual of the relation of others to the overall job. These ills are susceptible of cure and can be corrected by a unification measure which will provide control and direction at the Cabinet level.

The Bill proposes a form of military organization which we think is adapted to dealing with the problems that face us, viz, a unified control over a coordinate organization having three departments—Army, Navy, and Air Force—each headed by a civilian secretary and tied together by strong interorganizational links under the control and direction of a Secretary of Cabinet rank.

This form will, in our opinion, foster civilian and congressional influence and control over the military departments. It will favor sound and efficient balance in the development of each arm of the service; it will furnish a broader basis for considerations of military and foreign policy and will be more responsive to new developments in the scientific field.

In answer to the second question: The question of the form of organization of our military forces must be viewed in its proper perspective as only one part of a much larger picture encompassing many elements, military and civilian, governmental and private, which contribute to our national security and defense.

Our goal should be to bind them together in such a way as to achieve the most productive and harmonious whole. This calls for coordination as well as command; for parallel as well as subordinated effort. Where to use one and where to use the other are questions of balanced judgment and adjustment to be determined by the principles and traditions of our form of government, the lessons of experience and the basic policies and objectives to be achieved.

The necessity of integrating all these elements into an alert, smoothly working and efficient machine is more important now than ever before. Such integration is compelled by our present world commitments and risks, by the tremendously increased scope and tempo of modern warfare and by the epochal scientific discoveries culminating in the atomic bomb.

This involves organizational ties between the Department of State and the Military Establishment: ties between the military departments in strategy and logistics; ties between the Military Establishment and the agencies responsible for planning and carrying out mobilization of our industrial and human resources; between the gathering of information and intelligence and its dissemination and use; between scientific advances and their military application.

The next war will probably begin with little or no warning and will almost immediately achieve its maximum tempo of violence and destruction. Contrasting with the shortened opportunity for defensive preparation is the increased length of time necessary to prepare the complicated offensive and defensive weapons and organizational structure essential to modern warfare. The nation not fully prepared will be at a greater disadvantage than ever before.

The great need, therefore, is that we be prepared always and all along the line, not simply to defend ourselves after an attack but through all available political, military and economic means, to forestall any such attack. The knowledge that we are so prepared and alert will in itself be a great influence for world peace.

Much has been said about the importance of waging peace as well as war. The proposed organizational structure is adapted to both purposes.

In view of the critical state of affairs in the world today we cannot delay necessary measures required to put our house in order. There is a lot of hard work and much study needed to put our Armed Forces in condition to meet our responsibilities as a World power and, if necessary, to defend our way of life at a moment's notice.

A unification measure is a first step in the reorganization of the National Defense Establishment. It is a necessary step which will affect the safety of our country more than anything else short of abolishing war itself.

In support of the above a joint agreement has been reached between the War and Navy Departments and, although it is a compromise agreement, it is supported by each. Both Departments believe that the terms of the agreement are the best possible solution attainable at this time. Both Departments believe that the terms of the agreement, as expressed in the Bill, will work: that it will serve the best interests of the Nation and that it is a necessary measure for improving National Security.

Appendix 8

Executive Order 9877
Functions of the Armed Forces

By virtue of the authority vested in me by the Constitution and laws of the United States, and as President of the United States and Commander in Chief of the Armed Forces of the United States, I hereby prescribe the following assignment of primary functions and responsibilities to the three armed services.

Section I—The Common Missions of the Armed Forces of the United States are:

1. To support and defend the Constitution of the United States against all enemies, foreign or domestic.

2. To maintain, by timely and effective military action, the security of the United States, its possessions and areas vital to its interest.

3. To uphold and advance the national policies and interests of the United States.

4. To safeguard the internal security of the United States as directed by higher authority.

5. To conduct integrated operations on the land, on the sea, and in the air necessary for these purposes.

In order to facilitate the accomplishment of the foregoing missions the armed forces shall formulate integrated plans and make coordinated preparations. Each service shall observe the general principles and fulfill the specific functions outlined below, and shall make use of the personnel, equipment and facilities of the other services in all cases where economy and effectiveness will thereby be increased.

Section II—Functions of the United States Army

General

The United States Army includes land combat and service forces and such aviation and water transport as may be organic therein. It is organized, trained and equipped primarily for prompt and sustained combat incident to operations on land. The Army is responsible for the preparation of land forces necessary for the effective prosecution of war, and, in accordance with integrated joint mobilization plans, for the expansion of peacetime components of the Army to meet the needs of war.

The specific functions of the United States Army are:

    1. To organize, train and equip land forces for:

        a. Operations on land, including joint operations.

        b. The seizure or defense of land areas, including airborne and Joint amphibious operations.

        c. The occupation of land areas.

    2. To develop weapons, tactics, technique, organization and equipment of Army combat and service elements, coordinating with the Navy and the Air Force in all aspects of joint concern, including those which pertain to amphibious and airborne operations.

    3. To provide, as directed by proper authority, such missions and detachments for service in foreign countries as may be required to support the national policies and interests of the United States.

    4. To assist the Navy and Air Forces in the accomplishment of their missions, including the provision of common services and supplies as determined by proper authority.

Section III—Functions of the United States Navy

General

    The United States Navy includes naval combat and service forces, naval aviation, and the United States Marine Corps. It is organized, trained and equipped primarily for prompt and sustained combat at sea. The Navy is responsible for the preparation of naval forces necessary for the effective prosecution of war, and in accordance with integrated joint mobilization plans, for the expansion of the peacetime components of the Navy to meet the needs of war.

The specific functions of the United States Navy are:

    1. To organize, train and equip naval forces for:

        a. Operations at sea, including joint operations.

        b. The control of vital sea areas, the protection of vital sea lanes, and the suppression of enemy sea commerce.

        c. The support of occupation forces as required.

        d. The seizure of minor enemy shore positions capable of reduction by such landing forces as may be comprised within the fleet organization.

        e. Naval reconnaissance, antisubmarine warfare, and protection of shipping. The air aspects of those functions shall be coordinated with the Air Force, including the development and procurement of aircraft, and air installations located on shore, and use shall be made of Air Force personnel, equipment and facilities in all cases where economy and effectiveness will thereby be increased. Subject to the above provision, the Navy will not be restricted as to types of aircraft maintained and operated for these purposes.

f. The air transport necessary for essential internal administration and for air transport over routes of sole interest to naval forces where the requirements cannot be met by normal air transport facilities.

2. To develop weapons, tactics, technique, organization and equipment of naval combat and service elements, coordinating with the Army and the Air Force in all aspects of joint concern, including those which pertain to amphibious operations.

3. To provide, as directed by proper authority, such missions and detachments for service in foreign countries as may be required to support the national policies and interests of the United States.

4. To maintain the U.S. Marine Corps whose specific functions are:

a. To provide Marine Forces together with supporting air components, for service with the Fleet in the seizure or defense of advanced naval bases and for the conduct of limited land operations in connection therewith.

b. To develop, in coordination with the Army and the Air Force those phases of amphibious operations which pertain to the tactics, technique and equipment employed by landing forces.

c. To provide detachments and organizations for service on armed vessels of the Navy.

d. To provide security detachments for protection of naval property at naval stations and bases.

e. To provide, as directed by proper authority, such missions and detachments for service in foreign countries as may be required to support the national policies and interests of the United States.

5. To assist the Army and the Air Force in the accomplishment of their missions, including the provision of common services and supplies as determined by proper authority.

Section IV—Functions of the United States Air Force

General

The United States Air Force includes all military aviation forces, both combat and service, not otherwise specifically assigned. It is organized, trained, and equipped primarily for prompt and sustained air offensive and defensive operations. The Air Force is responsible for the preparation of the air forces necessary for the effective prosecution of war except as otherwise assigned and, in accordance with integrated joint mobilization plans, for the expansion of the peacetime components of the Air Force to meet the needs of war.

The specific functions of the United States Air Force are:

1. To organize, train and equip air forces for:

a. Air operations including joint operations.

b. Gaining and maintaining general air supremacy.

c. Establishing local air superiority where and as required.

d. The strategic air force of the United States and strategic air reconnaissance.

e. Air lift and support for airborne operations.

f. Air support to land forces and naval forces. including support of occupation forces.

g. Air transport for the armed forces, except as provided by the Navy in accordance with paragraph 1f of Section III.

2. To develop weapons, tactics, technique, organization and equipment of Air Force combat and service elements, coordinating with the Army and Navy on all aspects of joint concern, including those which pertain to amphibious and airborne operations.

3. To provide, as directed by proper authority, such missions and detachments for service in foreign countries as may be required to support the national policies and interests of the United States.

4. To provide the means for coordination of air defense among all services.

5. To assist the Army and Navy in accomplishment of their missions, including the provision of common services and supplies as determined by proper authority.

HARRY S. TRUMAN

The White House

July 26, 1947

Appendix 9

The National Security Act of 1947
(Public Law 253—80th Congress)
(Chapter 343—lst Session)
(S. 758)

An Act

To promote the national security by providing for a Secretary of Defense; for a National Military Establishment; for a Department of the Army, a Department of the Navy and a Department of the Air Force; and for the coordination of the activities of the National Military Establishment with other departments and agencies of the Government concerned with the national security.

BE IT ENACTED BY THE SENATE AND HOUSE OF REPRESENTATIVES OF THE UNITED STATES OF AMERICA IN CONGRESS ASSEMBLED.

SHORT TITLE

That this Act may be cited as the "National Security Act of 1947".

Table of Contents

Declaration of Policy

Sec. 2. In enacting this legislation, it is the intent of Congress to provide a comprehensive program for the future security of the United States, to provide for the establishment of integrated policies and procedures for the departments, agencies and functions of the Government relating to the national security; to provide three military departments for the operation and administration of the Army, the Navy (including naval aviation and the United States Marine Corps), and the Air Force, with their assigned combat and service components; to provide for their authoritative coordination and unified direction under civilian control but not to merge them; to provide for the effective strategic direction of the armed forces and for their operation under unified control and for their integration into an efficient team of land, naval, and air forces.

Title 1—Coordination For National Security

National Security Council

Sec. 101. (a) There is hereby established a council to be known as the National Security Council (hereinafter in this section referred to as the "Council").

The President of the United States shall preside over meetings of the Council: PROVIDED, That in his absence he may designate a member of the Council to preside in his place.

The function of the Council shall be to advise the President with respect to the integration of domestic, foreign, and military policies relating to the national security so as to enable the military services and the other departments and agencies of the Government to cooperate more effectively in matters involving the national security.

The Council shall be composed of the President; the Secretary of State, the Secretary of Defense, appointed under section 202; the Secretary of the Army, referred to in section 205; the Secretary of the Navy; the Secretary of the Air Force, appointed under section 207; the Chairman of the National Security Resources Board, appointed under section 103; and such of the following named officers as the President may designate from time to time: The Secretaries of the executive departments, the Chairman of the Munitions Board appointed under section 213, and the Chairman of the Research and Development Board appointed under section 214; but no such additional member shall be designated until the advice and consent of the Senate has been given to his appointment to the office the holding of which authorizes his designation as a member of the Council.

(b) In addition to performing such other functions as the President may direct, for the purpose of more effectively coordinating the policies and functions of the departments and agencies of the Government relating to the national security, it shall, subject to the direction of the President, be the duty of the Council—

(1) to assess and appraise the objectives, commitments, and risks of the United States in relation to our actual and potential military power in the interest of national security, for the purpose of making recommendations to the President in connection therewith; and

(2) to consider policies on matters of common interest to the departments and agencies of the Government concerned with the national security, and to make recommendations to the President in connection therewith.

(c) The Council shall have a staff to be headed by a civilian executive secretary who shall be appointed by the President, and who shall receive compensation at the rate of $10,000 a year. The executive secretary, subject to the direction of the Council, is hereby authorized, subject to the civil-service laws and the Classification Act of 1923, as amended, to appoint and fix the compensation of such personnel as may be necessary to perform such duties as may be prescribed by the Council in connection with the performance of its functions.

(d) The Council shall, from time to time, make such recommendations, and such other reports to the President as it deems appropriate or as the President may require.

Central Intelligence Agency

Sec. 102. (a) There is hereby established under the National Security Council a Central Intelligence Agency with a Director of Central Intelligence, who shall be the head thereof. The Director shall be appointed by the President, by and with the advice and consent of the Senate from among the commissioned officers of the armed services or from among individuals in civilian life. The Director shall receive compensation at the rate of $14,000 a year.

(b) (1) If a commissioned officer of the armed services is appointed as Director then—

(A) in the performance of his duties as Director, he shall be subject to no supervision, control, restriction, or prohibition (military or otherwise) other than would be operative with respect to him if he were a civilian in no way connected with the Department of the Army, the Department of the Navy, the Department of the Air Force, or the armed services or any component thereof; and

(B) he shall not possess or exercise any supervision, control powers, or functions (other than such as he possesses, or is authorized or directed to exercise, as Director) with respect to the armed services or any component thereof, the Department of the Army, the Department of the Navy, or the Department of the Air Force, or any branch, bureau, unit or division thereof, or with respect to any of the personnel (military or civilian) of any of the foregoing.

(2) Except as provided in paragraph (1), the appointment to the office of Director of a commissioned officer of the armed services, and his acceptance of and service in such office, shall in no way affect any status, office, rank, or grade he may occupy or hold in the armed services, or any emolument, perquisite, right, privilege, or benefit incident to or arising out of any such status, office, rank, or grade. Any such commissioned officer shall, while serving in the office of Director, receive the military pay and allowances (active or retired, as the case may be) payable to a commissioned officer of his grade and length of service and shall be paid, from any funds available to defray the expenses of the Agency, annual compensation at a rate equal to the amount by which $14,000 exceeds the amount of his annual military pay and allowances.

(c) Notwithstanding the provisions of section 6 of the Act of August 24, 1912 (37 Stat. 555), or the provisions of any other law, the Director of Central Intelligence may, in his discretion, terminate the employment of any officer or employee of the Agency whenever he shall deem such termination necessary or advisable in the interests of the United States, but such termination shall not affect the right of such officer or employee to seek or accept employment in any other department or agency of the Government if declared eligible for such employment by the United States Civil Service Commission.

(d) For the purpose of coordinating the intelligence activities of the several Government departments and agencies in the interest of national security, it shall be the duty of the Agency, under the direction of the National Security Council—

(1) to advise the National Security Council in matters concerning such intelligence activities of the Government departments and agencies as relate to the national security;

(2) to make recommendations to the National Security Council for the co-ordination of such intelligence activities of the departments and agencies of the Government as relate to the national security;

(3) to correlate and evaluate intelligence relating to the national security and provide for the appropriate dissemination of such intelligence within the Government using where appropriate existing agencies and facilities: PRO-VIDED, That the Agency shall have no police, subpoena, law-enforcement powers. or internal security functions: PROVIDED FURTHER, That the departments and other agencies of the Government shall continue to collect, evaluate, correlate, and disseminate departmental intelligence: AND PROVIDED FURTHER, That the Director of Central Intelligence shall be responsible for protecting intelligence sources and methods from unauthorized disclosure;

(4) to perform, for the benefit of the existing intelligence agencies, such additional services of common concern as the National Security Council determines can be more efficiently accomplished centrally;

(5) to perform such other functions and duties related to intelligence affecting the national security as the National Security Council may from time to time direct.

(e) To the extent recommended by the National Security Council and approved by the President, such intelligence of the departments and agencies of the Government, except as hereinafter provided, relating to the national security shall be open to the inspection of the Director of Central Intelligence, and such intelligence as relates to the national security and is possessed by such departments and other agencies of the Government, except as hereinafter provided, shall be made available to the Director of Central Intelligence for correlation, evaluation, and dissemination: PROVIDED, HOWEVER, That upon the written request of the Director of Central Intelligence, the Director of the Federal Bureau of shall make available to the Director of Central Intelligence such information for correlation, evaluation, and dissemination as may be essential to the national security.

(f) Effective when the Director first appointed under subsection (a) has taken office—

(1) the National Intelligence Authority (11 Fed. Reg. 1337, 1339, February 5, 1946) shall cease to exist; and

(2) the personnel, property and records of the Central Intelligence Group are transferred to the Central Intelligence Agency and such Group shall cease to exist. Any unexpected balances of appropriations. allocations or other funds available or authorized to be made available for such Group shall be available and shall be authorized to be made available in like manner for expenditure by the Agency.

National Security Resources Board

Sec. 103. (a) There is hereby established a National Security Resources Board (hereinafter in this section referred to as the "Board") to be composed of the Chairman of the Board and such heads or representatives of the various departments and independent agencies as may from time to time be designated by the President to be members of the Board. The Chairman of the Board shall be appointed from civilian life by the President, by and with the advice and consent of the Senate, and shall receive compensation at the rate of $14,000 a year.

(b) The Chairman of the Board, subject to the direction of the President, is authorized, subject to the civil-service laws and the Classification Act of 1923, as amended, to appoint and fix the compensation of such personnel as may be necessary to assist the Board in carrying out its functions.

(c) It shall be the function of the Board to advise the President concerning the coordination of military, industrial, and civilian mobilization, including—

(1) policies concerning industrial and civilian mobilization in order to assure the most effective mobilization and maximum utilization of the Nation's manpower in the event of war;

(2) programs for the effective use in time of war of the Nation's natural and industrial resources for military and civilian needs, for the maintenance and stabilization of the civilian economy in time of war, and for the adjustment of economy to war needs and conditions;

(3) policies for unifying, in time of war, the activities of Federal agencies and departments engaged in or concerned with production, procurement, distribution, or transportation of military or civilian supplies, materials, and products;

(4) the relationship between potential supplies of, and potential requirements for, manpower, resources, and productive facilities in time of war;

(5) policies for establishing adequate reserves of strategic and critical material, and for the conservation of these reserves;

(6) the strategic relocation of industries, services, government, and economic activities, the continuous operation of which is essential to the Nation's security.

(d) In performing its functions, the Board shall utilize to the maximum extent the facilities and resources of the departments and agencies of the Government.

Title II—The National Military Establishment

Establishment of the National Military Establishment
Sec. 201. (a) There is hereby established the National Military Establishment, and the Secretary of Defense shall be the head thereof.

(b) The National Military Establishment shall consist of the Department of the Army, the Department of the Navy, and the Department of the Air Force, together with all other agencies created under title II of this Act.

Secretary of Defense

Sec. 202. (a) There shall be a Secretary of Defense, who shall be appointed from civilian life by the President, by and with the advice and consent of the Senate: PROVIDED, That a person who has within ten years been on active duty as a commissioned officer in a Regular component of the armed services shall not be eligible for appointment as Secretary of Defense. The Secretary of Defense shall be the principal assistant to the President in all matters relating to the national security. Under the direction of the President and subject to the provisions of this Act he shall perform the following duties:

(1) Establish general policies and programs for the National Military Establishment and for all of the departments and agencies therein;

(2) Exercise general direction, authority, and control over such departments and agencies;

(3) Take appropriate steps to eliminate unnecessary duplication or overlapping in the fields of procurement, supply, transportation, storage, health, and research;

(4) Supervise and coordinate the preparation of the budget estimates of the departments and agencies comprising the National Military Establishment; formulate and determine the budget estimates for submittal to the Bureau of the Budget; and supervise the budget programs of such departments and agencies under the applicable appropriation Act: PROVIDED, That nothing herein contained shall prevent the Secretary of the Army, the Secretary of the Navy, or the Secretary of the Air Force from presenting to the President or to the Director of the Budget, after first so informing the Secretary of Defense, any report or recommendation relating to his department which he may deem necessary: and PROVIDED FURTHER, That the Department of the Army, the Department of the Navy, and the Department of the Air Force shall be administered as individual executive departments by their respective Secretaries and all powers and duties relating to such departments not specifically conferred upon the Secretary of Defense by this Act shall be retained by each of their respective Secretaries.

(b) The Secretary of Defense shall submit annual written reports to the President and the Congress covering expenditures, work, and accomplishments of the National Military Establishment, together with such recommendations as he shall deem appropriate.

(c) The Secretary of Defense shall cause a seal of office to be made for the National Military Establishment, of such design as the President shall approve, and judicial notice shall be taken thereof.

Military Assistants to the Secretary

Sec. 203. Officers of the armed services may be detailed to duty as assistants and personal aides to the Secretary of Defense, but he shall not establish a military staff.

Civilian Personnel

Sec. 204. (a) The Secretary of Defense is authorized to appoint from civilian life not to exceed three special assistants to advise and assist him in the performance of his duties. Each such special assistant shall receive compensation at the rate of $10,000 a year.

(b) The Secretary of Defense is authorized, subject to the civil-service laws and the Classification Act of 1923, as amended, to appoint and fix the compensation of such other civilian personnel as may be necessary for the performance of the functions of the National Military Establishment other than those of the Departments of the Army, Navy, and Air Force.

Department of the Army

Sec. 205. (a) The Department of War shall hereafter be designated the Department of the Army, and the title of the Secretary of War shall be changed to Secretary of the Army. Changes shall be made in the titles of other officers and activities of the Department of the Army as the Secretary of the Army may determine.

(b) All laws, orders, regulations, and other actions relating to the Department of War or to any officer or activity whose title is changed under this section shall, insofar as they are not inconsistent with the provisions of this Act, be deemed to relate to the Department of the Army within the National Military Establishment or to such officer or activity designated by his or its new title.

(c) The term "Department of the Army" as used in this Act shall be construed to mean the Department of the Army at the seat of government and all field headquarters, forces, reserve components, installations, activities, and functions under the control or supervision of the Department of the Army.

(d) The Secretary of the Army shall cause a seal of office to be made for the Department of the Army of such design as the President may approve, and judicial notice shall be taken thereof.

(e) In general the United States Army, within the Department of the Army, shall include land combat and service forces and such aviation and water transport as may be organic therein. It shall be organized, trained, and equipped primarily for prompt and sustained combat incident to operations on land. It shall be responsible for the preparation of land forces necessary for the effective prosecution of war except as otherwise assigned and, in accordance with integrated joint mobilization plans, for the expansion of peacetime components of the Army to meet the needs of war.

Department of the Navy

Sec. 206. (a) The term "Department of the Navy" as used in this Act shall be construed to mean the Department of the Navy at the seat of government; the headquarters, United States Marine Corps; the entire operating force of the United States Navy, including naval aviation, and of the United States Marine Corps, including the reserve components of such forces; all field activities, headquarters, forces, bases, installations, activities, and functions under the control or supervision of the Department of the Navy; and the United States Coast Guard when operating as a part of the Navy pursuant to law.

(b) In general the United States Navy, within the Department of the Navy, shall include naval combat and service forces and such aviation as may be organic therein. It shall be organized, trained, and equipped primarily for prompt and sustained combat incident to operations at sea. It shall be responsible for the preparation of naval forces necessary for the effective prosecution of war except as otherwise assigned, and, in accordance with integrated joint mobilization plans, for the expansion of the peacetime components of the Navy to meet the needs of war.

All naval aviation shall be integrated with the naval service as part thereof within the Department of the Navy. Naval aviation shall consist of combat and service and training forces, and shall include land-based naval aviation, air transport essential for naval operations, all air weapons and air techniques involved in the operations and activities of the United States Navy, and the entire remainder of the aeronautical organization of the United States Navy, together with the personnel necessary therefor.

The Navy shall be generally responsible for naval reconnaissance, antisubmarine warfare, and protection of shipping.

The Navy shall develop aircraft, weapons, tactics, technique, organization and equipment of naval combat and service elements; matters of joint concern as to these functions shall be coordinated between the Army, the Air Force, and the Navy.

(c) The United States Marine Corps, within the Department of the Navy, shall include land combat and service forces and such aviation as may be organic therein. The Marine Corps shall be organized, trained, and equipped to provide fleet marine forces of combined arms, together with supporting air components, for service with the fleet in the seizure or defense of advanced naval bases and for the conduct of such land operations as may be essential to the prosecution of a naval campaign. It shall be the duty of the Marine Corps to develop, in coordination with the Army and the Air Force, those phases of amphibious operations which pertain to the tactics, technique, and equipment employed by landing forces. In addition, the Marine Corps shall provide detachments and organizations for service on armed vessels of the Navy, shall provide security detachments for the protection of naval property at naval stations and bases, and shall perform such other duties as the President may direct: PROVIDED, That such additional duties shall not detract from or interfere with the operations for which the Marine Corps is primarily organized. The Marine Corps shall be responsible, in accordance with integrated joint mobilization plans for the expansion of peacetime components of the Marine Corps to meet the needs of war.

Department of the Air Force

Sec. 207. (a) Within the National Military Establishment there is hereby established an executive department to be known as the Department of the Air Force and a Secretary of the Air Force, who shall be the head thereof. The Secretary of the Air Force shall be appointed from civilian life by the President, by and with the advice and consent of the Senate.

(b) Section 158 of the Revised Statutes is amended to include the Department of the Air Force and the provisions of so much of Title IV of the Revised Statutes as now or hereafter amended as is not inconsistent with the Act shall be applicable to the Department of the Air Force.

(c) The term "Department of the Air Force" as used in this Act shall be construed to mean the Department of the Air Force at the seat of government and all field headquarters, forces, reserve components, installations, activities, and functions under the control or supervision of the Department of the Air Force.

(d) There shall be in the Department of the Air Force an Under Secretary of the Air Force and two Assistant Secretaries of the Air Force, who shall be appointed from civilian life by the President by and with the advice and consent of the Senate.

(e) The several officers of the Department of the Air Force shall perform such functions as the Secretary of the Air Force may prescribe.

(f) So much of the functions of the Secretary of the Army and of the Department of the Army, including those of any officer of such Department as are assigned to or under the control of the Commanding General, Army Air Forces, or as are deemed by the Secretary of Defense to be necessary or desirable for the operations of the Department of the Air Force or the United States Air Force, shall be transferred to and vested in the Secretary of the Air Force and the Department of the Air Force: PROVIDED, That the National Guard Bureau shall, in addition to the functions and duties performed by it for the Department of the Army, be charged with similar functions and duties for the Department of the Air Force, and shall be the channel of communication between the Department of the Air Force and the several States on all matters pertaining to the Air National Guard: AND PROVIDED FURTHER, That, in order to permit an orderly transfer. the Secretary of Defense may, during the transfer period hereinafter prescribed, direct that the Department of the Army shall continue for appropriate periods to exercise any of such functions, insofar as they relate to the Department of the Air Force, or the United States Air Force or their property and personnel. Such of the property, personnel, and records of the Department of the Army used in the exercise of functions transferred under this subsection as the Secretary of Defense shall determine shall be transferred or assigned to the Department of the Air Force.

(g) The Secretary of the Air Force shall cause a seal of office to be made for the Department of the Air Force, of such device as the President shall approve and judicial notice shall be taken thereof.

United States Air Force

Sec. 208. (a) The United States Air Force is hereby established under the Department of the Air Force. The Army Air Forces, the Air Corps, United States Army, and the General Headquarters Air Force (Air Force Combat Command), shall be transferred to the United States Air Force.

(b) There shall be a Chief of Staff, United States Air Force, who shall be appointed by the President, by and with the advice and consent of the Senate, for a term of four years from among the officers of general rank who are assigned to or commissioned in the United States Air Force. Under the direction of the Secretary of the Air Force, the Chief of Staff, United States Air Force, shall exercise command over the United States Air Force and shall be charged with the duty of carrying into execution all lawful orders and directions which may be transmitted to him. The functions of the Commanding General, General Headquarters Air Force (Air Force Combat Command), and of the Chief of the Air Corps and of the Commanding General, Army Air Forces, shall be transferred to the Chief of Staff, United States Air Force. When such transfer becomes effective, the offices of the Chief of the Air Corps, United States Army, and Assistants to the Chief of the Air Corps, United States Army, provided for by the Act of June 4, 1920, as amended (41 Stat. 768), and Commanding General, General Headquarters Air Force, provided for by section 5 of the Act of June 16, 1936 (49 Stat. 1525), shall cease to exist. While holding office as Chief of Staff, United States Air Force, the incumbent shall hold a grade and receive allowances equivalent to those prescribed by law for the Chief of Staff, United States Army. The Chief of Staff, United States Army, the Chief of Naval Operations, and the Chief of Staff, United States Air Force, shall take rank among themselves according to their relative dates of appointment as such, and shall each take rank above all other officers on the active list of the Army, Navy, and Air Force: PROVIDED, That nothing in this Act shall have the effect of changing the relative rank of the present Chief of Staff, United States Army, and the present Chief of Naval Operations.

(c) All commissioned officers, warrant officers, and enlisted men, commissioned, holding warrants, or enlisted, in the Air Corps, United States Army, or the Army Air Forces, shall be transferred in branch to the United States Air Force. All other commissioned officers, warrant officers, and enlisted men, who are commissioned, hold warrants, or are enlisted, in any component of the Army of the United States and who are under the authority or command of the Commanding General, Army Air Forces, shall be continued under the authority or command of the Chief of Staff, United States Air Force, and under the jurisdiction of the Department of the Air Force. Personnel whose status is affected by this subsection shall retain their existing commissions, warrants, or enlisted status in existing components of the armed forces unless otherwise altered or terminated in accordance with existing law; and they shall not be deemed to have been appointed to a new or different office or grade, or to have vacated their permanent or temporary appointments in an existing component of the armed forces, solely by virtue of any change in status under this subsection. No such change in status shall alter or prejudice the status of any individual so assigned, so as to deprive him of any right, benefit, or privilege to which he may be entitled under existing law.

(d) Except as otherwise directed by the Secretary of the Air Force, all property, records, installations, agencies, activities, projects, and civilian personnel under the jurisdiction, control, authority, or command of the Commanding General, Army Air Forces, shall be continued to the same extent under the jurisdiction, control, authority, or command, respectively, of the Chief of Staff, United States Air Force, in the Department of the Air Force.

(e) For a period of two years from the date of enactment of this Act, personnel (both military and civilian), property, records, installations, agencies, activities, and projects may be transferred between the Department of the Army and the Department of the Air Force by direction of the Secretary of Defense.

(f) In general the United States Air Force shall include aviation forces both combat and service not otherwise assigned. It shall be organized, trained, and equipped primarily for prompt and sustained offensive and defensive air operations. The Air Force shall be responsible for the preparation of the air forces necessary for the effective prosecution of war except as otherwise assigned and, in accordance with integrated joint mobilization plans, for the expansion of the peacetime components of the Air Force to meet the needs of war.

Effective Date of Transfers

Sec. 209. Each transfer, assignment, or change in status under section 207 or section 208 shall take effect upon such date or dates as may be prescribed by the Secretary of Defense.

War Council

Sec. 210. There shall be within the National Military Establishment a War Council composed of the Secretary of Defense, as Chairman, who shall have power of decision; the Secretary of the Army; the Secretary of the Navy; the Secretary of the Air Force; the Chief of Staff, United States Army; the Chief of Naval Operations; and the Chief of Staff, United States Air Force. The War Council shall advise the Secretary of Defense on matters of broad policy relating to the armed forces, and shall consider and report on such other matters as the Secretary of Defense may direct.

Joint Chiefs of Staff

Sec. 211. (a) There is hereby established within the National Military Establishment the Joint Chiefs of Staff, which shall consist of the Chief of Staff, United States Army; the Chief of Naval Operations; the Chief of Staff, United States Air Force; and the Chief of Staff to the Commander in Chief, if there be one.

(b) Subject to the authority and direction of the President and the Secretary of Defense, it shall be the duty of the Joint Chiefs of Staff—

(1) to prepare strategic plans and to provide for the strategic direction of the military forces;

(2) to prepare joint logistic plans and to assign to the military services logistic responsibilities in accordance with such plans;

(3) to establish unified commands in strategic areas when such unified commands are in the interest of national security;

(4) to formulate policies for joint training of the military forces;

(5) to formulate policies for coordinating the education of members of the military forces;

(6) to review major material and personnel requirements of the military forces, in accordance with strategic and logistic plans; and

(7) to provide United States representation on the Military Staff Committee of the United Nations in accordance with the provisions of the Charter of the United Nations.

(c) The Joint Chiefs of Staff shall act as the principal military advisers to the President and the Secretary of Defense and shall perform such other duties as the President and the Secretary of Defense may direct or as many as prescribed by law.

Joint Staff

Sec. 212. There shall be, under the Joint Chiefs of Staff, a Joint Staff to consist of not to exceed one hundred officers and to be composed of approximately equal numbers of officers from each of the three armed services. The Joint Staff, operating under a Director thereof appointed by the Joint Chiefs of Staff shall perform such duties as may be directed by the Joint Chiefs of Staff. The Director shall be an officer junior in grade to all members of the Joint Chiefs of Staff.

Munitions Board

Sec. 213. (a) There is hereby established in the National Military Establishment a Munitions Board (hereinafter in this section referred to as the "Board").

(b) The Board shall be composed of a Chairman, who shall be the head thereof, and an Under Secretary or Assistant Secretary from each of the three military departments, to be designated in each case by the Secretaries of their respective departments. The Chairman shall be appointed from civilian life by the President, by and with the advice and consent of the Senate, and shall receive compensation at the rate of $14,000 a year.

(c) It shall be the duty of the Board under the direction of the Secretary of Defense and in support of strategic and logistic plans prepared by the Joint Chiefs of Staff—

(1) to coordinate the appropriate activities within the National Military Establishment with regard to industrial matters, including the procurement, production, and distribution plans of the departments and agencies comprising the Establishment;

(2) to plan for the military aspects of industrial mobilization;

(3) to recommend assignment of procurement responsibilities among the several military services and to plan for standardization of specifications and for the greatest practicable allocation of purchase authority of technical equipment and common use items on the basis of single procurement;

(4) to prepare estimates of potential production procurement and personnel for use in evaluation of the logistic feasibility of strategic operations;

(5) to determine relative priorities of the various segments of the military procurement programs;

(6) to supervise such subordinate agencies as are or may be created to consider the subjects falling within the scope of the Board's responsibilities;

(7) to make recommendations to regroup, combine, or dissolve existing interservice agencies operating in the fields of procurement production, and distribution in such manner as to promote efficiency and economy;

(8) to maintain liaison with other departments and agencies for the proper correlation of military requirements with the civilian economy, particularly in regard to the procurement or disposition of strategic and critical material and maintenance of adequate reserves of such material, and to make recommendations as to policies in connection therewith;

(9) to assemble and review material and personnel requirements presented by the Joint Chiefs of Staff and those presented by the production, procurement, and distribution agencies assigned to meet military needs, and to make recommendations thereon to the Secretary of Defense: and

(10) to perform such duties as the Secretary of Defense may direct.

(d) When the Chairman of the Board first appointed has taken office, the Joint Army and Navy Munitions Board shall cease to exist and all its records and personnel shall be transferred to the Munitions Board.

(e) The Secretary of Defense shall provide the Board with such personnel and facilities as the Secretary may determine to be required by the Board for the performance of its functions.

Research and Development Board

Sec. 214. (a) There is hereby established in the National Military Establishment a Research and Development Board (hereinafter in this section referred to as the "Board"). The Board shall be composed of a Chairman, who shall be the head thereof, and two representatives from each of the Departments of the Army, Navy, and Air Force, to be designated by the Secretaries of their respective Departments. The Chairman shall be appointed from civilian life by the President, by and with the advice and consent of the Senate, and shall receive compensation at the rate of $14,000 a year. The purpose of the Board shall be to advise the Secretary of Defense as to the status of scientific research relative to the national security, and to assist him in assuring adequate provision for research and development on scientific problems relating to the national security.

(b) it shall be the duty of the Board, under the direction of the Secretary of Defense—

(1) to prepare a complete and integrated program of research and development for military purposes;

(2) to advise with regard to trends in scientific research relating to national security and the measures necessary to assure continued and increasing progress:

(3) to recommend measures of coordination of research and development among the military departments and allocation among them of responsibilities for specific programs of joint interest;

(4) to formulate policy for the National Military establishment in connection with research and development matters involving agencies outside the National Military Establishment;

(5) to consider the interaction of research and development and strategy, and to advise the Joint Chiefs of Staff in connection therewith; and

(6) to perform such other duties as the Secretary of Defense may direct.

(c) When the Chairman of the Board first appointed has taken office the Joint Research and Development Board shall cease to exist and all its records and personnel shall be transferred to the Research and Development Board.

315

(d) The Secretary of Defense shall provide the Board with such personnel and facilities as the Secretary may determine to be required by the Board for the performance of its functions.

Title III—Miscellaneous

Compensation of Secretaries

Sec. 301. (a) The Secretary of Defense shall receive the compensation prescribed by law for heads of executive departments.

(b) The Secretary of the Army, the Secretary of the Navy, and the Secretary of the Air Force shall each receive the compensation prescribed by law for heads of executive departments.

Under Secretaries and Assistant Secretaries

Sec. 302. The Under Secretaries and Assistant Secretaries of the Army, the Navy, and the Air Force shall each receive compensation at the rate of $10,000 a year and shall perform such duties as the Secretaries of their respective departments may prescribe.

Advisory Committees and Personnel

Sec. 303. (a) The Secretary of Defense, the Chairman of the National Security Resources Board, and the Director of Central Intelligence are authorized to appoint such advisory committees and to employ, consistent with other provisions of this Act, such part-time advisory personnel as they may deem necessary in carrying out their respective functions and the functions of agencies under their control. Persons holding other offices or positions under the United States for which they receive compensation while serving as members of such committees shall receive no additional compensation for such service. Other members of such committees and other part-time advisory personnel so employed may serve without compensation or may receive compensation at a rate not to exceed $35 for each day of service, as determined by the appointing authority.

(b) Service of an individual as a member of any such advisory committee, or in any other part-time capacity for a department or agency hereunder, shall not be considered as service bringing such individual within the provisions of section 109 or 113 of the Criminal Code (U.S.C. 1940 edition, title 18, secs. 198 and 203), or section 19 (e) of the Contract Settlement Act of 1944, unless the act of such individual, which by such section is made unlawful when performed by an individual referred to in such section, is with respect to any particular matter which directly involves a department or agency which such person is advising or in which such department or agency is directly interested.

Status of Transferred Civilian Personnel

See. 304. All transfers of civilian personnel under this Act shall be without change in classification or compensation, but the head of any department or agency to which such a transfer is made is authorized to make such changes in the titles and designations and prescribe such changes in the duties of such personnel commensurate with their classification as he may deem necessary and appropriate.

Saving Provisions

Sec. 305. (a) All laws, orders, regulations, and other actions applicable with respect to any function, activity, personnel, property, records, or other thing transferred under this Act, or with respect to any officer, department, or agency from which such transfer is made, shall except to the extent rescinded, modified, superseded, terminated, or made inapplicable by or under authority of law, have the same effect as if such transfer had not been made; but, after any such transfer, any such law, order, regulation, or other action which vested functions in or otherwise related to any officer, department, or agency from which such transfers was made shall, insofar as applicable with respect to the function, activity, personnel, property, records or other thing transferred and to the extent not inconsistent with other provisions of this Act, be deemed to have vested such function in or relate to the officer, department, or agency to which the transfer was made.

(b) No suit, action, or other proceeding lawfully commenced by or against the head of any department or agency or other officer of the United States. in his official capacity or in relation to the discharge of his official duties, shall abate by reason of the taking effect of any transfer or change in title under the provisions of this Act; and, in the case of any such transfer, such suit, action, or other proceeding may be maintained by or against the successor of such head or other officer under the transfer, but only if the court shall allow the same to be maintained on motion or supplemental petition filed within twelve months after such transfer takes effect, showing a necessity for the survival of such suit, action, or other proceeding to obtain settlement of the questions involved.

(c) Notwithstanding the provisions of the second paragraph of section 5 of title I of the First War Powers Act, 1941, the existing organization of the War Department under the provisions of Executive Order Number 9082 of February 28, 1942, as modified by Executive Order Number 9722 of May 13, 1946, and the existing organization of the Department of the Navy under the provisions of Executive Order Numbered 9635 of September 29, 1945, including the assignment of functions to organizational units within the War and Navy Departments, may, to the extent determined by the Secretary of Defense, continue in force for two years following the date of enactment of this Act except to the extent modified by the provisions of this Act or under the authority of law.

Transfer of Funds

Sec. 306. All unexpended balances of appropriations, allocations, nonappropriated funds, or other funds available or hereafter made available for use by or on behalf of the Army Air Forces or officers thereof, shall be transferred to the Department of the Air Force for use in connection with the exercise of its functions. Such other unexpended balances of appropriations, allocations, nonappropriated funds, or other funds available or hereafter made available for use by the Department of War or the Department of the Army in exercise of functions transferred to the Department of the Air Force under this Act, as the Secretary of Defense shall determine, shall be transferred to the Department of the Air Force for use in connection with the exercise of its functions. Unexpended balances transferred under this section may be used for the purposes for which the appropriations, allocations, or other funds were originally made available, or for new expenditures occasioned by the enactment of this Act. The transfers herein authorized may be made with or without warrant action as may be appropriate from time to time from any appropriation covered by this section to any other such appropriation or to such new accounts established on the books of the Treasury as may be determined to be necessary to carry into effect provisions of this Act.

Authorization for Appropriations

Sec. 307. There are hereby authorized to be appropriated such sums as may be necessary and appropriate to carry out the provisions and purpose of this Act.

Definitions

Sec. 308. (a) As used in this Act, the term "function" includes functions, powers and duties.

(b) As used in this Act, the term "budget program" refers to recommendations as to the apportionment, to the allocation and to the review of allotments of appropriated funds.

Separability

Sec. 309. If any provision of this Act or the application thereof to any person or circumstances is held invalid, the validity of the remainder of the Act and of the application of such provision to other persons and circumstances shall not be affected thereby.

Effective Date

Sec. 310. (a) The first sentence of section 202 (a) and sections 1, 2, 307, 308, 309, and 310 shall take effect immediately upon the enactment of this Act.

(b) Except as provided in subsection (a), the provisions of this Act shall take effect on whichever of the following days is the earlier: The day after the day upon which the Secretary of Defense first appointed takes office, or the sixtieth day after the date of the enactment of this Act.

Succession to the Presidency

Sec. 311. Paragraph (1) of subsection (d) of section I of the Act entitled "An Act to provide for the performance of the duties of the office of President in case of the removal, resignation, death, or inability both of the President and Vice President", approved July 18, 1947, is amended by striking out "Secretary of War" and inserting in lieu thereof "Secretary of Defense", and by striking out "Secretary of the Navy."

Approved July 26, 1947.

Appendix 10

Army Air Forces
United States Air Force

Headquarters Staff

Chief of Air Corps

Maj Gen George H. Brett
May 30, 1941–Dec 8, 1941

Maj Gen Walter R. Weaver [Acting]
Dec 8, 1941–Mar 9, 1942

Assistant Chief of Air Corps

Brig Gen Davenport Johnson
Oct 2, 1940–Aug 8, 1941

Brig Gen Muir S. Fairchild
Aug 8, 1941–Mar 9, 1942

Commanding General, Air Force Combat Command

Lt Gen Delos C. Emmons
Mar 1, 1939–Dec 17, 1941

Maj Gen Carl A. Spaatz
Jan 27, 1942–Mar 8, 1942

Maj Gen Millard F. Harmon [Actg]
Dec 17, 1941–Jan 26, 1942

Chief, Army Air Forces

Maj Gen/Lt Gen Henry H. Arnold
June 20, 1941–Mar 9, 1942

Commanding General, Army Air Forces

Lt Gen/Gen Henry H. Arnold*
Mar 9, 1942–Feb 9, 1946

General Carl A. Spaatz
Feb 9, 1946–Sept 26, 1947

Chief of Staff, United States Air Force

General Carl A. Spaatz
Sept 26, 1947–Apr 30, 1948

Vice Chief of Staff

General Hoyt S. Vandenberg
Oct 10, 1947–Apr 28, 1948

Assistant Vice Chief of Staff

Maj Gen William F. McKee
Sept 27, 1947–May 11, 1953

Chief of Air Staff; Deputy Commander and Chief of Air Staff

Brig Gen Carl A. Spaatz
Jun 20, 1941–Jan 26, 1942

Maj Gen/Lt Gen Barney M. Giles[†]
Jul 26, 1943–Apr 30, 1945

Maj Gen Millard F. Harmon
Jan 27, 1942–Jul 6, 1942

Lt Gen Ira C. Eaker
Apr 30, 1945–Aug 31, 1947

Maj Gen George E. Stratemeyer
Jul 6, 1942–Jul 26, 1943

Deputy Chief of Air Staff

Maj Gen Charles C. Chauncey
June 2, 1945–Oct 1, 1947

Brig Gen Reuben C. Hood
Jan 18, 1945–Feb 19, 1947

---

*Became General of the Army (temporary) December 21, 1944. Appointed to permanent rank of General of the Army, March 25, 1946, and appointed General of the Air Force May 7, 1949, both actions by Act of Congress.

[†]Giles was Chief of Air Staff, July 1943–Apr 1945. He became Deputy Commander as well as Chief of Air Staff, in May 1944.

321

Deputy Chiefs of Staff*

Brig Gen Laurence S. Kuter
Mar 9, 1942–Oct 17, 1942

Brig Gen Thomas J. Hanley
Oct 17, 1942–Jun 25, 1943

Brig Gen LaVerne G. Saunders
Mar 29, 1943–Aug 25, 1943

Brig Gen William E. Hall
Mar 29, 1943–Sep 4, 1944

Brig Gen Edwin S. Perrin
Jun 25, 1943–Apr 29, 1944

Brig Gen Hoyt S. Vandenberg
Aug 25, 1943–Mar 16, 1944

Brig Gen Haywood S. Hansell, Jr.
Oct 23, 1943–Aug 20, 1944

Brig Gen Patrick W. Timberlake
Apr 29, 1944–Jul 3, 1945

Brig Gen Donald Wilson
May 10, 1944–Sept 2, 1944

Brig Gen Roy L. Owens
July 3, 1944–May 15, 1945

Brig Gen/Maj Gen Lauris Norstad
Aug 20, 1944–May 8, 1945

Brig Gen Frederick H. Smith
Sept 2, 1944–Jan 15, 1945

Deputy Chief of Staff, Research & Development

Maj Gen/Lt Gen Curtis E. LeMay
Dec 5, 1945–Oct 9, 1947

Chief, Plans; Assistant Chief, Air Staff, Plans

Lt Col/Col Harold L. George
Jun 20, 1941–Mar 9, 1942

Col Howard A. Craig
Mar 9, 1942–Jul 18, 1942

Col/Brig Gen Orvil A. Anderson
Jul 18, 1942–Jul 8, 1943

Brig Gen/Maj Gen Laurence S. Kuter
Jul 8, 1943–May 8, 1945

Brig Gen Joe L. Loutzenheiser [actg]
May 8, 1945–June 27, 1945

Maj Gen Lauris Norstad
Jun 27, 1945–Jun 15, 1946

Brig Gen Frank F. Everest
Jun 15, 1946–Jun 27, 1946

Maj Gen Otto P. Weyland
Jun 27, 1946–Oct 9, 1947

Director of Information

Lt Gen Harold L. George
Mar 12, 1946–Aug 13, 1946

Brig Gen Emmett O'Donnell, Jr.
Aug 13, 1946–Sept 28, 1947

---

*The number varied through the years.

Secretary-General, The Air Board

Maj Gen Hugh J. Knerr
Mar 4, 1946–Jan 1948

Assistant Chief, Air Staff,
Operations, Commitments and Requirements;
Assistant Chief, Air Staff, Operations and Training

Lt Gen Hoyt S. Vandenberg
Jun 25, 1945–Jan 26, 1946

Maj Gen Earle E. Partridge
Jan 26, 1946–Oct 9, 1947

Assistant Chief Air Staff, Personnel

Brig Gen Ralph P. Cousins
Jul 7, 1941–Jan 12, 1942

Col F. Trubee Davison
Jan 12, 1942–Mar 29, 1943

Brig Gen/Maj Gen James M. Bevans
Mar 29, 1943–Feb 20, 1945

Maj Gen Hubert R. Harmon
Feb 20, 1945–Jun 7, 1945

Maj Gen Frederick L. Anderson
Jun 7, 1945–Sept 30, 1947

Assistant Chief, Air Staff, Intelligence

Brig Gen Martin F. Scanlon
Jun 20, 1941–Feb 21, 1942

Col Robert L. Walsh
Feb 21, 1942–May 30, 1942

Brig Gen Hume Peabody
May 30, 1942–Jun 22, 1942

Col/Brig Gen Edgar P. Sorensen
Jun 22, 1942–Oct 21, 1943

Maj Gen Clayton L. Bissell
Oct 21, 1943–Jan 5, 1944

Brig Gen Thomas D. White
Jan 5, 1944–Sept 2, 1944

Maj Gen James P. Hodges
Sept 2, 1944–Jul 7, 1945

Maj Gen Elwood R. Quesada
Jul 7, 1945–Feb 1946

Brig Gen George C. McDonald
Feb 1946–Oct 9, 1947

Assistant Chief, Air Staff, Materiel, Maintenance and Distribution;
Assistant Chief, Air Staff, Materiel and Services;
Assistant Chief, Air Staff, Materiel

Col Edgar P. Sorensen
Jun 20, 1941–Jan 4, 1942

Col/Brig Gen Thomas J. Hanley
Jan 4, 1942–Oct 17, 1942

Col Richard H. Ballard
Oct 17, 1942–Mar 29, 1943

Brig Gen/Maj Gen Edward M. Powers
Apr 27, 1945–Oct 9, 1947

Maj Gen Oliver Echols
Mar 29, 1943–Apr 27, 1945

Deputy Chief of Staff, Personnel and Administration

Lt Gen Idwal H. Edwards
Oct 10, 1947–Apr 28, 1948

Deputy Chief of Staff, Operations

Lt Gen Lauris Norstad
Oct 10, 1947–Mar 1, 1950

Deputy Chief of Staff, Materiel

Lt Gen Howard A. Craig
Oct 10, 1947–Sep 15, 1949

Air Inspector

Brig Gen Herbert A. Dargue
Jun 20, 1941–July 24, 1941

Maj Gen Follet Bradley
Mar 28, 1943–Jul 13, 1943

Col Edmund W. Hill
Jul 24, 1941–Jul 18, 1942

Brig Gen/Maj Gen Junius W. Jones
Jul 13, 1943–Oct 9, 1947

Col John F. Whiteley
Jul 18, 1942–Mar 28, 1943

Air Adjutant General

Col William W. Dick
Jun 20, 1941–Sept 19, 1942

Lt Col H. H. Hewitt [Acting]
Dec 15, 1943–Dec 27, 1943

Col Fred Milner
Sept 19, 1942–Sept 28, 1943

Col T. A. FitzPatrick
Dec 27, 1943–May 8, 1944

Col John B. Cooley
Sept 28, 1943–Dec 15, 1943

Col Hugh G. Culton*
Jun 8, 1945–Oct 9, 1947

---

*No AAG from May 8, 1944, to Jun 8, 1945.

Appendix 11

[63 Stat.]

PUBLIC LAW 216—August 10, 1949

Public Law 216   Chapter 412

An Act

To reorganize fiscal management in the National Military Establishment to promote economy and efficiency, and for other purposes.

Be it enacted by the Senate and House of Representatives of the United States of America in Congress assembled.

SHORT TITLE

Section 1. This Act may be cited as the "National Security Act Amendments of 1949".

Sec. 2. Section 2 of the National Security Act of 1947 is amended to read as follows:

"Sec. 2. In enacting this legislation, it is the intent of Congress to provide a comprehensive program for the future security of the United States; to provide for the establishment of integrated policies and procedures for the departments, agencies, and functions of the Government relating to the national security; to provide three military departments, separately administered, for the operation and administration of the Army, the Navy (including naval aviation and the United States Marine Corps), and the Air Force, with their assigned combat and service components; to provide for their authoritative coordination and unified direction under civilian control of the Secretary of Defense but not to merge them; to provide for the effective strategic direction of the armed forces and for their operation under unified control and for their integration into an efficient team of land, naval, and air forces but not to establish a single Chief of Staff over the armed forces nor an armed forces general staff (but this is not to be interpreted as applying to the Joint Chiefs of Staff or Joint Staff)."

CHANGE IN COMPOSITION OF THE NATIONAL SECURITY COUNCIL

Sec. 3. The fourth paragraph of section 101 (a) of the National Security Act of 1947 is amended to read as follows:
"The Council shall be composed of—
  "(1) the President;
  "(2) the Vice President;
  "(3) the Secretary of State;
  "(4) the Secretary of Defense;
  "(5) the Chairman of the National Security Resources Board; and
  "(6) The Secretaries and Under Secretaries of other executive departments and of the military departments, the Chairman of the Munitions Board, and the Chairman of the Research and Development Board, when appointed by the President by and with the advice and consent of the Senate, to serve at his pleasure."

CONVERSION OF THE NATIONAL MILITARY ESTABLISHMENT INTO AN EXECUTIVE DEPARTMENT

Sec. 4. Section 201 of the National Security Act of 1947 is amended to read as follows:

"Sec. 201. (a) There is hereby established, as an Executive Department of the Government, the Department of Defense, and the Secretary of Defense shall be the head thereof.

(b) There shall be within the Department of Defense (1) the Department of the Army, the Department of the Navy, and the Department of the Air Force, and each such department shall on and after the date of enactment of the National Security Act Amendments of 1949 be military departments in lieu of their prior status as Executive Departments, and (2) all other agencies created under title II of this Act.

"(c) Section 158 of the Revised Statutes, as amended, is amended to read as follows:

"Sec. 158. The provisions of this title shall apply to the following Executive Departments:

"First. The Department of State.

"Second. The Department of Defense.

"Third. The Department of the Treasury.

"Fourth. The Department of Justice.

"Fifth. The Post Office Department.

"Sixth. The Department of the Interior.

"Seventh. The Department of Agriculture.

"Eighth. The Department of Commerce.

"Ninth. The Department of Labor.

"(d) Except to the extent inconsistent with the provisions of this Act, provisions of title IV of the Revised Statutes as now or hereafter amended should be applicable to the Department of Defense."

THE SECRETARY OF DEFENSE

Sec. 5. Section 202 of the National Security Act of 1947, as amended, is further amended to read as follows:

"Sec. 202. (a) There shall be a Secretary of Defense, who shall be appointed from civilian life by the President, by and with the advice and consent of the Senate: Provided, That a person who has within ten years been on active duty as a commissioned officer in a Regular component of the armed services shall not be eligible for appointment as Secretary of Defense.

"(b) The Secretary of Defense shall be the principal assistant to the President in all matters relating to the Department of Defense. Under the direction of the President, and subject to the provisions of this Act, he shall have direct authority, and control over the Department of Defense.

"(c) (1) Notwithstanding any other provision of this Act, the combatant functions assigned to the military services by sections 205 (e), 206 (b), 206 (c), and 208 (f) hereof shall not be transferred, reassigned, abolished, or consolidated.

"(2) Military personnel shall not be so detailed or assigned as to impair such combatant functions.

"(3) The Secretary of Defense shall not direct the use and expenditure of funds of the Department of Defense in such manner as to effect the results prohibited by paragraphs (1) and (2) of this subsection.

"(4) The Departments of the Army, Navy, and Air Force shall be separately administered by their respective Secretaries under the direction, authority, and control of the Secretary of Defense.

"(5) Subject to the provisions of paragraph (1) of this subsection no function which has been or is hereafter authorized by law to be performed by the Department of Defense shall be substantially transferred, reassigned, abolished or consolidated until after a report in regard to all pertinent details shall have been made by the Secretary of Defense to the Committees on Armed Services of the Congress.

"(6) No provision of this Act shall be so construed as to prevent a Secretary of a military department or a member of the Joint Chiefs of Staff from presenting to the Congress on his own initiative, after first so informing the Secretary of Defense, any recommendation relating to the Department of Defense that he may deem proper.

"(d) The Secretary of Defense shall not less often than semiannually submit written reports to the President and the Congress covering expenditures, work and accomplishments of the Department of Defense, accompanied by (1) such recommendations as he shall deem appropriate, (2) separate reports from the military departments covering their expenditures, work and accomplishments, and (3) itemized statements showing the savings of public funds and the eliminations for unnecessary duplications and overlappings that have been accomplished pursuant to the provisions of this Act.

"(e) The Secretary of Defense shall cause a seal of office to be made for the Department of Defense, of such design as the President shall approve, and judicial notice shall be taken thereof.

"(f) The Secretary of Defense may, without being relieved of his responsibility therefor, and unless prohibited by some specific provision of this Act or other specific provision of law, perform any function vested in him through or with the aid of such officials or organizational entities of the Department of Defense as he may designate."

DEPUTY SECRETARY OF DEFENSE;
ASSISTANT SECRETARIES OF DEFENSE;
MILITARY ASSISTANTS; AND CIVILIAN PERSONNEL

Sec. 6 (a) Section 203 of the National Security Act of 1947 is amended to read as follows:

"Sec. 203. (a) There shall be a Deputy Secretary of Defense, who shall be appointed from civilian life by the President, by and with the advice and consent of the Senate: Provided, That a person who has within ten years been on active duty as a commissioned officer in a Regular component of the armed services shall not be eligible for appointment as Deputy Secretary of Defense. The Deputy Secretary shall perform such duties and exercise such powers as the Secretary of Defense may prescribe and shall take precedence in the Department of Defense next after the Secretary of Defense. The Deputy Secretary shall act for, and exercise the powers of the Secretary of Defense during his absence or disability.

"(b) There shall be three Assistant Secretaries of Defense, who shall be appointed from civilian life by the President, by and with the advice and consent of the Senate. The Assistant Secretaries shall perform such duties and exercise such powers as the Secretary of Defense may prescribe and shall take precedence in the Department of Defense after the Secretary of Defense, the Deputy Secretary of Defense, the Secretary of the Army, the Secretary of the Navy, and the Secretary of the Air Force.

"(c) Officers of the armed services may be detailed to duty as assistants and personal aides to the Secretary of Defense, but he shall not establish a military Staff other than that provided for by section 211 (a) of this Act."

"(b) Section 204 of the National Security Act of 1947 is amended to read as follows:

"Sec 204. The Secretary of Defense is authorized, subject to the civil service laws and the Classification Act of 1923, as amended, to appoint and fix the compensation of such civilian personnel as may be necessary for the performance of the functions of the Department of Defense other than those of the Departments of the Army, Navy, and Air Force."

CREATING THE POSITION OF CHAIRMAN OF THE JOINT CHIEFS OF STAFF AND PRESCRIBING HIS POWERS AND DUTIES

Sec. 7. (a) Section 210 of the National Security Act of 1947 is amended to read as follows:

"Sec. 210. There shall be within the Department of Defense an Armed Forces Policy Council composed of the Secretary of Defense, as Chairman, who shall have power of decision; the Deputy Secretary of Defense; the Secretary of the Army; The Secretary of the Navy; the Secretary of the Air Force; the Chairman of the Joint Chiefs of Staff; the Chief of Staff, United States Army; the Chief of Naval Operations; and the Chief of Staff, United States Air Force. The Armed Forces Policy Council shall advise the Secretary of Defense on matters of broad policy relating to the armed forces and shall consider and report on such other matters as the Secretary of Defense may direct."

"(b) Section 211 of the National Security Act of 1947 is amended to read as follows:

"Sec 211. (a) There is hereby established within the Department of Defense the Joint Chiefs of Staff, which shall consist of the Chairman, who shall be the presiding officer thereof but who shall have no vote; the Chief of Staff, United States Army, the Chief of Naval Operations: and the Chief of Staff, United States Air Force. The Joint Chiefs of Staff shall be the principal military advisers to the President, the National Security Council, and the Secretary of Defense.

"(b) Subject to the authority and direction of the President and the Secretary of Defense, the Joint Chiefs of Staff shall perform the following duties, in addition to such other duties as the President or the Secretary of Defense may direct:

"(1) preparation of strategic plans and provision for the strategic direction of the military forces;

"(2) preparation of joint logistic plans and assignment to the military services of logistic responsibilities in accordance with such plans;

"(3) establishment of unified commands in strategic areas;

"(4) review of major material and personnel requirements of the military forces in accordance with strategic and logistic plans;

"(5) formulation of policies for joint training of the military forces;

"(6) formulation of policies for coordinating the military education of members of the military forces; and

"(7) providing United States representation on the Military Staff Committee of the United Nations in accordance with the provisions of the Charter of the United Nations.

"(c) The Chairman of the Joint Chiefs of Staff (hereinafter referred to as the 'Chairman') shall be appointed by the President, by and with the advice and consent of the Senate from among the Regular officers of the armed services to serve at the pleasure of the President for a term of two years and shall be eligible for one reappointment, by and with the advice and consent of the Senate, except in time of war hereafter declared by the Congress when there shall be no limitation on the number of such reappointments. The Chairman shall receive the basic pay and basic and personal money allowances prescribed by law for the Chief of Staff, United States Army, and such special pays and hazardous duty pays to which he may be entitled under other provisions of law.

"(d) The Chairman, if in the grade of general, shall be additional to the number of officers in the grade of general provided in the third proviso of section 504 (b) of the Office Personnel Act of 1947 (Public Law 381, Eightieth Congress) or, of [sic] in the rank of admiral, shall be additional to the number of officers having the rank of admiral provided in section 413 (a) of such Act. While holding such office he shall take precedence over all other officers of the armed services: Provided, That the Chairman shall not exercise military command over the Joint Chiefs of Staff or over any of the military services.

"(e) In addition to participating as a member of the Joint Chiefs of Staff in the performance of the duties assigned in subsection (b) of this section, the Chairman shall, subject to the authority and direction of the President and the Secretary of Defense, perform the following duties:

"(1) serve as the presiding officer of the Joint Chiefs of Staff;

"(2) provide agenda for meetings of the Joint Chiefs of Staff and assist the Joint Chiefs of Staff to prosecute their business as promptly as practicable; and

"(3) inform the Secretary of Defense and, when appropriate as determined by the President or the Secretary of Defense, the President, of those issues upon which agreement among the Joint Chiefs of Staff has not been reached."

"(c) Section 212 of the National Security Act of 1947 is amended to read as follows:

"Sec. 212. There shall be, under the Joint Chief of Staff, a Joint Staff to consist of not to exceed two hundred and ten officers and to be composed of approximately equal numbers of officers appointed by the Joint Chiefs of Staff from each of the three armed services. The Joint Staff, operating under a Director thereof appointed by the Joint Chiefs of Staff, shall perform such duties as may be directed by the Joint Chiefs of Staff. The Director shall be an officer junior in grade to all members of the Joint Chiefs of Staff."

CHANGING THE RELATIONSHIP OF THE SECRETARY OF DEFENSE TO THE MUNITIONS BOARD

Sec. 8. Section 213 of the National Security Act of 1947 is amended to read as follows:

"Sec. 213. (a) There is hereby established in the Department of Defense a Munitions Board (hereinafter in this section referred to as the "Board").

"(b) The Board shall be composed of a Chairman, who shall be the head thereof and who shall, subject to the authority of the Secretary of Defense and in respect to such matters authorized by him, have the power of decision upon matters falling within the jurisdiction of the Board, and an Under Secretary or Assistant Secretary from each of the three military departments, to be designated in each case by the Secretaries of their respective departments. The Chairman shall be appointed from civilian life by the President, by and with advice and consent of the Senate, and shall receive compensation at the rate of $14,000 a year.

"(c) Subject to the authority and direction of the Secretary of Defense, the Board shall perform the following duties in support of strategic and logistic plans and in consonance with guidance in those fields provided by the Joint Chiefs of Staff, and such other duties as the Secretary of Defense may prescribe:

"(1) coordination of the appropriate activities with regard to industrial matters, including the procurement, production, and distribution plans of the Department of Defense;

"(2) planning for the military aspects of industrial mobilization;

"(3) assignment of procurement responsibilities among the several military departments and planning for standardization of specifications and for the greatest practicable allocation of purchase authority of technical equipment and common use items on the basis of single procurement;

"(4) preparation of estimates of potential production, procurement, and personnel for use in evaluation of the logistic feasibility of strategic operations;

"(5) determination of relative priorities of the various segments of the military procurement programs;

"(6) supervision of such subordinate agencies as are or may be created to consider the subjects falling within the scope of the Board's responsibilities;

"(7) regrouping, combining, or dissolving of existing interservice agencies operating in the fields of procurement, production, and distribution in such manner as to promote efficiency and economy;

"(8) maintenance of liaison with other departments and agencies for the proper correlation of military requirements with the civilian economy, particularly in regard to the procurement or disposition of strategic and critical material and the maintenance of adequate reserves of such material, and making of recommendations as to policies in connection therewith; and

"(9) assembly and review of material and personnel requirements presented by the Joint Chiefs of Staff and by the production, procurement, and distribution agencies assigned to meet military needs, and making of recommendations thereon to the Secretary of Defense.

"(d) When the Chairman of the Board first appointed has taken office, the Joint Army and Navy Munitions Board shall cease to exist and all its records and personnel shall be transferred to the Munitions Board.

"(e) The Secretary of Defense shall provide the Board with such personnel and facilities as the Secretary may determine to be required by the Board for the performance of its functions."

CHANGING THE RELATIONSHIP OF THE SECRETARY OF DEFENSE TO THE RESEARCH AND DEVELOPMENT BOARD

Sec. 9. Section 214 of the National Security Act of 1947 is amended to read as follows:

"Sec 214. (a) There is hereby established in the Department of Defense a Research and Development Board (hereinafter in this section referred to as the 'Board'). The Board shall be composed of a Chairman, who shall be the head thereof and who shall, subject to the authority of the Secretary of Defense and in respect to such matters authorized by him, have the power of decision on matters falling within the jurisdiction of the Board, and two representatives from each of the Departments of the Army, Navy, and Air Force, to be designated by the Secretaries of their respective Departments. The Chairman shall be appointed from civilian life by the president, by and with the advice and consent of the Senate, and shall receive compensation at the rate of $14,000 a year. The purpose of the Board shall be to advise the Secretary of Defense as to the status of scientific research relative to the national security, and to assist him in assuring adequate provision for research and development on scientific problems relating to the national security.

"(b) Subject to the authority and direction of the Secretary of Defense, the Board shall perform the following duties and such other duties as the Secretary of Defense may prescribe:

"(1) preparation of a complete and integrated program of research and development for military purposes;

"(2) advising with regard to trends in scientific research relating to national security and the measures necessary to assure continued and increasing progress;

"(3) coordination of research and development among the military departments and allocations among them of responsibilities for specific programs;

"(4) formulation of policy for the Department of Defense in connection with research and development matters involving agencies outside the Department of Defense; and

"(5) consideration of the interaction of research and development and strategy, and advising the Joint Chiefs of Staff in connection therewith.

"(c) When the Chairman of the Board first appointed has taken office, the Joint Research and Development Board shall cease to exist and all its records and personnel shall be transferred to the Research and Development Board.

"(d) The Secretary of Defense shall provide the Board with such personnel and facilities as the Secretary may determine to be required by the Board for the performance of its functions."

COMPENSATION OF SECRETARY OF DEFENSE, DEPUTY SECRETARY OF DEFENSE, SECRETARIES OF MILITARY DEPARTMENTS, AND CONSULTANTS

Sec. 10. (a) Section 301 of the National Security Act of 1947 is amended to read as follows:

"Sec. 301. (a) The Secretary of Defense shall receive the compensation prescribed by law for heads of executive departments.

"(b) the Deputy Secretary of Defense shall receive compensation at the rate of $14,000 a year, or such other compensation plus $500 a year as may hereafter be provided by law for under secretaries of executive departments. The Secretary of the Army, the Secretary of the Navy, and the Secretary of the Air Force shall each receive compensation at the rate of $14,000 a year, or such other compensation as may hereafter be provided by law for under secretaries of executive departments."

(b) Section 302 of the National Security Act of 1947 is amended to read as follows:

"Sec. 302. The Assistant Secretaries of Defense and the Under Secretaries and Assistant Secretaries of the Army, the Navy and the Air Force shall each receive compensation at the rate of $10,330 a year or at the rate hereafter prescribed by law for assistant secretaries of executive departments and shall perform such duties as the respective Secretaries may prescribe."

(c) Section 303 (a) of the National Security Act of 1947 is amended to read as follows:

"(a) The Secretary of Defense, the Chairman of the National Security Resources Board, the Director of Central Intelligence, and the National Security Council, acting through its Executive Secretary, are authorized to appoint such advisory committees and to employ, consistent with other provisions of this Act, such parttime advisory personnel as they may deem necessary in carrying out their respective functions and the functions of agencies under their control. Persons holding other offices or positions under the United States for which they receive compensation, while serving as members of such committees, shall receive no additional compensation for such service. Other members of such committees and other parttime advisory personnel so employed may serve without compensation or may receive compensation at a rate not to exceed $50 for each day of service, as determined by the appointing authority."

REORGANIZATION OF FISCAL MANAGEMENT TO PROMOTE ECONOMY AND EFFICIENCY

Sec. 11. The National Security Act of 1947 is amended by inserting at the end thereof the following new title:

. . . .

[Ed. Note] Material omitted (Title IV) can be found in: Alice C. Cole, et al, eds., *The Department of Defense: Documents on Establishment and Organization, 1944–1978*, (Washington, D.C.: OSD Historical Office, 1978), pp. 100–106, or in: Joint Army and Air Force Bulletin Number 22, 22 August 1949.

Notes

Chapter 1

Roots of AAF Organization

1. Memo, Lt Gen Ira C. Eaker to Herman S. Wolk, Feb 3, 1977.

2. Intvw, Lt Col Joe B. Green with Lt Gen Ira C. Eaker, Washington, D.C., Feb 11, 1967.

3. Gen Peyton C. March, USAF, "Lessons of World War I," *War Department Annual Reports*, 1919 (Washington, 1920), pp 471–78.

4. Maj Carl A. Spaatz, "An Air Force," 1923, Gen Carl A. Spaatz, Colln, MD, LC.

5. Raymond R. Flugel, "United States Air Power Doctrine: A Study of the Influence of William Mitchell and Giulio Douhet at the Air Corps Tactical School, 1921–1935" (Ph.D. dissertation, University of Oklahoma, 1965), p 185.

6. Aircraft in National Defense, *Senate Documents,* 69th Cong, 1st sess (Washington, 1926), p 29.

7. Alfred F. Hurley, *Billy Mitchell: Crusader for Air Power* (New York, 1964, pg 101.

8. James H. Doolittle Dissent to *Final Report of War Department Special Committee on Army Air Corps* (Washington, 1934), Baker Board Report, RG 18, MMB, NA.

9. Maj John F. Shiner, "Birth of the GHQ Air Force," *Military Affairs,* Oct 78, pp 113–120.

10. AR 95–10, *Air Corps Troops,* Mar 10, 1928, RG 18, 321.9, MMB, NA.

11. Report of Browning Board, Jan 7, 1936, AAG 334.7, Boards General, cited in Chase C. Mooney, *Organization of Military Aeronautics, 1935–1945* (AAF Hist Study 46, Washington, 1946).

12. *Ibid.*

13. File, AG 320.2 (5–5-36) Misc (Ret)-MC, May 8, 1936, cited in AAF Hist Study 46, p3.

14. Ltr, Maj Gen Frank M. Andrews, CG, GHQ Air Force, to TAG, Apr 26, 1937, in Personal Papers of Maj Gen Hugh J. Knerr, Air Bd Gen File, RG 340, SAF, Box 10, MMB, NA.

15. "The Air Force Crucible," *Air Corps Newsletter,* Jun 15, 1935, in Ofc/AF Hist.

16. Ltr, Andrews to TAG, Apr 26, 1937.

17. *Ibid.*

18. Maj Gen Oscar Westover, "The Army Is Behind Its Air Corps," *Air Corps Newsletter,* Oct 1, 1937, pp 1–5.

19. Lecture, Maj Muir S. Fairchild, "Air Warfare," ACTS, Maxwell AFB, Ala., Oct 39, Gen Muir S. Fairchild Colln, Box 15, MD, LC.

20. Lecture, Brig Gen Haywood S. Hansell, Jr., "The Development of the United States Concept of Bombardment Operations," AWC, AU, Maxwell AFB, Ala., Sep 19, 1951.

21. Ltr, Secy of War Henry L. Stimson to Chmn, House and Senate Mil Affairs Cmtes, in AAF Hist Study, 46, p 19.

22. AR 95–5, *Army Air Forces,* Jun 20, 1941, para 2(a).

23. *Ibid.,* para 4(d).

24. *Ibid.,* para 5(c).

25. Forrest C. Pogue, *George C. Marshall: Ordeal and Hope* (New York, 1966), p 290.

26. *Ibid.*

27. Summary of Patch-Simpson Board Interview with Gen Marshall, Sep 5, 1945, Patch-Simpson Bd Files, RG 165, MMB, NA.

28. General Arnold's plan is published in Maj Gen Otto L. Nelson, Jr., USA, *National Security and the General Staff* (Washington, 1946) pp 337–342.

29. *Ibid.,* pp 338–39.

30. WD Cir 59, War Department Reorganization, Mar 2, 1942, pp 4–5, para 6(b).

31. *Ibid.,* pp 5–6, para 6(c).

32. Nelson, p 335.

33. Wesley F. Craven and James L. Cate, eds, *The Army Air Forces in World War II,* 7 vols (Chicago, 1948–1958), Vol VI: *Men and Planes* (1955), p 23.

34. FM 100–20, Command and Employment of Air Power, Jul 21, 1943, Sec I, para 1.

35. *Ibid.,* Sec I, para 3.

36. *Ibid.,* Secs I, II.

37. Memo, CSA, subj: A Single Department of War in the Post-War Period, n.d., atch to memo, Col William T. Sexton, Secy, WDGS, for Secretariat, Joint US Chiefs of Staff, subj: A Single Department of War in the Post-War Period, Nov 2, 1943; App, WDGS, to Sexton memo, Subj: A Single Department of War, n.d., RG 218, Rcrds of the US JCS, MMB, NA.

38. App, WDGS, subj: A Single Department of War, n.d., RG, Rcrds of JCS, CCS, 040, 11/2/43, Sec 1, MMB, NA.

39. *Ibid.*

40. Ltr, Prof. I. B. Holley, Jr., to Herman S. Wolk, Aug 10, 1980.

41. WD Cir 347, Aug 25, 1944, p 5.

42. *Ibid.,* p 4.

43. *Ibid.,* p 5.

44. James E. Hewes, Jr., *From Root to McNamara: Army Organization and Administration, 1900–1963* (Washington, 1975), Chap IV.

45. App, WDGS, subj: A Single Department of War, n. d., RG 218, Rcrds of JCS, CCS, 040, 11/2/43, Sec 1, MMB, NA.

46. *Ibid.*

47. *Ibid.*

48. Hearings before the Select Committee on Post-War Military Policy, House of Representatives, *Proposal to Establish a Single Department of Armed Forces,* Testimony of Brig Gen William F. Tompkins, USA, Dir/Sp Plng Div, WDGS, in Apr 44, 78th Cong, 2d sess (Washington, 1944), pt 1, p 23.

49. Report of the Chief of Staff to the Secretary of War, atch to memo, Maj Gen William F. Tompkins USA, Dir/Sp Plng Div, WDGS, to CSA, May 9, 1945, RG 165, ACS, 319.1, Sec 1, Case 7, Box 193, MMB, NA.

50. *Ibid.*

51. *Ibid.*

52. Testimony of Gen Dwight D. Eisenhower, USA, in Oct 45 before the Senate Committee on Military Affairs.

53. Memo, Eaker to Herman S. Wolk, Feb 3, 1977.

54. Memo for CSA fr Gen H. H. Arnold, CG, AAF, subj: Re-Survey of the Troop Basis for the Post-War Army, Mar 31, 1945, RG 18, AAF, AAG, Mail & Rcrds Div, Decimal File 1945, 381, Box 189, Postwar File, Vol 2, MMB, NA.

55. Intvw, Herman S. Wolk with Lt Gen Ira C. Eaker, Washington, D.C., Aug 27, 1974; intvw, Herman S. Wolk with Maj Gen Haywood S. Hansell, Jr., Washington D.C., Oct 7, 1974; ltr, Lt Gen Ira C. Eaker to Herman S. Wolk, Oct 22, 1974; Margaret Truman, *Harry S. Truman* (New York, 1973), p 273.

56. Henry H. Arnold, *Third Report of the Commanding General of the Army Air Forces to the Secretary of War* (Baltimore, 1945), p 33.

57. Ltr, Gen Henry H. Arnold to Gen Carl A. Spaatz, Aug 19, 1945, Spaatz Colln, Box 21, File Aug 45, MD, LC.

58. Gen Henry H. Arnold, "Air Power and the Future," in *Third Report of the Commanding General of the Army Air Forces to the Secretary of War,* Nov 45.

59. Memo for Dr. Theodore von Karman fr Gen Henry H. Arnold, subj: AAF Long Range Development Program, Nov 7, 1944, Spaatz Colln, Box 58, MD, LC.

60. Thomas A. Sturm, *The USAF Scientific Advisory Board: Its First Twenty Years, 1944–1964* (Washington, 1967), Chap 1.

61. Arnold, *Third Report of the Commanding General of the Army Air Forces to the Secretary of War.*

62. *The New York Times,* Oct 6, 1945, p 12.

63. Report by Marshal of the Royal Air Force the Viscount Trenchard, *The Principles of Air Power on War,* May 45, Lt Gen Ira C. Eaker Colln, Box 26, MD, LC.

64. Gen Carl A. Spaatz, "Strategic Air Power: Fulfillment of a Concept," *Foreign Affairs,* Apr 46, pp 385–396.

65. Memo, Spaatz to Asst Secy of War for Air, subj: United States Contribution to United Nations Security Forces, Feb 4, 1947, OSAF 7a, Size and Composition of the Air Force, Bk I, 1945–49, MMB, NA.

66. Address, Asst Secy of War for Air Stuart Symington to Oklahoma City Chamber of Commerce, Dec 9, 1946.

67. Memo, Lt Gen James H. Doolittle to Lt Gen Ira C. Eaker, Oct 25, 1945, Eaker Colln, MD, LC.

Chapter 2

Planning for 70 Groups

1. Ltr, Gen Jacob E. Smart to H. S. Wolk, 17 Jul 1996.

2. Brig Gen Orvil A. Anderson, A Study to Determine the Minimum Air Power the United States Should Have at the Conclusion of the War in Europe, Apr 43, RG 18, AAF, OC/AS, Scientific Advsy Gp 1941–Aug 47, Box 12, MMB, NA.

3. *Ibid.*

4. *Ibid.*

5. Memo for Dep Cmdr, AAF, and Ch/Air Stf fr Maj Gen Laurence S. Kuter, ACAS/Plans, subj: Re-Survey of the Troop Basis for the Post-War Army, Mar 30, 1945, RG 18, AAF, AAG, Mail & Rcrds Div, Decimal File 1945, Box 189, Postwar File, Vol 2, MMB, NA.

6. *Ibid.*

7. *Ibid.*

8. Memo for Brig Gen Laurence S. Kuter by Col Reuben C. Moffat, subj: Post War Air Force, Dec 12, 1943, RG 18, Box 189, MMB, NA; for Gen Henry H. Arnold fr Brig Gen Laurence S. Kuter, ACAS/Plans, subj: Post War Air Force, Dec 24, 1943, RG 18, Box 189, MMB, NA.

9. Memo for Arnold fr Kuter, Dec 24, 1943.

10. Memo for Gen Henry H. Arnold fr Maj Gen Laurence S. Kuter, ACAS/Plans, subj: Status of Plans for the Post-War Air Force, Jan 17, 1945, RG 18, Box 189, MMB, NA.

11. *Ibid.*

12. See note 5.

13. See note 10.

14. Memo for Ch/Air Staff fr Brig Gen Byron E. Gates, Ch, Mgt Con, subj: Organization to Accomplish Redeployment Plans, Sep 4, 1944, RG 18, AAG, Mail & Rcrds Div, Decimal File, Jun 1944–1946,

Folder "325 Optns 5 Post War Planning, June Through Sept 1944," Box 1515, MMB, NA.

15. *Ibid.*

16. See note 10.

17. War Department Basic Plan for the Post-War Military Establishment, Mar 13, 1945, p 2, RG 18, 1945, AAG 381, Post-war, MMB, NA.

18. *Ibid,* p 3.

19. *Ibid.*

20. *Ibid.*

21. *Ibid.*

22. Paper by Gen George C. Marshall for Biennial Report of the Secretary of War, May 9, 1945, RG 165, 319.1, May 45, MMB, NA.

23. *Ibid.*

24. *Ibid.*

25. See note 5.

26. See note 5.

27. Memo for CSA (Attn: Sp Plng Div) fr Lt Gen Barney M. Giles, Dep Comdr, AAF, and Ch/Air Stf, subj: Report of Progress on Re-Survey of the Troop Basis for the Post-War Army, Jan 15, 1945, RG 18, Box 189, MMB, NA.

28. Draft memo, Col Reuben C. Moffat to CSA (Attn: Sp Plng Div), subj: Report of Progress on Re-Survey of the Troop Basis for the Post-War Army, Jan 14, 1945.

29. *Ibid.*

30. *Ibid.*

31. Memo for CSA fr Gen Henry H. Arnold, CG, AAF, subj: Re-Survey of the Troop Basis for the Post-War Army, Mar 31, 1945, RG 18, AAF, AAG, Mail & Rcrds Div, Decimal File 1945, 381, Box 189, Postwar File, Vol 2, MMB, NA.

32. *Ibid.*

33. *Ibid.*

34. *Ibid.*

35. *Ibid.*

36. *Ibid.*

37. Memo for CG, AAF, fr Gen Thomas T. Handy, Dep CSA, subj: Re-Survey of the Troop Basis for the Post-War Army, May 5, 1945, RG 18, Box 189, MMB, NA.

38. *Ibid.*

39. *Ibid.*

40. Memo for Dep CSA fr Maj Gen William F. Tompkins, Dir/Sp Plng Div, subj: Attached Report of the Commanding General AAF—Re-Survey of the Troop Basis for the Post-War Army, Apr 7, 1947, RG 18, Box 189, MMB, NA.

41. *Ibid.*

42. *Ibid.*

43. War Department Views Concerning Single Department of National Defense, atch to memo, Maj Gen William F. Tompkins, Dir/Sp Plng Div, subj: Attached report of the Commanding General AAF—Re-Survey of the Troop Basis for the Post-War Army, Apr 7, 1945, RG 18, Box 189, MMB, NA.

44. *Ibid.*

45. Presentation, Maj Gen William F. Tompkins, Dir/Sp Plng Div, to Senate Armed Svcs Cmte, May 1, 1945, RG 18, 325, UMT Gen, MMB, NA.

46. *Ibid.*

47. *Ibid.*

48. *Ibid.*

49. *Ibid.*

50. AAF Study, Universal Military Training, May 45, RG 18, 325, UMT Gen, MMB, NA.

51. *Ibid.*

52. Memo to Ch/Air Stf Plng Div, WDSS, fr Brig Gen F. Trubee Davison, Ch/Sp Projs Div, AAF, subj: AAF V–J Plan as of July 1945, Jul 26, 1945, RG 18, 1945, AAG 370.01 Conc-Mob-Demob, Vol 3/175; memo for Maj Gen Orvil A. Anderson fr Col William P. Berkeley, Exec to DCAS/Plans, subj: Chronological Summary of Pertinent Documents, Available in AC/AS–5, on Air Force Troop Basis and Organization, Sep 19, 1946, RG 341, Plans & Ops 320.2 (Apr 4, 1944), 129A, MMB, NA.

53. Harry S. Truman, *Memoirs,* Vol II: *Years of Trial and Hope* (Garden City, N.Y., 1956), p 48.

54. Memo for Gen Henry H. Arnold fr Lt Gen Hoyt S. Vandenberg, ACAS–3, subj: Daily Activity Report of the AC/AS–3, Aug 28, 1945, RG 18, AAG 319.1, OC&R DARs, 1945/369, MMB, NA.

55. *Ibid.*

56. Memo to Ch/Air Stf fr Maj Gen Lauris Norstad, ACAS/Plans, subj: AAF V–J Plan, Sep 5, 1945, 145.86–52 [45–46], AFSHRC; memo to Ch/Air Stf fr Brig Gen F. Trubee Davison, subj: AAF V–J Plan, Aug 31, 1945, 145.86.52, AFSHRC; memo for Lt Gen Hoyt S. Vandenberg, ACAS/OC&R, fr Col Joseph J. Ladd, subj: Period II Troop Basis, Aug 27, 1945, RG 18, 1945 AAG 320.2, Troop Basis, Vol 3, Box 96, MMB, NA; see note 53.

57. Memo for Lt Gen Hoyt S. Vandenberg fr Brig Gen George McCoy, Jr., subj: Bombardment Program in Interim Air Force, Aug 21, 1945, RG 18, AAG 1945, 452.1, Vol 4/231, MMB, NA; memo for Gen Henry H. Arnold fr Lt Gen Hoyt S. Vandenberg, ACAS–3, subj: Deployment of VHB Groups to European Theater, Aug 24, 1945, RG 18, AAG 370, Employment 1945, Vol 5/174, MMB, NA.

58. Memo for Dep CG, AAF, fr Lt Gen Hoyt S. Vandenberg, ACAS–3, subj: VHB Deployment, Aug 30, 1945, RG 18, AAG 370, Employment 1945, Vol 5/174, MMB, NA.

59. Memo for Lt Gen Hoyt S. Vandenberg fr Brig Gen William A. Matheny, Ch/Commitments Div, ACAS–3, subj: Item of Interest for Gen Arnold, Oct 1, 1945, RG 18, AAG 300.6, Memoranda and Notes, 1945, Vol 3, MMB, NA; memo for Gen Henry H. Arnold fr Maj Gen Harold M. McClelland, Actg ACAS–3, subj: Daily Activity report of AC/AS–3, Dec 27, 1945, RG 18, AAG 319.1, OC&R DARs, 1945/369, MMB, NA.

60. R&R Sheet, Cmt 1, Maj Gen Lauris Norstad, ACAS–5, subj: Proposed Organization and Deployment of the Post-War Air Force (70-Group Program), Sep 11, 1945, RG 18, AAG 370, Employment, 1945, Vol 5/174, MMB, NA.

61. MR, Col Jacob E. Smart, subj: Decisions Reached at Meeting in Gen Eaker's Office with Respect to Budget Estimates for Army Air Forces Program, Aug 28, 1945.

62. R&R Sheet, Col John S. Hardy, ACAS–1 (Mil Pers Div), to ACS–3 (Orgn Div), subj: AAF Troop Program for 1 July 1946, Nov 26, 1945, RG 18, 1945 AAG 320.2, AAF Prgm/91, MMB, NA; memo for Anderson fr Berkeley, Sep 19, 1946; R&R Sheet, Col Joseph J. Ladd, ACAS–3 (Orgn Div), to ACAS–1, subj: AAF Troop Program for 1 Jul 1946, Nov 21, 1945 RG 18, 1945 AAG 320.1, AAF Prgm/91, MMB, NA.

63. Memo, Davison to Ch/Air Staff, 31 Aug 31, 1945; memo, Norstad to Ch/Air Staff, Sep 5, 1945; Assumptions and Ground Rules Pertaining to the Interim and Peacetime Air Forces Plans, Dec 26, 1945.

64. Revision of Assumptions and Ground Rules of AAF VJ Plan as of 15 July 1945, Sep 19, 1945, AFHRA 145.86–90, AFHRA.

65. *Ibid.*

66. *Ibid.*

67. Memo fr Dep Comdr, AAF, fr Maj Gen Lauris Norstad, ACAS–5, subj: Comments on "AF V–J Plan of 15 July 1945, 145.86–52 (1045–46), AFHRA.

68. Interim Report of the Special War Department Committee on the Permanent Military Establishment of the Army of the United States (Bessell Committee), Sep 45, RG 165, SPD, 334, Sp WD Cmte on PME, MMB, NA.

69. *Ibid.*

70. *Ibid.*

71. *Ibid.*

72. Memo for Brig Gens William E. Bessell, Jr., Edwin W. Chamberlain, Gordon E. Textor, Glen C. Jamison, Reuben E. Jenkins, and Henry C. Wolfe fr Brig Gen Henry I. Hodes, Asst DCSA, subj: Strength of Permanent Military Establishment, Oct 15, 1945, 145–86–50, AFHRA.

73. *Ibid.*

74. Tab A to memo for Sp Cmte on Str of PME, fr Brig Gen Henry I. Hodes, Asst DCSA, subj: Procedures and Policies for the Preparation of Revised Report, Oct 15, 1945, 145–86–50, Oct–Dec, AFHRA.

75. Memo, Brig Gen Henry I. Hodes, Asst DCSA, subj: Special Committee on the Strength of the Permanent Military Establishment, Nov 6, 1945, 145.86–50, Oct–Dec 45, AFHRA.

76. *Ibid.* (Brig Gen Glen C. Jamison's handwritten comment on margin); MR, Col Jacob E. Smart, Secy of Air Stf, subj: Minutes of Staff Meeting, Oct 18, 1945, RG 18, AAG–37, 1945, Vol 9/156, MMB, NA.

77. Memo for Brig Gen Edwin W. Chamberlain fr Brig Gen Glen C. Jamison, subj: Special Committee on the Strength of the Permanent Military Establishment, Nov 17, 1945, 145–86–50, Oct–Dec 45, AFHRA.

78. Minority Report of AAF Member of Special War Department Committee on the Permanent Military Establishment, enclosure to memo for CSA fr Gen Henry N. Arnold, CG, AAF, subj: Revised Report on the Strength of the Permanent Military Establishment, Dec 4, 1945, RG 341, P&O 320.1 (Apr 4, 1944), Sec 2/129A, MMB, NA.

79. *Ibid.*
80. *Ibid.*
81. *Ibid.*
82. *Ibid.*

83. Address Before a Joint Session of the Congress on Universal Military Training, Oct 23, 1945, in *Public Papers of the President of the United States: Harry S. Truman, 1945* (Washington, 1961), p 406.

84. *Ibid.,* p 410.

85. Memo for CSA fr Gen Arnold, Dec 4, 1945.

86. *Ibid.*
87. *Ibid.*

88. AAF Sum Sheet for Ch/Air Stf fr Brig Gen Reuben C. Hood, Jr., subj: JCS 1478/6 (Postwar Military and Naval Strength), Dec 3, 1945, RG 341, P&O, PD 009 (Aug 17, 1945), Annex 1/22, MMB, NA; memo for Ch/Air Stf Brig Gen William F. McKee, Dep ACAS–3, subj: JCS 1478/6 (Postwar Military and Naval Strength), Nov 26, 1945.

89. *Ibid.*

90. Memo for CG, AAF, fr Maj Gen Idwal H. Edwards, ACS/G–3, WD, subj: JCS 1478/6 (Postwar Military and Naval Strength), Dec 14, 1945, RG 18, 1945, AAG 381, Postwar File, Vol 2, Box 189, MMB, NA; memo for Ch/Air Stf fr Gen McKee, Nov 26, 1945.

91. AAF Sum Sheet for Ch/Air Stf fr Gen Hood, Dec 3, 1945.

92. Assumptions and Ground Rules Pertaining to the Interim and Peacetime Air Forces Plans, Dec 26, 1945, RG 18, AAG Central File 391, File War Plans Misc Nat Def, Vol 2, Box 189, MMB, NA.

93. *Ibid.*
94. *Ibid.*
95. *Ibid.*
96. *Ibid.*
97. *Ibid.*
98. *Ibid.*

99. Memo for Anderson fr Berkeley, Sep 19, 1946.

100. Memo for Brig Gen Glen C. Jamison fr Lt Col Kenneth L. Garrett, subj: Material for Briefing of Generals Arnold and Eisenhower, Dec 8, 1945, 145.86–50, AFHRA.

101. *Ibid.*
102. *Ibid.*

103. *Ibid.;* Ltr, Maj Gen Lauris Norstad, ACAS–5, to Gen George C. Kenney, CG, PACUSA, Dec 17, 1945.

104. Memorandum to Asst Sec of War for Air, CG, AAF, Dep Cmdr, AAF, Chief of Air Staff, *et al*, from Col R. C. Moffatt, Chief Special Planning Div (by command of Gen Arnold), 26 Dec 1945, subj: Assumptions and Ground Rules Pertaining to the Interim and Peacetime Air Forces Plan (26 Dec 1945), in RG 18, AAG 381, Postwar File 1945, MMB; AAF Ltr 20–91, Lt Gen Ira C. Eaker, Dep Cmdr to Major AAF Commands and CGs and Commanders of Independent Air Force Facilities, 15 Dec 1945, subj: Interim and Peacetime Air Force Plans, in RG 18, 321, Interim Postwar & Peacetime AFs, Box 603.

105. Atch, Composition and Development of Interim Air Force, Postwar Div, 21 Nov 1945 to AAF Ltr, 20–91, 14 Feb 1946 (Supersedes previous Ltr 20–91), in RG 18, AAG, 321, Interim Postwar and Peacetime Air Forces, Box 603.

106. R&R Sheet, Maj Lauris Norstad, AC/AS–5 to Chief of Air Staff, Oct 3, 1945, subj: Interim Command Organization of Army Air Forces in the Pacific, in RG 18/1945, 321, AAF–2/97.

107. Tab C, "Breakdown of the 400,000 Troop Program," to Memorandum for the Chief, Requirements Division, by Col P. T. Collen, Chief, Policy and Tactical Employment Br., 19 Feb 1946, subj: Post War Air Force, in RG 18, AAG 321, Interim and Peacetime Air Forces, Box 603, MMB, NA.

108. *The New York Times,* Oct 28, Sec IV, p 10.

109. *Ibid.*

110. Memorandum for the Chief of Staff, Feb 14, 1946, subj: Mobilization in a National Emergency Without Universal Military Training, in RG 341, AAF File, MMB, NA.

111. *Ibid.*

112. *Ibid.*

113. *Ibid.*

114. Draft, "Universal Military Training," Dec 46, War Dept Training Division, in RG 28, Decimal File 325, UMT, General, MMRB, NA.

115. *Ibid.*

Chapter 3

Unification and a Separate Air Force

1. Ltr, Robert A. Lovett, Asst S/W for Air, to Gen Carl A. Spaatz, CG; USAFE, Mar 25, 1945, Spaatz Colln, File Mar 45 Personal, Box 21, MD, LC.

2. Hearings before the Select Committee on Post-War Military Policy, House of Representatives, *Proposal to Establish a Single Department of Armed Forces,* 78th Cong. 2d sess (Washington, 1944), pt 1, p 71.

3. *Ibid.,* p 50.

4. *Ibid.,* p 49.

5. Hearings before the War Contracts Subcommittee, Committee on Military Affairs, Senate, *Hearings on Contract Termi-* *nation,* 78th Cong, 2d sess (Washington, 1944), pp 533–34.

6. Memo, Robert P. Patterson, Under S/W, to S/W, May 4 1944, Robert P. Patterson Papers, Folder Postwar Plng 2, Box 162, MD, LC.

7. Report of the Joint Chiefs of Staff Special Committee for Reorganization of National Defense, Apr 11, 1945, p 1, RG 340, Air Board General File, 1945-48, Box 12, MMB, NA.

8. *Ibid.,* p 7.

9. *Ibid.,* p 18.

10. *Ibid.,* Encl B, p 14.

11. *Ibid.,* Encl B, p 12.

12. *Ibid.,* p 2.

13. *Ibid.,* p 5.

14. *Ibid.,* p 10.

15. Report of the Joint Chiefs of Staff Special Committee for Reorganization of National Defense, Apr 11, 1945. Minority Report of Admiral James O. Richardson, p 45.

16. *Ibid.*

17. *Ibid.*

18. *Ibid.,* Encl B, p 12.

19. *Ibid.*

20. Reorganization of National Defense, memo, CSA to CINC Army and Navy, Encl B to memo for Pres fr Adm William D. Leahy, C/S to CINC of Army and Navy, Oct 16, 1945, RG 218, Rcrds of US JCS, CCS 040, Nov 2, 1943, Sec 3, MMB, NA; Reorganization of National Defense memo, CNO, Encl D to memo for Pres fr Adm William D. Leahy, C/S to CINC of Army and Navy, Oct 16, 1945, RG 218, Rcrds of US JCS.

21. See note above.

22. See note 20.

23. See note 20, Encl B.

24. Hearings before the Committee on Military Affairs, Senate, *Department of Armed Forces and Military Security: Hearings on S. 84 and S. 1482.* Statement by Fleet Adm Chester W. Nimitz, on Nov 17, 1945, 79th Cong, 1st sess (Washington, 1945), p 383 [hereafter cited as *Hearings on S. 84 and S. 1482*].

25. *Ibid.*

26. *Ibid.*

27. See note 20, Encl D.

28. See note 20, Encl D.

29. See note 20, Encl D.

30. See note 20, Encl D.

31. See note 20, Encl D.

32. Statement by Adm Ernest J. King, CNO, Oct 23, 1945, Hearings on S. 84 and S. 1482.

33. Statement by General of the Army Henry H. Arnold, Oct 19, 1945, Hearings on S. 84 and S. 1482.

34. *Ibid.*

35. *Ibid.* Also see note 61, Chap I; memo for CSA fr Gen Henry H. Arnold, CG, AAF, subj: Revised Report on the Strength of the Permanent Military Establishment, Dec 4, 1945, RG 341, P&O 320.2 (Apr 4, 1944), Sec 2/129A, MMB, NA.

36. See note 33. See also memo, Gen Henry H. Arnold to Dep Cmdr, AAF, Subj: Reorganization of National Defense, Oct 22, 1945, RG 18, 1945, 321, AAF 2/97, MMB, NA.

37. Reorganization of National Defense, memo, CG, AAF, Encl E to memo for Pres fr Adm William D. Leahy, C/S to CINC of Army and Navy, Oct 16, 1945, RG 218, Rcrds of US JCS, CCS 040, Nov 2, 1943, Sec 3, MMB, NA; Also see memo for Gen George C. Marshall fr Gen Henry H. Arnold, subj: Required Legislation is Obtained for Permanent Post-War Establishment, Aug 28, 1945, Gen Henry H. Arnold Colln, MD, LC.

38. Arnold, *Third Report of the Commanding General of the Army Air Forces to the Secretary of War,* (11), Integration of Air Power into National Defense.

39. Reorganization of National Defense, memo, CG, AAF, Encl E to memo for Pres fr Adm William D. Leahy, C/S to CINC of Army and Navy, Oct 16, 1945.

40. *Ibid.*

41. Statement by General of the Army George C. Marshall, Oct 18, 1945, *Hearings on S. 84 and S. 1482.*

42. *Ibid.*

43. *Ibid.*

44. *Ibid.*

45. Memo CSA, atch to memo for Secy, JCS, fr Lt Col F. T. Newsome, Asst Secy, WDGS, subj: Reorganization of National Defense, Sep 26, 1945, RG 165, Rcrds of WD Gen and Sp Stfs, Sp Plng Div, WDSS 334, Plng Bd for Postwar Posts to Sp Nat Def Comsn, MMB, NA.

46. See note 41.

47. Statement by S/W Robert P. Patterson, Oct 17, 1945, *Hearings on S. 84 and S. 1482*, p 14.

48. *The New York Times*, Oct 6, 1945, p 12.

49. Unification of the War and Navy Departments, a Report to the Secretary of the Navy James V. Forrestal by Ferdinand Eberstadt, Sep 25, 1945, p 3, OSD Hist Ofc Archives.

50. *Ibid.*, pp 6–8

51. Statement by SECNAV James V. Forrestal, Oct 22, 1945, *Hearings on S. 84 and S. 1482*, p 97.

52. *Ibid.*, p 99.

53. *Ibid.*, p 99.

54. *Ibid.*, pp 100–101.

55. *Ibid.*, p 101.

56. *Ibid.*, p 102.

57. *Ibid.*, p 102.

58. Presentation of Collins Committee Report to the Army Staff and the Chief of Staff, subj: Conference on Outline of Proposed Organization of a Unified Department of Armed Forces, Lt Gen J. Lawton Collins, presiding, Oct 16, 1945, RG 165, 320, Sep–Dec 46, MMB, NA.

59. *Ibid.*

60. *Hearings on S. 84 and S. 1482*, p 362.

61. Hearings before the Committee on Armed Services, Senate, *National Defense Establishment (Unification of the Armed Services): Hearings on S. 758, Statement of Gen Dwight D. Eisenhower on Mar 25, 1947, 80th Cong, 1st sess, (Washington, 1947)*.

62. *Hearings on S. 84 and S. 1482*, p 363.

63. *Ibid.*, p 367.

64. *Ibid.*, p 360.

65. Memo, Gen Dwight D. Eisenhower, to ACS, G–1, et al, subj: Responsibilities of Staff Officers, Scope, Approach and Execution (Comments of Chief of Staff before Staff Officers, 5 Dec 1945), Dec 10, 1945, RG 165, Rcrds of WD Gen and Sp Stfs, ACS, Patch-Simpson Bdm Minutes and Comments, Box 922, MMB, NA. Also see intvw, William R. Porretto, hist, ATC, with Lt Gen Barney M. Giles, San Antonio, Tex., Oct 21, 1966. According to Giles, Eisenhower's view was that "the Air Force boys should keep their shirts on and start planning for separate air power."

66. Memo, Eisenhower to ACS, G–1, *et al,* Dec 10, 1945.

67. *Hearings on S. 84 and S. 1482*, p 361.

68. *Ibid.*

69. Harry S. Truman, Memoirs, Vol II: *Years of Trial and Hope* (Garden City, N.Y., 1956), p 46.

70. *Ibid.*

71. *The New York Times,* Aug 31, 1945, p 16.

72. Special Message to the Congress Recommending the Establishment of a Department of National Defense, Dec 19, 1945, in *Public Papers of the Presidents of the United States: Harry S. Truman, 1945* (Washington, 1961), p 547.

73. *Ibid.*

74. *Ibid.*, p 548.

75. *Ibid.*, p 551.

76. *Ibid.*, p 555.

77. *Ibid.*, p 559.

78. Memo for Lt Gen Ira C. Eaker fr Col Jacob E. Smart, Secy of Air Stf, Sep 18, 1945, RG 18, AAG, 320.2. File Postwar, 1945, MMB, NA.

79. *Ibid.*

80. *Ibid.*

81. R&R Sheet, Lt Gen Ira C. Eaker, Dep Comdr, AAF, to ACAS–5 (Maj Gen Lauris Norstad), subj: Study on Single Department of National Defense and/or a Separate Air Force, RG 18, AAG 320.2, File Postwar, 1945, MMB, NA.

82. R&R Sheet, Maj Gen Lauris Norstad, ACAS–5, to Dep Cmdr, AAF, subj: Study on Single Department of National Defense and/or a Separate Air Force, Oct 10, 1945, MMB, NA; memo, Maj Gen

Lauris Norstad, ACAS/Plans, to Air Judge Advocate, subj: Study on Single Department of National Defense and/or Separate Air Force, Nov 13, 1945, RG 18, 1945, AAG 381, War Plans Misc, Nat Def Vol 2/189, MMB, NA.

83. R&R Sheet to ACAS–1, 2, 3, 4, 5, and Air Judge Advocate fr Lt Gen Ira C. Eaker, Dep Comdr, AAF, fr Col Desmond O'Keefe, Air Judge Advocate, Nov 19, 1945, RG 8, 1945, AAG 381, War Plans Misc, Nat Def Vol 2/189, MMB, NA.

84. Ltr, Brig Gen Frank F. Everest to Lt Gen Nathan F. Twining, CG, Twentieth AF, Oct 20, 1945, RG 18, AAG 322, MMB, NA.

85. Memo, Gen Henry H. Arnold to Dep Comdr, AAF, subj: Reorganization of National Defense, Oct 22, 1945, RG 18, 321, AAF 2/97, MMB, NA.

86. Memo for Gen Henry H. Arnold fr Maj Gen Lauris Norstad, ACAS/Plans, subj: Daily Activity Report, Dec 11, 1945, RG 18, AAG 319.1, Plans Daily Activity Rprts, 1945, 370, MMB, NA.

87. Memo for Gen George C. Marshall, CG, AAF, subj: Required Legislation to Insure the Continuation of Present War Department Organization Until Legislation is Obtained for Permanent Postwar Establishment, Aug 28, 1945, Gen Henry H. Arnold Colln, MD, LC.

88. Memo for Gen Henry H. Arnold fr Gen George C. Marshall, CSA, subj: Legislation, Aug 30, 1945, RG 165, ACS, Patch-Simpson Bd, Minutes and Comments, Box 922, MMB, NA.

89. Intvw, Patch Bd with Gen Henry H. Arnold, CG, AAF, Sep 18, 1945, RG 165, Rcrds of WD Gen and Sp Stfs, CSA, Patch-Simpson Bd Files, MMB, NA.

90. Hewes, *From Root to McNamara*, pp 148–49.

91. Memo, Gen Thomas T. Handy, Dep CSA, to Lt Gen Alexander M. Patch, Jr., subj: General Eisenhower's Plan for Reorganization of the War Department, Sep 10, 1945, in Hewes, p 149.

92. Statement by Gen Dwight D. Eisenhower to Patch Bd, Sep 23, 1945, RG 165, Rcrds of WD Gen and Sp Stfs, CSA, Patch-Simpson Bd File, Box 927, MMB, NA.

93. Testimony of Gen Carl A. Spaatz to Patch Bd, Sep 17, 1945, RG 165, Rcrds of WD Gen and Sp Stfs, CSA, Patch-Simpson Bd File, Box 927, MMB, NA.

94. *Ibid.*

95. Memo for ACAS–1 fr Col Newcomer, subj: Promotion of AAF Officers, Dec 7, 1945, RG 18, 1945, AAG 21, Interim Postwar and Peacetime Air Forces, 2/99, MMB, NA.

96. *Ibid.*

97. See note 93.

98. See note 94.

99. MR, Gen Carl A. Spaatz, Sep 17, 1945, Spaatz Colln, File Sep 45, Box 22, MD, LC.

100. Memo for CSA fr Gen Henry H. Arnold, CG, AAF, subj: Report of Board of Officers on Recognition of the War Department, Nov 14, 1945, RG 165, ACS, Patch-Simpson Bd, Minutes and Comments, Box 922, MMB, NA.

101. *Ibid.*

102. *Ibid.* Also see memo for Ch/Postwar Div fr Brig Gen Charles P. Cabell, Ch/Strategy & Policy Div, ACAS–5, subj: Comments on Patch Report, Nov 6, 1945, RG 341, P&O, PD 020 (11-2-43), Sec 2/23A, MMB, NA.

103. Memo for Ch/Postwar Div fr Cabell, Nov 6, 1945.

104. See note 100.

105. Memo for Lt Gen William H. Simpson fr Gen Henry H. Arnold, subj: Statement of the Position of the Army Air Forces Concerning the Reorganization of the War Department, Dec 21, 1945, RG 341, P&O, PD 020 (11-23-43), Sec 2/23A, MMB, NA.

106. Ltr, Spaatz to Arnold, Dec 3, 1944, Spaatz Papers, Box 58, MD, LC.

107. Statement of My Personal Opinion as to Why AAA Should Not be Integrated with the Air Forces, Brig Gen Aaron Bradshaw, Jr., to Patch Bd, Sep 17, 1945, RG 615, Rcrds of WD Gen and Sp Stfs, CSA, Patch-Simpson Bd File, MMB, NA.

108. *Ibid.*

109. *Ibid.*

110. See note 105.

111. Memo, Gen Carl A. Spaatz to Lt Gen William H. Simpson, subj: Statement of the Position of the AAF Concerning the Reorganization of the WD, Dec 45, Spaatz Colln, File Dec 45, Box 24, MD, LC.

112. Memo for CSA fr Gen Carl A. Spaatz, subj: Relationship of Program for Single Department of Common Defense Sponsored by the President and the War Department to Proposed Implementation of Simpson Board Report, Feb 1, 1946, RG 165, ACS, Patch-Simpson Bd, Box 922, MMB, NA. Also see memo to Ch/Air Stf fr Brig Gen John A. Samford, DCAS–2, subj: Air Force Autonomy Within the War Department, May 23, 1946, RG 341, P&O, PD 020, MMB, NA.

113. See note above.

114. See note 112.

115. Memo for Lt Gen William H. Simpson, Pres, Bd of Offs on Orgn of the WD, CG, AAF, CG, AGF, CG, ASF, *et al*, fr Brig Gen Henry I. Hodes, Asst DCAS, subj: Statement of Approved Policies to Effect Increased Autonomy of the AAF Within the War Department Structure, Apr 4, 1946, RG 165, ACS, Patch-Simpson Bd, Box 922, MMB, NA.

116. *Ibid.*

117. *Ibid.*

118. *Ibid.*

119. *Ibid.*

120. Memo, Brig Gen Glen C. Jamison, DCAS–5, to Maj Gen Lauris Norstad, ACAS–5, subj: The Simpson Board Recommendations for the Reorganization of the War Department, May 3, 1946, RG 341, P&O, PD 020 (Nov 2, 1943), Sec 2/448, MMB, NA.

121. Memo for DCAS fr Gen Carl A. Spaatz, CG, AAF, subj: Statement of Approved Policies to Effect Increased Autonomy of the Army Air Forces Within the War Department Structure, Mar 28, 1946, RG 165, ACS, Patch-Simpson Bd, Box 922, MMB, NA.

122. See note 115.

123. See note 115.

124. See note 115.

Chapter 4

Organizing the Postwar Air Force

1. R&R Sheet, Maj Gen Howard A. Craig, ACAS–3, to Mgt Con (Brig Gen Byron E. Gates), subj: Reorganization of Zone of Interior Command Organization, Aug 23, 1944.

2. *Ibid.;* R&R Sheet, Maj Gen Laurence S. Kuter, ACAS/Plans, to Mgt Con (thru Gen Craig), subj: Reorganization of Zone of Interior Command Organization, Aug 21, 1944, RG 18, 1945, AAG 321, CAF/98, MMB, NA.

3. Memo for CSA fr Gen Henry H. Arnold, CG, AAF, subj: Activation of Headquarters Continental Air Force, Oct 22, 1944, RG 18, 1945, AAG 321, CAS/98, MMB, NA.

4. Memo for Gen Henry H. Arnold fr Lt Gen Thomas T. Handy, Dep CSA, subj: Activation of Headquarters Continental Air Forces, Oct 25, 1944, RG 18, 1945, AG 321, CAF/98, MMB, NA.

5. Memo for Lt Gen Thomas T. Handy, Dep CSA, fr Gen Henry H. Arnold, CG, AAF, subj: Activation of Headquarters Continental Air Forces, Oct 28, 1944, RG 18, 1945, AAG 321, CAF/98, MMB, NA.

6. *Ibid.*

7. Notation by Gen Handy, Nov 17, 1944, to memo for Handy fr Arnold, Oct 18, 1944; AAFL 20–9, to CGs, All AFs and All Independent and Subordinate AAF Comds, fr Lt Gen Barney M. Giles, Dep Comdr, AAF, and Ch/Air Stf, Activation of Headquarters Continental Air Forces, Dec 16, 1944.

8. AAFL 20–9, Dec 16, 1944.

9. AAFR 20–1, Jun 1, 1945, in Chase C. Mooney and Edward C. Williamson, *Organization of the Army Air Arm, 1935–1945* (USAF Hist Study 10, Maxwell AFB, Ala., 1956), p 58.

10. Chauncey E. Sanders, *Redeployment and Demobilization* (USAF Hist Study 77, Maxwell AFB, Ala., 1952), pp 40–43; Albert E. Haase, *Manpower Demobilization* (Offutt AFB, Nebr., 1946).

11. Intvw, Arthur K. Marmor with Maj Gen Leon W. Johnson, Apr 14, 1954, Ofc/AF Hist.

12. Memo, Maj Gen Donald Wilson, ACAS–3, to Brig Gen Byron E. Gates, Ch/Mgt Con, AAF: Organization of Continental Air Defense Commands, Jun 6, 1945; ltr, Gates to CG, CAF, subj: Organization of Continental Air Defense, Jun 15, 1945.

13. Third Ind, HQ CAF to CG, AAF, Oct 10, 1945, to ltr, HQ 3d AF to CG, Eastern Defense Command, subj: "Joint Air Defense" Eastern Defense Command, Gulf Sea Frontier, Aug 20, 1945.

14. Memo for CG, AAF, fr Brig Gen George L. Eberle, Actg ACS/OPD, WDGS, subj: Statement of Composition and Interim Mission of the General Reserve, Mar 28, 1946, RG 18, AAG 326, Misc 1946–47, Vol 1/607, MMB, NA.

15. Ltr, Col Godwin Ordway, Jr., Ch/Troop Con Sec, OPD, WDGS, to CGs AAF, AGF, and ASF, subj: General Reserve, Apr 12, 1946.

16. Memo for Asst Ch/Air Stf and Ops Plan Div fr Brig Gen Reuben C. Hood, Jr., Dep Ch/Air Stf, subj: Army Air Forces Strategic Reserve, Jul 31, 1945, RG 18, 320.2, Orgn and Tac Units, Vol 9, MMB, NA.

17. Memo for CGs AAF, AGF, and ASF fr Maj Gen Idwal H. Edwards, ACS, G–3 (Orgn and Tng), subj: Strategic Striking Force and Inactivation of Units, Sep 8, 1945, RG 18, 322, Orgn and Tac Units, Vol 9, MMB, NA.

18. MR, Col Bourne Adkison, Actg Ch/Orgn Div, Asst Ch/Air Stf, subj: Strategic Striking Force and Inactivation of Units, Sep 25, 1945, RG 18, 322.....; ltr, Col Bourne Adkison, Actg Ch/Orgn Div, to G–3, WDGS, subj: Strategic Striking Force and Inactivation of Units, Sep 14, 1945, RG 18, 322.....

19. Memo for CGs, AAF, AGF, and ASF fr Maj Gen Idwal H. Edwards, ACS, G–3 (Orgn and Tng), subj: Reserve, Nov 17, 1945, RG 18, 322....

20. Ltr, Brig Gen William A. Matheny, Ch/Commitments Div, ACAS–3, to CG, AAF, subj: VHB, Units for SSF and General Reserve, Dec 27, 1945, RG 18, 322.....

21. Minutes of the Second Meeting of Ad Hoc Committee on AAF Reorganization, Dec 12, 1945, RG 18, AAG 319.1, PDAR 1945, 370, MMB, NA.

22. Memo to ACAS/Plans, and Ad Hoc Cmte on AAF Reorgn of the AF, fr Col Reuben C. Moffat, subj: Establishment of the Air Force Combat Command, Dec 13, 1945, RG 18, AAG 319.1, PDAR, 1945, 370, MMB, NA.

23. *Ibid.*

24. *Ibid.*

25. Spaatz Bd Rprt, Effect of the Atomic Bomb on Employment, Size, Organization, and Composition of the Post-

war Air Force, Oct 23, 1945, RG 341, AFOAT 1945, 334, Spaatz Bd/1.

26. Rprt by Jt Strat Sur Cmte, Overall Effect of Atomic Bomb on Warfare and Military Organization, Oct 26, 1945.

27. Testimony of Maj Gen Curtis E. Le-May before the War Department Equipment Board, Jan 3, 1946.

28. Memo for Lt Gen Ira C. Eaker fr Lt Gen Hoyt S. Vandenberg, ACAS–3, subj: The Establishment of a Strategic Striking Force, Jan 2, 1946, File 145.86–90 (45–6), AFHRA.

29. *Ibid.*

30. *Ibid.*

31. R&R Sheet, Cmt 2, Maj Gen Lauris Norstad, ACAS–5, to Dep Cmdr, AAF, subj: Atomic Bomb Striking Force, Dec 14, 1945, RG 18/471.6, Bombs, Vol 7/1945, Box 259, MMB, NA.

32. R&R Sheet, Cmt 2, Lt Gen Hoyt S. Vandenberg, ACAS–3, to Dep Comdr, AAF, subj: Atomic Bomb Striking Force, Dec 17, 1945, RG 341, AFOAT 1945, 322, ABSF/1, MMF, NA.

33. R&R Sheet, Cmt 2, Col John G. Moore, Dep ACAS–4, to Dep Comdr, AAF, Subj: Atomic Bomb Striking Force, Dec 11, 1945, RG 341, AFOAT 1945, ABSF/1, MMB, NA.

34. *Ibid.*

35. R&R Sheet, Cmt 2, Brig Gen John A. Samford, Dep ACAS/ Intelligence, subj: Atomic Bomb Striking Force, Dec 6, 1945, RG 18, AAG 370.22, Campaigns and Expeditions, 1945/178, MMB, NA.

36. *Ibid.*

37. R&R Sheet, Cmt 2, ACAS–3, to Comdr, AAF, subj: Atomic Bomb Striking Force, n.d.

38. Ltr, Maj Gen Curtis E. LeMay, DCAS/R&D, to CG, SAC, subj: Mission of the 58th Bombardment Wing, Jun 13, 1946, RG 18, 1946-47, AAG 320, Misc Vol 1/632, MMB, NA.

39. Ltr, Maj Gen Curtis E. LeMay, DCAS/R&D, to Lt Gen Nathan F. Twin-

ing, CG, AMC, Jun 18, 1946, RG 341, AFOAT 1946, S 322, Kirtland AFB/2, MMB, NA.

40. Memo, Maj Gen Leslie R. Groves, MED, subj: Our Army of the Future—As Influenced by Atomic Weapons, Jan 2, 1946, in *Foreign Relations of the United States, 1946,* I, 1198.

41. *Ibid.,* 1199.

42. *Ibid.,* 1199.

43. Memo for CG, MED, fr Maj Gen Curtis E. LeMay, DCAS/R&D, subj: Inter-Branch Responsibility for the Atomic Bomb Project, Jul 1, 1946, RG 341, AFOAT 1946, 312.1, Manhattan District/2, MMB, NA.

44. *Ibid.*

45. Memo to Gen Henry H. Arnold fr Maj Gen Lauris Norstad, ACAS–5, subj: Daily Activity Report, Dec 11, 1945, RG 18, AAG 319.1, Plans Daily Reports, 1945/370, MMB, NA.

46. Second Meeting of the Air Board, 4–6 June 1946, p 170, RG 340, Meetings of the Air Board, Box 13, MMB, NA.

47. R&R Sheet, Cmt 1, Brig Gen Glen C. Jamison, Dep ACAS–5, subj: Committee on the Reorganization of the Air Forces, Jan 2, 1946, RG 18, 1944-46, AAG 334, Jan–Mar 46, Jan 1–Feb 15, 1946/1555, MMB, NA.

48. Ltr, Maj Gen Lauris Norstad, ACAS–5, to Lt Gen John K. Cannon, CG, USAFE, Jan 17, 1946, RG 18, 1944–46, AAG 320, WD Jul 45–1946/1442, MMB, NA.

49. *Ibid.*

50. *Ibid.*

51. Ltr, Lt Gen Ira C. Eaker, Dep Comdr, to Gen Carl A. Spaatz, subj: Special Organizational Planning for the AAF, Nov 14, 1945, RG 18, AAG 321, AAF, Vol 2/97, MMB, NA.

52. *Ibid.*

53. See note 60, Chap 2.

54. DF, Col Alfred D. Starbird, Ch/European Sec, Theater Gp, to ACS, G–

3, subj: Answers to Questionnaire for Key Commanders on the Effects of Strategic and Tactical Air Power on Military Operations, ETO, Sep 18, 1945, RG 165, WDGS, O&T Div, G–3 WDGCT 452.1 (Sep 18, 1945)/127, MMB, NA.

55. Ltr, Maj Gen Samuel E. Anderson, C/S, CAF, to CG, AAF, subj: Formation of an Operational Air Force in the United States, Jun 20, 1945, RG 18, AAG Central File, 322, Box 104, MMB, NA.

56. *Ibid.*

57. Memo, Brig Gen William F. McKee, Dep ACAS–3, to ACAS–5, subj: Requirement and Organization of Postwar Tactical Air Commands, Oct 29, 1945, RG 18 (AAF), AAG, Decimal File, 322, Box 104, MMB, NA. See also memo for ACAS–3 fr Brig Gen Alfred R. Maxwell, Ch/Rqmts Div, ACAS–3, same subj, Oct 5, 1945, RG 18 (AAF), AAG Box 104, MMB, NA.

58. See note above.

59. Memo, Col Reuben C. Moffat to Brig Gen William F. McKee, subj: Requirement and Organization of Postwar Tactical Air Commands, Oct 30, 1945, RG 18....Box 104.

60. *Ibid.*

61. Discussion, atch to memo, Brig Gen William F. McKee, Dep ACAS–3, to ACAS–5, Oct 29, 1945, RG 18 (AAF).....Box 104.

62. Ltr, Maj Gen Samuel E. Anderson, C/S, CAF, to CG, AAF, subj: Interim Air Force, Sep 8, 1945, RG 18.....Box 104.

63. Ltr, Maj Gen St. Clair Streett, Dep CG, CAF, to CG, AAF, subj: Proposed Army Air Forces Structure, Nov 14, 1945, HD 145.86–36, AFHRA.

64. Ltr, Maj Gen Lauris Norstad, ACAS–5, to Lt Gen Ira C. Eaker, Dep Comdr, AAF, subj: AAF VJ Day Plan as of 15 July 1945, Aug 10, 1945, HD 145–86–52 (1945–46), AFHRA.

65. R&R Sheet, Col Reuben C. Moffat, Ch/Sp Plng Div, to ACAS–3 (Orgn Div), subj: Strategic Striking Force and Inactivation of Units, Dec 6, 1945, RG 18, 1945, 322, Units Misc, MMB, NA.

66. Intvw, Herman S. Wolk with Lt Gen Ira C. Eaker, Aug 27, 1974; ltr, Lt Gen Ira C. Eaker, Dep Comdr, AAF, to Air Staff and Major Commands, subj: Organization—Army Air Forces, Jan 29, 1946, RG 18, CAF, 221, Box 114, MMB, NA.

67. Memo for SECDEF fr Gen Dwight D. Eisenhower, subj: Tactical Air Support, Nov 3, 1947, RG 18, AAG, 322, Box 104, MMB, NA.

68. *Ibid.*

69. Ltr, Eaker to Air Staff and Major Commands, Jan 29, 1946.

70. Intvw, Brig Gen Noel F. Parrish and Alfred Goldberg with Gen Carl A. Spaatz, Feb 21, 1962; R&R Sheet, Cmt 2, Maj Gen Lauris Norstad, Jan 30, 1946, RG 18, 1944–46, RG 18, 1944–46, AAG 320.3, Charts 1487, MMB, NA.

71. Intvw, Lt Cols Steven W. Long, Jr., and Ralph W. Stephenson, with Lt Gen Elwood R. Quesada, Washington, D.C., May 12, 1975, USAF Oral Hist Tape K239.0512–838, AFHRA.

72. Second Meeting of the Air Board, 4–6 June 1946, p 177, RG 340, Meetings of the Air Board, Box 113, MMB, NA.

73. Memo, Lt Gen Ira C. Eaker, Dep Comdr, AAF, to A–5, Sp Stf, *et al*, subj: Organization—Army Air Forces, with atch, Organization Chart, RG 18, 1944–46, AAG 321, Charts 1487, MMB, NA.

74. R&R Sheet, Cmt 1, Brig Gen Glen C. Jamison, Dep ACAS–5, subj: Committee on Reorganization of the Air Force, Feb 14, 1946, RG 18/AAG Eaker Personal, Reading File ACAS–5, MMB, NA.

75. Ltr, AG 322 (Mar 21, 1946), OB–1–AFCOR–(971–d)–M, Maj Gen Edward F. Witsell, TAG, to CGs AAF and CAF, subj: Establishment of Air Defense, Strategic Air And Tactical Air Commands; Redesignation of the Headquarters, Continental Air Forces and Certain Other

Army Air Forces Units; Activation, Inactivation and Assignment of Certain Army Air Forces Units, Mar 21, 1946, RG 18, MMB, NA.

76. Ltr, Maj Gen Charles C. Chauncey, Dep Ch/Air Stf, to CG, CAF, subj: Organization—Army Air Forces, Mar, 1946, RG 18, AAG, 322, Box 104, MMB, NA.

77. Ltr, Maj Gen Elwood R. Quesada, CG, TAC, to CG, AAF, subj: Organizational Plan of the Tactical Air Command, Apr 12, 1946, RG 18, 322 (Apr 12, 1946), MMB, NA.

78. Quesada intvw, May 12, 1975.

79. Ltr, Lt Gen Ira C. Eaker to Lt Gen Ennis C. Whitehead, CG, PACUSA, Apr 3, 1946, RG 341, Air OPD 312.1 (Nov 21, 1945), Box 72, MMB, NA.

80. See note 75.

81. Army Air Forces Monthly Organization Chart, Apr 46, RG 18.....Box 104.

82. Ltr, Gen Carl A. Spaatz, CG, AAF, to CG, SAC, subj: Interim Mission, Mar 12, 1946.

83. See notes 75 and 77.

84. See note 75; Second Meeting of the Air Board, Jun 4, 1946, pp 4–5.

85. AAFR 20–14, Organization—AAF Proving Ground Command, Mar 7, 1946.

86. AAFR 20–61, Organization—Air University, Apr 5, 1946.

87. Ltr, Dep Comdr, AAF, to CG, Air Transport Command, subj: Mission of the Air Transport Command, Mar 18, 1946.

88. Ltr, Maj Gen Charles C. Chauncey, Dep Ch/Air Stf. to CG, AMC, Apr 10, 1946, RG 18, 322, Commands and Organization, MMB, NA.

89. Ltr, Dep Comdr, AAF, to CG, ATC, subj: Mission of the Air Training Command, Mar 21, 1946.

90. Army Air Forces Announcement (Gen Spaatz), Mar 12, 1946, Spaatz Colln, File Feb 46, Box, 25, MD, LC.

91. WD Cir 138, War Department Reorganization, May 14, 1946, p 15.

92. Memo for Ofcs of the Air Stf, ACASs, Sp Ofcs of Air Stf, Chs/Divs, fr Lt Gen Barney M. Giles, Dep Comdr, AAF, and Ch/Air Stf, subj: Principles for AAF Future Action, Jan 29, 1945.

93. *Ibid.*

94. *Ibid.*

95. See Chase C. Mooney and Edward C. Williamson, *Organization of the Army Air Arm, 1935–1945* (USAF Hist Study 10, Maxwell AFB, Ala., 1956), p 62.

96. Memo, Dr. Edward L. Bowles to Gen Henry H. Arnold, Nov 26, 1945; ltr, Maj Gen Laurence C. Craigie, Ch/Engrg Div, Wright Field, to Aero Bd, USN, subj: Project RAND, Oct 11, 1946.

97. Memo for Gen Henry H. Arnold fr Robert A. Lovett, Asst S/W for for Air, subj: A. Need for Improved and Increased Business Management Procedures; B. Solution Through Establishment of Office of Air Comptroller General, Oct 5, 1945, RG 18, 322, 11-7-45, MMB, NA.

98. *Ibid.*

99. *Ibid.*

100. *Ibid.*

101. Memo for Robert A. Lovett, Asst S/W for Air, fr Lt Gen Ira C. Eaker, Dep Comdr, AAF, Nov 7, 1945, RG 18, 322, 11-7-45, MMB, NA; memo for Maj Gen Curtis E. LeMay fr Lt Gen Ira C. Eaker, Nov 7, 1945, RG 18, 322, 11-7-45, MMB, NA.

102. Memo, Col Jacob E. Smart, Secy of Air Stf, subj: Minutes of Air Staff Meeting, Nov 29, 1945, RG 18, AAG 337, Conf 1945, Vol 9/156, MMB, NA.

103. Memo for Maj Gen Hugh J. Knerr fr Lt Gen Ira C. Eaker, Dep CG, AAF, subj: Air Force Board, Feb 12, 1946, RG 340 (SAF), Air Bd, Interim Rprts and Working Papers, 1946–48, Box 20, MMB, NA.

104. Memo for Air Stf, AAF, Cen, fr Col Harry E. Wilson, C/S, AAF Cen, subj: Organizational and Functional Charts, Mar 5, 1946; General Order 1, APGC, Jul 17,

1946, in Robert F. Futrell, *Ideas, Concepts, Doctrine: A History of Basic Training in the United States Air Force, 1907–1964* (Maxwell AFB, Ala., 1974), p 106.

105. See note above; remarks by Lt Gen Ira C. Eaker, Dep CG, AAF, to First Meeting of the Air Board, in Report of the First Meeting of the Air Board, Apr 16, 1946 (Verbatim Report), RG 340 (SAF), Air Bd, Minutes of Mtgs, 1945–48, Box 13, MMB, NA.

106. See note above.

107. Statement by Gen Dwight D. Eisenhower to Patch Board, Sep 23, 1945, RG 165, Patch-Simpson Board File, MMB, NA.

108. See note 103; Notes on Proposed Air Board by Maj Gen Hugh J. Knerr, in First Interim Report of the Air Board, Apr 16, 1946, RG 340 (SAF), Air Bd, Interim Rprts and Working Papers, 1946–48, Box 20, MMB, NA.

109. Notes on Proposed Air Board.

110. *Ibid.*

111. *Ibid.,* pt II.

112. *Ibid.,* pt II.

113. *Ibid.,* pt II.

114. *Ibid.,* pt II.

115. *Ibid.,* pt II.

116. *Ibid.,* pt II.

117. Memo, Gen Carl A. Spaatz, CG, AAF, to members of Air Bd, Apr 16, 1946,

in First Interim Report of the Air Board, Interim Rprts and Working Papers, 1946–48, Box 20, MMB, NA.

118. *Ibid.*

119. WD Cir 138, May 14, 1946, paras 1, 2.

120. *Ibid.,* para 2.

121. *Ibid.,* para 2(b).

122. *Ibid.,* para 10 (d).

123. *Ibid.,* para 2.

124. *Ibid.,* para 30.

125. *Ibid.,* AppI, para 1.

126. Memo, Gen Carl A. Spaatz, CG, AAF, to Lt Gen Charles P. Hall, Dir/Orgn and Tng, WDGS, subj: Organization of the War Department, Nov 22, 1946, RG 165, WDGS, Ops and Tng Div, G–3, 320 (Nov 15, 1946), CSN 640–8, Box 215, MMB, NA.

127. Memo, Brig Gen Henry I. Hodes, DCSA, to Dirs of Pers and Admin, Intel, *et al,* subj: Reorganization of the War Department, Nov 15, 1946, RG 165, Orgn and Tng Div, G–3, 320 (Nov 15, 1946), CSN 640–8, Box 215, MMB, NA.

128. Memo, Brig Gen Glen C. Jamison, Dep ACAS–5, to Maj Gen Lauris Norstad, ACAS–5, subj: The Simpson Board Recommendations for the Reorganization of the War Department, May 3, 1946, RG 341, P&O, PD 020 (Nov 2, 1943), Sec 2/448, MMB, NA.

Chapter 5

Moving Toward Autonomy

1. Ltr, SECNAV James V. Forrestal to Samuel Rosenman, Dec 18, 1945, in Richard F. Haynes, *The Awesome Power: Harry S. Truman as Commander-in-Chief* (Baton Rouge, La., 1973), p 98.

2. Ltr, Maj Gen Lauris Norstad, ACAS/Plans, to Gen Henry H. Arnold, Mar 20, 1946, Gen Lauris Norstad Colln, MMB, NA.

3. Memo for all Div Chs fr Maj Gen Lauris Norstad, subj: Unification, May 15, 1946, RG 341, P&O, PD 020 (Nov 2, 1943), Sec 2/448, MMB, NA.

4. Diary of Fleet Admiral William D. Leahy, Feb 8, 1946, William D. Leahy Papers, MD, LC.

5. See note 3.

6. Memo for Br Chs fr Col Elmer J. Rogers, Jr., May 21, 1946, RG 341, P&O, PD 020 (Nov 2, 1943), Sec 2/448, MMB, NA.

7. Ltr, Stuart Symington, Asst S/W for Air, to Gen George C. Kenney, CG, SAC, May 30, 1947, Spaatz Colln, Box 28, MD, LC.

8. *Ibid.*

9. Minutes of War Council Meeting, May 16, 1946, folder War Council Meetings, Box 23, Robert P. Patterson Papers, MD, LC.

10. Ltr, Robert P. Patterson, S/W, and SECNAV James V. Forrestal, to Pres Harry S. Truman, May 31, 1946, RG 319, Rcrds of the Army Stf, P&O 320, Sec VIII, Cases 32–45, MMB, NA.

11. *Ibid.*

12. *Ibid.*

13. *Ibid.*

14. JCS 1478/10, Memorandum by CG, AAF, Mar 15, 1946, RG 218, CCS 370 (8-19-45), Box 121, MMB, NA.

15. Ltr, Gen Carl A. Spaatz, CG, AAF, to James E. Webb, Dir/Bureau of Budget, Dec 6, 1946, Papers of James E. Webb, Truman Library.

16. JCS 1478/9, Memorandum by Chief of Naval Operations, Mar 6, 1946, RG 218, CCS 370 (8-19-45), Sec 3, Box 121, MMB, NA.

17. See note 14.

18. JCS 1478/11, Memorandum by Chief of Staff, U.S. Army, Mar 16, 1946, RG 218, CCS 370 (8-19-45), Sec 3, Box 121, MMB, NA.

19. JCS 1478/17, Memorandum by Acting Chief of Staff, U.S. Army, May 14, 1946, RG 218, CCS 370...Sec 5...NA; JCS 1478/19, Memorandum by Chief of Naval Operations, May 23, 1946, RG 218, CCS 370...Sec 5...NA.

20. See note 2.

21. Ltr, Pres Harry S. Truman to S/W Robert P. Patterson and SECNAV James V. Forrestal, Jun 15, 1946, RG 341, P&O, PD 020 (Nov 2, 1943), Sec 2/448, MMB, NA.

22. *Ibid.*

23. *Ibid.*

24. *Ibid.*

25. Stephen Jurika, Jr., ed, *From Pearl Harbor to Vietnam: The Memiors of Admiral Arthur W. Radford* (Palo Alto, 1980), p 83.

26. Diary of Fleet Admiral William D. Leahy, Jun 4, 1946, William D. Leahy Papers, MD, LC.

27. Memo for Stuart Symington, Asst S/W for Air, fr Col John B. Montgomery, Nov 1, 1946, RG 18, AG Bulky File, 381, Unification, MMB, NA.

28. *Ibid.*

29. Analysis of Notes, atch to Sum Sheet, Maj Gen Lauris Norstad, WD Dir/Plans and Ops, subj: The Unified Air Force, Jan 9, 1947, RG 319, P&O 320, Sec XII, Cases 62–78, MMB, NA.

30. *Ibid.*

31. *Ibid.*

32. *Ibid.;* memo for Col Sims fr W. Stuart Symington, Asst S/W for Air, Nov 18, 1946, RG 319, P&O 320, Sec XII, Cases 62–78.

33. Gen Eisenhower's Testimony before the Patch Board, Sep 23, 1945, RG 165, Patch-Simpson Board File, MMB, NA.

34. Intvw, Hugh Ahmann with Gen Lauris Norstad, USAF, Ret, Feb, Oct 1979. K239.0512–1116.

35. *Ibid.*

36. Ltr, Maj Gen Lauris Norstad, Dir/Plans and Ops, to Lt Gen J. E. Hill, HQ AFMIDPAC, Sep 6, 1946, Gen Lauris Norstad Colln, MMB, NA.

37. JCS 1259/26, Dec 5, 1946, RG 218, 323.361, 1946–47 (2-26-45), MMB, NA; JCS 1259/27, Dec 11, 1946, RG 218, 323.361, 1946–47 (2-26-45), MMB, NA.

38. Gen Lauris Norstad, "The National Security Act of 1947: Implications and Interpretations," in Paul R. Schratz, ed, *Evo-*

lution of the American Military Establishment Since World War II (Lexington, Va, 1978), pp 24–25.

39. Outline Command Plan, atch to memo for Pres fr Fleet Admiral William D. Leahy, C/S to CINC, Dec 12, 1946, para 4.

40. *Ibid.,* paras 5–6.

41. *Ibid.,* handwritten signature by Harry S. Truman, Dec 14, 1946.

42. JCS 1259/27, Joint Chiefs of Staff, Unified Command Plan, Dec 11, 1946, para 4, RG 218, 323.361, 1946–47 (2-26-45), MMB, NA.

43. JCSM–34–49, Memorandum for the Chief of Staff, USAF, from Joint Chief of Staff, Jan 7, 1949.

44. Msg, JCS to CG, SAC, WARX–87110, Apr 13, 1949, cy in SAC Hist Ofc.

45. *Ibid.*

46. See note 34.

47. *Ibid.*

48. Ltr, Robert P. Patterson, S/W, and SECNAV James V. Forrestal, to Pres Harry S. Truman, Jan 16, 1947.

49. Ltr, Pres Harry S. Truman to S/W Robert P. Patterson and SECNAV James V. Forrestal, Jan 16, 1947.

50. Memo for CG, AAF, CG, AGF, *et al,* fr Brig Gen Henry I. Hodes, WD Asst Dep C/S, subj: Board of Officers to Determine Army and Air Force Organizational Matters Under Unification, Jan 20, 1947, RG 340 (SAF), Air Bd, Gen File, 1945–48, Box 12, MMB, NA.

51. Report to Chief of Staff, USA, on Army and Air Force Organizational Matters Under Unification, Mar 14, 1947, Sec A [hereafter referred to as Hall Board Report], RG 340 (SAF), Air Bd, Gen File, 1945–48, Box 12, MMB, NA.

52. Hall Board Report, pt 1, Sec A, pp 2–3.

53. *Ibid.,* p 5.

54. *Ibid., p 7.*

55. Hearings before the Committee on Armed Services, Senate, *National Defense Establishment (Unification of the Armed Services): Hearings on S. 758,* 80th Cong, 1st sess (Washington, 1947), RG 340 (SAF), Air Bd, Gen File, 1945–48, Box 12, MMB, NA.

62. *Ibid.*

57. *Ibid.*

58. See note 15.

59. See note 15.

60. Paper for Chief of Naval Operations, subj: Naval Shore-Based Aviation for Naval Reconnaissance and Anti-Submarine Warfare, Jun 4, 1946, RG 218, Rcrds of the US JCS, Chmn's File 124, MMB, NA.

61. Diary of James V. Forrestal, Vol VI, Oct 46 to Mar 47, Entry Nov 12, 1946, Forrestal Papers, OSD Hist Ofc.

62. Memo for S/W fr W. Stuart Symington, Asst S/W for Air, Oct 15, 1946, RG 340 (SAF), 321, Unification, MMB, NA.

63. Ltr, Stuart Symington to Clark M. Clifford, the White House, Dec 14, 1946, Papers of James E. Webb, Truman Library.

64. Memo for Gen Carl A. Spaatz fr Maj Gen Hugh J. Knerr, Secy-Gen, Air Bd, subj: Roles and Missions, Apr 11, 1947, RG 340 (SAF), Air Bd, Secy-Gen File, 1942–49, Maj Gen Knerr's Personal Papers, Box 10, MMB, NA.

65. *Ibid.*

66. See note 61, Chap 3.

67. See note 61, Chap 3.

68. See note 61, Chap 3.

69. Memo, Gen Dwight D. Eisenhower, CSA, to Gen Carl A. Spaatz, CG, AAF, Mar 21, 1947, RG 340 (SAF), Air Bd, Gen File, 1945–48, Box 12, MMB, NA.

70. See note 61.

71. See note 61.

72. See note 61, Chap 3.

73. EO 9877, Functions of the Armed Forces, Jul 16, 1947, Sec III, para 1e.

74. *Ibid.,* Sec III, para 1f.

75. *Ibid.,* Sec IV, para 1a–g.

76. *Ibid.,* Sec IV, para 4.

77. *Ibid.,* Sec II, paras 1, 2.

78. *Ibid.*, Sec II, para 4.

79. *Ibid.*, Sec III, para 1(f).

80. Sixth Meeting of the Air Board, "Roles and Missions," Sep 9–10, 1947, RG 340 (SAF), Air Bd Gen File, Box 18, MMB, NA.

81. *Ibid.*

82. *The National Security Act of 1947,* Jul 26, 1947, Sec 2, Declaration of Policy.

83. *Ibid.*, Sec 202(a), Secretary of Defense.

84. *Ibid.*, Sec 202(a), Secretary of Defense.

85. *Ibid.*, Sec 206(a), Department of the Navy.

86. *Ibid.*, Sec 206(a), Department of the Navy.

87. *Ibid.*, Sec 208(f), United States Air Force.

88. *Ibid.*, Sec 207(a), (d), (f), Department of the Air Force.

89. *Ibid.*, Sec 208, United States Air Force.

90. *Ibid.*, Sec 208c, United States Air Force.

91. *Ibid.*, Sec 211(a), Joint Chiefs of Staff.

92. *Ibid.*, Sec 210, War Council.

93. Intvw, Thomas A. Sturm and Herman S. Wolk with Lt Gen Ira C. Eaker, Nov 17, 1972.

94. Ltr, Stuart Symington, Asst S/W for Air, to James E. Webb, Bureau of the Budget, Feb 3, 1947, C4–3 Folder, Papers of James E. Webb, Truman Library.

95. Intvw, Hugh A. Ahmann and Herman S. Wolk with Stuart Symington, May 2, 1978.

96. Ltr, Stuart Symington, Asst S/W for Air, to Lt Gen Ennis C. Whitehead, CG, FEAF, Sep 10, 1947, Spaatz Colln, Box 264, File SAF, LC.

97. MR, Lt Gen Lauris Norstad, subj: Conference with General Eisenhower, May 1, 1948, Gen Lauris Norstad Colln, MMB, NA.

98. *Ibid.*

99. *Ibid.*

100. Diary of Fleet Admiral William D. Leahy, Jul 16, 1947, William D. Leahy Papers, LC.

101. *The New York Times,* Jul 27, 1947, Sec IV, p 8.

Chapter 6

Independence and Organization

1. Ltr, Gen Carl A. Spaatz, CG AAF, to Vannevar Bush, May 14, 1946; memo for Dir/Orgn and Tng, WDGS, fr Lt Gen Ira C. Eaker, Dep Comdr, AAF, Nov 1, 1946.

2. Minutes of the Sixth Meeting of the Air Board, Sep 9–10, 1947, p 28, RG 340 (SAF), Air Bd, Gen File, 1945–48, Box 18, MMB, NA.

3. Intvw, Thomas A. Strum and Herman S. Wolk with Col Kenneth F. Gantz, USAF, Ret, Montgomery, Ala., Feb 15, 1972.

4. Intvw, Thomas A. Sturm and Herman S. Wolk with Stuart Symington, Washington, D.C., Feb 18, 1972.

5. *Final Report of the War Department Policies and Programs Review Board* (Washington, 1947), p 22, RG 340 (SAF), Meetings of the Air Bd, Interim Rprts and Working Papers, Box 22, MMB, NA.

6. *Ibid.,* p 24.

7. Annex G to *Final Report of the War Department Policies and Programs Review Board,* Extracts from the Report of the President's Advisory Commission on Universal Training, *A Program for National*

Security, May 29, 1947 (Washington, 1947), RG 340 (SAF), Mtgs of the Air Bd, Interim Rprts and Working Papers, 1946–48, Box 22, MMB, NA.

8. Memo, Gen Dwight D. Eisenhower to All Members of the Army, Jul 26, 1947, RG 165, Rcrds of the WD Gen and Sp Stfs, 320, Bk 1, Cases 1–15, MMB, NA.

9. Hearings before the Select Committee on Post-War Military Policy, House of Representatives, *Proposal to Establish a Single Department of Armed Forces,* Statement of Robert A. Lovett, Asst S/W for Air, on Apr 26, 1944, 78th Cong, 2d sess (Washington, 1944), RG 107, Rcrds of the Asst S/W for Air, MMB, NA.

10. *Ibid.*

11. Msg to Arnold fr Symington and Spaatz, AGACG 650, Sep 18, 1947, Arnold Colln, Box 25, File Independent Air Force, MD, LC.

12. Minutes of the Sixth Meeting of the Air Board, Sep 9–10, 1947 p 1.

13. *Ibid.,* p 1.

14. *Ibid.,* p 2.

15. First Meeting of the Aircraft and Weapons Board, Aug 19, 1947, RG 341, DCS/Rqmts, Box 181, MMB, NA.

16. Memo for Asst S/W for Air fr S/W Robert P. Patterson, subj: Unification, Apr 11, 1946, RG 341, P&O, PD 020, See 3/23A, MMB, NA.

17. Se note 2, Chap 5.

18. Flora Lewis, "The Education of a Senator," *The Atlantic,* Dec 71, p 56.

19. *Ibid.*

20. Address to the First Annual Convention of the Air Force Association, Columbus, Ohio, Secretary-Designate of the Air Force Stuart Symington, Sep 15, 1947; Symington intvw, May 78.

21. Address to the First Annual Convention of the Air Force Association.

22. *Ibid.;* Secy Symington's statement before the President's Air Policy Commission, Nov 26, 1947, Spaatz Colln, Box 263, MD, LC; Symington memo to Forre-

stal, Apr 21, 1948, OSAF File 520, A53–307, Sp File 9, MMB, NA.

23. Hist, OSAF, Sep 18, 1947–Jun 30, 1950, I, 1–2.

24. *Ibid.,* 2; Sixth Meeting of the Air Board, "Roles and Missions," Sep 9–10, 1947, p 26, RG 340 (SAF), Air Bd, Gen File, Box 18, MMB, NA.

25. *Annual Report of the Secretary of the Air Force, FY 1948* (Washington, 1948); hist, OSAF, Sep 18, 1947–Jun 30, 1950, I, 3.

26. Hist, OSAF, Sep 18, 1947–Jun 30, 1950, I, 4.

27. *Ibid.,* 2.

28. Sixth Meeting of the Air Board, Sep 9–10, 1947, p 5.

29. Stf paper, The Officer Personnel Act of 1947, Sep 47, RG 340 (SAF), Air Bd, Gen File, Box 10, MMB, NA.

30. Gen Carl A. Spaatz, Tomorrow's Soldier Must be Different, Air Bd Working Papers, Box 13, MMB, NA; see note 29.

31. Memo for Lt Gen Barney M. Giles, Dep Comdr, AAF, and Ch/Air Stf, to Ofcs of Air Stf, Asst Chs/Air Stf, *et al,* subj: Principles for AAF Future Action, Jan 29, 1945.

32. Ltr, Maj Gen Frederick L. Anderson, ACAS–1, to Col Marvin F. Stalder, Dep Ch/Procurement Sec, Pers and Admin Div, WDGS, Apr 25, 1947, RG 18, AAG 008, Policy 1946–47, Box 561, MMB, NA.

33. Air Force Officer Opportunities Under Unification, encl to memo, Brig Gen Reuben C. Hood, Jr., Dep Ch/Air Stf, to Ch/Air Stf, subj: Assignment of Responsibility for Service Units, Dec 10, 1945.

34. *Ibid.*

35. Annual Rprt, Ch/NGB,, FY 1947, pp 102–103; AAF Plan for the National Guard, Jun 47, App B; ltr, Lt Col Cecil J. Looke, Jr., Exec, ACAS–3, to ADC, subj: Interim Ceiling on National Guard Organization, Mar 14, 1947.

36. Army Air Forces Plan for the Air Reserve, Jun 19, 1946, approved by WD,

Jul 12, 1946; ADC Plan to Activate the Air Reserve Program, May 14, 1946.

37. Hist, ADC, Mar 46–Jun 47, pp 61–75; DOD Selected Manpower Statistics, May 78, p 98; *Annual Report of the Secretary of the Air Force, FY 1948*, p 165.

38. Memo for Maj Gen Hugh J. Knerr, Secy-Gen, Air Bd, fr Lt Gen Ira C. Eaker, Dep CG, AAF, Apr 16, 1946, RG 340 (SAF), Air Bd, Interim Rprts and Working Papers, Box 20, MMB, NA.

39. Air Board Review and Comment on Organization, in First Interim Report of Air Board, Apr 16, 1946, RG 340 (SAF), Air Bd, Interim Rprts and Working Papers, Box 20, MMB, NA.

40. *Ibid.*

41. *Ibid.*

42. Memo, Maj Gen Hugh J. Knerr, Secy-Gen, Air Bd, to Gen Carl A. Spaatz, CG, AAF, subj: Post-Unification Organization, Mar 22, 1946, RG 340 (SAF), Air Bd, Interim Rprts and Working Papers, 1946–48, Box 20, MMB, NA.

43. *Ibid.*

44. *Ibid.*

45. See note 42.

46. Second Meeting of Air Board, Jun 4–6, 1946, RG 340 (SAF), Air Bd, Gen File, 1945–48, Box 13, MMB, NA.

47. Fourth Meeting of Air Board, Dec 3–4, 1946, RG 340 (SAF), Air Bd, Gen File, 1945–48, Box 13, MMB, NA.

48. *Ibid.*

49. *Ibid.*

50. *Ibid.*

51. *Ibid.*

52. Fourth Meeting of Air Board, Dec 3–4, 1946, RG 340 (SAF) Air Bd, Gen File, 1945–48, Box 13, MMB, NA.

53. *Ibid.*

54. *Ibid.*

55. *Ibid.*

56. *Ibid.*

57. Fifth Meeting of Air Board, Jun 5–6, 1947, RG 340 (SAF), Air Bd, Gen File, 1945–48, Box 13, MMB, NA.

58. Hall Board Report, p 4.

59. *Ibid.*, pt I.

60. Memo for Lt Gen Ira C. Eaker, Dep CG, AAF, fr Maj Gen Hugh J. Knerr, Secy-Gen, Air Bd, n.d. [ca. Mar 47], Air Bd, Gen File, 1945–48, Box 12, MMB, NA.

61. Memo for Gen Carl A. Spaatz, CG, AAF, fr Gen Dwight D. Eisenhower, CSA, Mar 21, 1947, RG 340 (SAF), Air Bd, Gen File, 1945–48, Box 12, MMB, NA.

62. *Ibid.*

63. Memo for Air Stf fr Lt Gen Ira C. Eaker, Dep CG, AAF, Mar 25, 1947, RG 340 (SAF), Air Bd, Gen File, 1945–48, Box 12, MMB, NA.

64. Memo for CSA fr S/W Robert P. Patterson, subj: Army and Air Force Organizational Matters Under Unification, Apr 11, 1947, RG 340 (SAF), Air Bd, Gen File, 1945–48, Box 12, MMB, NA.

65. Memo, Maj Gen William E. Hall to CSA, subj: Board of Officers to Determine Army Matters Under Unification, Apr 18, 1947, RG 340 (SAF), Air Bd, Gen File, 1945–48, Box 12, MMB, NA.

66. Memo for CSA fr S/W Robert P. Patterson, subj: Army and Air Force Organizational Matters Under Unification, Apr 23, 1947, RG 340 (SAF), Air Bd, Gen File, 1945–48, Box 12, MMB, NA.

67. Memo, Maj Gen William E. Hall to CSA, subj: Army and Air Force Organizational Matters Under Unification, Apr 25, 1947.

68. Memo for Dep Comdr, USAF, fr Maj Gen Hugh J. Knerr, Secy-Gen, Air Bd, Sep 25, 1947; ltr, Spaatz to Bush, May 14, 1946; memo for Dir/Orgn and Tng, WDGS, fr Lt Gen Ira C. Eaker, Dep CG, AAF, Nov 1, 1946; Sixth Meeting of the Air Board, Sep 9–10, 1947, p 114, RG 340 (SAF), Air Bd, Gen File, Box 18, MMB, NA.

69. Memo to Air Stf fr Maj Gen Charles C. Chauncey, Dep Ch/Air Stf, subj: Organization of the Air Forces Upon

Unification, Jun 13, 1947, RG 340 (SAF), Air Bd, Gen File, 1945–48, Box 12, MMB, NA.

70. Briefing, Maj Gen Earle E. Partridge, ACAS–3, to Gen Carl A. Spaatz, CG, AAF, and the Air Staff, subj: Organization, Nov 6, 1946.

71. *Ibid.*

72. Memo for Dep Comdr, AAF, fr Brig Gen August W. Kissner, Actg ACAS–5, subj: Transfer of Functions and Personnel from Plans and Optns Div to the Air Force, Aug 28, 1947, RG 341, OPD 320.5, Jul 14, 1947, Sec 1, Box 130, MMB, NA; see note 32.

73. See note 70.

74. Assignment of Table of Organization and Equipment, Troop Basis, Activation and Training Responsibility for Units of the Technical Services and Army Service Forces Staff Divisions Having Troops, encl to memo for CSA, subj: Assignment of Responsibility for Service Units, Nov 20, 1945.

75. *Ibid.*

76. Ltr, Spaatz to Bush, May 14, 1946; memo for Dir/Orgn and Tng, WDGS, fr Lt Gen Ira C. Eaker, Dep Comdr, AAF, Nov 1, 1946.

77. Ltr, Gen Carl A. Spaatz, CG, AAF, to CG, SAC, subj: Air Force Attitude Toward Officers of Other Branches of the Service Serving with the Air Forces, Jan 2, 1947.

78. *Ibid.*

79. Sixth Meeting of the Air Board, Sep 9–10, 1947, RG 340 (SAF), Air Bd, Gen File, 1945–48, Box 10, MMB, NA; memo for Dep Comdr, USAF, fr Maj Gen Hugh J. Knerr, Secy-Gen, Air Bd, subj: Organization, Sep 25, 1947.

80. Fifth Meeting of the Air Board, Jun 5–6, 1947, Prefatory Remarks of Maj Gen Hugh J. Knerr, p 2.

81. *Ibid.*

82. *Ibid.;* ltr, Lt Gen Ira C. Eaker, Dep Comdr, AAF, to ACAS–1, subj: AAF Policy—Integration of Technical Services, Jul 9, 1946, RG 18, AAG 008, Policy 1946–48, Box 561, MMB, NA.

83. Fifth Meeting of the Air Board, Jun 5–6, 1947.

84. *Ibid.*

85. *Ibid.*

86. *Ibid.*

87. *Ibid.*

88. AAF Policy Letter, unnumbered, in Sixth Meeting of Air Board, Sep 9–10, 1947, RG 340 (SAF), Air Bd, Gen File, 1945–48, Box 10, MMB, NA; also see ltr, Lt Gen Ira C. Eaker, Dep Comdr, AAF, to ACAS–1, Jul 9, 1946.

89. Sixth Meeting of Air Board, Sep 9–10, 1947.

90. *Ibid.*

91. *Ibid.*

92. *Ibid.*

93. Memo for Mr. Garver fr Lt Col Hayden W. Withers, Ch/Plans Br, Med Plans and Svcs Div, Ofc of Air Surgeon, subj: Medical Service for the United States Air Force, Dec 12, 1947.

94. *Ibid.*

95. See note 65, Chap 5.

96. *Ibid.*

97. *Ibid.*

98. *The National Security Act of 1947,* Jul 26, 1947, Sec 207 (a), (f), Sec 208; Sixth Meeting of the Air Board, Sep 9–10, 1947, pp 26–27.

99. For example, see memo for Lt Gen J. Lawton Collins, Actg WD Dep C/S, fr Maj Gen Curtis E. LeMay, DCAS/R&D, and Cloyd H. Marvin, Actg Dir/R&D, WDGS, subj: Proposed Action for Separation of Army and Air Force Research & Development, Aug 26, 1947, RG 341, OPD 320.5 (Jul 14, 1947), Sec 1, Box 130, MMB, NA.

100. *Ibid.*

101. *Annual Report of the Secretary of the Army, 1948* (Washington, 1949) p 30.

102. *Army-Air Force Agreements: As to the Initial Implementation of the National*

Security Act of 1947 (Washington, 1947), RG 165 (C/S 320–1947), MMB, NA.

103. R&R Sheet, Lt Gen Hoyt S. Vandenberg, Actg Dep Comdr, AAF, to Asst Chs/Air Stf, *et al*, subj: Recent Agreements Concerning Adjustment Between the Army & Air Force under the Unification Act, Aug 22, 1947, RG 341, OPD 320.5 (Jul 14, 1947), Sec 1, Box 130, MMB, NA.

104. Memo, Lt Gen J. Lawton Collins, WD Dep C/S, to Dirs/WDGS Divs, *et al*, subj: Separation of Air Force from U.S. Army, Sep 16, 1947, RG 341, OPD 320–5, (Jul 14, 1947), Sec 1, Box 130, MMB, NA.

105. Memo for S/W fr Gen Dwight D. Eisenhower, CSA, subj: Separation of the Air Force from the U.S. Army, Sep 15, 1947; memo for Secretary-Designate of Defense fr Kenneth C. Royall, S/W, subj: Separation of the Air Force from the U.S. Army, Sep 15, 1947.

106. *Army-Air Force Agreements.*

107. Sixth Meeting of the Air Board, Sep 9–10, 1947, pp 48–49; *Army-Air Force Agreements;* memo, Col Ralph P. Swofford, Jr., Exec to Dep Comdr, AAF, to Air Staff, subj: Interpretation of Agreements Between Spaatz & Eisenhower, Sep 2, 1947, RG 341, OPD 320.5 (Jul 14, 1947), Sec 1, Box 130, MMB, NA.

108. Memo for Dirs/WDGS Divs, Chs/WDSS Divs, *et al*, fr Lt Gen J. Lawton Collins, Actg WD Dep C/S, subj: Basic Agreements on the Preparation of the Army and the Air Force, Aug 29, 1947, RG 341, OPD 320.5 (Jul 14, 1947), Sec 1 Box 130, MMB, NA.

109. Memo for Dirs/Pers and Admin, R&D, *et al*, fr Lt Gen J. Lawton Collins, Actg Dep CSA, Aug 4, 1947, RG 341, OPD 320.5 (Jul 14, 1947), Sec 1, Box 130, MMB, NA; *Army-Air Force Agreements;* memo, Col Ralph P. Swofford, Jr., Exec to Dep Comdr, AAF, to Air Stf, subj: Inter-

pretation of Agreements Between Spaatz & Eisenhower, Sep 2, 1947.

110. Sixth Meeting of the Air Board, Sep 9–10, 1947, pp 48–49.

111. Memo for CG, AAF, fr Brig Gen John E. Upston, DCAS–1, and Maj Gen Willard S. Paul, GSC, Dir/Pers and Admin, subj: Separation of the Air Force from the Army, Aug 25, 1947, RG 341, OPD 320.5 (Jul 14, 1947), Sec 1, Box 130, MMB, NA.

112. Sixth Meeting of the Air Board, Sep 9–10, 1947, p 55.

113. *Ibid.*, pp 50–51.

114. *Ibid.*, p 54.

115. *Ibid.*, p 53.

116. *Ibid.*, pp 61–62.

117. Memo, SECDEF James V. Forrestal to Secys of Army and Air Force, Oct 14, 1947.

118. Policies and Procedures Applicable to the Separation of the Air Force from the Army, Dec 10, 1947, signed by Eisenhower and Spaatz, RG 341, OPD 320.5 (Jul 14, 1947), Sec 1, Box 130, MMB, NA.

119. Transfer Order 1, SECDEF, Order Transferring Certain Functions, Personnel and Property from the Department of the Army to the Department of the Air Force, Sep 26, 1947.

120. *Ibid.*

121. *Ibid.*

122. *Ibid.*

123. *Annual Report of the Secretary of the Air Force, FY 1948* (Washington, 1948), p 21; memo, Lt Gen Lauris Norstad, DCS/Ops, to Dir/Intel, *et al*, subj: Transfer of Functions from the Army to the Air Force, Mar 17, 1948; memo, Gen Hoyt S. Vandenberg, VCS, to DCS/Ops, *et al*, subj: Transfer of Functions from the Army to the Air Force, Mar 12, 1948, RG 341, OPD 320.5 (Jul 14, 1947), Sec 1, Box 130, MMB, NA.

124. Transfer Order 40, SECDEF, Jul 22, 1949.

Chapter 7

Epilogue

1. Bernard Brodie, "The Atomic Bomb and American Security," *Yale Institute of International Studies,* Nov 1, 1945.

2. Ltr, Alexander de Seversky to S/W Robert P. Patterson, Oct 4, 1946, Spaatz Colln, Box 264, MD, LC.

3. Memo for Col Harold W. Bowman fr Maj Donald T. Sheehan, Plans and Plcys, Ofc of Info Svcs, subj: Public Relations "White Paper," sep 17, 1945, RG 18, AAF Ofc of Info Svcs, Personal Narratives Div, 1942–45, Folder Current and Future Public Relations Plan, MMB, NA.

4. Memo fr Gen Dwight D. Eisenhower to All Members of the Army, Jul 26, 1947, RG 165, Rcrds of WD Gen and Sp Stfs, 320, Bk I, Cases 1–15.

5. Intvw, Hugh A. Ahmann and Herman S. Wolk with Stuart Symington, Washington, D.C., Dec 12, 1978.

6. *First Report of the Secretary of Defense, 1948* (Washington, 1948), p 141.

7. 70-Group Program, atch to ltr, Gen Carl A. Spaatz, CSAF, to Lt Gen Ennis C. Whitehead, CG, FEAF, Oct 6, 1947, RG 18, AAG 312.1, Ops Ltrs 1946–47, Vol 2, MMB, NA.

8. Statement by Stuart Symington, SAF, to the President's Air Policy Commission, Nov 26, 1947, Folder B 24–2, Box 16, files of PAPC, Harry S. Truman Library.

9. *Ibid.*

10. Ltr, Stuart Symington, SAF, to James E. Webb, Dir/Bureau of the Budget, Dec 16, 1947, Papers of Clark M. Clifford, Harry S. Truman Library.

11. Memo for SECDEF James V. Forrestal fr SAF Stuart Symington, Dec 16, 1947, Papers of Clark M. Clifford, Harry S. Truman Library; ltr, Stuart Symington to Clark M. Clifford, Dec 16, 1947, Clifford Papers, Truman Library.

12. *Survival in the Air Age: A Report by the President's Air Policy Commission* (Washington, 1948), p 9.

13. Memo for Ch/Info fr Col S. L. A. Marshall, subj: Present Doctrine of the Army, Apr 9, 1948, RG 218, CCS 020 (Oct 4, 1944), Sec 1, MMB, NA.

14. *Ibid.*

15. *Public Papers of the Presidents of the United States: Harry S. Truman, 1948* (Washington, 1964), pp182–186.

16. Memo, Harry S. Truman to SEC-DEF, May 13, 1948, Gen Hoyt S. Vandenberg Colln, Box 40, MD, LC.

17. Memo fr Pres Harry S. Truman to CSAF, May 13, 1948, Gen Hoyt S. Vandenberg Colln, Box 40, MD, LC.

18. *Annual Report of the Secretary of the Air Force, FY 1948,* p 4.

19. *Ibid.,* pp 4–5.

20. *Ibid.,* pp 4, 7.

21. Memo fr SAF Stuart Symington to SECDEF James V. Forrestal, Apr 21, 1948, RG 340, OSAF File 520, A53–307, Special File 9, MMB, NA.

22. MR, Lt Gen Lauris Norstad, DCS/Ops, subj: Conference with General Eisenhower—May 1948, May 7, 1948, Gen Lauris Norstad Colln, 1945–48, Box 6, MMB, NA.

23. Memo, Adm Daniel V. Gallery, Asst Ch/Naval Ops, Guided Missiles, to Dep Ch/Naval Ops, Air, subj: Comment on Final Report "War Department Policies and Programs Review Board" (Aug 11, 1947), Dec 17, 1947.

24. *Ibid.*

25. Memo for SA thru Dep CSA fr Lt Gen Lauris Norstad, Dir/Plans and Ops,

WD, subj: Differences Between the Department of the Army and the Department of the Navy, Oct 2, 1947, RG 18, AAG File F–750 thru F–1000, MMB, NA.

26. Memo to SECDEF fr SA Kenneth C. Royall, Feb 28, 1948, RG 341, AAG File, MMB, NA.

27. Memo for SECDEF fr SECNAV John L. Sullivan, Mar 10, 1948, RG 341, AAG File, MMB, NA.

28. See memo for SECNAV John L. Sullivan fr SAF Stuart Symington, Mar 15, 1948, RG 341, AAG File, MMB, NA; memo for SECDEF James V. Forrestal fr SAF Stuart Symington, Mar 12, 1948, RG 341, AAG File, MMB, NA; memo to SECDEF James V. Forrestal fr SA Kenneth C. Royall, Mar 12, 1948; memo for SECDEF James V. Forrestal fr SECNAV John L. Sullivan, Mar 10, 1948, RG 341, AAG File, MMB, NA.

29. Memo, SAF Stuart Symington to SECDEF James V. Forrestal, Apr 2, 1948, RG 340, OSAF Special File 9, MMB, NA.

30. *Ibid.*

31. Memo for SA, SECNAV, SAF, and JCS fr SECDEF James V. Forrestal, subj: Organization and Mission of Military Air Transport Service (MATS), May 3, 1948.

32. GO 1, MATS, Assumption of Command, Jun 1, 1948.

33. Ltr, Stuart Symington to Clark M. Clifford, Jun 18, 1948, Clifford Papers, Truman Library.

34. *Ibid.;* ltr, Stuart Symington to Ferdinand Eberstadt, June 30, 1948, Clifford Papers, Truman Library.

35. Comments by Symington to Eberstadt Committee, atch to ltr, Symington to Eberstadt, Jun 30, 1948; memo to Stuart Symington fr W. Barton Leach, Clifford Papers, Truman Library.

36. Questions and Answers, incl to ltr, Gen Carl A. Spaatz to Ferdinand Eberstadt, Chmn, Cmte on Nat Scty Orgn, Washington, D.C., Sep 16, 1948.

37. MR, Norstad, May 7, 1948.

Glossary

AAA	Antiaircraft Artillery
AAF	Army Air Forces
AAFL	Army Air Forces Letter
AAFR	Army Air Forces Regulation
AAG	Air Adjutant General
ACAS	Assistant Chief of Air Staff
ACAS/	Assistant Chief of Air Staff for
ACAS–1	Assistant Chief of Air Staff, Personnel
ACAS–2	Assistant Chief of Air Staff, Intelligence
ACAS–3	Assistant Chief of Air Staff, Operations, Commitments, and Requirements.
ACAS–4	Assistant Chief of Air Staff, Materiel
ACAS–5	Assistant Chief of Air Staff, Plans
ACS	Assistant Chief of Staff
ACTS	Air Corps Tactical School
ADC	Air Defense Command
admin	administration
aero	aeronautical
AF	Air Force
AFB	Air Force base
AFCC	Air Force Combat Command
AFHRA	Air Force Historical Research Agency, formerly the Albert F. Simpson Historical Research Center, Maxwell Air Force Base, Alabama
AFMIDPAC	United States Army Forces, Middle Pacific
AG	Adjutant General
AGF	Army Ground Forces
ALCOM	Alaskan Command
AMC	Air Materiel Command
ANG	Air National Guard

APGC	Air Proving Ground Command
app	appendix
AR	Army Regulations
ASF	Army Service Forces
asst	assistant
ASWAAF	Arms and Services with the Army Air Forces
ATC	Air Training Command
atch	attachment
ATSC	Air Technical Service Command
AU	Air University
B–9	Two-engine, all-metal, low-wing monoplane bomber with retractable landing gear. Four crewmembers (pilot, navigator/ bombardier, 2 gunners). Fitted with one .30-caliber machinegun each in front and rear cockpits. Could carry 2,000 pounds of bombs at a top speed of 186 miles-per-hour. Service ceiling, 20,000 feet. Combat range, 600 miles.
B–10	Besides design features of the B–9, this bomber had an enclosed cockpit, front and rear turrets, and newly designed engine cowling. Crew of four (pilot, radio operator, 2 gunners). Armament consisted of one 30-caliber Browning machinegun each in the nose and rear turrets and in the floor behind the bomb bay. Bombload, 2,260 pounds. Top speed was around 210 miles-per-hour with a service ceiling of over 21,000 feet and a combat range of 600 miles. The B–10B version's service ceiling was 24,200 feet and its range was 1,240 miles.
B–17	Four-engine, midwing bomber, developed by Boeing. Used widely during World War II in Europe and the Mediterranean area. Nine crewmembers. The combat version of the B–17 gave up the graceful lines of thc YB–17. The slim rudder yielded to a broad dorsal fin enclosing twin .50-caliber machineguns in the tail. Top and belly turrets with jutting guns bulged from the fuselage. Gunners stood at open side hatches to train their .50s on enemy planes.
B–24	Four-engine, midwing bomber developed by Consolidated Vultee and used in World War II. Eight to 10 crewmembers. Flew in all combat theaters but was especially useful in the Pacific theater where long-range missons were usual, serving as a bomber tanker and transport. First model used operationally by Army Air Forces units was the B–24D in 1942. The D had a wing span of 110 feet, a length of 66 feet, 4 inches and a height of 17 feet, 11 inches. Maximum takeoff weight, 60,000 pounds. Top speed, 303 miles per hour at 25,000 feet. Service ceiling,

	32,000 feet. Combat range, 2,850 miles. Later Ds carried ten .50-caliber Browning machineguns and a bombload of 12,800 pounds. Some had a Briggs-Sperry two-gun ball turret aft of the bomb bay. Others carried two 4,000-pound bombs externally under each wing.
B–29	Built by Boeing, the B–29 featured a pressurized cabin, highly advanced-remote gun-firing system, and a bomb capacity of 20,000 pounds. Powered by four Wright R–3350 radial engines in low-drag nacelles. Ten crewmembers. The A–model had a wing span of 141 feet, 3 inches. Length, 99 feet. Height, 29 feet 7 inches. Maximum takeoff weight, 141,100 pounds. Top speed, 358 miles-per-hour at 25,000 feet. Service ceiling, 31,850 feet. Combat range, 4,100 miles. Armament was concentrated in remotely controlled turrets, two above and two below the fuselage, each containing two .50-caliber machineguns. Two .50-caliber and one .20-mm (or three .50-caliber) guns in tail turret. Technological breakthroughs of the B–29 presaged a new era of strategic air power.
bd	board
bk	book
br	branch
CAF	Continental Air Forces
CCS	Combined Chiefs of Staff
CDF	central decimal file
cen	center
CG	commanding general
ch	chief
Ch/	chief of
chap	chapter
chmn	chairman, chairmen
CIA	Central Intelligence Agency
CinCAFPAC	Commander in Chief. Army Forces in the Pacific
CinCPAC	Commander in Chief, Pacific Command
cir	circular
cmte	committee
CNO	Chief of Naval Operations
colln	collection
comd	command

comdr	commander
comsn	commission
con	control
conf	conference
CONUS	Continental United States
coord	coordination
C/S	chief of staff
CSA	Chief of Staff, United States Army
CSAF	Chief of Staff, United States Air Force
DAR	daily activity report
DCAS	Deputy Chief of Air Staff
DCAS/	Deputy Chief of Air Staff for
DCS/	Deputy Chief of Staff for
DCSA	Deputy Chief of Staff, United States Army
def	defense
dep	deputy
DF	disposition form
dir	director
Dir/	Director of
div	division
encl	enclosure
engrg	engineering
EO	executive order
exec	executive
FEAF	Far East Air Forces
FM	field manual
fr	from
gen	general
GHQ	General Headquarters
GSC	General Staff Corps

hist	historical, history, historian,
HQ	headquarters
H.R.	
(with number)	House Bill
ibid	*ibidem*, in the same place
incl	inclosure
indep	independent
intel	intelligence
intvw	interview
IPWAF–1	Initial Postwar Air Force
JCS	Joint Chiefs of Staff
JCSM	Joint Chiefs of Staff Memorandum
LC	Library of Congress, Washington, D.C.
ltr	letter
maint	maintenance
MATS	Military Air Transport Service
MD	Manuscript Division, Library of Congress, Washington, D.C.
MED	Manhattan Engineer District
memo	memorandum
mgt	management
mil	military
misc	miscellaneous
MMB	Modern Military Branch, National Archives, Washington, D.C.
MR	memorandum for record
mtg	meeting
NA	National Archives (National Archives and Records Service), Washington, D.C.
nat	national
NGB	National Guard Bureau
NSC	National Security Council
NSRB	National Security Resources Board

OCAC   Office of the Chief of the Air Corps

OC&R   operations, commitments, and requirements

OPD   Operations Division (G3), War Department General Staff

Ops   operations

organ   organization

OSAF   Office of the Secretary of the Air Force

OSD   Office of the Secretary of Defense

P–47   Powered by a single radial engine, the P–47 was developed by
                Republic and used in World War II as a fighter and fighter-
                bomber. The D–model's wing span was 40 feet, 9 inches.
                Length 36 feet, 1 inch. Height, 14 feet, 2 inches. Maximum
                takeoff weight, 19,400 pounds. Top speed of 428 miles-per-hour
                at 30,000 feet. Service ceiling, 42,000 feet. Combat range, 475
                miles. Armament, eight .50-caliber machineguns and one 500-
                pound bomb. One crewman. Affectionately known as the "Jug,"
                the P–47 was reputed to be the toughest fighter of the war, able
                to absorb tremendous punishment.

P–51   Prop-driven low-wing monoplane, powered by a single liquid-
                cooled engine. Buiit by North American and widely used in
                World War II. One crewman. Escorted B–17s and B–24s on
                bombing missions over Germany. The D–model had a wing
                span of 37 feet. Length, 32 feet, 3 inches. Height, 12 feet, 2
                inches. Maximum takeoff weight, 11,600 pounds. Top speed,
                437 miles-per-hour at 25,000 feet. Service ceiling, 41,900 feet.
                Combat range, 950 miles. Armament, six .50-caliber machine-
                guns and two 1,000-pound bombs. Designated as the F–51, the
                Mustang served in the Korean War. .

P–80   Developed by Lockheed, the P–80 was the first jet aircraft
                accepted for operational service with the Air Force. A small
                low-wing monoplane with a thin, laminar-flow wing section
                and an air-intake on each side of the fuselage ahead of the wing
                leading edge. The A–model's wing span was 39 feet, 11 inches.
                Length, 34 feet, 6 inches. Height, 11 feet, 4 inches. Maximum
                takeoff weight, 14,500 pounds. Top speed of 558 miles-per-
                hour at sea level. Service ceiling, 45,000 feet. Combat range,
                540 miles. Armament, six .50-caliber machineguns.
                One crewman.

PV–2   Prop-driven, twin-engine, Navy patrol bomber. Four crew-
                members. Wing span, 75 feet. Length, 52 feet, 1 inch. Height,
                13 feet, 3 inches. Maximum takeoff weight, 36,000 pounds.
                Top speed, 282 miles-per-hour at 13,700 feet. Service ceiling,
                23,900 feet. Combat range, 1,790 miles.

GLOSSARY

PACOM	Pacific Command
PACUSA	Pacific Air Command, United States Army
PAPC	President's Air Policy Commission (Finletter Commission)
para	paragraph
pers	personnel
Ph.D.	Doctor of Philosophy
plng	planning
PME	permanent military establishment
pres	president
prgm	program
prof.	professor
proj	project
pt	part
PWAF	Postwar Air Force
RAF	Royal Air Force
RAND	Research and Development (The RAND Corporation. Santa Monica, California)
R&D	research and development'
R&R	routing and record
reorgn	reorganization
RG	record group
ROTC	Reserve Officer Training Corps
rprt	report
rqmt	requirement
S.	Senate Bill (with number)
SA	Secretary of the Army
SAC	Strategic Air Command
SAF	Secretary of the Air Force
scty	security
sec	section
SECDEF	Secretary of Defense
SECNAV	Secretary of the Navy
secy	secretary

SECNAV	Secretary of the Navy
secy	secretary
sp	special
SPD	Special Planning Division, War Department General Staff
SSF	Strategic Striking Force
stf	staff
stmt	statement
str	strength
strat	strategic
subj	subject
sum	summary
sur	survey
sv	service
S/W	Secretary of War
tac	tactical
TAC	Tactical Air Command
TAG	The Adjutant General
tech	technical
tng	training
UMT	Universal Military Training
US	United States (of America)
USA	United States Army
USAF	United States Air Force
USAFE	United States Air Forces in Europe
USN	United States Navy
USSAFE	United States Strategic Air Forces in Europe
VCS	vice chief of staff
VHB	very heavy bomb
WD	War Department
WDGS	War Department General Staff
WDSS	War Department Special Staff

XB–17

Boeing started work on the prototype for this four-engine, mid wing bomber in 1934 and first flew it in 1935. The plane's flying characteristics were outstanding for the time. It could carry 2,500 pounds of bombs, 2,260 miles and could attack closer targets with up to 9,000 pounds of ordnance. Accepted by the military in January 1937 as the B–17 Flying Fortress, the aircraft had a top speed of 256 miles-per-hour at 14,000 feet. Service ceiling was 30,600 feet. Loaded with 10,496 pounds of bombs, its maximum range was 1,377 miles.

ZI

Zone of Interior

Bibliographic Note

Governmental Sources

National Archives of the United States

The major sources concerning planning for the post–World War II Army Air Forces are to be found in the Modern Military Branch of the National Archives, Washington, D.C.

This planning, done by the AAF during 1943–47, concentrated on the primary objective of gaining independence for the Army Air Forces. The planning, including consideration of the 70-group program, and the March 1946 reorganization, was sustained and complex. The records reflect this.

Records pertaining to postwar planning in the Modern Military Branch, National Archives, are massive yet sometimes difficult to locate. This is because pertinent clusters of documents have sometimes been filed under subjects unrelated to the general topic of postwar planning.

Nonetheless, the National Archives' record groups that have considerable documentation on this subject are readily determined. They are RG 18, records of Headquarters Army Air Forces; RG 165, records of the War Department General and Special Staffs; RG 218, records of the U.S. Joint Chiefs of Staff; RG 319, records of the Army Staff; RG 340, records of the Office of the Secretary of the Air Force; and RG 341, records of Headquarters United States Air Force.

Record Group 18, Headquarters AAF, contains a wealth of material relating to the AAF's postwar planning. The decimal correspondence files of the Office of the Air Adjutant General (under the Office of the Chief of the Air Staff) have documentation covering early postwar planning in 1943–44, done by the Post War Division under Brig. Gen. Laurence S. Kuter, Assistant Chief of Air Staff, Plans. These files include considerable material describing the planning in 1945 for what eventually became the AAF's 70-group program. These decimal files also contain correspondence on the War Department's Basic Plan for the Post-War Military Establishment and on the subject of Universal Military Training, featuring correspondence between the War Department's Special Planning Division and AAF headquarters. Also, the subjects of postwar organization of Continental Air Forces and the major Army Air Forces' commands are in evidence here. Further, there is material on the establishment of an atomic striking force.

Among the relevant decimal files are 221, 300.6, 312.1, 319.01, 320.01, 320.1, 320.2, 320.3, 321, 322, 325, 334, 370, 370.01, 381, 391, 452.1, and 471.6.

The files of the Office of the Assistant Chief of Air Staff, Plans (RG 18) also afford significant information on postwar planning of the Army Air Forces.

RG 165, records of the War Department's General and Special Staffs, documents the War Department's position on the various issues affecting postwar planning. Here are the Patch-Simpson Board files; records of the Special War Department Committee on the Permanent Military Establishment, known as the Bessell Committee; and correspondence bearing on the Collins Committee report regarding unification of the armed forces. The researcher will also find high-level War Department papers on unification, including those reflecting Army Chief of Staff Eisenhower's views during the 1946–47 period. The key decimal indicators include 319.1, 320, 334, and 452.1.

Also crucial to the story of postwar planning is Record Group 218, documents of the Joint Chiefs of Staff. Besides positions taken on unification and force structure by the military services in the early phases of postwar planning, this record group has valuable papers describing the services' movement towards unified planning and the first so-called Unified Command Plan of December 1946. The appropriate JCS numbered papers are in the JCS 521, JCS 1259, and JCS 1478 series. The numerical designators under RG 218 are CCS 020, CCS 040, CCS 323.361, and CCS 370.

Records of the Army Staff (RG 319) contain some significant high-level documents dealing with unification issues during 1945–46, which can be found in 320, the Plans and Operations files.

Record Group 340 (Office of the Secretary of the Air Force) has been especially important in this study. Among the special documentary categories are the records of the Air Coordinating Committee; the Air Board, 1946–48; minutes of all Air Board meetings, 1946–48; as well as interim reports of board meetings and working papers. The report of the board on Army and Air Force Organizational Matters Under Unification (Hall Board) is in RG 340. This record group also contains the Report of the JCS Special committee for Reorganization of National Defense; the Final Report of the War Department Policies and Programs Review Board; and personal papers of Maj. Gen. Hugh J. Knerr, Secretary-General of the Air Board.

Moreover, of great interest to the historian is a large volume of correspondence between Secretary of the Air Force Symington and Secretary of Defense Forrestal during 1947–49. These documents are among those of the Office of the Administrative Assistant, Correspondence Control Division, OSAF File 520 ("Special Interest" files).

Additional important material treating of the struggle for autonomy, force structure, and organization exists under these decimals: Plans and Operations

009, 020, 312.1, 320.2, and particularly 320.5. On the atomic bomb striking force, see AFOAT 1946, numbers 312.2 and 322.

The papers of General Lauris Norstad are also in the National Archives (as well as on file in the Air Force History Support Office and the Air Force Historical Research Agency), a considerable collection depicting Norstad's role both in the unification drive and AAF reorganization. These documents are noteworthy in giving the historian an insight into some of General Norstad's keenly penetrating views on unification, roles and missions, and Air Force relations with the Navy.

Library of Congress

The Manuscript Division, Library of Congress, holds the collections of the Chiefs of Staff of the United States Air Force.

The General Henry H. (Hap) Arnold collection contains important documentation describing Arnold's, and the AAF's, role in the battle for an independent Air Force. The collection also offers a wealth of material on postwar organizational planning. The General Carl A. Spaatz collection complements the Arnold source material and gives the researchers a view of the interchange of ideas between Arnold and Spaatz. The latter's opinions on postwar organization and the Air Force's struggle with the Navy over roles and missions are also evident.

Compared to the Arnold and Spaatz collections, there is less material on postwar planning in the Hoyt S. Vandenberg, Ira C. Eaker, and Muir S. Fairchild papers. The Vandenberg collection has interesting 1948 memorandums from President Harry S. Truman to the service chiefs and the Secretary of Defense. In them, Truman admonishes all concerned to put their disagreements aside for the greater well-being of the country. The Fairchild papers have some reveling transcripts of lectures delivered to the Air Corps Tactical School, shedding considerable light on the ideas and doctrine of the Army Air Corps prior to World War II.

There are additional collections in the Manuscript Division that proved valuable to this study. The Robert P. Patterson collection includes documents pertaining to the autonomy drive and to roles and missions. Minutes of War Council meetings are also available here. The Admiral William D. Leahy papers acquaint the researcher with the sharp views on the roles and missions battle by President Roosevelt's military adviser.

Harry S. Truman Library

Holdings in the Harry S. Truman Library, Independence, Missouri, cover the immediate post–World War II years. The Clark M. Clifford papers and those of James E. Webb were especially helpful to the chronicling of this study for the years 1946–48. Both collections contain a number of letters from Air Force Secretary Stuart Symington that are particularly revealing of his opinions on the budget and the Navy.

Air Force Historical Research Agency

The massive archives of the Air Force Historical Research Agency house many documents pertinent to this work. This material is vital to the 1943–45 period when the Army Air Forces accomplished much early postwar planning, and to the years 1946–47 culminating in establishment of the United States Air Force. Much of the Agency Archives is on microfilm in the Air Force History Support Office, Washington, D.C.

Historical Studies

Historical studies dealing with Air Force organization and doctrine, and the development of aircraft have been useful, especially those published by the Historical Division of the Air University.

Bald, Ralph D., Jr. *Air Force Participation in Joint Army–Air Force Training Exercises, 1947–50.* USAF Historical Study 80. Maxwell Air Force Base, Ala,: USAF Historical Division, Air University, 1952

Finney, Robert. *History of the Air Corps Tactical School, 1920–1940.* USAF Historical Study 100. Maxwell Air Force Base, Ala.: USAF Historical Division, Air University, 1955.

Futrell, Robert F. *Command of Observation Aviation: A Study in Tactical Control of Air Power.* USAF Historical Study 24, Maxwell Air Force Base, Ala.: Research Studies Institute, Air University, 1952.

Gleckner, Robert F. *The Development of the Heavy Bomber.* USAF Historical Study 6. Maxwell Air Force Base, Ala.: USAF Historical Division, Air University, 1951.

Greer, Thomas H. *The Development of Air Doctrine in the Army Air Arm, 1917–1941.* USAF Historical Study 89. Maxwell Air Force Base, Ala.: USAF Historical Division, Air University, 1953.

Holley, Irving B. Jr. *Evolution of the Liaison Type Airplane, 1917–1944.* USAF Historical Study 44. Maxwell AFB, Ala.: USAF Historical Division, Air University, 1946.

McClendon, R. Earl. *Autonomy of the Air Arm.* Maxwell Air Force Base, Ala.: Documentary Research Division, Air University, 1954. [Reprint, Air Force History and Museums Program, 1996]

Mooney, Chase C. *Organization of Military Aeronautics, 1935–1945.* AAF Historical Study 46. Washington: AAF Historical Office, 1946.

Mooney, Chase C., and Layman, Martha E. *Organization of Military Aeronautics, 1907–1935*. AAF Historical Study 25. Washington: AAF Historical Division, 1944.

Mooney, Chase C., and Williamson, Edward E. *Organization of the Army Air Arm, 1935–1945*. USAF Historical Study 10. Maxwell Air Force Base, Ala.: Research Studies Institute, Air University, 1956.

Sanders, Chauncey E. *Redeployment and Demobilization*. USAF Historical Study 77. Maxwell Air Force Base, Ala.: USAF Historical Division, Air University, 1952.

Williams, Edwin L., Jr. *Legislative History of the AAF and USAF, 1941–1951*. USAF Historical Study 84. Maxwell Air Force Base, Ala.: USAF Historical Division, Air University, 1955.

Also useful in this study was: Haase, Albert E. *Manpower Demobilization in the AAF*. SAC Historical Study, Offutt Air Force Base, Nebr.: Historical Office, Strategic Air Command, 1946.

Reports

Annual Report of the Chief of the Air Corps, 1930s.

Annual Report of the Secretary of the Air Force, Fiscal Year 1948. Washington: Government Printing Office, 1948.

Annual Report of the Secretary of the Army, 1948. Washington: Government Printing Office. 1949.

Arnold, Henry H. *First Report of the Commanding General of the Army Air Forces to the Secretary of War*. Washington: War Department, 1944.

_____ . *Second Report of the Commanding General of the Army Air Forces to the Secretary of War*. Washington: War Department, 1945.

_____. *Third Report of the Commanding General of the Army Air Forces to the Secretary of War*. Washington: War Department, 1945.

Doolittle, James H. Dissent to the *Final Report of the War Department Special Committee on the Army Air Corps*. Washington: Government Printing Office, 1934.

Final Report of the War Department Policies and Programs Review Board. Washington: War Department, 1947.

First Report of the Secretary of Defense, 1948. Washington: Government Printing Office, 1949.

March, Gen Peyton C. "Lessons of World War I." *War Department Annual Reports, 1919*. Washington: Government Printing Office, 1920.

Survival in the Air Age: A Report by the President's Air Policy Commission. Washington: Government Printing Office, 1948.

Regulations, Circulars, Letters, Orders

Air Corps News Letter, 1930s.

Army Air Forces Letter 20–9, December 16, 1944.

Army Air Forces Letter 20–91, February 14, 1946.

Army Air Forces Regulation 20–1, *Army Air Forces.* June 1, 1945.

Army Air Forces Regulation 20–14, *AAF Proving Ground Command.* March 7, 1946.

Army Air Forces Regulation 20–61, *Air University.* April 5, 1946.

Army Regulation 95–5, *General Provisions.* June 20, 1941.

Army Regulation 95–10, *Air Corps Troops.* March 10, 1928.

Executive Order 9877, *Functions of the Armed Forces.* July 16, 1947.

Field Manual 100–20, *Command and Employment of Air Power.* July 21, 1943.

War Department Circular 59, *War Department Reorganization.* March 2, 1942.

War Department Circular 138, *War Department Reorganization.* May 14, 1946.

War Department Circular 347, Section III, *Military Establishment.* August 25, 1944.

War Department Letter, AG 322, March 21, 1946.

Interviews

Selected oral history interviews have been important to the writing of this study. Several deserve special mention. In the early 1970s, Lt. Col. Joe B. Green, USAF, conducted a series of extensive interviews with Lt. Gen. Ira C. Eaker at the Army War College, Carlisle Barracks, Pa. In these interviews, General Eaker provided many pertinent insights into the history of the Army Air Corps between the wars; into strategy, operations, and command problems of the strategic air war in the European theater during World War II; also into the major issues of the immediate postwar years. Eaker's interviews can be recommended to anyone with an interest in Air Force history.

I am personally grateful to General Eaker. On several occasions he gave most generously of his time to this writer, recalling especially his command of air forces in the European theater and describing his part during 1945–47 in planning for the postwar Air Force. He also responded with substantive memorandums to a number of specific questions that I posed following our interviews.

Maj. Gen. Haywood S. Hansell, Jr., was kind enough to recall with me his experience as a major war planner and bomber commander. He also gave numerous insights into prewar air planning and training.

In addition, Gen. Curtis E. LeMay graciously granted me an interview in Washington, wherein he cleared up a number of points relating to operations during World War II and to planning for the postwar Air Force.

The first Secretary of the Air Force, Stuart Symington, consented to an interview in May 1978 and another in December 1978. They were conducted by this writer and Hugh A. Ahmann of the Albert F. Simpson Historical Research Center. Symington ranged over his career as industrialist and as a government official, dwelling on his years as Assistant Secretary of War for Air and as Secretary of the Air Force, 1947–50.

Besides the above interviews, I found interviews with the following to be most helpful (transcripts of almost all of them are available at the Air Force Historical Research Agency and in the Air Force History Support Office):

Maj. Gen. Edward P. Curtis	Lt. Gen. James H. Doolittle
Thomas K. Finletter	Col. Kenneth F. Gantz
Roswell L. Gilpatric	Maj. Gen. Leon W. Johnson
Gen. George C. Kenney	Maj. Gen. Hugh J. Knerr
Gen. Laurence S. Kuter	Robert A. Lovett
Gen. Earle E. Patridge	Lt. Gen. Elwood R. Quesada
Gen. Carl A. Spaatz	Gen. Otto P. Weyland
Eugene M. Zuckert	

Congress

Most important to this study were congressional hearings of the 78th and 79th Congresses. The House of Representatives Select Committee on Post-War Military Policy held hearings in 1944 on a *Proposal to Establish a Single Department of Armed Forces*. High-ranking officials of the War Department and the Army Air Forces presented their views on postwar military policy to this committee.

During the 79th Congress, War and Navy Department officials testified in September and October 1945 before the Senate Committee on Military Affairs, relative to unification problems. Reports of these hearings contain much significant information. This brief list holds some of the most relevant testimony:

House. Hearings before the Select Committee on Post-War Military Policy. *Proposal to Establish a Single Department of Armed Forces*. 78th Cong, 2d sess. Washington: Government Printing Office, 1944.

Senate. Hearings before the War Contracts Subcommittee, Committee on Military Affairs. *Hearings on Contract Termination*. 78th Cong. 2d sess. Washington: Government Printing Office, 1945.

Senate. Hearings before the Committee on Military Affairs. *Department of Armed Forces and Military Security: Hearings on S. 84 and S. 1482.* 79th Cong, 1st sess. Washington: Government Printing Office, 1945.

Senate. Hearings before the Committee on Military Affairs. *National Defense Establishment (Unification of the Armed Services): Hearings on S. 758.* 80th Cong, 1st sess. Washington: Government Printing Office, 1947.

Presidential Papers

Public Papers of the President of the United States: Harry S. Truman, 1945. Washington: Office of the Federal Register, National Archives and Records Service. 1961.

Public Papers of the President of the United States: Harry S. Truman, 1946. Washington: Office of the Federal Register, National Archives and Records Service. 1962.

Public Papers of the President of the United States: Harry S. Truman, 1947. Washington: Office of the Federal Register, National Archives and Records Service. 1963.

Public Papers of the President of the United States: Harry S. Truman, 1948. Washington: Office of the Federal Register, National Archives and Records Service. 1964.

Books

Brodie, Bernard, and Galloway, Eilene. *The Atomic Bomb and the Armed Services.* Public Affairs Bulletin 55. Washington: Government Printing Office, 1947.

Carter, Kit C., and Mueller, Robert. *The Army Air Forces in World War II: Combat Chronology, 1941–45.* Washington: Office of Air Force History, 1973.

Cline, Ray S. *The War Department, Washington Command Post: The Operations Division.* Washington: Office of the Chief of Military History, Department of the Army, 1951.

Cole, Alice C., Goldberg, Alfred, Tucker, Samuel A., Winnacker, Rudolph A., eds. *The Department of Defense: Documents on Establishment and Organization 1944–1978.* Washington: Historical Office, Office of the Secretary of Defense, 1978.

Condit, Kenneth W. *The History of the Joint Chiefs of Staff: The Joint Chiefs of Staff and National Policy, 1947–1949.* Vol II. Washington: Historical Division, Joint Secretariat, Joint Chiefs of Staff, 1977. (Also published by Michael Glazier, Inc, Wilmington, Del.).

Craven, Wesley F., and Cate, James L., eds. *The Army Air Forces in World War II.* 7 vols. Chicago: University of Chicago Press, 1948–1958.

Davis, Richard G. *Carl A. Spaatz and the Air War in Europe.* Washington: Center for Air Force History, 1993.

Emerson, William R. *Operation Pointblank: A Tale of Bombers and Fighters*. The Fourth Harmon Memorial Lecture. Colorado Springs, Colo.: United States Air Force Academy, 1962.

Futrell, Robert F. *Ideas, Concepts, Doctrine: A History of Basic Thinking in the United States Air Force, 1907–1964*. Maxwell Air Force Base, Ala.: Air University, 1974.

Gropman, Alan L. *The Air Force Integrates, 1945–1964*. Washington: Office of Air Force History, 1978.

Hewes, James E., Jr. *From Root to McNamara: Army Organization and Administration, 1900–1963*. Washington: United States Army Center of Military History, 1975.

Holley, Irving B., Jr. *Buying Aircraft: Materiel Procurement for the Army Air Forces*. Washington: Office of the Chief of Military History, Department of the Army, 1964.

Knaack, Marcelle S. *Encyclopedia of U.S. Air Force Aircraft and Missile Systems*. Vol I: *Post-World War II Fighters, 1945–1973*. Washington: Office of Air Force History 1978.

Matloff, Maurice. *Strategic Planning for Coalition Warfare, 1943–1944*. [U.S. Army in World War II, The War Department]. Washington: Office of the Chief of Military History, Department of the Army, 1959.

Maurer, Maurer. *The U.S. Air Service in World War I*. 4 vols. Washington: Office of Air Force History, 1978–1979.

Moody, Walton S. *Building a Strategic Air Force, 1945–1953*. Washington: Air Force History and Museums Program, 1996.

Palmer, Michael A. *Origins of the Maritime Strategy: American Naval Strategy in the First Postwar Decade*. Washington: Naval Historical Center, 1988.

Rearden, Steven L. *History of the Office of the Secretary of Defense*. Vol I: *The Formative Years, 1947–1950*. Washington: Historical Office, Office of the Secretary of Defense, 1984.

Schnabel, James F. *The History of the Joint Chief of Staff: The Joint Chiefs and Staff and National Policy, 1945–1947*. Vol I. Washington: Historical Division, Joint Secretariat, Joint Chiefs of Staff, 1979. (Also published by Michael Glazier, Inc, Wilmington, Del.).

Sherry, Michael S. *Preparing for the Next War: American Plans for Postwar Defense, 1941–1945*. New Haven: Yale University Press, 1977.

Shiner, John F. *Foulois and the U.S. Army Air Corps, 1931–1935*. Washington: Office of Air Force History, 1982.

Sturm, Thomas A. *The USAF Scientific Advisory Board: Its First Twenty Years, 1944–1964*. Washington: USAF Historical Division Liaison Office, 1967.

Watson, George M., Jr., *The Office of the Secretary of the Air Force, 1947–1965.* Center for Air Force History, 1993.

Webster, Charles K., and Frankland, Nobel. *The Strategic Air Offensive Against Germany, 1939–1945.* 4 vols. London: Her Majesty's Stationery Office, 1961.

Articles

Cate, James L. *"Development of Air Doctrine, 1917–41." Air University Quarterly Review* I (Winter 1947).

Futrell, Robert F. "Preplanning the USAF: Dogmatic or Pragmatic?" *Air University Review* XXI (January–February 1971).

Greenwood, John T. "The Emergency of the Postwar Strategic Air Force, 1945–1953." *Air Power and Warfare.* Proceedings of the 8th Military History Symposium, United States Air Force Academy, October 18–20, 1978. Washington: Office of Air Force History and the United States Air Force Academy, 1979.

Huston, John W. "The Wartime Leadership of Hap Arnold." *Air Power and Warfare.* Proceedings of the 8th Military History Symposium, United States Air Force Academy, October 18–20, 1978. Washington: Office of Air Force History and the United States Air Force Academy, 1979.

Maurer, Maurer. "The Constitutional Basis of the United States Air Force." *Air University Review* XVI (January–February 1965).

Quesada, Elwood R. "Tactical Air Power." *Air University Quarterly Review* XI (Spring 1959).

Wolk, Herman S. "The Defense Unification Battle, 1947–50: The Air Force." *Prologue: Journal of the National Archives* (Spring 1975).

————. "Men Who Made the Air Force." *Air University Review* XXIII (September–October 1972).

————. "The Uses of History in the Nuclear Age." *Air University Review* XXII (November–December 1971).
Non-Governmental Sources

Non-Governmental Sources

Books

Acheson, Dean. *Present at the Creation: My Years in the State Department.* New York: W. W. Norton & Co, 1969.

Ambrose, Stephen E. *Rise to Globalism: American Foreign Policy Since 1938*. Baltimore: Penguin Books, 1971. Paperback.

Arnold, Henry H. *Global Mission*. New York: Harper & Bros, 1949.

————. *Winged Warfare*. New York: Harper & Bros, 1941.

Arnold, Henry H., and Eaker, Ira C. *This Flying Game*. 3d rev ed. New York: Funk & Wagnalls Co, 1936.

Baldwin, Hanson W. *The Crucial Years, 1939–1941*. New York, Harper & Row, 1976.

Barlow, Jeffrey G. *Revolt of the Admirals: The Fight for Naval Aviation, 1945–1950*. Washington: Naval Historical Center, 1994.

Berger, Carl. *B–29: The Superfortress*. New York: Ballantine Books, Inc, 1970.

Borden, Norman E., Jr. *The Air Mail Emergency*. Portland, Maine: The Bond Wheelwright Co., 1958.

Brodie, Bernard. *Strategy in the Missile Age*. Princeton University Press, 1959.

————., ed. *The Absolute Weapon: Atomic Power and World Order*. New York: Harcourt, Brace & Co, 1946.

Buchan, Alastair. *The End of the Postwar Era: A New Balance of World Power*. New York: E. P. Dutton & Co, 1974.

Butow, Robert J. C. *Japan's Decision to Surrender*. Palo Alto: Stanford University Press, 1954.

Byrd, Martha. *Chennault: Giving Wings to the Tiger*. Tuscaloosa: University of Alabama Press, 1988.

Caraley, Demetrios. *The Politics of Military Unification: A Study of Conflict and the Policy Process*. New York: Columbia University Press, 1966.

Chennault, Claire L. *Way of a Fighter: The Memoirs of Claire Lee Chennault*. New York: G. P. Putnam's Sons, 1969.

Churchill, Winston S. *The Second World War*. 6 vols, Boston: Houghton, Mifflin Co, 1948–1953.

Coletta, Paolo E. *The United States Navy and Defense Unification 1917–1953*. Newark, Del.: University of Delaware Press, 1981.

Collier, Basil. *A History of Air Power*. New York: Macmillan Publishing Co, Inc, 1974.

Copp, Dewitt S. *A Few Great Captains: The Men and Events that Shaped the Development of U.S. Air Power*. Garden City, N.Y.: Doubleday & Co, 1980.

Davis, Burke. *The Billy Mitchell Affair*. New York: Random House, 1967.

Davis, Vincent. *Post Defense Policy and the U.S. Navy, 1943–1946*. Chapel Hill: The University of North Carolina Press, 1966.

THE STRUGGLE FOR AIR FORCE INDEPENDENCE

Divine, Robert A. *Roosevelt and World War II*. Baltimore: Penguin Books, 1969. Paperback.

Dorwart, Jeffrey M. *Eberstaat and Forrestal: A National Security Partnership, 1909–1949*. College Station: Texas A&M University Press, 1991.

Douhet, Giulio. *The Command of the Air*. Translated by Dino Ferrari. 1942 ed. New York: Arno Press, 1972. [Reprint, Office of Air Force History, 1991].

Edmonds, Walter D. *They Fought With What They Had: The Story of the Army Air Forces in the South West Pacific, 1941–1942*. Boston: Little, Brown & Co, 1951.

Eisenhower, Dwight D. *Crusade in Europe*. Garden City, N.Y.: Doubleday & Co, 1952.

———. *The Papers of Dwight David Eisenhower: The War Years*. Baltimore: The Johns Hopkins University Press. 1970.

Emme, Eugene M., ed. *The Impact of Air Power: National Security and World Politics*. Princeton: D. Van Nostrand Co, 1959.

Feis, Herbert. *The Atomic Bomb and the End of World War II*. Princeton: Princeton University Press, 1966.

Forrestal, James. *The Forrestal Diaries*. Walter Millis, ed. New York: The Viking Press, 1951.

Foulois, Benjamin D., and Glines, Carroll V. *From the Wright Brothers to the Astronauts: The Memoirs of Benjamin D. Foulois*. New York: McGraw-Hill Book Co, 1968.

Fredette, Raymond H. *The Sky on Fire: The First Battle of Britain, 1917–1918, and the Birth of the Royal Air Force*. New York: Harcourt, Brace, Jovanovich, 1976.

Freeman, Roger A. *The Mighty Eighth: Units, Men, and Machines: A History of the U.S. Eighth Army Air Force*. Garden City, N.Y.: Doubleday & Co, 1970.

Gaddis, John Lewis. *The United States and the Origins of the Cold War, 1941–1947*. New York: Columbia University Press, 1972.

Gardner, Lloyd C. *Architects of Illusion: Men and Ideas in American Foreign Policy, 1941–1949*. Chicago: Quadrangle Books, 1970.

Goldberg, Alfred, ed. *A History of the United States Air Force, 1907–1957*. Princeton: D. Van Nostrand Co, Inc, 1957.

Greenfield, Kent R. *American Strategy in World War II: A Reconsideration*. Baltimore: The Johns Hopkins University Press, 1963.

Hammond, Paul Y. *Organizing for Defense: The American Military Establishment in the Twentieth Century*. Princeton: Princeton University Press, 1961.

Halle, Louis J. *The Cold War as History*. New York: Harper & Row Publishers. Inc, 1967.

Hansell, Haywood S., Jr. *The Air Plan that Defeated Hitler*. Atlanta: Higgins-McArthur/Longino & Porter, 1972.

382

Hart, B. H. Liddell. *History of the Second World War.* New York: G. P. Putnam's Sons, 1970.

Haynes, Richard F. *The Awesome Power: Harry S. Truman as Commander in Chief.* Baton Rouge: Louisiana State University Press, 1973.

Herz, Martin F. *Beginnings of the Cold War.* New York: McGraw-Hill Book Co, 1966. Paperback.

Higham, Robin. *Air Power: A Concise History.* New York: St. Martins Press, 1973.

Hinton, Harold B. *Air Victory: The Men and the Machines.* New York: Harper & Bros, 1948.

Holley, Irving B. Jr. *Ideas and Weapons.* New Haven: Yale University Press, 1961. Paperback.

————. *General John M. Palmer, Citizen Soldiers, and the Army of a Democracy.* Westport: Greenwood Press, 1982.

Hoopes, Townsend and Douglas Brinkley. *Driven Patriot: The Life and Times of James Forrestal.* New York: Knopf, 1992.

Huntington, Samuel P. *The Common Defense: Strategic Programs in National Politics.* New York: Columbia University Press, 1961. Paperback.

Hurley, Alfred F. *Billy Mitchell: Crusader for Air Power.* New York: Franklin Watts, Inc. 1964.

Huzar, Elias. *The Purse and the Sword: Control of the Army by Congress Through Military Appropriations, 1933–1950.* Ithaca: Cornell University Press, 1950.

Infield, Glenn B. *The Poltava Affair.* New York, Macmillan Publishing Co, 1973.

Jurika, Stephen, Jr., ed. *From Pearl Harbor to Vietnam: The Memoirs of Admiral Arthur W. Radford.* Palo Alto: Hoover Institution Press, 1980.

Kenney, George C. *General Kenney Reports: A Personal History of the Pacific War.* New York: Duell, Sloan & Pearce, 1949.

King, Ernest J., and Whitehill, Walter M. *Fleet Admiral King: A Naval Record.* New York: W. W. Norton & Co, 1952.

Kolko, Gabriel, and Kolko, Joyce. *The Limits of Power: The World and United States Foreign Policy, 1945–1954.* New York: Harper & Row Publishers, Inc, 1972.

Kuter, Laurence S. *Airman at Yalta.* New York: Duell, Sloan & Pearce, 1955.

Lafeber, Walter. *America, Russia, and the Cold War, 1945–1966.* New York: John Wiley & Sons, Inc, 1968.

LeMay, Curtis E. and Kantor, MacKinlay. *Mission With LeMay: My Story.* Garden City, N. Y.: Doubleday & Co, 1965.

Loosbrock, John F., and Skinner, Richard M., eds. *The Wild Blue: The Story of American Airpower*, New York: G. P. Putnam's Sons, 1961.

Lukacs, John. *A History of the Cold War*. New York: Doubleday & Co, 1961.

Lukas, Richard C. *Eagles East: The Army Air Forces and the Soviet Union, 1941–1945*. Tallahassee: Florida State University Press, 1970.

MacIsaac, David. *Strategic Bombing in World War II: The Story of the United States Strategic Bombing Survey*. New York: Garland Publishing Co, 1976.

Mahan, Alfred Thayer. *The Influence of Sea Power Upon History, 1660–1783*. Boston: Little, Brown & Co, 1918.

Millis, Walter. *Arms and Men: A Study in American Military History*. New York: G. P. Putnam's Sons, 1956.

————., ed. *American Military Thought*. New York: The Bobbs-Merrill Co, 1966.

Millis, Walter, Mansfield, Harvey C., and Stein, Harold. *Arms and the State: Civil-Military Elements in National Policy*. New York: Twenteith Century Fund, 1958.

Nelson, Otto L., Jr., Maj. Gen., USA. *National Security and the General Staff*. Washington: Infantry Journal Press, 1946.

Perret, Geoffrey. *Winged Victory: The Army Air Forces in World War II*. New York: Random House, 1993.

Pogue, Forrest, C. *George C. Marshall: Education of a General, 1880–1939*. New York: The Viking Press, Inc, 1963.

————. *George C. Marshall: Ordeal and Hope*. New York: The Viking Press, Inc, 1966.

————. *George C. Marshall: Organizer of Victory, 1943–1945*. New York: The Viking Press, Inc, 1973.

Potter, E. B. *Nimitz*. Annapolis: Naval Institute Press, 1976.

Quester, George H. *Deterrence Before Hiroshima: The Airpower Background of Modern Strategy*. New York: John Wiley & Sons, Inc, 1966.

Reitzel, William, Kaplan, Morton A., and Coblenz, Constance G. *United States Foreign Policy, 1945–1955*. Washington: The Brookings Institution, 1956.

Rogow, Arnold A. *James Forrestal: A Study of Personality, Politics, and Policy*. New York: The Macmillan Co, 1963.

Sallagar, Frederick M. *The Road to Total War*. New York: Van Nostrand Reinhold Co, 1969.

Schratz, Paul R., ed. *Evolution of the American Military Establishment Since World War II*. Lexington, Va: George C. Marshall Research Foundation, 1978.

Sherry, Michael S. *Preparing for the Next War: American Plans for Postwar Defense, 1941–45*. New Haven: Yale University Press, 1977.

Sherwin, Martin J. *A World Destroyed: The Atomic Bomb and the Grand Alliance.* New York: Alfred A. Knopf, Inc, 1975.

Sherwood, Robert E. *Roosevelt and Hopkins.* New York: Harper & Bros, 1948.

Sixsmith, E. K. G. *Eisenhower as Military Commander.* New York: Stein & Day, 1972.

Smith, Perry McCoy. *The Air Force Plans for Peace, 1943–1945.* Baltimore: The Johns Hopkins University Press, 1970.

Speer, Albert. *Inside the Third Reich: Memoirs by Albert Speer.* Translated by Richard and Clara Winston. New York: The Macmillan Co, 1970.

Stanley, Timothy W. *American Defense and National Security.* Washington: Public Affairs Press, 1956.

Stein, Harold, ed. *American Civil-Military Decisions: A Book of Case Studies.* Tuscaloosa: The University of Alabama Press, 1963.

Truman, Harry S. *Memoirs.* Vol II: *Years of Trial and Hope.* Garden City, New York: Doubleday & Co, 1956.

Truman, Margaret. *Harry S. Truman.* New York: William Morrow & Co, 1973.

Ulam, Adam B. *The Rivals: America and Russia Since World War II* New York: The Viking Press, Inc, 1971.

Weigley, Russell F. *History of the United States Army.* New York: The Macmillan Co, 1967.

———. *The American Way of War: A History of United States Military Strategy and Policy.* New York: Macmillan Publishing Co, Inc, 1973.

Weinberg, Gerhard L. *A World at Arms: A Global History of World War II.* Cambridge: Cambridge University Press, 1994.

Wheeler, Gerald E. *Prelude to Pearl Harbor: The United States Navy and the Far East, 1921–1931.* Columbia: University of Missouri Press, 1968.

Yergin, Daniel H. *Shattered Peace: The Origins of the Cold War National Security State.* Boston: Houghton Mifflin Co, 1977.

Articles

Bernstein, Barton J. "Roosevelt, Truman, and the Atomic Bomb, 1941–1945: A Reinterpretation." *Political Science Quarterly* 90 (Spring 1975).

Brodie Bernard. "The Atomic Bomb and American Security," *Yale Institute of International Studies,* November 1, 1945.

———. "The Atomic Bomb as Policy Maker." *Foreign Affairs,* October 1948.

Goldberg, Alfred. "General Carl A. Spaatz." Field Marshal Sir Michael Carver, ed. *The War Lords: Military Commanders of the Twentieth Century*. Boston: Little, Brown & Co, 1976.

Gorrell, Edgar S. "An American Proposal for Strategic Bombing in World War I." *Air Power Historian*, April 1958.

Hansell, Haywood S., Jr. "General Laurence S. Kuter, 1905–1979." *Aerospace Historian*, Summer 1980.

———. "Strategic Air Warfare." *Aerospace Historian*, Winter 1966.

Holley, I. B., Jr. "An Air Force General: Laurence Sherman Kuter." *Aerospace Historian*, Summer 1980.

Hopkins, George E. "Bombing and the American Conscience During World War II." *Historian*, May 1966.

Krauskopf, Robert W. "The Army and The Strategic Bomber, 1930–1939." *Military Affairs*, Summer 1958.

Kuter, Laurence S. "How Hap Arnold Built the AAF." *Air Force Magazine*, September 1973.

Lewis, Flora. "The Education of a Senator." *The Atlantic*, December 1971.

Olson, Mancur, Jr. "The Economics of Strategic Bombing in World War II." *Airpower Historian*, April 1966.

Ransom, Harry H. "The Battleship Meets the Airplane." *Military Affairs*, Spring 1959.

Shiner, John F. "Birth of the GHQ Air Force." *Military Affairs*, October 1978.

Spaatz, Gen Carl A., USAF. "Air Power in the Atomic Age." *Collier's*, December 8, 1945.

———. "Strategic Air Power: Fulfillment of a Concept." *Foreign Affairs*, April 1946.

Taylor, Joe Gray. "They Taught Tactics." *Aerospace Historian*, Summer 1966.

Twining, Nathan F. "The Twentieth Air Force." *Military Review* 26 (June 1946).

Wells, Samuel F., Jr. "William Mitchell and the *Ostfriesland*: A Study in Military Reform." *Historian*, August 1964.

Wolk, Herman S. "Building the Peacetime Air Force." *Air Force Magazine*, September 1980.

———. "Independence and Responsibility: USAF in the Defense Establishment." Paul R. Schratz, ed. *The American Military Establishment Since World War II*. Lexington, Va.: George C. Marshall Research Foundation, 1978.

———. "Prelude to D–Day: The Bomber Offensive—The Overlord Air Dispute." *Air Force Magazine*, June 1974.

———. "Roots of Strategic Deterrence." *Aerospace Historian*, September–October 1972.

———. "The B–29, the A–Bomb, and the Japanese Surrender." *Air Force Magazine,* February 1975.

———. "The Strategic World of 1946." *Air Force Magazine*, February 1971.

———. "Founding the Force." *Air Force Magazine*, September 1996.

Ph.D. Dissertations

These Ph.D. dissertations were especially helpful in the writing of this study:

Boyle, James M. "The XXI Bomber Command: Primary Factor in the Defeat of Japan." Saint Louis University, 1964.

Flugel, Raymond R. "United States Air Power Doctrine: A Study of the Influence of William Mitchell and Giulio Douhet at the Air Corps Tactical School, 1921–1935." University of Oklahoma, 1965.

Green, Murray. "Stuart Symington and the B–36." American University, 1960.

Gross, Charles J. "Origins and Development of the Air National Guard." The Ohio State University 1976.

Legere, Lawrence J. "Unification of the Armed Forces." Harvard University, 1951.

Shiner, John F. "The Army Air Arm in Transition: General Benjamin D. Foulois and the Air Corps, 1931–1935." The Ohio State University, 1975.

Index

ISBN 0-16-049066-9

90000

9 780160 490668